EXPLORER RACE

RACE

AND BEYOND

Explorer Race Roots, Friends and All That Is

with

Zoosh through Robert Shapiro

EXPLORER RACE
and Beyond

Zoosh and Others
through Robert Shapiro

Light Technology Publishing

Michael Tyree, Illustrator
Margaret Pinyan, Editor

ISBN 1-891824-06-6

Published by
Light Technology Publishing
P.O. Box 1526
Sedona, AZ 86339
1-800-450-0985

Printed by
MI**SS**ION
PO**SS**IBLE
COMMERCIAL
PRINTING
P.O. Box 1495
Sedona, AZ 86339

Other Books by Robert Shapiro

The Explorer Race Series
The Explorer Race
ETs and the Explorer Race
Explorer Race: Origins and the Next 50 Years
Explorer Race: Creators and Friends—Mechanics of Creation
Explorer Race: Particle Personalities
Explorer Race and Beyond

The Sedona Vortex Guidebook
(with other channels)

Shining the Light Series
Shining the Light
Shining the Light II: The Battle Continues
Shining the Light III: Humanity Gets a Second Chance
Shining the Light IV: Humanity's Greatest Challenge
Shining the Light V: Humanity Is Going to Make It!

Contents

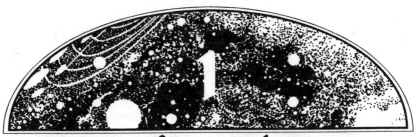

Creator of Pure Feelings and Thoughts, One Circle of Creation

January 21, 1997

ell, all right, Zoosh speaking. What's on the agenda for tonight?
How about the being who gave the Creator that sense of impatience? Can that being talk?

You mean the being that was all of you?
Yes.

You mean from that time frame?
Yes.

But you're talking about the part of Creator . . .
The part of the Explorer Race that agitated the Creator.

I'll see. [Pause.] This is essentially the root of the Explorer Race.
The root, the total, the seed—I don't know how you would put it.

Maybe "the seed" is a good term.
Whatever wanted to do it—who or what.

We'll have to see if we can track that. You understand, it might not have a great deal of experience.
But it had a lust and a desire.

Seed of the Explorer Race

All right. We are the seed being to which you have referred. At one time we were simply a portion of the being you have come to know as your Creator. And when that was the case, we were that being also. But there was a moment—not by chance but apparently by plan—when we felt something impact us. We, of course, thought that it had impacted *all* of the being we were in. We did not realize that it had impacted only ourselves, as the portions of Creator who have become you and all beings here.

After that feeling of impact we were very excited, and we conveyed that excitement to the rest of the being that was ourselves at that time. But the rest of the being was not really interested. This energy was very much like a . . . how can we put it in the language of the day? . . . it was an energy of impetus. It seemed to tear us from our moorings and wanted us to hurtle out into space and find a place to create something—at that time we knew not what.

We felt ourselves trying to do that, when all of a sudden the being we were in [this Creator] seemed to have realized the urgency for us, and moved with us onto a journey that He has described in the previous session [see chapter 15 of *Explorer Race: Particle Personalities*]. We have had a long time to consider where that energy came from, and I think you will be able to hear from that source this night. Any questions?

No. If we can hear from that source, that would be wonderful.

Then I will see if I can stand aside and create a reverse trace to that being.

I am that which encompasses all your known, unknown and potential existence. From the beginning of my awareness I realized that it was my job to provide structure, organization, individuality, variety, philosophy, cause, purpose, effects, responsibility and many of the other things you have come to take as being part of the natural course of events. In the early days when I was in my infancy, I felt very enthusiastic about life. I felt, however, that I was primarily potential yet to be filled. If you were to have seen me then, I would have looked very transparent, though a thorough examination would have revealed a transparency that seemed to surround a vast space with no apparent objects filling that space.

In the beginning I felt this was me, and that is all. But gradually I began to want to see what I could do. I noticed that every time I had a thought there would be forms, sometimes simple shapes, other times vast shapes. I began to realize that my thoughts crystallize into substance, and they were not simply the pursuit of self-identification.

When I realized that these thoughts had the capacity to endure, I began to organize my thoughts in some form where each thought was pure unto its own self and could, as a result of its own experience, build upon what it started out its life as being. I then discovered that what I had assumed were thoughts were actually feelings. Feelings are, at the very core of their being, a foundation to thought.

When I discovered that, I went through every pure feeling I could find within myself. Then I began to add beliefs and ideas to those feelings, and I realized how complex a creation was possible. I decided it would be essential to have assistants not unlike apprentices, who would have the authority to create whole universes of their own and consult with other beings; to have some level of autonomy and still be able to consult with me if there were no other source of answers. I have noticed that these beings have come to be called creators, and I feel that is a good word for them.

After establishing that principle, I decided that the foundation for all creators must be pure feeling, that the primal feeling must be love and that everything must begin and end with love. In this way little harm could be done. Allowing for their potential to grow, I could not prevent all harm, but I could limit it with this essential programming.

So at the core of all creators is feeling. And when that feeling is attuned to pure love—and sometimes spontaneity, sometimes ideas, sometimes the sheer desire to define one's world—it is that energy, those feelings, that are the progenitor to these creators' apparitions or creations. I have often considered the pattern of what I have begun, and I do assume that it is a result of my having been placed here.

My Origin

I *do* remember my origin. Before I was here I existed in a place that was . . . I can only describe it as pure ecstatic feeling. It is a place so fulfilling that one cares not to leave it, nor does one have any need, for pure ecstatic feeling feeds all needs. Yet one day this source of pure ecstatic feeling, of which I was a portion, separated like the way leaves separate from a tree at the end of their season, each one moving out in its own direction with the intention of establishing its own creation.

The one exception is that it was intended that whatever we created, whatever path all beings would take within that creation, they would work toward ecstatic feeling and would tap the source of ecstatic feeling to begin. This is why, when creation takes place even on the biological level, ecstatic feeling must be involved. If ecstatic feeling is not involved, then you are not in any creation I know of. This feeling ties you all together.

As a being, I feel at the moment that I am about three-quarters of the way through this creation. Beings within this creation will not, however, replace me. What will occur is that ultimately this creation is intended to reach a higher level than that which was my source. That is why I have allowed a certain amount of tension you might call creative impetus.

As far as I know, all other fellow beings like myself have done the same thing. The original reason for our departure from the source of pure ecstatic feeling was not to improve on it (for I am not aware of any improvement that is available), but rather to create the ultimate varieties of it so that there would be a progression that beings can take from pure ecstatic feeling through many things and eventually return to pure ecstatic feeling—and also to see if it is possible to create an even higher level of this ecstatic feeling.

If it is not possible, then so be it. If on the other hand it is possible, we will all come to know this in about (in terms of your experiential time) three and a half billion years. This might seem like a long time to you, but as you are immortals, you will all live to see it. That's when we will find out if there could be something more.

What is the extent of your creation? Is it the circle in the center of union?

It is all that you have heard of so far.

Do the circles of union belong to your creation, or is yours within one circle, this circle?

I encompass all that you know and have heard of as well as more that has not yet been discussed.

Okay, so you are beyond that buffer that sends sentient beings?

How I Accelerated the Process

Yes. It was my intention, when I sent that energy to the seed of yourselves, to accelerate the process. The process had settled down to be very gradual, so gradual that it was almost coming to a stop. This is why I needed to do something to stimulate the growth process. That's where you, the Explorer Race, come in.

This is an experiment, then, from the ultimate. This is the only time you've done this?

Yes. It is the only time it has been necessary. I do not think it will be necessary again. I have checked with the other beings like me, and all of them have at one time or another had to do something similar. It appears that I was the next to last being to have done this.

The attempt to move to a higher level of ecstatic feeling is what will happen when we achieve that tenfold expansion of consciousness?

This we do not know. We hope that that will happen, but it will not be immediate. It will radiate out, but it will take some time to radiate out to the entire creation that is within me. When that happens, then we will see.

So you're the one who sent the stream of inspiration past our Creator?

Yes. Although you as the seed being had all the energy that was necessary to create, you did not have all the tools that were necessary to function as a creator. It was necessary to send that which would support and sustain your creation within the Creator you resided in, but also to have enough to interest that Creator. So that was patterned in as well.

And the friends of the Creator were sort of inspired by you to be where they happened to meet the Creator.

They are portions of myself.

Whether they are aware of it or not.

I think on deep levels they are aware of it.

Zoosh as well.

Yes.

Youthful Enthusiasm Enabled You to Choose Suffering

What was the Explorer Race lacking? Maturity? What did the Creator have that the Explorer Race didn't have, so that it had to go through the Creator?

The seed being that you were then had youthful enthusiasm, but did not have the core responsibility that all creators have. You could have made a creation without wisdom. The creators necessarily have wisdom, because all creators are a combined total. They are all connected to other creators. You as a portion of a creator did not have that status or authority, so while you had some means to create, you might have gone too far with some creations in your youthful enthusiasm.

Why did we need that youthful enthusiasm—in order to put up with the suffering, the experiment, the whole game?

Yes, because no being would consciously choose suffering unless they were filled with youthful enthusiasm, which has within it a sense of its own immortality, or unless they were serving some greater cause that allowed it to be somewhat self-sacrificial to serve the higher purpose. You were filled with that. Even today one sees that—courage and self-sacrifice for the betterment of all or even for some.

After we take over this creation and run it, will we have gained the maturity and wisdom to do our own creation?

Becoming Responsible by Managing Creation

Yes. It is intended that you have the responsibility that will come as a result of managing (if I might use that word) this creation, because only when you feel this entire creation as yourself will you understand all the subtleties of what you have contributed to. Yes, Earth is shielded largely from influencing other planets that cannot tolerate such extreme energy, but it is not a complete and total shield. Some of this energy is intended to escape, but with it goes a degree of minor discomfort. This has grossly affected many beings and many civilizations, some of whom you will not really meet as individuals but will come to know when you reconnect as your total being. You will need to purify those beings as well, so there will be much to do. Some things will have to be uncreated. Other things will have to be re-created. Still more things will have to be created entirely anew.

If you create creators and they all have this wisdom and responsibility, what did you do to the seed part of us that made us different?

Your Ignorance and Discovery Enabled by My Shielding

It was necessary to treat your *system* of being different. I had to encapsulate even your own Creator somewhat, so that your Creator could and would operate on faith but not necessarily have the whole picture. It was also necessary to encapsulate you even while you were within your Creator so that you could experiment with ignorance and discovery, which in my experience are the tools of quantum expansion. Thus it was necessary to apply a degree of shielding to both your Creator and you within your Creator. When you recombine as your total self, you will not experience that shielding. That's how you will know where to go, what to do, who to help, who to leave alone.

But there's almost a sense that our growth was stunted or that something was missing—or is it all explained by this shielding?

Your growth has been purposely controlled so that you could benefit from your own creation. If you and your Creator were allowed to know all, you would not have been able to apply ignorance and discovery. If you had known all, you would have known how ignorance and discovery would affect the populations in your immediate sphere of influence as well as populations well beyond. If you had known that there would be suffering, you would never have been able to institute that which could lead to suffering.

After the Quantum Leap, Chaos Elsewhere

It was therefore necessary to install blinders upon you, as it were, so that you could make the choice, give the gift, live the gift and in time restructure the gift. For when that quantum leap of ten times consciousness takes place, there will be much to do afterward. Many beings will not have any idea what has happened. The farther reaches of the universe are not involved in this experiment at all. In one moment they will be conscious to the degree they are, and in the next moment they will suddenly have ten times that consciousness. So there will be some chaos and confusion, and you will need to be almost everywhere at once.

This will happen in all of the creations within this circle of creation, the other universes?

Yes. And as it affects other universes, you will need to send expeditionary portions of yourself there, or you will have to support the creators in those universes as they assist their own beings. You will be busy for a time. [Chuckles.]

You got this theory of ignorance and discovery from your peers? That was the technique they used in their creations?

No, we did not share.

Then you invented it?

I decided to take a chance with it. It wasn't so much an invention as an application that required taking a chance. When I was considering taking a chance with it, I initially considered doing it myself. But I knew that I would not be able to do it as thoroughly as other beings might do, because I would know all the effects it would have.

You couldn't be ignorant.

Answering the Call for Volunteers

No. But if some beings were chosen to partake of this creation, they could (if their souls agreed) have this experience themselves for a time. So I basically put out a call for volunteers. I was *very* surprised at how many beings volunteered. There were volunteers from all over. I was quite stunned. I had to go through a weeding-out process. My primary tool for this process was who would stay with it the longest, who would be willing to exist in this process for billions of billions of years in experiential time.

Ultimately, since you were living in a voidlike place within your Creator, the idea of being involved [chuckles] in a great mass of creation excited you, and that is how I made my choice. I recognized that your excitement could create some confusion at some point; nevertheless, I felt that was a reasonable risk.

You Existed Before I Did, in Pure Liquidity

So did we have a history before this? Was there a conscious history of who we were before that quickening inside the Creator?

Yes. You had existed before my existence. Understand that my existence began, from my perception, from that moment of separation from complete Ecstasy; before that I was a portion of something else. When I was involved in creating creators and conditions for creations, I had to call various feelings from various places and I had to create the purest feelings to function as the foundation for creators, yes? Youthful enthusiasm is a feeling, and when I was focusing on that I could hear you calling as a seed race, asking if you could come and accept the mantle of youthful enthusiasm, which appealed to you. I said yes, of course.

So you came from a far-off place. I believe it is a place that consists almost entirely of liquid—liquid elements, for it is not exactly water, though water exists there. It is a place of pure liquidity. You came in that form and I told you that you could keep that in creation or in your creative ability, but you might also have to become light. Since light flows, you decided you could accept that. You could not accept any existence that did not at the very least flow. Eventually you will resume pure liquidity, but that will be long after your responsibilities here.

Is the place where we were within the source from which you came?

It was not in pure Ecstasy. It is a different place, perhaps a place worthy of hearing from next time.

(You're doing something—I'm shaking all over. There's something happening here.) So we came forth and we moved into the Creator while He was in the Void?

Yes.

We went through the centrifuge? How did that work?

No, you were sent to where this Creator was, who came to be your own. This Creator had love within the core of Its being, of course, but It also had tremendous patience—an obvious place for youthful enthusiasm.

So it's a wonderful drama, far beyond anything that we have caused. It was all sort of staged, yet you didn't know the outcome.

Your Eventual Ability to Uncreate; Your Root of Youthful Enthusiasm

No. The best plans, in my experience, do have the outcome as a mystery. This way, when you are able to uncreate, you can bring things together without any real sense of exactly what will happen, though you will have a vague sense. You will see what happens, and if it isn't right, you have the responsibility and the ability to uncreate. When one has achieved quantum mastery, uncreation is achievable. I have done this and a little bit more.

What would you call us—a race, a being? How would you describe what we are in totality?

You are essentially a feeling. You are your full enthusiasm, and no matter how old you are as an individual, you all have that within you, though sometimes you forget. Even when you are very old as a physical being, it is exactly youthful enthusiasm that allows you to feel the sense of adventure that one often feels in what is called senility—to leap out of the body in your spirit-body form and dash around to discover there is more yet to be had. It is exactly your youthful enthusiasm that makes the perpetuation of life such a pleasure.

There is no other feeling like us in any of the other creations within your creation?

There is no other race of beings that has youthful enthusiasm at its core, though there are certainly other races of beings that are utilizing it. After all, you too utilize other feelings: You have joy, love, excitement, happiness—and those and other feelings might be the root of other races. So although you might utilize other emotions and thoughts, your root is youthful enthusiasm, and there are no other beings or races that have that as a root, though there are several that have similar feelings—spontaneity being an example.

Have we ever heard of you? Do you have an identity? Has there ever been a whisper of who or what you are in our religion or mythology?

I don't think so, because if I were well-known, it would cause you all to feel separated more from the All. Therefore I have not gone out of my way [chuckles] to make my presence known. But now as you evolve toward greater consciousness, you can begin to hear about beings such as myself without being in the least bit intimidated.

What can we call you? What would you choose to be known by?

I do not use a name or a sound or color, because I am all of those and more, so what can I say? I will let you name me, eh? But do not name me Spot or anything like that.

[Laughs.] Let's talk about you. The little bit that we got before was that there was a circle of union [see chapter 12 in Explorer Race: Particle Personalities*] around everything that we knew of in creation, that there were several unions, and then we got to the golden light [see chapter 13 in* Particle Personalities*] that fed this creation. I gather that's an agent of yours?*

Yes.

Then we heard of the one who made shapes, then the buffer [see chapter 7 in Particle Personalities*] where the personalities were nurtured.*

My Internal Structure

Yes. There is a great deal of structure within me, and this is very important. We cannot have creations feeding back into places where they were before they became what they are. There is a large number of safety mechanisms to keep you moving in your proper direction.

Can you help us understand what else is in your creation? Is this the only circle of union in your creation that has creations in it, or are there many?

There are other creations that have union. Generally speaking, that which exists in some form of mass between creations is often union. Not always, but often, as it is a material that supports and sustains while acting as an insulator.

Shiva is connected to you in some way because he was your architect for the orbs, right?

This is an assistant.

What is beyond the buffer? The personalities come from you, but can you describe anything beyond that?

Beyond union?

Beyond the buffer zone. We know that the personalities are nurtured there and that the being who makes dense, compressed light uses it, but we don't know what's beyond that.

What is beyond that is primarily what I call raw feelings, meaning a vast array of feelings, a few of which could be loosely termed tinctures of thoughts (tinctures meaning a form of pure thought), but in condensed streams—the raw material that this being you have referred to utilizes. This raw material might be loosely referred to as the core of my being.

Which flows out, but is somehow constantly replenished from your source?

Yes, because pure Ecstasy has within it all thought and feeling that sustains and nurtures life. It does not, however, have within it criticism, discomfort, any of that. I had to call on something else to . . .

Discomfort: Culling It from a Creator's Rejects

I was going to ask you that, because a particle of union said it had everything except discomfort.

Yes, I had to actually dredge that up [chuckles] from someplace else. When I sent you to your Creator, you did not have it yet. When I sent the energy burst that got you going, I included a very small amount of the energy of stress. I'm calling it stress in the mechanical sense, which means, perhaps more precisely, resistance, which is at the source of all discomfort. It is built in this way because it is your job to create, refine and largely utilize discernment in its purified form. You cannot fulfill that end without having some challenge to work with, and this small amount of resistance has compounded itself into all of the discomforts you feel.

And where did you get it?

I culled it from a being who was sent out from another level of creation. This was not a being so much as a collection of odds and ends that didn't work in that particular creation. It was rejected by one of the other beings like myself who, noticing these bits that were unresolved, gathered up all that was unresolved from its creation and expelled it. When it was moving toward the auric field of Ecstasy, where it would have been transformed into pure loving energy, I sampled a small amount of it and let it be on its way. I took a very small amount, but I must admit that I did not realize its capacity for self-regeneration. When I realized this fully, it was a little too late. Being a quantum master and a little more, I have resolved all that is *my* responsibility, and I will allow you to resolve all that is *yours*.

Pure Ecstasy, My Source; Other Levels

I sort of lost the picture there. You said you separated as a leaf would separate, so did pure Ecstasy separate into several beings like you?

No, the core of pure Ecstasy remains, but other beings, parts of pure Ecstasy like myself, separated at the same time and went to other places away from pure Ecstasy, but not so far that we cannot feel its radiations.

How many? Two, or millions, billions, hundreds?

Oh, I think there are only 91.

Ninety-one. And they are all doing the same thing you are, creating creators?

I have not really checked. We do not check on each other. I think most of them are involved in some level of creationism.

And the source of pure Ecstasy is one of many sources? There are others like him?

You would have to ask that being.

All right, if that's possible.

Yes, perhaps another night.

What brings you joy? Watching your creations unfold?

Joy is my natural state of being, but what brings me a special joy is watching the level of cherishment that parents have for children. This is my favorite part. In most places children are cherished like treasures. Even on your own planet this is often the case, though not always, because of your particular challenges. But I'd say that what gives me the greatest joy is that cherishment.

You mentioned levels of creation. Are there levels above and beyond you that you aspire to?

Aspire, no. I cannot say that aspiration is a personally experienced emotion within me. I am reasonably happy and fulfilled doing what I am doing.

Are there levels above you?

Are there other levels such as you experience dimensions? I do not think so. I think that at this place where we are, dimensions are created from this point on. I am not aware of other variations of this existence in some other expression.

Like the fellow who had anticipation but not curiosity, they're down the line, right? [Laughs.] They're down the line from you, not upline?

Yes.

The Future of My Creations, How I Interact with Them

Is there a cycle? Will you at some point learn everything there is to know and shut this down to do something else? How does your cycle play out at your level?

I believe that at some point I will allow these creations within me to be entirely autonomous, at which time I will simply take a little nap.

Then what?

I'll decide when I wake up.

Oh, all right. [Laughs.] But there are other possibilities, other adventures even at your level?

Possibly I might find someone to fill in for me, but I don't think it's intended. I believe it is intended that you all become autonomous in some way at some point. After all, what is the point of creating creators if they do not eventually have autonomy?

How do they not have autonomy now?

Well, they are within me; that's where they are. They do not simply leave me and go out to create a creation elsewhere. Their primary restriction is that they must stay within myself.

How do you interact with them? You give them inspiration, you send them love, you send them energy, you send them light?

I send them, generally speaking, what they need. If they need to learn something, then I let them find it. Anything that anyone needs to learn can be found and experienced within myself, or you would not need to learn it—for all needs shall be fulfilled.

How would you make creators autonomous, by somehow allowing them to move beyond what you are?

Yes. I would simply inform them all that should any of them desire to move beyond my boundaries, they would be welcome to do so.

What are your boundaries like?

[Chuckles.] It's hard to put that in your numbers. The closest I can give you would be . . .

I don't mean numbers; just describe what happens. Do you fall off an edge? Is there a barrier? Is there more light?

If you were to approach it (you'd have to be a creator to do so), you would simply lose interest in going any farther. You would lose the impetus to go farther.

How would you change that when someone desires to go farther?

I simply would not reduce the energy flow to creators.

Oh, that's what you do?

Yes. I reduce the energy flow so that they would choose to stay within me at this time. I would eliminate that clause [chuckles].

If they were to move, is there a space there, or would they run into one of the other 91 beings like you or whatever is out there?

There is infinite space. The chances of their running into another one of the 91 beings is very unlikely, though it is possible. If they were to approach another one of the beings, it would say, "Not here; this space is taken." [Chuckles.]

You said, "I believe it's intended that you all become autonomous." You didn't say, "I intend that you all should be autonomous." Where does this intention come from?

It comes from Ecstasy. Ecstasy originally released myself and the others with an allowance for *us* to be autonomous, so I simply extrapolate that that is an intention.

My Perception of Some Other Beings

Are there other beings we missed who are mechanics in making this creation work? Are there other beings there who have responsibilities or functions to make this work?

It is possible, yes, that there are other beings. Some of them might not be too practical to communicate with, such as pure tone, for instance, or pure emotion or even pure thought. A pure thought would be focused in *one thought* and anything you asked it would be answered within the parameters of that thought. I believe the beings you have spoken with so far are the ones who are most easily assimilated into your thought patterns.

I see. What about the friends of the Creator and Zoosh? They had histories before. What is your version? What is your perception of them?

Zoosh, as a being, as a persona, has, in its root (the progenitor of Zoosh and its progenitor) existed somewhat outside of my being, but Zoosh itself did not exist as a personality until it came to be within myself. Much the same can be said for the other beings, with the exception of the Master of Discomfort, who is distantly related to that discomfort energy that I sampled slightly to send with you.

Coming into Me from Beyond Me

So, like the Explorer Race, then, the friends of the Creator came from beyond your creation, from someplace else?

Their precursors did, that which preceded them, but the personalities they now have represented to you were all generated within this mass creation.

Can you help me understand the concept of the progenitors and of moving from someplace else to within you?

Yes. An example, if you were to experience it physically, would be . . . have you ever been around a child who is young enough to directly reflect the personality and opinions of its parents? It would be like that. The Zoosh personality is the child of the progenitor of Zoosh and its progenitor.

Who were created someplace else?

Yes.

Were Zoosh and the other friends of the Creator all created in a certain place, or did they come from diverse places?

I believe from diverse places.

From the other 91 creators?

No.

Ah, so there's someplace else where beings are created?

There are, to my understanding, infinite places of creation. It is a very large loop.

Well, this is the Beyond book. We're going to check it out, right?

That's right.

You are stimulating something in me, because my body is shaking and I'm finding it hard to breathe. What are we stimulating, memory?

Well, it is not my intention to give you discomfort . . .

No, no, it's wonderful!

Perhaps we'll see what happens.

My Appearance

All right. Do you have shape? Are you circular or spherical?

I initially said that I was transparent. I am translucent, because of all that is within me. If you were to see me, I would look . . . let's see if I can draw it. [Draws.] I will indicate, for the sake of some clarity, a gap at the bottom. See this as a circular thing. There are lines on the other side too, but I am showing you roughly a side view.

The gap is my allowance for all that is within me to have its own cycle of growth, so that I alone do not influence you. There is a certain amount of protection, so that what is appropriate to stay within stays there and what is inappropriate to come in stays without. But if there is something that needs to come in that I have not allowed for due to your own evolutionary growth, I have allowed for that.

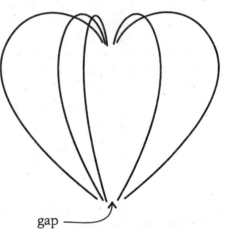

gap

Is that where the beings from outside your creation come in? Like the Explorer Race and the friends of the Creator?

No, they would come in more from the top. You're seeing it in its expanded form now. At some point it will expand even more. When you have the ten times consciousness it will expand quite a bit. But picture the shapes; simply picture the gap at the bottom getting larger and everything swinging up from there.

Do all 91 of your peers look like this?

Variations of that, yes.

With your responsibility to this creation, can you go out and look around in other places? Do you have any interest in doing that?

I cannot go per se.

But can you see clairvoyantly or something?

I am able to do so, but I limit that within myself so that I do not . . . well, my whole focus is purity, refinement—we start with the purest source of whatever feeling or thought, and it continues to be refined either by its own experience or through some process of my own. So I am disinclined to stimulate myself too much with other people's creations.

My Connection to the Centers of Pure Feeling; How I See My Job

Beyond our Orb we have beings described as centers of pure feeling, which we draw on. Do you have some sort of connections to each of those; do you feed those?

I initially fed them with the pure feeling and gave them the ability to reproduce that pure feeling as they need to so it can create itself. The advantage of keeping those feelings pure is that it can easily re-create itself, yet not be easily affected by other feelings or thoughts. So purity is guaranteed, which means that the opening exists where the feelings exit, but there is no longer an entrance. There was an opening for entrance when I initiated these feelings, but now that opening has been closed and the feelings reproduce themselves.

Say more about the purity of feeling and thought.

It is not my intention to disrupt the evolution of beings, even if I have been largely involved in their creation. It is my intention to provide the clearest sources by which all creators and ultimately all beings can tap into and choose for themselves how to combine things. As I see it, my job is to create the essences, the foundational elements by which beings can then go to the market, if you would, and mix and match as they will.

Is that something that you contemplated, or when you individualized was it just there?

Because I had come from pure Ecstasy, which is the combination of *all* benevolent feelings, I felt strongly that feelings must be available in their pure source. It is my hope that ultimately all that is created within me will regenerate pure Ecstasy on its own as a primary feeling, honoring its source. But I decided from the very beginning that I would not underlay any being with that desire. I would simply see if it would come about in the natural course of events, allowing for where I came from and who I am. It is as if I am breaking myself down into my component parts, projecting variations of my component parts into creations within myself, allowing creators within me to utilize them in any way and see if it would all simply reproduce itself eventually into my point of origin.

Connections with My Source

Do you communicate with your source? It's feeding you, in a sense.

Not "in a sense"; it *does* feed me.

Is there any sort of father-son communication?

No, it is more like food.

Do you have emotional or mental interactions with your source?

Not mental. I had to create a lot of mental from scratch, because mental was not used very much because it always slows things down. But I could see it that would be useful within the creations within myself. One must find some means by which to separate the dimensions. And dimensions, if expressed by any creator, use a form of mental frequency to create the barriers that separate dimensions. So I do not think with my source; my source would consider that too slow. But there is a shared mutual love; I feel cherished by my source, and I cherish my source.

There's no interchange of information?

Information is thought.

It's a love exchange, right?

Pure feeling, yes. Pure feeling, not thought.

A feeling of oneness?

Pure love is a feeling of oneness, amongst other things.

Consultants in Your and My Creation

When we first started the book series, we had only our Creator here in our creation. Then what we call outside consultants came in and created the dimensions and did a lot of the engineering to make the creation work. Those beings are all your creation, right?

Yes, as they express themselves here, yes.

When you created your creation, did it happen spontaneously, or did you have the benefit of outside consultants?

It didn't spontaneously happen; it happened with consideration. And no, I did not have outside consultants. That is, it is pure Ecstasy's intention that portions of itself—myself and the 91—be relatively autonomous. The only exception is that pure Ecstasy feeds us.

Is your source in turn fed by something, or is it creating what it sustains you with?

It might very well be fed by something, but I do not think it is fed by its own. I believe it is creating pure ecstasy, but it is possibly being fed by something. You will have to ask it.

I've run out. What would you like to tell us?

Your Lineage

I will say this: You all come from a benevolent lineage: pure liquidity and all of the subtle influences of myself and beings within me. Your parents are truly pure Liquidity and total Ecstasy. I believe in your capacity to find your own path to rejoin this ultimate sense of home. I know that when you take over this creation you will by your very nature transform many planets into planets of liquid and joy that are now stark and barren, waiting for life. It is your nature to do so, and I will enjoy observing you in action.

That's why we needed a water planet, right?

Yes. Good night.

Thank you very, very much.

A ll right [sighs], Zoosh speaking.

Awesome, man, awesome! It took you longer to get back this time than it ever has, I think.

You have me on the clock, eh?

[Laughs.] No, you just look different. How was it different?

For me? You mean, was it good for me? [Everyone laughs.] I enjoyed hearing this being communicate in such a fashion because my normal communications with this being do not involve any level of the mental. So that was a pleasure.

So he had to focus in a different way to talk to us.

Yes.

Why is my body shaking? It feels like it's going to break the edges of the skin; something's going on.

Well, I am hopeful that it is simply a form of initiation.

Well, you choose the next one. You're doing great.

All right. We could either hear from the pure Ecstasy or the pure Liquidity.

Pure Ecstasy first.

All right, we'll do pure Ecstasy and then . . .

. . . learn more about his idea before we go to our source.

All right.

Thank you.

Good night.

The Liquid Domain

January 23, 1997

reator of purity: I can speak but briefly.

Mostly I would like you to draw a road map of where we are within you and what the creation looks like within you—where this vast circle of creation is in relation to your shape. And another road map of what you see when you look out from there. Do you see your source?

Purity's Map

Wait. Too many questions. Let me have the picture. [Reaches for the drawing made last session.]

Put a "you are here" and then draw in the things that . . .

[Draws a dot.] Allowing that this is not to scale, you are here.

Is that our universe, or is it the whole circle of creation? Show me the circle of creation.

You mean the orbs?

Yes.

I won't do this to scale, either, if you don't mind. Generally speaking . . . [draws a curve around the dot] there are the orbs, then factor the opposite on the other side.

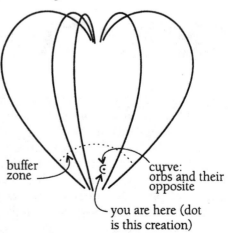

buffer zone

curve: orbs and their opposite

you are here (dot is this creation)

But it is not to scale—I would say they are much smaller.

What about everything else in the creation—the circles of union, the gold light, the buffer zone?

Yes, I understand, where is it all? [Draws a curved dotted line for the buffer.] There.

Okay, and what's up here [pointing to upper part of diagram]? Just you enjoying yourself?

There is room to grow in.

[Laughs.] There's room to grow! In that drawing would you put "you are there" to show your relationship to your source and the other 91? What do you see when you look out?

I generally look in, I don't look out.

All right, if you were to look out, like get above and look down?

If I were to look out, I would see the source of Ecstasy.

Behind you, above you, around you?

If I were to turn or to observe as you do, I would see the source of Ecstasy and not much else.

You wouldn't see the other 91?

No. They are at a distance.

So you're much closer to the source than they are?

No, I think they would see that, too. The source of Ecstasy is quite bright.

Based on what you told us, what would you feel would be the most intelligent way to go about talking to your source and some of the other 91? How could we learn the most?

Well, obviously, I think by going to the source of the Explorer Race in the liquid realm.

Thank you.

I speak as the liquid domain, which contains the essential personality of the beings you now know as Explorer Race. My liquidity is largely made up of minerals that in your realm you would experience as stone or ore, even what you might refer to as gems. This form of liquid is intended to prepare beings who pass through my being for some form of encapsulated life where it will be necessary for them to absorb nutrients or interact physically in some way with their environment. Not all beings who must do this pass through myself, but many, many years ago your essence did. Nevertheless, your mark has been left within me and I can still speak about you. Even now as I look at the result—what you have become—I can see that there has been very little change in your actual personalities, with the possible exception of the impact of experience on your personality.

So you're saying that we did not come from you, we just passed through you?

Versions of Water You Experienced
When You Passed through Me

Oh, yes. You came from somewhere else. [Chuckles.] Back, back back we go! But tonight it is perhaps *my* turn to say a little bit.

When you first arrived, your personality was very *excitable!* You were what you might call nervous. I think this was because you had never experienced any form of physical life, and to some extent you were excited at the prospect. You had always lived in realms (to the extent that I know) where you absorbed energy, but you never had to eat or touch or discern or do any of the things you now take for granted in your world. You were very excited, anticipating wondrous new things.

The thing [chuckles] I remember about you the most is that you had all these questions. It was never-ending questions, all based on the precept of "what will it be like?" It was pleasantly amusing. You went through a significant process when you came to be with me. You started out in an area that had to do with the variations of water. Though you did not encounter ice or even steam within me, you encountered variations on the experience, water. There was the water you now know, a thinner water and several levels of thicker water. This is because at some point in your travels you would live on planets that had these versions of water.

Now, the thin version of water is actually the most wholesome, for it contains no oxygen. Oxygen, as you know, does wear things out after a time. This water contains none of that, so you can consume as much as you want and it does only good, without any impact at all to erosion. Then you experienced the water that you now have.

After that you experienced a thicker water, which has properties of great spirituality. It also has a gloss. It does not need to have a sun reflect off of it; it glows on its own because it tends to absorb the kinetic and magnetic energy around it. It is that which tends to foster and nurture life. It was a very interesting experience for most of you.

Then there was water even thicker than that. This kind of water would have a consistency not unlike somewhat liquefied clay. This kind of water serves not only to satiate thirst, but is also a pure food. One essentially eats and drinks when one consumes it. It also tends to give one the experience of absolute total recall. You have all experienced this at one point in your evolution to your now point of being.

This, I believe, is a form of water found on Andromeda. Generally speaking, you will find things on Andromeda that tend to support thought.

Then there was one last version of water that was very thick, like cement. It didn't set up like cement but remained very thick. This was a very unusual property. You do not actually eat or drink this water, you float in it. Even a physical being such as yourself could float in it. It has an effect like osmosis: If you are hungry or thirsty, if you need love and nurturance, whatever your needs, by floating in this version of water all these needs will be sated after a time. This is a very highly evolved form of water.

Liquid Minerals Such as Diamond, Gold and Salt

That was your first experience of my liquid self. From there you moved through many different forms of minerals, not all of which you have on your Earth, which is known for its great variety of minerals. I will pick out a few as examples. I think one wherein you experienced one of the greatest pleasures was liquid diamond. In liquid diamond you experience all known and unknown (from my point of view) thoughts that could or might ever come in handy. All of this would go into the deepest levels of your unconscious to create a welcoming energy should those thoughts ever need to be processed by you in a form of application or even imagination. Thus it was more a tincture for the immortal unconscious.

Then there was another mineral that I believe had a startling effect on you: liquid gold. When you experienced liquid gold, many of you were utterly transformed. Those of you who were the most excitable became much more relaxed and rested. Even today you can get the same result by soaking a piece of pure gold in clear, pure spring water for at least a week. It would be best if it were a rod down the center of a bottle, but if not, just agitate the water once a day. Shake it or tip it back and forth for seven days (seven 24-hour periods) and place it where sunlight shines on the bottle at least two hours a day. Put it in the window like a plant. After a week you can drink small quantities (an ounce or half an ounce) and it will allow many of you to feel much more rested and help you release anxiety and nervousness.

Let's see, there was another mineral you found very beneficial, and that was liquid salt, the salt you use for table salt, sodium chloride. Many of you who had some form of discomfort from the past—delusions or disillusionments, such things as this—had it completely purified from you. I think for many of you that this was your first experience of being purified by what was apparently some *thing* rather than some *one*, and that was quite startling to you. I believe that even today many of your societies consider salt a purifying item.

How were you notified that we were coming? What was the communication to you and what was the request?

I was notified by your progenitor, that which preceded you, that you would be coming along. It was requested of me (beings are polite, you know) that I subject you to all forms of liquid that I had available for the journey upon which you would be going. As you approached to within (in terms of distance you can understand) about one and a half trillion miles, I would be able to feel the rest of your journey forward and would know what to expose you to. This was so, and I have done so. (I think that speaking to your progenitor might be the obvious choice for next time.)

Your Three and a Half Minutes within Me

How long were we there, in a time that we can understand?

In the time you can understand, yes—you were within me for about three and a half minutes.

Three and a half minutes?

Yes. It is interesting, is it not, because within me there is no time as you know it. Everything happens at once, so there is extremely intense experience. You experience multiple levels of your own being within me. You came as a group, remember, so you would experience first dimension, second dimension, third dimension, all the way up to ninety-second or ninety-fourth dimension—that would be the range. If only one of you were to experience it, then all of you would be exposed to it because you are united at your core. That allows you to have many more tools than you would have otherwise as an individual. So you experienced a very intense three and a half minutes. If I were to equate that to the experiential progressive experience in a given life that you might have now, approximately ten and a half lifetimes of sequential experience would be compacted into three and a half minutes of semi-instantaneous experience. This also tells you the intensity that you can tolerate when you are united.

Even though we were united, how many individuals were there?

Using Your Experience As Groups of Nine

At that time I think the sum total of your individuality was about nine. It hadn't gone beyond that yet. You arrived with nine core personalities, because to some extent you were going to be encouraged to understand that nine is a mystical number. Ultimately what you will discover with nine is not just groups of nine, but groups of nine times groups of nine—not quite to the infinite, but out there a ways. By experiencing groups of nine you will be able to utilize them to reconnect entirely with all of your beings, no matter where they are in this galaxy or this universe—all of you. You will have to conceptualize it in the form of groups of nine.

I will show you what is equal to ten. For the sake of simplicity I will do it like this. [Draws nine dots.] Here is nine, yes? Now I will draw a symbol for yourself. Making you a bigger symbol [draws a triangle above the dots, the whole drawing also in the shape of a triangle], I am making you the triangle, see? Think of yourself as a triangle—useful form, in any event—and that all other beings are out there in groups of nine. Then you can simply say that whoever "I" is reacts with groups of nine of the Explorer Race everywhere. This allows the "I" to be the tenth person, essentially encompassing all beings. The nine would not only be the nine that were within me, but groups of nine *everywhere* that are associated with the Explorer Race. Utilizing this in various meditations (I think others can provide those), you will be able to unite with all beings in the Explorer Race.

As you know, all of you are not presently on Earth. Shall I give you a percentage of how many of you are present on Earth at this time?
Please.

About 7%. Are you surprised?
Yes!

93% of Explorer Race Not on Earth

Everyone on Earth is associated with Explorer Race, yet only 7% of your total being is here. The reason people have had difficulty in uniting with all beings on Earth is that 93% of your totality is still scattered about the universe on other planets or in other dimensions! It is infinitely easier for you to unite with all beings on Earth if you say, "I would like to unite with all beings in the Explorer Race anywhere in this universe to give me the feeling of perfect unity with all beings of the Explorer Race on Earth."

How do you know so much about us? You have followed our history?

I know everything about your core personalities. I had to know where you were going and what you were going to do in order to expose you to the proper liquids, so I was given a road map of where you would go, what you would do (given certain variables) and what you would wind up doing. Even now I can see that.

Who gave it to you?

[Chuckles.] Your progenitor.

How I Perform for Beings

Ahh, progenitor. Let's talk about your creation a little bit. What do you do?

For all beings, whether they be the Explorer Race or beings doing other things in other places, I perform in the capacity I performed for you. For beings perhaps going to some other universe, they would come within me and I would expose them to the liquid forms of the experience they might have in their future.

Excuse me, coming to the universe in this creation, or . . .

In any creation.

There are billions of other creations out there beyond this circle of union, right?

Yes, and I am not alone. Other beings perform in capacities not unlike mine. Recently a group of beings passed through me, staying a little longer—about five minutes of your time. They were exposed entirely to thoughts, not to any elements as you were. I took the essence of thoughts and their precursors, which are inspirations, and liquefied them, then these beings moved through that, tinting their souls to be receptive when these thoughts or inspirations would come up for them as they developed in the future.

What sort of experience were they being aimed into?

They were being readied for a very massive universe just now getting started, of which they will be the core. As the core, they will function not unlike the brain functions in your body. It will be their job to provide guidance when it comes to all knowledge, but only if that knowledge has to do with thought. Other beings will be involved in all knowledge with feeling, for example, so their job is very specific. That universe will tend to grow out from them and other core units.

So where would they go to get imbued with feeling? Could you do that also?

I could also do that, yes. I have done that for other beings. To give you an example a little more relevant for you, very often guides who work with you day to day will often come to me to experience liquid emotion, liquid inspiration and liquid godlike material . . . no, no, I must be accurate: *liquid god material.* (If I say "godlike," that could be anything, yes?) For guides must be able to instantaneously recognize (sometimes even before the experience happens) what the person they are guiding is going through so that they can provide for that person's needs according to their job (because sometimes a person has more than one guide). You'd be very surprised, I think, if you realized how influential each person's guides are. I will put a percentage on it to give you some idea. Take an average person for an average life, all right?

In our universe?

How Much You're Influenced by Your Guides

On your Earth. Let's say there is a control group (and none like this has existed) where no guides are present. Then let's say there is a normal group where guides are present. The chances of change of decisions for the better for a person in the normal group is about 58%, whereas a person without guides does not have that opportunity to change even little decisions (what to eat, what to wear, who to be with), but has to do the best he can. Therefore guides have a minimum of a

58% impact on your individual life.

Now, that's for the average person. What about the person leading an intense life, perhaps a life of adventure or drama? A person like this could very easily have a 73% influence from their guides. Let's take the other extreme—a person living a very bland, predictable life. A safe life, but bland and predictable, might have a 33% influence from their guides.

In the here and now, those who are preparing to be guides can go through your . . . do we call it a planet, a creation? What is it that you have?

My Appearance

Well, I would say it is more of a mass. If you were to see me from a distance, it would appear to be a mass of color, but as you approached you would see the color moving and you wouldn't quite understand what it was. As you got very much closer, you would notice that it was definitely a liquid, very large. In terms of size, I can make myself larger to some degree—20% larger and 30% smaller than I am right now. To say how large am I right now, using the center of your sun as one of my boundaries and allowing for the fact that I am moving . . . I will draw you my shape for the moment. It varies, but I will just give you the example, yes?

Yes, please.

My current shape, roughly [draws] . . . I have made a sketch. If you took me lengthwise, using that drawing, and measured from the center of your sun, then my outermost perimeter would reach about 180,000 miles past Pluto.

So are you a creation within some other organized structure of creations?

Allowing for the fact that we are all within something, philosophically, I experienced myself as myself within space, but I do not experience myself on a regular basis as a portion of someone else. This tells me that whoever I am a portion of does not interfere directly in what I do. And since I am reasonably conscious, as far as I can tell I have not received any guidance from whoever I am a portion of, at least up to now. Now, that might change.

My First Awareness

What was your first experience of awareness?

I remember that initially when I came to be aware of myself, I was very small. I will give you an example. Let me think of something in your world . . . hmmm . . . about the size of an average grapefruit. Yes, this is when I became aware of myself. I realized I had been in this condition for some time, but I felt very much like, I suppose, the consciousness of an egg. As I became more aware of myself, I began stretching like you do when you wake up in the morning. And the more I stretched, the better I felt, until I got to about the size that you see in the drawing. Then I went about another 20% farther and realized I didn't want to go any farther than that. That's when I shrank down to about my present size, though the shape varies.

I didn't know what to do for a long time. I experienced myself as liquid, but I was what I would call my base liquid, my core liquid, which would be . . . how do we describe that to you? If you were to experience the sound . . . I'll say this, but you're not going to understand it at the moment: If you experience the sound of your Creator and all the other creators in unison, they would sound like that. (That doesn't mean anything to you, so let me come up with something else.) All right, for those of you who have had this near-death experience, as you call it, the choir you hear, which sounds like a thousand-voice choir singing in perfect harmony, is very much like this sound. I experience myself as a liquid sound of that angelic choir. That is my core.

My life's work started very much the way it is now. Someone, a being, a creator, spoke to me from afar and said, "I would like to send some beings to you to be in your midst. I believe you have the capacity to represent all elements, all experiences, all thoughts, all emotions (and so on) in liquid form. This will allow individual souls or beings to become instantaneously saturated with the full range of experience of that particular form of being. Would you like to try?"

I replied, "Very much." So they sent some beings to me. It was about several hundred experiences before they sent you. I think maybe they wanted to give me some training. [Chuckles.]

Your Initial Size and Mine

In relation to a human, what size were we when we came through you?

You were much smaller, even though you were the core of your being and there were nine of you. You were about the size . . . I'm going through my liquid memory. I could draw the size.

Sure. [He draws a tiny dot on a sheet of blank paper.] A dot? [Laughs.]

Yes. I don't think it made an impression on your paper. Well, you were about the size of a dot. Very small, but you were concentrated.

You were half the diameter of this solar system out past Pluto and we were a dot?

Yes, but you have expanded beyond those boundaries quite a bit. [Chuckles.]

There was enough mass there to experience and absorb what you had to offer them?

Oh, I've had *much* smaller sources of beings come through me! You were about average. I've had much smaller and on occasions much bigger, but that is rare. Generally speaking, when the core of beings passes through me, they are quite small because they largely represent a potential, which means they will become more. There is a great advantage in starting out small, because you start out not only with love, but with tremendous intimacy because you are, naturally, entirely engaged with each other in such a space.

You began as the size of a grapefruit, yet now you have every mineral known and every thought and every feeling—and it all came from that grapefruit?

Well, you have to understand that I have every mineral, even those unknown to you, and ideas and . . .

. . . in this creation, plus many that are in other creations—the essence of all of those are within you in your expanded state?

Yes, including thoughts, feelings, fantasies, emotions, actions . . .

. . . that you never had, as far as you know.

I have not had them personally, no.

But they are there.

Yes, because the beings who pass through me need them. Anytime beings pass through me, I am left with an impression, so I have it available to me. Should I have some time between jobs, I can kind of amuse myself. [Chuckles.]

The Being I'm Inside Of

Could you ask, "I request that where I came from—my progenitor, my creator, my precursor, my source—talk to me"? Would you try that now and see if somebody talks to you?

I cannot do this, and I'll tell you why. I did it visually, but I can't say it. If I said it, it would begin, and that would be it. With me, once something begins, it never ends. So I respectfully decline to do that. But I did go so far as to look, and I can see that I am, in fact, within  some greater thing, which is roughly a cone shape, but more rounded than a cone. It looks a bit like a pod, but open on one end. I will give you an example here. Generally the being I'm in looks like this [draws]. I'm drawing indeed, but I do not claim to be as good as your people.

Are you the only one in there?

No, there are a great many. And where am I? say you.

Yeah, you are here.

I am here [puts a dot in the upper middle of the conical shape].

That's wonderful. How do we understand what you just said: "If something starts, it never ends"?

For me, once something begins, such as when you came through to experience the forms of liquid you need, I always have that. To put it in your vernacular, I do not have a subconscious or an unconscious. I have a total conscious. So anything that I experience in any way is always with me in some way; I can access it immediately or I can choose to let it be there and do something else.

If I were to begin a dialogue with that from which I have come, the dialogue would be never-ending. Because of my natural fascination with this idea, I think I would be inclined to engage in that dialogue for some time. So I think I will wait until I have been replaced and can begin that dialogue or wait until I have enough time off between assisting other beings that I can begin that dialogue and maintain it for some time. There are many things I'm going to want to discuss.

Oh, how wonderful! So that's something to look forward to?

Yes. Because you are cut off from instant conscious knowledge of who you are and where you're from, you might wonder why so many beings like myself do not even consider where we're from. That is because out here, life, while it is cherished, is almost taken for granted. When you hear "life is," that's what it means. "Life is" means that we accept that life is, and the associated feeling is taking it for granted, not in any abusive way, but "this is life, this is what it is." We don't think about where we came from because we feel united. I have felt all this time united to that being, but I haven't really been conscious of its shape.

Beings Who Need My Help (Functional Mastery)

I certainly don't want to intrude. I was just interested in what lies beyond you. So you are within it, but out beyond that are all these other creations that call on your life skills, your reason for being?

Yes, and it is a most benevolent experience, because it often allows me to come into contact with beings that I never would have otherwise, and of course any teacher understands that feeling.

We've talked a little about levels of mastery—spiritual mastery, material mastery, quantum mastery. Do you know what level you have attained or that you're working on?

A moment . . . I think a little past quantum mastery to . . . I want to say this the right way so that it doesn't sound wrong. To me it sounds like "the master of all beings," but that sounds godlike, and I don't want to project that. Mastery, you understand, means the ability to fully experience, which means that I have the ability to fully experience all beings, all things, all ideas, all forms. This is, I believe, about one notch past quantum mastery.

Is there a name for that level? I don't think we've come across it yet.

I'm not aware of a name for that, no. Perhaps you can get one from your Zoosh.

Well, this is exciting. It's as if we were adopted and now we're trying to find our natural father. [*Laughs.*]

I have it! Your Zoosh told me: *functional mastery.*

Aha, that's the first time we've heard that. Thank you. What excites you, then, is the experiences of the beings who come to you, right?

Yes, it is fascinating! Not only do I get to experience them, but I get to *be* something for them, and sometimes I will be something that I have never been before. I become what they need, so in that sense I am a reactive being. And by becoming what they need, occasionally I will become something that I've never been before and discover some new level of myself. So not only do I provide something for them, but they often provide something for me. It is very well balanced.

So they want something, and you know that you have literally everything within you, even though you haven't called it out before or even known it was there.

Reacting to Needs

Yes, I don't have to think about it. I react to their needs. They can be a trillion miles away or so, but when they're anywhere from about one and a half to three trillion miles away, depending on the type of being, where they're going to go and what they're going to do, I can become right then what they need. Beings or groups of beings go through me one at a time. I don't have more than one group of beings within me at any time.

Because you need to be what they need.

That's right. I need to be it completely so they can have a total experience of what they need. I cannot do two at once, just one at a time.

Your mass is so huge, though, and the beings are so small.

But they must have a total experience while they are encapsulated within my being, and if there's any other portion of my being doing anything else but being what they need, it will not feel like totality to them and thus create a distraction. That could permanently mark their ability to receive and act upon inspirations, ideas and so on. They could have what would amount to a blank spot, so that if some inspiration came to them later on as an individual, there might be a gap in their ability to have a place to build from. If it were an inspiration they needed, for example, it would go unheeded by every single being in their race. So I need to be totally what they need.

When you look at the vast spectrum of creation and all the different parts each one of them choose to focus on, you must be connected to something so close to the source of everything, perhaps some of each one of those things . . .

The Limit of My Knowledge and Yours

I don't want to cause you alarm, but because you are involved now on this Earth planet with such a very specific purpose that within the context of all life, even such as I might know—and I'm sure I know a small portion of what exists—if what I know is equal to 360°, what you know is equal to about one-thirteenth of a degree. That does not mean that you do not have the capacity to know more. You choose to know what you need to know when you have a purpose, and your purpose is very specific. Let's take that one more step. Let's say that all of the knowledge that exists (I'm getting this guidance from someone, who is the being who preceded the progenitor of Zoosh, a very wise being), that if all the knowledge that even this being is aware of were 360°, then the knowledge I have would be equal to about one six-millionth of a degree. This tells you, obviously, that I also am involved in a very specific endeavor and that the massive amount of potential experience is beyond digitizing.

My God! Well, we've got some adventures left out there, right? [Laughs.]

As far as I know, it is truly infinite!

But it's never been brought to me with such force as with your numbers just now.

It is colorful, I will say that.

Do you have a guide? Do you have someone who guides you without your really knowing it?

I have not a direct guide, but when I need to know something, as I just did, I will have volunteers. I have not had this particular being volunteer before. I have been in touch with your Zoosh before, naturally, because Zoosh is involved with you, yes. But I have not been involved with the being who preceded the progenitor of Zoosh before, because it wasn't necessary. If I need something like that it will often come—in your case, from a version of who knows you, but in the case of other beings, if I'm interacting with them, a guide who will come from a version of who knows them. You want your consultants to be at least more worldly than yourself.

How are you using the word "progenitor"? How is it different from creator or . . .

Progenitor would be the nucleus of the personality of that being, whereas what preceded the nucleus of the personality of that being would be the potential for the personality. The potential would mean that the personality does not exist yet, only its potential. All the bits and pieces that might make up its root personality exist.

You have such intensity, you have such a wonderful energy! I can see how you were able to give us youthful exuberance—or did we have that before we came?

I think I was influential in that. You had some of it, but it was what you might call raw. Your nervousness, your anxiety, your excitement—all of this was channeled more into more constructive methods. Now, you still have those emotions, but youthful exuberance allows you to adapt in order to get the best out of something and enjoy it. I would like to see more adults allow that to come through them, because you do have it within you, but because of manners and the ways of being of any society, you do not often show it.

Expressing and Suppressing Emotion Affects How
Much You Can Feel

I'll tell you something interesting in terms of creation. If you show the emotions you are experiencing, especially if they are benevolent emotions, they can build and you get more. If you suppress them, they do not build and you get less. Let's say you get an inspiration and you become youthfully exuberant about it. If you allow that exuberance to show, you will get much more—quantum amounts more will be available to you. But if you suppress it for any reason, you will have quantum amounts *less* than what you originally received! Visually speaking [draws an oval], if this is the idea and you allow youthful exuberance, it easily becomes this [draws much larger orb]. If you do not allow it, if you suppress it in some way, then [draws small circle below] it becomes that.

That looks like the orbs. [Laughs.]

It does look a bit like that, yes.

Back to the joys, though, of your being. You said you had about 200 different visitations of beings who needed your services?

A couple of hundred before you came.

Since then you've had . . .

Thousands.

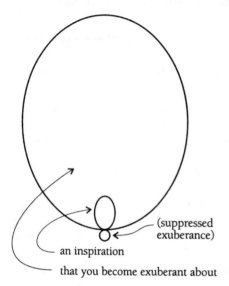

(suppressed exuberance)

an inspiration

that you become exuberant about

And you can follow where every single one of those beings went and watch their evolution?

Yes, because it is important for me to know where they are going to go, what they are going to do in order to consciously engage my ability to provide. I do not think about becoming what they need, it just happens. It's a reaction. But after they are gone I get the chance to consider it and think about it.

But can you see where they are as well as be told beforehand?

Yes, I can see, as you say.

You can see us on Earth.

Yes, I can see you, not with eyes, but I can see you, yes.

What an incredible thing! You can look at every one of these and say, "Look, I helped them be that! Part of me is in them!"

It is exciting, isn't it? It's exciting, and I like that. Maybe that's one of the reasons they sent you through me, because one of my natural emotions is exuberance. [Chuckles.] I think you can tell!

[Laughs.] Exuberance, yes, but there's also a beautiful intensity of energy there that I love. Give us a couple of stories about some of the beings totally different from us who have come through you, and how their evolution has worked out.

Other Beings Who Have Come through Me

Understand that there must be some similarity or it would simply not be able to translate to your experience. Let's find something that's really different. Some beings came through once who were primarily expressing themselves in the experience of what you might call wind. They were in constant motion, and they have gone on to create societies that run at fantastic speeds. They enjoy doing everything quickly. [Chuckles.] Some of you can identify with that.

Let's give you an example. If you were to sleep, get up in the morning and go to work, do your work and then come home at the night, a workday for you might take six, eight, ten, twelve hours, depending on what you are doing. Though the time is not directly comparable, a workday for them might last eight-tenths of a second, something like that, so their great joy then is doing what they do with absolute perfection as fast as it can be done. It is not competitive per se, but there is a constant attempt to better oneself in terms of speed without losing any accuracy. You can identify with that a little bit.

A tiny bit, yes. What do they do the rest of the time?

That's what they do *all* the time.

They don't run out of things?

Although you might consider eight-tenths of a second to be hardly worth mentioning, their cycle is about eight hours darkness and about twenty-eight hours light. Think of how many eight-tenths of a second there are in that period. Generally speaking, as beings they live one cycle of light and dark. But if we say eight-tenths of a second is a day, in terms of their experience they live much longer than you do.

Yes, it's a different method of counting time. That's a great example. Give us another one, something that's so far beyond—if you don't mind.

No, it's all right. Let's see what comes to mind that is sufficiently unlike you, but enough like you to make reasonable sense. Oh yes, a group of beings came through before you did who were expressing themselves as varietal shapes having to do with animals. They were very interested in providing potential animal shapes (what you call breeds) to wherever they would go. Whether the beings would fly, swim, walk, apparently not move at all or all of the above and more, they would provide the shapes to creators wherever they go—which they are still doing, I might add—variations of shapes and versions of animals. And to each animal in their universe they give one pure, absolute emotion.

They have been to this planet and originally did that here, giving your animals one pure emotion. Sometimes a group of animals would get the same emotion. Many of them have love. Some of them have curiosity as a core emotion, you understand. Some of them have almost a testiness about them. Some of them have great loyalty. I think you can imagine what that animal might be.

Cats? [Laughs as she looks at her cat.]

[Chuckles.] Some people might say dogs. In any event, I think it is safe to say that these beings have been *very* influential in your universe. Your Creator was very taken with these beings and utilized a great many of their suggestions for life forms, many of which are no longer with you at this time, but most of which . . .

. . . are in this creation someplace?

Yes. Most of which are somewhere, yes. But your Creator also referred other creators to these beings, so they are now traveling all over. So the idea and the experience of animals is getting out.

What did they gain from you? Diversity of the possibilities, or what?

When they came, I became all shapes and many densities (allowing for different tissues and so on). I also became all emotions, because that is something they would plan to do, and (this will surprise you) also all variations of the emotion humor. Very often—and you can look at this in your own animal world—animals are amusing. Although I was all emotions, I wasn't necessarily all variations of those emotions; but I *was* all variations of humor. These beings felt very strongly that in order for animals to be accepted and to be in the lives of all beings, they would need to have a common experience that would tend to endear them. You know, sometimes animals are not particularly endearing in their own right, but when they do something endearing, suddenly you expand your whole perspective of that being.

I didn't realize other creations had animals.

Whales, for example, used to be fearsome creatures on your planet, whereas now they're considered benevolent and loving because they've done some things over the years that endeared them to people. Yes, other creations are now beginning to have animals. When you look at all animals you could say they are extraterrestrials, but animals, especially on Earth, tend to be more of a core or a very specific type of being, and most of them don't need to have a tremendous amount of thought (though some do).

Tarantulas and Sting Rays, Masters of Profound Thought

One animal that is perhaps more involved in thought than most other animals on Earth is the tarantula spider. These beings have so much thought that they will sometimes simply stop. They'll be walking along and stop to consider something, very often at the most inopportune moment. They can have a thought, experience multiple levels of that thought, then see how that thought connects to other thoughts they have had. That kind of experience is so profound that one very often has to stop and think about it.

Sometimes the most innocuous beings are much more than they look. Sting rays and tarantulas are perhaps the most profound thinkers on your planet. You must understand that some animals are known for being profound. Perhaps you haven't realized it, but some day as people connect more to these sting rays and tarantulas, the solutions to many of your problems will become instantly obvious.

They don't have room for a brain, but they have a great mental body?

Yes, the mental body is the mass of their being, and their mental body ranges out well past the perimeters of their physical body. This is largely because they are intended to survive and act essentially as reference libraries for other beings who need to solve problems. Thus they have massive amounts of profound knowledge, wisdom and philosophy that they as beings do not need, but that are engaged within their mental being or connected in some way. Therefore when your more profound spiritual beings or thinkers connect spiritually with these beings, you will be able to solve what has been heretofore unsolvable.

That's an awesome contribution, thank you! That's incredible!

Provided for Your Education, but You Must Connect

Let me add that if you can make the connection with spiders in general in a way that is benevolent for you, they can teach you a great deal about meditation. The spider's energy tends to move out spherically, whereas you tend to move your energies either vertically or horizontally. Because their energy moves in all directions, it might help to try a meditation with a spider spirit sometime.

To think that someone so far away from here and almost unrelated knows what's going on here at such great depth!

So many things have been provided. Beings and things have been provided for your education, but ofttimes you must prove your worthiness of this education by taking the spiritual and mental step to create union between yourself and something else. Then all that extra knowledge will be available to you. It is a great way, I might add, that creators have for gauging the spiritual evolution of a society. (From my perspective, a society would be a universe.) Sometimes extraterrestrials come to your society and engage it at a distance on the basis of how spiritually evolved you are. They don't even think about your technological evolution. Spiritual evolution is the primary means to gauge any race's advancement.

Because we're in ignorance, we play a series of reincarnational lives, but at your level do you think you'd ever close shop and go off and do something else? Is that even a possibility?

I cannot conceive of doing that. I am so blessed to have this job. It is total fulfillment all the time. Can you imagine walking away from total fulfillment? I must say, I think the answer to your question is no. [Chuckles.]

Well, from our level of ignorance, you know, we project our concepts out, and they don't always fit the larger reality.

Eye and I

When you drew the nine dots and triangle to show members of the Explorer Race how to connect with the rest of our race by using groups of nine, you showed the "I" as a triangle. I saw mentally the Masonic symbol of the pyramid with the eye in the capstone. So "I" means both e-y-e, the all-seeing eye, and the "I" as self. Was that a code they deliberately used?

I believe that these beings have been privy to profound wisdom. My understanding of this organization is that not every member at every level has this information, but there has been some effort to code into various societies such knowledge as will allow for spiritual evolution of the individual within the context of all beings. I believe it was intentional on their part.

Were you referring to e-y-e or I?

Oh, I was referring to the letter I—the self, this personality.

In my mind's eye I saw the picture on our dollar bills.

Yes. A good hint, eh? The all-seeing eye is really just a reference to "I."

Which is who we are when we get to see, right?

Yes. "I" becomes a greater amount. Understand that initially "I" was all of you, yes? And it is still all of you, but you need to use tactics and meditations to connect. Then "I" simply becomes more, and a great many rewards go with that. Think of all of the Explorer Race all over the universe . . .

. . . that we could contact! Aha!

And become—have all their knowledge, all their wisdom shared. They can share yours. Would that not be wonderful?

You know how to get us going! [Laughs.] You've never talked through another human being like this before, have you?

No, not another human being, no.

But you've talked through other beings?

I have occasionally spoken through other beings in concordance with those who have passed through me, yes. But not to humanity.

It must be sort of disconcerting talking to people who know so little.

Not at all, because I do not see you that way. I see you in your totality. As I speak to you I see you as a spokesperson of the total you; I see you as your total being. As I say, the essence of you has not changed so much. It has been impacted by what you have learned, but I do not in any way think of you as less-than. I see you as being improved.

My Perspective of the Explorer Race Experiment and the Origin of the Idea of Suffering

What is your perspective of the Explorer Race experiment?

I think it is a bold and very worthy experience. I understand that the intention is to expand all beings by ten times what they are. I do not know if it will get out to where I am, but if it does, well, it could be exciting! I certainly approve of the experiment.

As it turns out, suffering is one main thing everyone seems to mention about what we set up. It was not the Creator who did it; we influenced the Creator. From your point of view, do you see that the suffering provided the tension, which was its original intent? Do you see it as a worthwhile thing? Or was there another way this could have been done without the suffering?

I honestly cannot say how you could have done it. Perhaps it could have been done with some kind of kinetic tension, but that would have necessitated something from beyond you yourselves. I can see your reason for doing this, but I must admit that I am inclined to agree with your Creator.

That there's too much suffering.

Too much suffering, yes. But I can see your point clearly.

Okay, I want to get this clear: Was suffering the idea of the creator of all creations, the one who talked earlier tonight?

Oh, no.

Was it our idea?

I think it preceded *all* of us. I think you have to go back a few steps, or at least one step, to find out where the idea came from. You're talking about the core idea that was floated past your Creator and where it came from?

I thought it came from this being [Creator of Purity] who talked before you tonight, who created everything that we know of as creations—the orbs, everything out to the level . . . here, he looks like this [shows the first drawing].

I can see that in your mind's eye. Are you asking, did that being create the idea of the Explorer Race?

The idea of wanting to expand.

I must say honestly that I'm not sure whether this being created it or molded it to its personality. Let me see the sequence.

Well, he said he was the last of the 91 of these beings who separated from the purity of his source to get the idea of this expansion.

A moment . . . you are right. This being created this.

And we volunteered without realizing the consequences? We volunteered without realizing what we were getting ourselves into?

I wouldn't say that, no, never. I cannot say I'm the last word on this, but I think you knew what you were getting into at its core. That's probably why you were excited and nervous when you were within me, even though it would take a great deal of time before you would actually experience an impact from anything serious.

We'll trace that down, but I value your perceptions. I've about run out of intelligent things to ask. Tell us whatever else you'd like to tell us.

You Are Part of All You Are Within, and Have Its Capacities

Only this: All the creators—beings such as myself and others who exist in all existence that I am aware of and more—are a portion of you. *If you are within it, you are a portion of all of it.* This tells you that since you are a portion of all of it, you can unite totally with all of it and have these same capacities. I know that if I focused on uniting with all, I would have much greater capacities than I do, but I know well enough that I might lose some interest in my job and then not get as much pleasure out of it, perhaps not even do it as well. So I'm enjoying what I do.

I say this to you, however, because you are the seekers, and as all seekers know, you always look for what is around the next corner as well as want to solve the mystery, whatever it is. So know that you are ultimately a portion of the great mystery, and in time you will surely have the pleasure of discovering many, many answers. Good night.

❖ *Robert's Comments on His Experience*

Oh boy, had to go way out for that guy.

He was wonderful.

That's great.

You feel you go out to meet the being?

I sort of merge in a way with the being, and I'm left with . . . it's sort of like being stamped with the essence of that being, visually and in other ways that are not readily apparent. Doing all this Explorer Race book channeling has definitely had its impact on me, all these creators and so on.

You have walked where no human has gone before! What impact do you feel?

It's hard to describe, but it sort of makes me more broad-minded. I feel more universal. It makes me more thoughtful or, as some people might say, dreamy. There are just so many beings, there's just so much! It's a feeling of vastness, for lack of a better term.

Did you get the numbers? We know one-thirteenth of a six-millionth of one degree of everything that's out there. [Laughs.] We've got a long ways to go to meet our neighbors!

When that was being said, I had the impression that it wasn't that we had so little knowledge up to this point in time, but it's because of who we are and what we're doing.

Because of the ignorance! We chose it.

But I think that outside the context of this experience we have much more.

Sure, but this is who we are encapsulated.

Yeah, right.

Well, human knowledge is one-thirteenth of a degree compared to that being's 360° (representing its entirety), but its knowledge is still only one six-millionth of the knowledge of the being who preceded Zoosh's progenitor. This means that we have some things to explore yet.

The Double-Diamond Portal Who Imprinted the Explorer Race's Six Core Qualities

Tuesday, January 28, 1997

We are the quadrant bodies representing the multilevel qualities of the Explorer Race. That which is myself represents the origin of the descriptive qualities of the Explorer Race. These qualities also represent the body (the "body" being the personality, or beginning, of the Explorer Race)—all incarnations of all beings who are, have been or ever will be incarnating as a member of the Explorer Race. If you were to see me in my component parts, the visual representation would look like this [draws].

What do the dots represent?

The dots represent six qualities: *curiosity, impetuousness, eternal optimism, urgency, wonder* and, for lack of a better term, *senselessness*, which really means indefatigability, the ability to persevere regardless of provability. Those are the six core elements of the Explorer Race personality. [Draws.] In a direct side view would be these stars, these six points. However, one of them would be like this, yes [points to vertical line on the left]? The

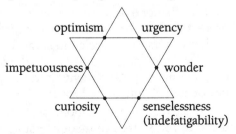

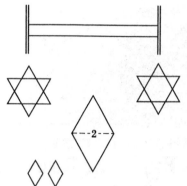

other one would be the opposite, though it is not obvious. It seems to be the same thing, but if you transpose them, there would be two triangles [halves of one diamond] on top of each other. This is the way it's represented here; it's just that there's a thickness of two. (I'll put a 2 in the center there to show there are two.)

The Temporary Foundational Elements of the Explorer Race Personality

That [referring to the blue tetrahedron that had been removed from its hanging position] is a third-dimensional representation, but I am referring primarily to a philosophical representation having to do with the coordinated foundational elements of the Explorer Race personality. Simply put, the Explorer Race starts here; there is no precursor to the Explorer Race beyond this point. This does not mean that you and your souls did not exist before this. It means that you were not members of the Explorer Race before this; you were something else.

I am a temporary function, not unlike a logarithm or a formula that exists until the complete function can be worked out or evolves to its natural state. As the beings you are familiar with like to say, you were needed by somebody down the line from here. The purest, most driven feelings ascribed to here could not be put together down the line because these feelings needed to be a platform upon which everything else would be built; that is, they needed to come together in a place where there was absolutely no other distraction.

one diamond atop the second diamond

When this occurred I was in my natural state—the two diamonds. I'll show it from a slightly oblique view [draws] giving some thickness. I was in this state of being. If you were to look at me, I would appear to be a staged diamond, solid, yet with some depth.

The Diamond Shape

The diamond shape represents a shape that allows that which is needed to flow through it. That which is no longer needed will flow back into it and be recycled in some form, either as component parts or to someplace where it is needed. The diamond is thus a perfect portal, enabling me to pull elements into being that are the foundation of the personality of you as the Explorer Race.

I created a temporary mold, stamping these qualities as a foundation on all of you so that your souls, your personalities and whatever would follow would be built on that. I could not create an artificial matrix, because it already is artificial: If your souls were to evolve in the normal, natural ways, this would not be the foundation upon which they would be built. They would instead be built upon whatever you had experienced along the way that was most significant.

This is a sidestep for you—to be the Explorer Race. I could not create this matrix without participating myself, so I separated myself into my component parts, which would be two triangles per diamond, formed into the star shape. If you were to see me now, since you are still on the Explorer Race avenue—not on the line that you were on before and not on the line that you will be someday—I would appear to be a beam of light with two six-pointed stars at either end [see second drawing, top of previous page]. So I am not in my natural state of being, either. Since it is not my natural state of being, I am able to hold what is unnatural (this is not to say that it is inappropriate or unworthy), including holding something for you that is not *your* natural state of being.

The foundational elements of the Explorer Race—the qualities you all have to one degree or another along with other qualities—are therefore not your natural state. You have been told that you have been on the Explorer Race route for a long time although you have been other places, and that you existed before this in other things. You all volunteered for this Explorer Race job because it is worthy. It was worth doing, and it is still perceived to be worth doing.

It is important for you to note, however, that at some point the job will be over. Others will take over for you and you will continue along your way. When that occurs you will return to your natural state and I too will return to my natural state. Understand that in good conscience I could not create a matrix that was unnatural, though worthy, for a mass group of beings without taking on a similar context for myself. How could I possibly perform service to others without putting myself through some level of the strain that you yourselves are in?

Answering the Call to Become the Explorer Race

When you volunteered (and you all did) to become the Explorer Race, you came from all over. Some of you were pursuing feeling, some color, tone, thought or essence (something that hasn't been previously talked about too much, which has more to do with a sensation). Some of you were pursuing things that were so esoteric compared to your now existence that it is literally impossible to put them into any language, even an archaic language of your peoples. When you are done serving the purpose and cause of the Explorer Race, regardless of the outcome, you will all return to what you were doing before.

I'm talking about great lengths of time, as you understand time. I'm also talking about what existed before and what will exist after, because my primary focus and connection with you has to do with who you were before. In my natural state as the diamonds, I am more comfortable and compatible with you in your natural states [chuckles]. Since you are in a somewhat strained state now (not a natural state for who you really are), then I am also strained. You had asked for my contribution and I contributed to your unnatural state of being so you could be the Explorer Race. I have chosen to participate on some level with you because I know you all very well—who you were and who you will be when this vast experience of the Explorer Race is over.

This Creator had received, as all creators do, an inspiration that was primarily based in the future, meaning a change that would turn into a desirable result. Since component parts were needed to produce this, the needs for what it would take radiated out spherically in all directions, dimensions and times. This message went out well past me before it reached most of you! (In terms of space, I am now closer physically to your planet, though very far away, than you were when this happened.) The message passed through me and my consciousness *well* before it hit any of you who volunteered to participate as beings, essentially sparks of life, before becoming fully ensouled by your Creator.

What You Were Before

When you came to be with your Creator (the being you consider your Creator now), you were sparks of life that were added to your Creator. However, as sparks of life, you were not the limited context of a soul. As you know souls now, souls are essentially personality, but what you were before this was . . . words fail me. I will simply say this: Even though you have been ensouled by your Creator, you were so much more before, that you are now perhaps a single note in the scale (*do, re, mi* and so on). Let us say that you are *do* now; that is what your Creator has made you. Before, you were fully three octaves. Temporarily, therefore, during the Explorer Race experience you have had to become very focused to become that single note. Looking at it from my perspective, you had to simply become less.

It is important for you to truly know how much more you are in your natural state. From my perspective, there is so little knowledge of who you really are because you had to become less to be in this creation at all. The mad pursuit to find out who you are *is not available in this creation.* This means that you can never know who you are while you are in this creation, but you will know eventually. Those who occasionally exit the Explorer Race between lives and go on to be who you are even for a moment elsewhere do remember. It is perhaps these experiences that revitalize your resolve to continue with the experiment, because you can see its value more clearly at these more expanded levels of yourself.

When you think about it, it is very strange, even in your cultures, that people do not have a greater understanding of who they are. There is so little known about the death experience, as you call it (which is truly the birth experience [chuckles]), because you are dealing with an unnaturally limited existence even *after* a physical life. I am not trying to say that you are so much more magnificent than the Creator who has focused you, but you are so much *more!*

Creator Inspired by One Alternative Benevolent Future

Who gave this Creator the inspiration?

The inspiration came from the alternative positive future, using the polarized term. This means, you understand, that there are alternative benevolent futures in existence and that they constantly vary based on who the individual is who might be getting the inspiration. They are also based on all of the infinite beings that relate to it. So even where you are, you are constantly receiving alternate potentials for your future: what could be, what might be and so on. Sometimes it feels like thought, sometimes fantasy, sometimes just subconscious feelings. This process is also there at other levels, but just more complex. Like all other beings, this particular creator you mentioned was receiving these alternate potentials for futures all the time, but none of them particularly resonated with this being.

Then one did resonate. I recognize that you are saying, "But where did *that* potential future come from? Did it come from one being?" I do not think so. Now, I'm not asking you to accept that there is order to chaos, but I think there is less randomness to chaos than is apparent. This was a future that happened to strike this being as a wonderful possibility. It resonated with this future in a particularly personal fashion; this being could feel the real value of it. Even though It continued to get more alternate futures after this inspiration, this being has not had another experience such as that. That was a moment of ecstatic feeling where the being wanted to say, "No, no, I don't want this to just go by. I feel the value in this, and I want to see it happen." You understand, I am saying that it came from one of the many.

Creator got the inspiration, put out a call, and we responded to the need. Now, how did you fit in?

In order to create an Explorer Race, all of the necessities—the tools, the stock, the material—needed to be in place before anybody showed up. That's why I and others were essentially formulated (you might say programmed) in place before the message got to any volunteers who would participate as actual subjects in the experiment. I volunteered to produce essential foundational elements that would be in *all* beings of the Explorer Race.

It is my understanding that all basic qualities, emotions, feelings, actions, results and so on of the Explorer Race are built on these six foundational elements. These foundational elements act as a means to unite you all, as a common ground. If you can understand that everyone has some connection to these elements, on the measurable personality scale it is ultimately this that is your common ground. Oh, I know, as with all beings, that your common ground to be valued and treasured is love, joy and happiness, but in terms of quantifiable personality characteristics, these six points represent your common ground.

The Six Core Qualities—from the Future

Who determined what those six qualities would be? Were you inspired, or were you told?

I was essentially told by that Creator who reacted to that particular inspiration, so I did not invent them. These qualities were sent out. It was like a mass program, and it was what I could do. I do this from a great distance from you. I will continue to generate these qualities, which I'm bringing from other places, because diamonds are essentially portals. [Chuckles]. Do you understand? Yes, I'm bringing them from the future—how you *will* be!

Remember that the being got the insight from the future, and since I am essentially a compound portal where things can go both ways and be recycled in both directions, I am bringing *from your future* the foundational elements that unite all of you in your quantifiable personality characteristics. I am therefore certain that I am not providing anything totally unnatural for you, but rather something that supports you in being less and which is also a portion of you that you are becoming.

The key element is that senselessness. Senselessness does account for a certain amount of mischief, but at the same time it allows beings to look past whatever their absolute dogma is. Dogma might be religion, but absolute dogma is often the beliefs and thoughts of the time. For instance, in the field of science it takes complete senselessness to say, "I don't care if gravity *is* a law, *I* know it can be defeated!" That is certainly senseless. On the other hand, we know that it is so. That is why that quality is the *key* quality and why, even though it has caused a great deal of mischief, it has allowed you to make tremendous breakthroughs in a much shorter time than almost all other civilizations that I am aware of for a single group.

You are a portal and have spent these eons flowing these qualities to us in our lightbody. What are the dynamics? How does it work?

I provide these qualities that are culled from the future to your essential personalities, which is the total you, speaking of you as a single being. I send it to the complete you, the sparkle you, the total you. That total you radiates these qualities to the temporary yous that you are now, meaning that which is off on this side course to be the Explorer Race.

Your Receiving the Call and Converging toward Here

When the call finally got to us, then what happened?

You were all over the place. Most of you were not involved in any common society or even a common endeavor. One of the primary necessities of the Explorer Race volunteers was that there be the maximum amount of variety. Some of you, in terms of what you were doing and who you were, were diametrically different from what others were. Many of you were involved in things so different from what others were involved in that there would be absolutely no shred of an ability to communicate. That also has helped you.

And some of those became men and some became women? [Laughs.]

Yes, and some became stubborn and some flexible and so on. It was believed that in order to achieve quantifiable and tremendously prodigious progress (high-speed stable progress), you would have to use something that was basically a paradox: You would have to use entirely different components, components that had absolutely no familiarity with the other components. Therefore all of you were *completely* different, in completely different places, different areas. It took a vast amount of time to get the message to everyone, and then, even moving at the quickest rate, it took a *huge* amount of time for you all to get here.

To get to you?

To get to this general space where you have become involved in being the Explorer Race. You didn't pass through me; none of you did. I'm not a portal for you. You passed near me, so I could see you at a distance. But I didn't function as a portal; I am more the qualities.

What did we look like when we passed near you?

All different ways. Some of you didn't have any physical appearance at all. You were essences—meaning feelings, essential elements. Some of you were masses of color, some were tone, some a taste and some an aroma. Just think of all of the different qualities of your life; you were all of these different things and more. Some of you were shapes, some were shapeless—everything you can think of and its opposite as well as its unknown, in the sense that you have your conscious mind, your subconscious mind and your unconscious mind. The unconscious mind is the unknown. It was like that.

So we were, like you, just going about our business and then this inspiration came to us?

Yes, the inspiration went everywhere, and individuals such as myself volunteered to participate.

As the Liquid Domain did, right?

Yes, as all others did who are participating. You volunteered to participate as a directly applicable life form to be ensouled in a very specific fashion through your Creator. As I say, many of you were much more vast and profound than even your own Creator (that which you *consider* your Creator in this creation). Yet you felt that this was an experience you could not miss, considering that it was not only a great service, but also a personal experience of great value.

So somehow we came and sort of nestled in.

You came from all over!

We came directly to the Creator?

You came directly toward this general creation, not having a sense of your Creator at that time. I don't think that being had left Its original point yet. I don't think that being had even begun Its voyage out from what had begat It. That's how much earlier the whole thing started. Your Creator had not even been launched or been informed of the idea yet.

Or hadn't been inspired.

That's right. That's how much earlier it was necessary to get the component parts together and get a volunteer who would arrange it all. That's where your Creator came in. Your Creator is essentially management [chuckles]—inspired management.

We never knew that until a week ago [see chapter 15 of Explorer Race: Particle Personalities], when He talked about this part of Him that had such an impact on the creation.

When you think of the context of it all, of its vastness, how much cooperation is needed, how many beings are involved, it is really not a small thing. That is why many of you, regardless of how magnificent you were then, were very comfortable with the idea of temporarily giving up almost three octaves of your being to participate as the Explorer Race. You were willing to do so in consideration of the value to all existence as well as its personal value to yourself.

As we got this inspiration, we must have seen it, then, in its completeness?

That's right, because when the inspiration came to that other being who sent it out, it was colored only by that being's own enthusiasm for the project. Other than that addition, it was intact. So yes, everybody had a complete understanding of what would happen, modeled upon that future potential. Absorbing the enthusiasm of every being who became enthusiastic about it as it radiated out, it was so filled with enthusiasm by the time it got to you that it was almost pure ecstasy. Then you added your own to it. It was really hard to say no.

It sounds like the future generates everything, in a sense.

Encouragement to Persevere

Think about it. If we can use the model of a vast sphere for existence and then apply time to it (since you are referring to the future), at some point the sphere revolves or even has an orbit such as your own planet. At some point the sphere becomes larger, which would suggest a future. So perhaps the future version of this sphere, feeling its own value and joy, reaches back to previous or past versions of itself to encourage it to go on.

How many times have you been doing something difficult that you either dreaded or just had to plod through? Yet you told yourself that you could do it because at some point you would be done and then things would be better. This is truly an essential element of the Explorer Race as well as an essential element of all existence as I know it. I too have had that experience. I am actually having it now. Because I am being something slightly unnatural to me, I can hold this function knowing that I will be my total self again at some point, as you will be, and that perhaps there will be more for me also. I see more clearly as experience goes on that this expansion is going to be ten times in consciousness what everything was before. It is possible that the expansion will be exponential and that expansion *itself* will become a way of life.

What was your experience before the inspiration? What were you doing, what was your purpose, what were your feelings?

Life As a Recycler before the Explorer Race

I was in the double diamond shape. I was functioning, you might say, as a recycling point. I could pass through me what was needed somewhere if it was no longer needed someplace else. This would work both ways; I could take in or send out in both directions, one direction referring to the expanded and the other to the restricted—greater-than and less-than, more and less. I am loath to say past and future here because sometimes the past is more, as I have indicated in your particular case.

That was largely what I was doing. It was very interesting. I must admit that I think my future will be better, but it was very interesting and fulfilling because I was involved. Everyone was benefiting from what I was doing, so there was happiness. No matter what was passing through me, whatever direction it was going, everyone was happy about it. Sometimes beings would be giving up something they didn't need anymore and were happy to be done with, yet beings elsewhere were thrilled to have it.

These things were more qualities?

Anything. Qualities and possibly "stuff," physical things.

Stuff?

It could have been stuff, yes. For instance, some qualities become elements. I'll give you an example—to combine a few things, the quality or the experience of absolute protection, total faith and a certainty in the continuity and benefit of all life. These are feelings, thoughts, philosophies, yet if I were to give you the element for that, in your world it would be the metal gold. Sometimes a group of beings would have more gold than they needed and it would burden them because they wanted to do something more. At the level of those particular beings, gold was perhaps too physical, and they wanted to have the more resonant qualities, not so much the physical experience. Therefore they would give up some of the physical stuff, the gold, and when they would do that they would acquire more of the resonant qualities. As the recycler, I would pass the resonant qualities to them from somebody else and then pass the gold on to whoever wanted or needed it. So everybody was happy.

An Infinite History

That's wonderful! What was your first awareness?

This is a difficult question for me, because I have always been aware. I am not aware of having a first awareness. As a matter of fact—and this might have to do with my connection to all times, all places, all beings—as I apply my experience to the past, making it a linear experience, I can go back and back and back and back and there is no point of origin. It is an always. I could just keep going back.

It's possible that your function is so important as a portal that in whatever original creation, you were a part of that?

Let's just say this: I am unaware of, nor can I find, any point of origin.

How interesting! There's no creator, no progenitor, no slowly waking up?

No. Personally, I cannot identify with that.

And you've always been doing basically the same thing?

Yes, with the exception of this current job. Because I am at the current job, I am not really performing the duty I did before. I have to believe that someone else has filled in for me, because I must do what I am doing now for you.

But you're not aware of any peers who are also double portals?

I'm not aware of it, but I must believe that someone somewhere has taken over for me. I am unable to find that because I am really quite focused in what I am doing now. My best guess is that some future version of myself is functioning in the future to do this, which is covering this time as well.

There's no one that you can ask without distracting yourself?

Looking at it right now, I see the future version of myself doing this. I think perhaps that's what you are *all* doing. Even though most of you have seemingly shrunk or become less in order to be the Explorer Race and ultimately become more, perhaps somewhere you are still that more.

The Future of the Explorer Race

Is it your understanding that we will go back to what we did before, or that this will so alter our experience that we'll get our three octaves back and do something totally different?

Well, you might get thirty octaves.

Aha! That's right, the tenfold!

You see, you might get thirty octaves, and if the exponential expansion does occur, you might suddenly find that you have 300, then 3000 and so on. This I do not know, but it is possible. If that occurs, you probably will not have to go back. You will be able to be where you are and still have what you were. I believe that at that level going back will not be necessary.

Yeah, for us it's kind of like going back to the farm after you've . . .

Yes, that's true. You might not be interested in riding around on mules anymore, as it were.

Now that we've got our starships.

That's right, and more. Now that you *are* starships. Truly advanced beings do not use vehicles, but I understand your joke.

Because we came from so many different places, we didn't take a whole chunk of something that was necessary someplace else?

Exactly. This is also probably intended. Because you came from so many different places, since you directly benefit by what you do as well as what everyone else does, I would expect that those places you came from would also directly benefit, since you're spreading it around. It was a master plan, you know. It really is a master plan, and although we could say it's random, it certainly suggests that there is a level of organization to the randomness.

Yes, and it's always out there ahead of you; there's always more.

In your own life, just think how much more you are now than you were ten years ago. When you think of that, you can easily identify with the larger scale.

Since you flow these qualities, then you're intimately connected with us?

Intimately.

And you watch us and chuckle.

Sometimes I watch you individually. I have a tendency, as I always have, to relate to you as a single mass, meaning a primary personality that all of you are a part of even though you came as individuals from all over. You do tend to make up a core personality of which these six qualities are the foundation, so I still tend to relate to you as a single being made up of many. When you say that I can look at you from a distance, I do, but I relate more to your broad personality.

The other night someone said something that struck me—that only 7% of the Explorer Race is on Earth.

Oh, yes.

But they've all been on Earth at some time?

No. As the Explorer Race, you have traveled around in this creation, and certainly some of you will *never* incarnate on the Earth. I do think that many of you will—as many as possible—because it is such an intense school. Some of you will simply come close—*almost* incarnating, such as not being born but perhaps spending some time in your mother before a miscarriage.

Those Who Surround the Explorer Race

What about all the guides and golden beings who are supposed to be around us? Are they part of the Explorer Race, or are they part of the Creator?

I think they're part of the Creator and perhaps beyond Creator. There are masses of beings, some of whom are clearly learning from your experience and others who are clearly functioning in a supporting role. I can see that quite clearly. Those who are learning do not so much help you as learn from you and your experience. They do not drain you in any way; they are not a burden. Essentially, they learn not just cause and effect, but the difference between what seems like it should work and what actually works. That, you understand, is a very fine point indeed.

Where, in our limited view so far of creation, are these golden beings? There is this Circle of Creation, then the creator of that [Ecstasy, who created the 91 circles of creation/union] and God knows how many billions of others out there. So these beings learning from us could be from anywhere?

Oh, I thought you were talking about the guides around each of you.

Yes, I am. These golden beings around us that you said are learning the fine points—are they from . . .

Oh yes, anywhere, easily well past this creation as long as they are within an area that is somehow related to what you are doing. By this I mean that although they might not be able to directly apply what they learn, they would get some experience that might inspire them for what they might need to do elsewhere. Just by simply *being* gold beings and doing nothing, they tend to support and sustain you. Some of them advise you as your more personal guides, but others are simply here to observe and try to understand and extrapolate.

Think about it: As big as it is, this is really where you start. You won't be able to go back from this point and ask, "Where did the Explorer Race come from?" If you're going to go back, you will find out where you came from, but there you would not be the Explorer Race. You would instead be the more that you were then. Therefore you've made some progress. [Chuckles.]

What about the friends of the Creator? Were they part of that great volunteering mass? Where did they come from?

Some of them were, I think, because some of them had the capacity to travel. Again, we're not talking about traveling distances, but traveling at tremendous velocity and still taking quite awhile to get there. Yes, there were some who went well back, friends of the Creator. For example, is there not a being having to do with resonance [Master of Frequencies and Octaves; see chapter 21 of *Explorer Race: Creator and Friends*]?

Yes.

This being was *way* out—*way*, way out [chuckles], if I may use that term, and had to hitch a ride to get here quickly enough. This being could not move quickly enough on its own, so another volunteer who could travel about ten times faster took a slight side trip and picked up that being on the way. The resonant creator [Master of Frequencies and Octaves] had to hitchhike, essentially.

The Call and the Response

So there were two calls put out, then. One was to the beings who would be encapsulated into the Explorer Race and another to the friends of the Creator?

No, no. It was always simply one call. This is true even in your society. A person might stand at the front of a crowd of people and read printed words, yet every individual would hear it a little differently, because they will hear it based on who they are. Because the call had to do with the potential of how it would turn out, everything would strike each individual and continue to go on as though a signal were passing through you. Your decision to participate would depend upon the way you personally understood that call and whether you would fit into it or not.

I see. The call goes out for a Broadway musical and the choreographers, dancers and others come, each trained for specifics.

Exactly, and they see how they would do things from their perspective.

But they had to be inspired to be at certain places along the way to meet the Creator?

Yes. It wasn't like they were given a map; it was a feeling. First there was the call, and then they were traveling toward the feeling from the point where they perceived the call. It's like this: If something flashed at a great distance, you might be able to point your finger at it and say, "There, that's where the flash began." Yet within that place there might well be many miles, so you would go to where you felt it had originated and wait until someone came along who would say, "This way" or "Follow me." So they all simply went, then waited until something said, "Follow me." It felt like it was a portion of that call, so they came along. You had a lot of beings hurtling toward a central area, waiting for someone to say . . .

"Let's go!"

That's right, "I'm your ride."

Would it be sort of fun or would it serve any purpose to get the backgrounds of each of the eight friends of the Creator, since they influenced the creation so much?

It would probably be better to get it from them directly, since they could give you their personal perspectives.

We had them talk awhile back, but we had no way to talk about anything back this far.

You could ask them what they were doing when they heard the call.

I think I might do that.

Or where they were involved or who they were with and so on. It might be amusing.

Do you have any sense what the "more" might be for you?

I feel as if I will not only become more massive and be able to do more of what I've been doing, but I also feel as if I might become a body of myself, to offspring portions of myself. In short, I might be able to give birth, which I have never done.

So it would require more of you?

Yes, and although it's not clear to me, I feel I might simply be able to become more, and that every time I send out some portion of myself, be able to feel what that portion is doing as well. In other words, it would be to multiply or to expand the pleasure.

When you look out, what do you see? What's out there?

What I Can See from Here

[Chuckles.] Oh dear, it is so vast, and there is *so* much happiness! I can tell you that the discomfort you experience is just a tiny drop compared to your massiveness and that it is so unnatural to the rest of existence. It is not like your experience of a disease, where the tiniest drop can corrupt the whole organism. It is not like that at all. My understanding is that in order for a discomfort even to exist where you are now, a Herculean effort goes into perpetuating its existence so that it can be used for something useful. But if the Herculean effort were not being made, the joy and happiness of all existence would overwhelm it.

Try to imagine what I see. Try to imagine the feeling of total ecstasy, humor, happiness, camaraderie, the union of all beings and all knowledge of everything. Just think of all the qualities you would like to have, which of course you once had and will have again. I can only say that it is a great, abundant dance of joyous, thrilling life. Do I see individual characteristics? Oh, I could.

Do you see creations or galaxies or . . .

Beyond that.

Multidimensional clumps of creations?

Beyond that, including all of that down to individual cells in a single being as well as creations upon creations upon creations, from the largest to the smallest and from the most complex to the purest and most singular. All this and more. I believe that I can see this largely because of my personal participation with all these beings, acting as a go-between, as you say. That act allows me to not only give beings what they need, but to take from them what they no longer need. This creates a tremendous intimate connection between myself and all other beings, and that intimacy is a shared respect and love and friendliness. So I keep in touch.

Concerning the Potential Negative Future Anomaly

You have such a vast and wonderful perspective, I'd like to hear about this recent strange anomaly Zoosh informed us about, which has to do with beings from a potential negative future. It's like a ricocheting bullet into this time line. I don't know whether you have any involvement in bringing any aspects to them. [See Shining the Light IV, *chapters 43-45.]*

Yes, I understand that is an effort to speed up the natural benevolent qualities within *yourself*. You are polarized in this place where you are in existence. If anything should happen in a polarized being's existence that tends to put it out of balance in reference to one polarity or the other, the opposite polarity becomes much more powerful in order to re-create that balance. Thus the purpose of this alternative negative future, as we are calling it, or discomforting energy, is to stimulate its opposite to become much more powerful and thereby speed your trip forward. Do you understand?

Yes.

That is the intent. It is actually by way of creating faster and more powerful benevolence. Because of the discomforting imbalance, it creates an immediate velocity and expansion of benevolence and love. I think it is intended to act as a means to eventually increase your velocity toward your natural state of being, which is the ecstatic expression of your true natural qualities. Of course, in the immediate future it would be the benevolent expression of your more pleasant qualities. It is an attempt to function as a slingshot by reaching into the future and pulling something that is not a true thing, but is created truer by pulling it back into the present, thus giving it energy.

This energy will be used as a primer (such as one might use in an explosive charge) to instigate a more positive reaction. From my perspective that is the ultimate intent of many of your modern religions—to create a reaction of benevolence to any aspect of the religion that is malevolent or restrictive. As you all know, you don't like to be restricted, and the immediate reaction to restriction is to expand, after which *more* personal freedom is experienced than you had before. So I think there is a benevolent intent behind this.

Wonderful! Thank you so much!

You're welcome.

Obviously, from before the beginning you have watched civilizations rise and fall on this planet. You have watched the other 93% of the Explorer Race doing whatever they're doing.

Yes, and many of them have passed through some level of extremity, perhaps in an existence on Orion or even in the distant past of the Pleiades when they were experimenting with . . .

. . . violence?

Yes, although by your standards I'm sure you wouldn't consider it violence. You might consider it rudeness, which to them would have been violence. If someone stalks out of the house and slams the door, that would be violent to them, but to you it's just rude.

The Absent Members of the Explorer Race

I was dumbfounded to learn that all members of the Explorer Race were not on the planet. How do we get together? There must be trillions of them!

You have to understand that in real existence, space does not in any way represent distance or separation. As a matter of fact, what you call space is the stuff that *connects* all things.

Therefore, it matters not where members of the Explorer Race are; even if they are way out past where I am, it makes no difference, as it would on a voyage. Of course, there isn't anybody out that far, but if it were so, they would still be connected.

They could be in all dimensions right now? They're not necessarily down here in the third dimension?

Yes, looking from a distance at true members of the Explorer Race, there isn't anybody below 2.8 or above 9.

That's a pretty good spread, though.

It's a pretty good spread, but it's not really so big. It only seems big when you are less than you normally are. Then things look bigger, just as an adult appears to be gigantic to a child. It is all in the perspective, you know.

Are they all currently in this Creator's creation?

No. About 2 or 3% are beyond, elsewhere, but they are near enough.

That's interesting. What are they doing?

Well, some beings have been in the Explorer Race long enough to have done all they can do as individual personalities, so they are amusing themselves while they are waiting around for the rest of you. [Chuckles.]

For us slower ones, yes.

I wouldn't say slower ones, but those of you who have more to do. Some had less to do. You wouldn't tell them they had to sit in the corner and be quiet, would you?

Merging the Members into One Personality

[Laughs.] So we move to the fourth dimension and then the fifth. How do we all get to be one personality?

When you merge into becoming a creator of your own. When you do that, then the parts that are at some distance will all begin to start moving back toward the center of your being, and many of them will be in light. They will certainly not all be incarnated physically, and it will be more of your central personalities.

We come together into one. So when do we go back out to be individuals?

You go back out to become individuals after you have created someone to take over for you. When you have done that, then you are free to go.

But there's some benefit besides the expansion. It's my understanding that we somehow subsume the experiences that . . .

The expansion really happens when you replace your Creator. Your Creator goes up, and *that's* when the expansion takes place. If it becomes exponential expansion, then a lot of what I'm telling you will change. This means that if—and it's an if—it becomes exponential, then your experience of having to be in charge of this creation will be much shorter in terms of experiential time. If, on the other hand, it doesn't become exponential and is simply expanded by ten times, it will be just that much easier for you to manage this creation and reproduce someone to take over for you. Most likely you will reproduce someone who will be greater than the sum of your total self. Now, it seems that one cannot reproduce something greater than what one is, yet we know, at least from our philosophical point of view, that it can be done without even being paradoxical. After all, how many little women are running around with tall children?

You have really added some neat stuff here, stretched the boundaries.

Good, that is my intent.

What is your thinking on why we get to know this now? This information has never been available on this plane before.

If you think about it from the perspective of the fact that you are reacting constantly to discomfort, that suggests that your comfort side or your benevolent side or your loving side is constantly in reaction. I believe it is because the velocity has picked up so much.

Was it Zoosh's idea that we get all this information? He's running around making all these appointments with you guys, right?

Zoosh's and My View of Your Future

Zoosh believes *absolutely* in your ultimate success. I have never seen a single shred of doubt there. Because the velocity has picked up, from what Zoosh has said to me, he believes that what was scheduled to happen in the future will be happening sooner. This also means that time as you know it, as well as space and distance and experience itself, are speeding up. Therefore Zoosh believes that it is acceptable for you to know more about who you really are and where you came from, and that this will tend to create a personal connection for you with it so that you will not only want to be more, but you will feel pulled as well.

In the past you've been pushing yourself rather blindly because you knew that there was more, but you didn't know where to find it. Now you have something that pulls you and by which you pull yourself. When you are pulling and being pulled, after a while you stop pushing and directionlessness disappears, whereas objectivity and selectivity (meaning that one individual might be different from another) accelerate vastly. It's like dropping the anchor. Pushing is slow. That is why ships that travel between the stars and galaxies do not push themselves from place to place; they are pulled. And that is why your space program now is in its infancy, because it is pushing.

As you come more into a better understanding of who you are, you will drop all that and utilize vehicles that pull themselves from place to place—much easier.

Pushing (Masculine) vs. Being Pulled (Feminine)

Pulling and being pulled, of course, is a feminine characteristic. As you know, it is that characteristic that is much more quickly successful. The characteristic involved in pushing is the only way [chuckles] that you could have made sufficient mistakes quickly enough to learn as fast as you did so that you could return to being who you are. Ultimately, a school such as this is based on your ability to make mistakes and then correct them. That's why it was necessary to disconnect you somewhat from your feminine qualities, all of you. In this way you would make mistakes and then correct them. You would learn what is, learn what feels good, learn what doesn't feel good and learn how to correct them in many ways.

When you have learned as much as you have learned (and that is being accelerated now), you get to return to your natural state, which uses the feminine qualities naturally. I have separated these qualities for the sake of making it more understandable. One does not think of these qualities as polarized feminine when you are not polarized. One simply thinks of them as natural qualities, the way one does things. One calls them feminine qualities where *you* are now so that one can have a clear philosophical and intellectual understanding of them.

From your point of view, are entities or beings pulled to this particular focus we have here who will be put into books? Are beings gathering, beings who want to express themselves and speak to a lot of people?

I understand what you're saying. I don't think that that is the case. I think it is more that your Zoosh is acting as a talent agent. [Both laugh.]

He sends out his own messages, eh?

Yes, he taps on our etheric shoulders, as it were, and says, "Now it's your turn. Say whatever you would like." He does not try to prime us at all.

Nonphysical Visitors—the Gallery—to These Sessions

What about in the room? Are other nonphysical beings listening here who are learning? They don't know any more about this than we do.

Some of them are learning. Some of them are simply amused—certainly the ones who sit up there [indicates upstairs loft]. The ones who sit on the balcony are essentially those who like to laugh and make little jokes.

Who's sitting up there?

Oh, I don't think of them as individuals or as names, really. They call themselves the Gallery.

Are they cynics? I don't know what you're describing.

Oh, no—beings, just individual personalities in various shapes and forms. I suppose if you were to look at them physically, some of them look human and some of them decidedly do not.

But they're just interested in what the beings are saying through Robert?

They are amused, yes. They attend other speakers as well; they are not exclusive. Their loyalty is divided [chuckles] by whoever is saying the most things of interest.

Then we have a gallery here every night that Robert channels?

Yes, and occasionally they will stop by for other events.

Other events here?

Yes.

We don't have any other events.

Dreams As Events

Oh, I don't know about that. What would you say if I told you that dreams are other events? Dreams, you must remember, are essentially that which you remember within the context of your thoughts, that which you remember of what you were doing while your body rests. Sometimes these beings will observe your dream function when you are asleep. But as long as they are enlightened—you know, they are not parasites or anything like that—and as long as they have something to learn or have some connection to any of you, however tenuous, they are allowed to pay attention to your dream but must not in any way interfere. Nor are they allowed to connect directly to your energy or the energy of any other being you are involved with in your unconscious travels. They must observe at a distance.

Dreams, after all, are apparently convoluted, since they are rarely sequential except for moments. It might interest you to know that coming here to study dreams is considered a reward to some extent. Beings come from all over the universe to this planet to study the dreams of people here, respectfully, at a distance. Literally everyplace else, people's dreams have much more of a continuity with their wakefulness, which means that they might easily have a linear connection in a dream to something that happened in their daily experience. Here you would very often have to find an interpretation or a symbolic connection.

Because life is so complex here, the sleep state of the physical self requires that one's essential self (one's immortal personality, as your Zoosh says) have . . . let's compare the dreamer in the Andromeda galaxy to the dreamer here. The Andromedan dreamer might have a deep dream that connects, as a variation, to his existence on a daily basis. When the person wakes up he remembers the dream in its entirety, and it serves as a direct correlation to resolutions or potentials that could be directly applied in his life.

However, because so much is going on on so many levels here, one has to dream in quantity, literally a hundred times as much, because there are so many variables to life. Every one of you dreams a minimum of a hundred times more than people in other places—I've even run across fifty thousand times more in a single night. When you keep dream journals, that is often why there is so much jumping about, because so *much* goes on. You know, of course, that only a small shred (significantly less than 1% of your experience) can be interpreted into your conscious memory, even for the most avid and accomplished dream-journaling individual.

Beings will come from all over to study the complexities of your dreams and understand how a particularly complex and involved dream might in some way relate to the dreamer. They're also interested to see if all of your dreams in some way relate on a practical level to your daily life compared to the Andromedan dreamer. Of course, only a very small number do relate, really no more than 2%. Fully 10% of what you consider your dream life is involved in actual alternate realities and another 12% is involved in resolving other people's discomforts.

For some of you there is a significant amount of bilocation going on, especially to assist those who have recently died to get to other places. This suggests that some of you are training to be personal guides, at least on the rudimentary level, helping out just at deep levels of sleep. This often happens in the case of a sudden loss of life, as in a massive earthquake or airliner crash or some such thing. Often 50% or more of your actual dream time is spent interacting with beings around the universe, talking to them, helping them, helping them to understand.

Here is a place where things can be tested, and because beings in other parts of the universe cannot directly ask you to *do* something, they will sometimes ask you to dream a solution. Perhaps they have a problem they cannot resolve because where they are life does not offer them the opportunities, the competition, the stress, the urgency that you might have here—where resolution becomes a necessity and not just optional.

Ofttimes beings have come to rely on you from all over the universe, to ask you to dream a solution for them. They would give you the basic elements of their lives. Sometimes they will interpret them into some context of an Earth life, but it would be as a symbol or an Earth rendition, as if they were on Earth, and what their life would appear to be. They would give you a problem, and through the use of dream technology you would dream them a solution or an alternative. So you see, the idea of many more things going on in your house as well as in other houses is a given.

Just keep talking! [Laughs.] What do we need to know? What would you like to tell us at great length if you choose? We've got all night.

My View of What You Are Doing

The important thing right now is to remember that what you, this Explorer Race are doing is a wonderful, worthy thing, yet you are *so* much more than this. I want you to realize that even if you have a hundred or a hundred thousand or ten million lifetimes in this side road you've taken as the Explorer Race, it is a small percentage of the total you, the vast you, of what you have done, of what you are doing now at other levels, and of what you will do. You are all immortals, like everyone.

Understand that it is like a vast theater in which you participate, and that the drama, though it changes, follows certain basic lines of theater. I feel this is ultimately intended to give you tremendous variety, the chance to apply and see what works in different circumstances. For as you know, in one set of circumstances something works well, but in another it not only doesn't work, but actually hinders things. This gives you great discernment and tremendous flexibility.

Even at other levels of yourself, at the tremendous number of other levels of the totality of your complete being, what you are doing now is not in any way small or insignificant. It is so vast that the total you and the beings who are beyond your ability to comprehend at this moment in these lives, are being benevolently affected. Know that not only is this Explorer Race experiment worthy of you, but it will tend to be one of the defining moments of your immortal personality's total experience. It will be during this side road of being the Explorer Race that you will expand your own consciousness, creating an energy that will expand the consciousnesses of all beings.

Know that being the Explorer Race is ultimately a pleasure, a sense of amusement and bemusement and, yes, suffering and misery at times, but that is so brief in your total experience. I can assure you that when you are in the future looking back on having been involved in this, you will—all of you—be excited and thrilled at having done it. You will feel so great a sense of appreciation for having been involved in something worthwhile for yourself as well as for beings you will never physically meet (though you will be aware of them) that you will be thankful that you originally answered the call. Good night.

Thank you—from our hearts. Thank you.

❖ Robert's Comments on His Experience

I could see this being floating in space and sort of rays of light or what I call thick light coming . . . I don't know whether it's coming toward us or what. It was like rays . . . it looked like it was tethered, but now I think it was somehow radiating toward us.

Beautiful expressions this one had. Did you get a feeling for that?

I could really feel this being's sense of intimacy with us. There was a really intimate connection. You know, when the energy was with me, I could feel that sense of total relaxation such as you might feel with someone you've known for so long that it didn't matter what you said or did, because they were perfectly comfortable with you whatever you were.

I felt like that, too.

There was a feeling of familiarity.

He was a master speaker, too. There wasn't anything he couldn't say wonderful things about.

I had the feeling that this being could just . . .

. . . talk all night! [Laughs]

Yeah, keep on keeping on. The colors of the diamonds would change from time to time, but they weren't merged as a six-pointed star. It was more like two sets of triangles.

I didn't ask him if each quality had a color. I should have.

He told us that as a diamond shape, he separated the two triangles. He showed us how they were put together sideways. As you see from his drawing, from the side the triangles were vertical lines apparently connected by a beam of light. He had that beam going in two different levels, top to bottom instead of center.

It's possible that the six-pointed stars were a single merged thing, but the definition of the triangles themselves, because of the different colors, was so striking that they appeared to be separate. Maybe they weren't.

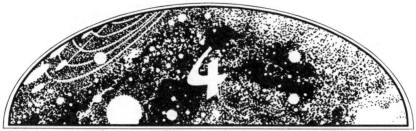

About the Other 93% of the Explorer Race

January 30, 1997

ll right, Zoosh speaking.

I'm totally fascinated that there's only 7% of the Explorer Race on Earth. I'd like to find out why. Where are the other 93%? Why aren't they here? Why are we here? Are we the laggards? What are they doing? Have they already been here? Have they been on some planet like this with a different purpose?

One question at a time, I'm not the Secretary-General of the U.N. Of the 93% of the Explorer Race that does not seem to be here on Earth, most are scattered about this universe.

This creation?

Yes, in this creation, because for them to wander beyond this creation, they would literally remove themselves from the context of whatever form they're incarnated in to be learning. So we'll have to jump around a bit, and we might not be able to do it all tonight. We're dealing largely with a group of beings, all of whom have had several Earth lives.

That would be in the earlier eighteen civilizations, then?

Yes, perhaps. But Earth is a very vital component in the Explorer Race's experience, and generally speaking, all (I can think of only one exception) members of the Explorer Race group have had at least one Earth life. The 93% have already had three or more Earth lives and could not gain any more wisdom within their own soul line, in terms of their personal goals or endeavors, by returning to Earth again. This is why from time to time you will hear (many of you have heard this in personal sessions) that this is your last Earth life. From some of you there is a mighty sigh of relief.

[Sighs.]

Yes, sighs heard all around. But that does not necessarily mean it is your last life associated with the Explorer Race or this universe. This Earth has been involved in one way or another with the Explorer Race for some time. As a result you have x amount of incarnated souls directly involved with the Explorer Race. Granted, there are some beings who are indirectly involved, meaning they influence you, they come into contact with you and you come into contact with them. (I am talking only about beings who are directly associated with the Explorer Race as a member in good standing.)

Where the 93% Is Now Located

Most of these beings have already done their Earth time, as it were, and they are practicing on other planets what they have learned or been exposed to here. One might expect that they would be practicing on planets and in galaxies that are or have been directly involved in your own genetic makeup, such as Sirius, Andromeda, Pleiades and so on. But interestingly enough, they are not in fact doing that. When the Explorer Race first goes out in ships, it is intended that you go to places like Pleiades, Orion, Sirius and so on, places that are not that far away, places where the general population will realize by that time that there is a distinct connection between you and them.

The 93% are therefore not in those familiar places. They are at the far-flung reaches of the universe. Some of them are on planets that could be casually compared to some of the planets in Sirius, in Pleiades, perhaps a few in Orion, but probably not anything like Andromeda, which is fairly unique. They have the opportunity to experience something like that, but they're not allowed to go to places with any connection to your genetic makeup. They're literally barred from going there because of the progression of your space explorations in the future. I will draw a casual picture of your universe (which, as you know, continually changes) that usually has a shape roughly something like this [draws a gourd shape].

That's not an unusual shape for your universe.

Do another "you are here" for where we are.

[Marks a dot near the bottom edge.] Most of the beings

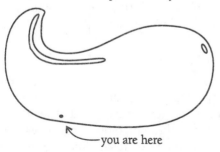

you are here

among that 93% will be over here—to represent their location I will draw a rough circle, or what you call a little squiggle here [draws a long curved enclosure]. There is another little bitty outcropping of them over here [puts a small oval near the right edge]. Generally speaking, that's where they are—quite a ways away, but not so terribly far away as to be literally out of touch. Of course, if you consider it in terms of light-years, it's quite a ways, yet it's not that far because it's in the same universe.

They are allowed to be as close as that so they can have telepathic contact with you and Earth ("you" meaning your higher selves). They don't have, nor are they allowed to have, telepathic contact with individuals who are functioning, living beings on this planet. Because of where and who they are now, they would be affected in some way that would interfere with their lives. But they can have contact with your higher selves; they are allowed to do that.

They are also allowed to practice what they have learned. They are allowed to conduct themselves on the basis of what they have learned and what they are learning, but even though they are concentrated in one space, they are not actually allowed to function in an evolutionary capacity as far as the Explorer Race goes. This means that they are not allowed to extrapolate or extenuate Explorer Race consciousness. Instead they are involved in their own personal growth cycles. They are individuals who are done with Earth and its environs and are basically waiting for the rest of you to be done.

Why aren't we done?

The 93% Had Past Simple Lives Here; You Here Now Have Complex Lives Requiring Deep Soul Wisdom

Well, [chuckles] some of you need more challenges than others. As you have suggested already, most of this 93% came and went with earlier civilizations. However, some of you wanted to get the maximum out of the experience and needed to be thrown into a situation where you *had* to learn. This 93% were more open to learning; there was no sense of reluctance. Those of you here now have had a demonstrated reluctance to learn what you chose to learn. One could very easily say that it's because what you chose to learn is so difficult and requires many Earth lives. Not only that, it requires some kind of intense life, a life in which whatever you're learning does not ever leave you and which you are always experiencing in some form.

I don't want you to read that as if you're slow learners. It's more that you needed to learn something absolutely and have great depth in learning it. It's not a small thing. Those who needed to do only what I would call small or uncomplicated things have come and gone. As is often the case, one leaves the complicated thing for the last so you can give it your full attention. That's why you're here and they're there, but all of you make up the Explorer Race. In a sense, the easy part is over, and those who were involved in the easy part are out there waiting. The tough part is happening now.

If we started with just a few beings and we're going to go back to a few beings, why are there so many individual choices of lessons? How can our lessons be so much harder, and why are we avoiding them?

Well, let's just use the physical body as a comparison. We know that the more complex aspects of the physical body such as the brain, the nervous system or the cardiovascular system are involved in absolutely essential processes within the physical self. This does not suggest that other parts of the physical self are not essential, but that some parts are so essential you can't do without them. [Chuckles.] The less complicated lessons were taken on by beings who in their own right have led relatively uncomplicated existences from the beginning, what you might call, if you were to observe them, simplistic and uncomplicated life forms.

On the other hand, some of you (most of you who are here now) have existed well before the Explorer Race was even conceived of and begun in any way. You had already done a lot and had been involved in a great deal, so you were not at all interested in participating unless you could have some *real* growth—learning something that would impact all of your previous existence as well as existence that might follow this experience within the context of time.

Was that before or during this creation?

If I'm saying that you existed before the Explorer Race was even conceived of, I'm backing up before the diamond, all right? If we understand that, we can see that the beings who are here now are involved in complexities that require a tremendous depth of at least soul wisdom. I'm not talking only about people involved in spiritual things, but about the average person living in these times, which are complex indeed. No one who is living in these times, with very few exceptions, has had what I would call uncomplicated existences. To greater or lesser degrees some of you have even been involved in creations yourself. If you think about it, beings who are that involved in complex interactions are not going to become involved in *any* project, no matter how worthy it is, if they have to give up some of their existence without any potential for growth. So those of you who are hanging around now in these times are beings of great complexity.

That certainly puts a different tone on it. We've always been told that we were the laggards, the ones who couldn't get it, who took forever to learn the lessons.

Well, that's never been my point of view because I've always seen this as a school—not a nursery school, but a Ph.D. program. Because it is a Ph.D. program, one must assume that the people in that graduate class have had a great deal of education and experience simply to *qualify*, to say nothing of actually living through it and producing what needs to be done to go on from there.

So yes, many of you preceded the time of the diamond portal. That diamond portal referred to beings who preceded even itself; and those beings are here now. That is why with just a simple glance even from a distance at your Earth as it exists now, it seems to be so complex. That is because you are such complex beings, and it is not possible for you to take anything and make it simple. Even your most helpful inventions are very complex; your philosophies are complex; your social relationships are complex. Generally speaking, everything about life is complex because *you* are complex.

Had many of us been through some of these eighteen civilizations and just kept coming back for more?

The Present Complex Civilization

Not really. If you are referring to the eighteen civilizations, I'd say that a lot of these civilizations that have risen and fallen on Earth (not necessarily destroyed, but went someplace else) were not that complex. The civilization in which you're living now is the most complex—not necessarily the most complex spiritually, but certainly in its varieties of expression and in the flexibility one has to have simply to live from one day to the next. This is because one is constantly surrounded by paradoxical situations where in order to do the best in one situation, one might be harming another situation; and in order to do the best in that situation, one might be harming the other one and so on. That is typical in your society today. You cannot live in a society like that if you've always had simple lives. You just don't have the depth for it.

Can we say that while the beings now on Earth came through the path of Orion, Sirius, Maldek and Mars, those in the previous eighteen civilizations came to Earth and left? Or was theirs more complex?

No, I'd say that before you even got to Orion, they had come to Earth and left. When they came to Earth, it was very much the Garden of Eden—Eden being another name for Earth in the past. I'm not overlooking that Eden is a name for a planet in Pleiades, but Eden is also another name for Earth in the past when it was a beautiful gardenlike place.

How many of these eighteen civilizations came and went on the Earth after it was brought here from Sirius? Did some of them exist on the Earth that was blown up when Maldek . . .

No, they all had to exist on the Earth *after* it came here. It doesn't count [chuckles] if they existed on Earth when it was part of Sirius.

Who Is *Not* the Explorer Race

There was a planet here before Maldek blew up, right?

Regardless, I'm saying that all of the beings of the Explorer Race, including the 93%, had to have some existence here on this Earth in this location.

After it came from Sirius?

Yes. They came and went rather quickly because what they needed to do was not complex.

Were there no civilizations on the planet that was here before the Earth came from Sirius to replace it? The one that got the big wedge in it when Maldek blew up?

I am talking only about Earth here. I am not counting that planet. What I am saying, to reiterate, *this planet here in this space.* The 93% had lives here on this planet here in this space.

But who had lives on the other planet that was here in this space before the one we are on now came from Sirius?

Many people, but the requirement is that all beings involved in the Explorer Race have lives here *on this planet,* otherwise you gain nothing. You might as well have a life on the Pleiades.

But there were civilizations that came and went on the planet that was here before?

We seem to be stuck on this one.

Well, you haven't answered it.

That's fine, but I'm talking about the Explorer Race and you're talking about somebody else. You're talking about the planet that was here that this Earth replaced. That has nothing to do with the Explorer Race.

What did it have to do with? I have no idea what it was called, but there was a planet here, and it got damaged.

The Explorer Race was not required to be involved in that planet. Did that planet have civilizations? Yes.

The Explorer Race was a particular group of people, yet you're saying the Pleiadians, the Arcturans and the Andromedans are not part of the Explorer Race. They're sentient beings on other planets, but they're not part of the Explorer Race?

I have said for rather long time that the Pleiadians are in no way connected with the Explorer Race other than the fact that you will contact them. They need to grow—is this not thoroughly understood by now?

Well, we're genetically connected to them.

Their genetics are involved in *you,* but . . .

. . . we're not involved in them.

You will be, but they are not the Explorer Race.

And they will never be part of it?

Well, never is a long time. *You* are the Explorer Race, all right? Earth is where the Explorer Race is happening. Even the 93% that isn't living here are not living on the Pleiades, either. They're not allowed to go there.

So the Andromedans, Arcturans, Sirians, all of these are created by the Creator and will leave with Him; they are part of His extrusion, His creation?

They're not going to leave with the Creator. You'll be taking over for the Creator and you'll inherit that creation.

You mean they'll be here?

Yes. Did you think that all of the people on all of the planets are just going to go *pouf!* and be off with the Creator and you are going to create all new people for all these planets?

Well, I never thought about it before.

If you take over a business run by somebody else, do you go through it with a giant broom and sweep all of the employees out and dump them someplace? No, you take over and manage those employees *and* the machines they use, yes?

You're getting very explicit with this. I didn't understand before that we're the managers and they're going to be managed.

Well, I don't like to make it sound like that.

I'll take that part out.

No, it's all right, I stimulated that.

I never did understand what you meant when you said, "They're coming here to learn from you." And if I didn't understand it, probably the readers didn't understand it.

Your Relationship to the Pleiadians

Going back here a ways, the Pleiadians backed off because it dawned on them through their teachers (*they* didn't get the glimmer; it came to them through their teachers) that they weren't in existence to teach you, but rather the other way around. If you're going to teach them, that tells you something right there. What's the obvious conclusion? They are not the Explorer Race.

Well, it makes sense of what Jehovah keeps saying, that when we wake up enough and find out what the Pleiadians have been doing to us, we're really going to be pissed off. But I didn't understand it in this way before.

Well, when you wake up I don't think that you will be angry. It's paradoxical, is it not? When you wake up, you're not going to be angry but you will be enlightened.

And we're going to say, "Oh, look what they did!" and forgive them.

I don't think you'll even have to forgive them; you'll simply understand them

Souls are not the same as the genetic lineage, something you talked about for the Origins book. So souls can pop in and out of the Explorer Race, depending on

when they incarnate, or what?

Yes. If the Pleiades and places like that weren't off-limits, one might conceivably have an Explorer Race existence here, then go off and be on the Pleiades and have a life there. But that's not allowed. Once you're involved in the Explorer Race and get into that stream, it's a stream you can't shake off. You can't just say, "Oh, I had a life on Arcturus and now I'm going to have a life on the Pleiades. I'm simply not going to think about my life on Arcturus." It doesn't work that way. Once you're involved in the Explorer Race, that's it, you're in. Which means that they're ain't no out from it.

You're saying that before we got to the Earth we might have had lives somewhere like Orion.

Explorer Race Flow Chart

Before you got involved in the Explorer Race, you might very well have had lives on Orion and places like that, and *after* the Explorer Race goes out and starts contacting Orion, the Pleiades and so on, you might also have lives there then.

I thought the Orions were part of the Explorer Race, but you're saying the Explorer Race didn't start until they created these prototype humans on this planet?

No, wait, wait, wait. Remember, there was [begins to draw] Orion, various places and so on.

But we were preparing for this, we were part of . . .

Flow chart, all right? [Points to top left circle, following line to Earth:] Orion, various places, Earth.

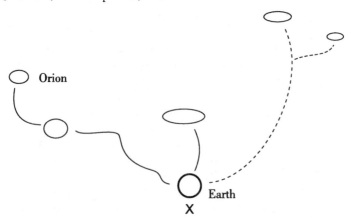

Once you've had your lives here [on the left], x marks the spot. Then you go out here [draws broken line] and you have your existences here or here [draws two ovals]. You hang out and wait for everybody to get done. You don't go back to Orion because you've already . . .

. . . done that, been there?

No, no, no. That is *not* it! You don't go back to Orion *because* you are involved in the Explorer Race! No one comes to Earth at this time who is not involved in the Explorer Race. Even if you hadn't planned on being involved in the Explorer Race, if you come to Earth at this time you *are* involved and you do not go back to Orion to live. Once you're involved in the Explorer Race, even if you say nothing, do nothing, think nothing, you are nevertheless emitting the experience of the Explorer Race.

If you went back to Orion right after this Explorer Race life here, you would emit that energy before the Explorer Race went out in starships and contacted these places. This energy would unsettle their society; the Orion people would feel like they needed to do something, but they wouldn't know what. But when the Explorer Race is ready and starts sending out spaceships [draws a line upward from Earth and a spaceship at its end], they'll go to Orion and other places, emitting Explorer Race stuff. You would also be saying and doing things; there'll be an exchange.

I got it!

Flow charts are essential! If you've come to Earth and had your life here, whether it's simple or not (though there are a few souls hanging around in those outer reaches who've done complex things, too), you basically have to wait until everybody else is done. What's happening right now, as you know, is a shift, and before too long you'll be sending out starships to these various galaxies. Once that contact takes place, those who are hanging around in the 93% will soon be able to incarnate on these places. But generally speaking, there will need to have been contact for at least ten or fifteen years so that their growth cycle will have begun.

Why is that? It is not only that you emit the Explorer Race energy, but *once you've been involved* in the Explorer Race's accelerated growth cycle, you actually need and require it, at least for some time. You cannot go someplace that doesn't have much of an accelerated growth cycle; you can't wander over to Pleiades to have a vacation life, because you will actually need and be exuding powerful growth-cycle energy. The Pleiadians, without interaction with people who are having a growth cycle, wouldn't know what to do with the energy—and *you* would become inordinately bored after two weeks.

So you must wait. Once Pleiades has had a contact for ten or fifteen years with members of the Explorer Race from Earth, their growth cycle will start to pick up. Then members of the 93%, if they want to incarnate there, will be able to do so.

A Period of Space Exploration, Then
Becoming a United Nations Planet

What happens to the Earth after we begin to start going out and exploring, sending out starships?

The Earth will be heading rapidly toward lock-in on the fourth dimension—we're talking about 4.0 Earth here. It very rapidly becomes a cosmopolitan, even political, center for this portion of the universe because the beings on 4.0 Earth will be sufficiently expanded and spiritually involved. Many beings from all over will be able to come here and walk amongst you, although some of them will have to wear protective devices. You will have, essentially, a United Nations planet—the United Nations of the cosmos.

As a result, Earth will take her *proper* place as an interactive educational place. People will come from the Pleiades, Orion, Arcturus—anyplace that has its genetics involved here even on a very minor scale. This will happen for the first time in 50 years or so, and after that you'll start to get contact from other people who have been observing you or have been even obliquely involved with you. That will continue for 500 to 600 years, and after that you'll start to get visitors from places that are in no way connected with you at all. First you will connect to familiars, then to beings that are *somewhat* familiar, and after that it's a free-for-all. [Chuckles.]

After the fourth dimension is reached, some of these 93% might even come back and incarnate here?

They might, though it's a big might. After the 4.0, you'll still be involved in an expanded, pell-mell growth cycle. It will probably be a greater growth cycle than they're ready for, but there are always a few who want to challenge the wheel, as it were, and come. But I should think not for at least 2500 years.

What's Next for Those Here Now

At the death of the current people who are going through this challenge, where are we going? Are we going to reincarnate here?

You mean at the end of the natural cycles of the people who are in existence here now?

Right.

Not everybody's going to go to the same place, obviously, but I'd say most of you will head out, at least for a time, to the areas where the 93% are. You'll swell the percentage a bit. You'll head out there because invariably the first stage of home is the other parts of yourself. The rest of yourself is in those two places where the 93% are hanging out. Remember that you are extrapolated from just a few beings. You're going to go there first, and after that you'll decide what you want to do. Of course, first you'll go through the veils and that process, but the most likely thing then is that you'll hang out with the 93% and swell their numbers.

But since you're on an accelerated growth pattern, especially right now in this time, a lot of you will probably go someplace where you can experience multilevel learning. Everybody who lives in these times has a pervasive, burning desire to know something.

Everything.

Not everyone has a burning desire to know everything, but generally everyone has a burning desire to know something that usually does not get satisfied within this life. So you'll probably have a life someplace where you can be exposed to massive amounts of information, as much as you want. Some of you will need to go to the outer areas of the universe to have what amounts to a vacation life, where everything is nicey-nicey.

The Gold-Crystal Library: A Place You Might Go Next

Okay, where are we going next for these multilevel lives? What are the possibilities?

Where, meaning names and descriptions of the kind of place? One of the places that will be very popular is a place that is really rather small—but when you're there, you're smaller, too. (Most souls aren't much bigger than particles. Although they might radiate light and look bigger, they're generally about the size of a particle.) There's one place that comes readily to mind. If you were to see it traveling through space, you'd say it looked like a chunk of rock or an asteroid or something. It's not big enough to be a planet, not even a moon, and it's not in orbit around anything. It has a wandering path like a comet, though it does not demonstrate itself to be a comet.

This pseudo asteroid is made up largely of chunks of highly refined or purified forms of crystals. Some of the crystals are crystals of ores that you experience here; even though you don't experience gold in a crystalline form, there are gold crystals. Some of you will go to these crystals; one would be a little bigger than a basketball, but it would weigh about one and a half times as much as this planet. That does not mean it is dense but that it exists in a framework that is not physical. Seen from the outside as a physical object, it looks like a bright, glimmering, multifaceted crystal object that does not in any way suggest how massive it is. But once you penetrate it and go amongst it, it is like being in the ultimate library.

Some of you have heard the term "library crystal." It is similar to that, but its capacity is that of the average library crystal to the 1686th power, roughly. It would have all knowledge that has existed from the beginning of this universe to its current status, whatever that is. It would also have the ability to extrapolate potential knowledge for the future. And since it would have been made up in this universe, it could connect to similar life forms in other universes. It would basically be a fountain of wisdom.

Many of you will want to go there, where entering it even as a sizable particle would make it seem massive. (The soul does not experience itself as a particle but as looking like its most recent past life, if it's within the function of time; if it's outside of the context of time, it tends to look like its favorite life [chuckles], but sometimes it will just be a spark of light.) Let's put it within the present context of what you know life as: It would seem to be a library in which there were no actual books, but something you could touch and then know everything.

For instance, you would ask a question or be curious about something and then touch it with some portion of yourself. Whatever you were interested in, you would receive the exact information you want, plus as much expansion on it that you cared to receive. The advantage of this is that it would allow you to experience life to some extent in a linear form, which many of you are somewhat attracted to. You can't live in time without being somewhat attracted or interested in sequence, so that many of you will experience this education in some sequential format. When you do, you will find it most interesting indeed.

There is an interesting side benefit: Once you've been in some vehicle or a library (if we can call it that), you will always have access to it. It's almost like a key to the executive washroom that you never lose; it's always there. Part of the reason these things exist in universes is because wherever creators are, they need to have plenty of sources for all knowledge at all times.

Let me see if I understand this: The beings on the planet now will either go out to the 93% or go to places like this?

Most beings on this planet will go to the 93% first, then they might go to places like this. Other places might be simply benevolent planets where one can have a pleasant, benevolent life.

Who Makes Up the Rest of the 7%?

So who's being born now? Who's going to be on this planet when it becomes the United Nations, and who's going out in the starships? Who are those beings?

They are the Explorer Race.

They are us, or some of the 93%?

Oh, I see what you're thinking. You're thinking that the 93% that is out there waiting is the rest of the Explorer Race and that the 7% is on Earth now. You're thinking that the net total is 100%. But in reality [chuckles], you beings being born (I think I've misled you here), who are in existence now and who will be in existence at least until you lock into the fourth dimension, will make up the rest of the 7%. So all the beings on Earth now (fewer than six billion) are not 7% of the Explorer Race, but about 1½%. [The other 5½% will come here from now till the next stage.] Shortly after you lock into the next stage of your spiritual evolution, you will start getting some reincarnational cycling from the 93%. Basically, from now until then the 7% [will incarnate].

I see. Not many of us who are here now are going to be here when it becomes the United Nations planet?

Probably not, because that is not dissimilar from what other planets are. You can go to other planets and find places on those planets like that.

The Current Challenge: The Tough Forty Years

So the big [sigh] powerful challenge, the hurdle, the thing to get through is right now?

Yes, for the past 15 years, plus for the next 25 or so, this is where the action is. This is the tough part, the complex and challenging part.

Is it going to get more challenging in the next 25 than it's been in the last 15?

I think that perhaps the next five years will be a little more challenging, then after that it will get a little easier. You've already been in that cycle a little bit now, but for about another five more years you have to use all the discernment that you've learned, plus learn a little more. You are in the time of application. You're past theory; now you're applying. This is the weeding-out time, and during the weeding-out time things invariably get more complex. You're still attached to theories that might not in fact be practical or work out in life. At the same time you are learning new things, so you are building levels; and anytime you're building levels of existence it gets complex. But that doesn't need to intimidate you because you have learned how to exist in complexity.

Technologically speaking, you're going through a veritable revolution. Many of those who are responsible for the present level of technology, including businesses, will gradually come full circle and find themselves attracted to natural things—natural plants, natural existences, natural responses, natural behaviors. Anybody in those fields, be alert, because corporations are going to come a-calling.

I understand much, much better now.

Much of the challenge of the Explorer Race phenomenon is not so much an understanding of the infinitesimal details as it is the day-to-day living of it. In the day-to-day living one actually gets to experience what works and what doesn't. One gets to experience quite a bit, yes, but the true complexity of living in these times is the subconscious reality, the unconscious reality, the multidimensional reality that is you.

Your Responsibility for Daydreams and Fantasies

As I've mentioned before, you have responsibility for your daydreams. You do not have absolute and exclusive responsibility for your night dreams, but you do have responsibility for your daydreams and fantasies. This is part of your multidimensional existence. As you begin to evolve and realize the manner in which you manifest things (connected with your thoughts, imaginations and, most important, feelings and inspirations), you will begin to act more like a creator.

A creator must be, first and foremost, *loving and responsible.* When one is responsible, one acts as if everything one does (including thoughts, feelings and actions) is all critically important. Right now a lot of the complexity of your life is happening outside the boundaries of your day-to-day experience—dreams and so on. But in your next five years especially, you're gradually going to release that need for having others take care of you. Even though those others are rarely there to take care of you, you will begin to release that need and find that you're getting more enamored with the idea that dreams, fantasies, daydreams, even thoughts have an existence toward manifestation in their own right.

For a while people will be attracted to discipline, not unlike the discipline one finds with religious fervor, for example. But that's not really it, because discipline invariably establishes limits within you. What you need to do is recognize that everything you think, daydream or fantasize about and everything you do is all directly connected with what actually happens. This will become increasingly obvious regardless of your philosophy, religion or even considerations in day-to-day life. This will come about largely because people will begin to notice the correlation between their fantasies and their actual life.

For instance, not many of you know this, but as an example, you might fantasize about something to a great extent because you can't (or perceive that you can't) or don't have it in your current life. What you don't always realize is that the fantasy life becomes so wonderful that you no longer have a physiological need to have it in reality. The fantasy life essentially replaces what you could have in some form.

Homework to Learn How Your Fantasizing Might Limit Your Reality

Here's some homework for you. Just for fun, pick some one thing that you fantasize about regularly and ask that you have some true, actual experience in your daily life with it. Then don't fantasize about it for 90 days, just mark it on your calendar. You will actually experience withdrawal, because some of you are so involved with these fantasies that they take on an actual life of their own, thus functioning nicely as a substitute for reality, becoming so wonderful that it literally feeds you.

So let's cut off that food and ask for that experience in your day-to-day life. Cut off that fantasy for 90 days and see what happens.

I'm not trying to get you to go cold turkey, but I want to remind you of the potential you have to create some real and wonderful experience in your life. It might not be exactly as you picture it in your fantasy, but it will certainly be some aspect of what you really want. And anytime you catch yourself fantasizing about it, don't beat yourself up; just say, "Oops, I forgot. Okay, stop." Then go on and think about something else. Those who can do this will have a startling revelation. You will discover that the fantasies have actually been physically *keeping* from you what you most desire. (That's my Explorer Race homework for today.)

I don't fantasize, but I watch Voyager. *If I shut that off for 90 days, will I get my own starship?*

Noooo. [Both laugh.] But you might have some experience. Fantasizing is different from watching entertainment. When you're fantasizing or making up a story in your own mind, that can become an end in itself. So I'll separate fantasies from entertainment.

So far you've mentioned just one place that would be popular to go to after this life. But you implied that there would be several places, not just the gold-crystal place. Is that true?

Three More Places You Might Go after This Life

Yes, several places will be popular. There is a place that is somewhat of a precursor to the work done on Sirius. I have mentioned that on Sirius a lot of the basic bodies or physiologies of beings are designed, but there is a place on the other side of the universe that exists sort of in a pre-Sirius existence. The stimulation for potential beings includes anything from what you now consider an animal to what you consider an advanced being—well past what you'd call a human being, having a great capacity to do many things. It is a place where beings are generated in prototype. It's an experience of a sort of junior creator school.

This will become a popular place, because when you're outside of the context of Earth with all the rest of your Explorer Race buddies, you understand that you're in creation training. The potential for this sort of Creator Jr. situation becomes *very* attractive, and many of you will go there to have what I would call an existence there. One doesn't actually have a life there; one exists there for a time, observing or participating in some way in this level of creation. In this level of creation the beings created in prototype there are all intended for this universe, so it is a place where your Creator expresses, in the form of prototypes, beings He might wish to populate this universe with. So by going there you will feel very close to the Creator. That will become a very popular place.

Another one?

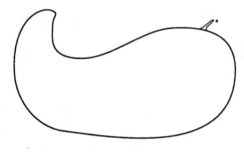

Let's see. There's a planet in the far-flung reaches of this universe. If I were to draw for a moment where this planet is (I'm drawing a picture of the universe), it's in kind of a funny location. Here's our sort of kidney-shaped universe. This is not to scale, but it gives you an idea. There's something like a little tail there. Out on the tip of this tail a planet is dangling. Now, that planet has an interesting function. Although it is involved in this universe, because of its particular location it is functioning very much in connection with other universes. So it is what I would call a junction or meeting point for many universes. It is possible to go there and have a sequential life like you're having now, but one in which you function consciously on a multidimensional basis.

For example, I'll pick out a life of a person there now, just a random person. Okay, I have a volunteer. This is a typical example, a person living consciously in thirteen dimensions at once and totally aware, without any problem at all, of all of the different facets of its existence at those thirteen levels, many of which are directly connected to other universes. So you see, this is a chance to fudge a little bit—to remain in this universe, yet have connections to other universes and consciously live a multidimensional life. That will be very popular.

God, you know it! Any more?

Let's see.

This is fascinating!

There's a place that is also like a library, but instead of holding knowledge, it has small groups or representations of all life forms. For instance, Zeta Reticulan beings would not be beings from Zeta who were moved there, but beings who would be *like* beings on Zeta Reticuli, kind of like a museum. Using that as an example, every planet anywhere within a given dimension that has any life form (including animals) would have a representational group of beings so that there is a cross section of any particular race of beings on this planet. It's actually a trinary planet because you can't fit them all in one.

There'll probably be a lot of interest in going there, because especially on Earth one does not get the chance to have the level of intimacy with animals you would like. How many of you would like to be able to talk directly with your dogs and cats and horses? On that planet you would be able to talk directly with them and find out anything you ever wanted to know about why cats act this way or that—or dogs or horses or tortoises, for that matter. You'll be able to go to that planet and exist there and talk to all of these beings. You'll be able to talk to a Zeta Reticulan being and find out everything about them. You'll be able to talk to a butterfly and find out everything it thinks and why it acts the way it does. That will also be a popular place.

We're talking about the beings on this planet now, when they leave their natural life cycles, within 5 years or 75 years?

Yes, certainly. Tomorrow or, as you say, 75 years from now. The reason these places are as popular as they are now is because they all have some connection or relationship to this planet, either directly (such as the place I just mentioned) or in contrast to Earth, such as the multidimensional place, because here you are fixed in your dimension. Granted, you are all moving en masse through a dimension now, but sometimes it's very frustrating for you because many of you feel you need to be doing so much more, but you can't. Where there is multidimensional experience, you can easily conduct your lives in many dimensions at once and feel totally free. That's what a lot of you are missing now. You feel like a prisoner because you are very focused in this one spot.

That's four destinations so far.

I think that's all I'll mention for now.

Is the term "human being" directed only to the third dimension? Will we still be called human beings in the fourth dimension?

That's an interesting question. I'd say you will probably have a different name for yourself by then, but "human being" is intended to explain what you are rather than signify a type. You will probably have other names for yourself having to do with geographical references, such as Pleiadians, Orions and so on. You will probably refer to yourself in accordance with this galaxy. The actual name as it now exists is not human being, it's *human*. "Human being" is an explanation. [Chuckles.] When people come from other planets, they don't call you human beings, they call you humans.

I've heard so many explanations of the "hu" part—that "man" is something beyond this dimension and the "hu" puts it in the third dimension.

I'd rather say, check your Latin. That's enough for me; it's not really that critical.

I think I learned more tonight than I have for a long time. It got some stuff out of my mind.

It is important to understand the details sometimes, and because we're trying to cover so much ground, hurtling along in this process as we are, sometimes it's necessary to get those details straight.

The Danger of "Us versus Them"

I'm going to tell you something. This is the wave of the future: The

Internet is really something that's exploded in the past 15 years or so. An awful lot of textbooks that will go to children in schools will be vastly integrated with people who've been stimulated by material from the Internet. To say nothing of the fact that within 25 years at the absolute most, there won't be any textbooks anymore, even in school districts that don't have much money. Everything will be on the computer, so it will be easy for children to be exposed to material that will stunt their growth.

Do you know (I'm sure you do) that anything prejudicial about any group of people (which is why I bend over backward to make the sinister secret government out to be people) does not create just a temporary complication. That is the number-one thing that blocks you in your spiritual evolution, because it creates, fosters and nurtures "us versus them." If you take just that one phrase, there is no greater single thing that keeps you from advancing spiritually. That is why I wax somewhat eloquent on these subjects.

It is very seductive even for people in the New Age movement who really ought to know a little better by now. You can't have an "us versus them" and still expand. As long as there is an enemy, that immediately says, "I do not have the power to change this for myself personally, and I must wear my armor and keep weapons handy to combat this." I assure you that at higher levels of spiritual evolution one does not wear armor. One does not need weapons. One sees and understands. I make such an issue of this and bring it up from time to time because it really has the capacity to slow you down.

And that's why the secret government stimulates it so much?

That's right. It's not only to divide and conquer, it's also the fact that even the sinister secret government is a "them."

I want to ask you something, because I think people are hooked on excitement. I think I am, and many others obviously are. It keeps a certain kind of movement going. How would you intrigue those who are drawn to excitement, which is reflected in the controversy of "us and them." How could you pull them forward with other kinds of excitement that would be more beneficial?

Basically, that's what I've *been* doing. There's a point at which I cannot drive you forward. I mean, I can talk about the stars and adventures and so on, but I cannot hold out the stick that says on it "exciting future, more exciting than you can imagine." If I tell you too much, there's a point at which I would basically be bribing you.

Or putting your thought form into our . . .

That's right. There's a point at which I can interfere with you. If you ask what I can do to encourage those who are addicted to excitement, there's not much more I can do than I've been doing. If people are going to remain addicted to excitement (which is, by the way, distraction, because excitement is a feeling, a sensation, but primarily a distraction), there's not much I can do about it. If you desire to be distracted, you will find a way, thank you very much.

Without getting addicted, though, what am I going to do when you run out of stories? [Laughs.]

Well, you know, if I ever feel you getting too excited, I will cut off your source of supply. Good night.

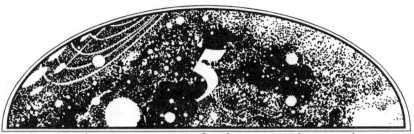

Synchronizer of Physical Reality and Dimensions

February 3, 1997

oosh: What shall we talk about tonight?

The 7% of the Explorer Race

All those questions I was asking last time were based on the assumption that 93% of the Explorer Race was out there and the other 7% were on the Earth. But you said, "Oh, you misunderstood. Only 1½% are here." So where are the other 5½%—in spirit? Are they even born?

Seven percent *are* on Earth, but this counts all the *dimensions* of Earth.

So the other 5½% don't have to come back to Earth in the third or fourth dimension unless they choose?

That's right. They might; it is not an absolute.

You said the people now on Earth were leaving and the 93% weren't coming back. I am asking, who is going to be here in the fourth dimension and go out to the planets?

Some of that 7% might. Understand that you've got maybe 5.6 or so billion people on the Earth now, which is an outrageously large number, but in the future you're not going to be so overpopulated. So it's very possible that you can have a circumstance in which not all the people on Earth come back in some dimension. But the Earth will continue to be populated.

With a much smaller number of people.

That's right, because the present population on Earth in your dimension alone is outrageous! It's much more than the Earth can take. Forty million people is the population Earth is comfortable with. She could handle 200 to 300 million, but that's the limit. So I think you'll find that there are plenty of people left to reincarnate on some level of Earth, but we're not going to have as many.

But we needed this number now for some sort of critical mass?

Yes, you needed a cathartic reaction, as you say, a critical mass, but that time has come and gone. That's part of the reason, aside from the exits I talked about awhile back that lasted a couple of weeks. It has actually prolonged itself and is still functioning in a low-keyed way. I'm referring to information [given September 1996] about folds in time and time windows [see *Shining the Light IV*, chapter 36]. Well, that situation still exists somewhat, and this is part of the reason a lot of people you might expect to be sticking around for a time are exiting, especially some individuals who had a lifetime of spiritual training. Some right here in your town have moved on, one perhaps slightly before her time.

In tonight's session I expect to talk to the friends of the Creator. Where were they when they heard the call? When I asked them questions before, I thought they were around this creation someplace. Will each one of them come in, or will you talk for them? How do you want to do it?

I think we'll have them come in one at a time as you mention them. Lead them through the questions. Do the best you can, and we'll keep it short tonight.

No, that's all right. We want this information out. I just don't know how fast I can think to ask the right questions.

Well, take your time.

The first one is the Synchronizer of Physical Reality and Dimensions. I feel better already. Its energy is kind of vibrating here.

Give a quick summation of this being's statements. It helps to make the connection.

He said, "I am the individual in charge of balancing, leveling and synchronizing physical-reality dimensions so that your Creator does not have to be responsible for this."

That's sufficient. Now we'll get to that being. These beings might show you a different facet of their personalities than last time, so don't be alarmed by that. They are multifaceted beings, all right?

Synchronizer of Physical Reality and Dimensions

O h, yes. We meet again.

Yes, and I'm looking forward to meeting you when I know who I am. Last October when I asked you about when you first became aware of reality, I had no idea that the Explorer Race or Creator's friends came from so far beyond this creation. Could you tell us what your life was like there or share other experiences?

Yes. My first recall of my beginning awareness involved what I would call a multiple-layered variation of light tones ranging from the whitest white light to the palest gold light. One might think there would not be many different tonalities, but it's surprising how many exist in this seemingly small range of color.

My Experience in Cycling Light Color Tones

I remember at the time becoming aware of a sense of harmony among equals, but equals who are not the same. In various portions there were strong similarities, but similar in cycles. There were about five complete cycles of similars, moving from the whitest white to the palest gold, which would appear to be a pale yellow to you, but if looked at closely you would see the gold tinge. I remember that one might expect beings to be compartmentalized.

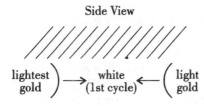

Side View

lightest gold) → white (1st cycle) ← (light gold

Let me draw roughly what it looked like . . . a picture floating in space. Roughly like this, yes? But there are layers of color. One would expect it to be leading from white to light gold, but it wasn't like that at all. There were five cycles, so we have five cycles superimposed over this broad-band spectrum.

We have, then, a circumstance where the first cycle would appear to be very light gold. As the whiteness becomes whiter, it tends to condense toward the center here (I'm trying to describe the way it looked). You have the light gold colors around the apparent edges. Let me draw arrows indicating that the white is moving inward, but it is not coming from the gold. If you were to look at it, you'd see white layered in the center, and you'd definitely see the lighter gold colors around the edges. But we're talking about five layers. If you look at the first layer or cycle separately, it would appear to be gold all the way across, light gold, and as you move toward the whiter colors, you see them more toward the center (we're looking at it from the side).

These cycles were very interesting because they were synchronized within each cycle, but the cycles were quite different from each other. One might expect that any being would be slotted in a place, either within a cycle or within a certain color tonation within a cycle, but it was not like that. All the beings who made this up were in constant progressive motion. Here's an overhead view for the sake of under-standing. [Draws again.] This is why the whites tend to dominate the picture. One might expect any being to be slotted in a given place (see the side view), but it was not that way at all [labels the lines in the second drawing].

Overhead View

———— 5th cycle
———————— 4th cycle
—————————— 3rd cycle
———————————— 2nd cycle
—————————————————————— 1st cycle

This would be the first cycle, go-ing up to the fifth. We were in con-stant motion from the first cycle all the way through the fifth cycle. I be-came aware of myself in there. This is probably where I learned synchro-nization so well, because in order to shift from cycle to cycle it was nec-essary to prepare ourselves well in advance before we made the move. It was a constant flowing motion, so I and the other beings would all prepare ourselves before the shift to the next cycle. Then we would move up and down (as it appears in the [first] drawing) and back and forth [second drawing] the length of these sets before we moved into the next cycle. It was a constant motion and a narrow enough range of color tonalities so that it was not overwhelming to make the shift from one color to another.

I believe that this sense of practical, applied synchronicity prepared me. In the very beginning when I became aware of myself, I was not at all aware that this cycle of sets covered all dimensions. I had the im-pression that it was a fixed resonance, but it was only when I actually left this place of self-awareness that I came to realize, as I moved away from it, that it became less visible or there was less of it to see.

Apparently when we were within it we would experience all dimen-sions, but as soon as we left even the auric field (which is very close to the total being itself), we would go into a specific dimension. I remember that when I left I stood off at a distance and went through all the dimen-sions. I could see portions of this total being in each dimension, but I could not experience the totality of the being unless I was within it.

When Things Changed for Me and I Left Home

You might ask, why did I leave? I felt, like many beings associated with your Creator, a sense of tremendous urgency. It was something that could not be ignored; it was overwhelming. I knew I had to go somewhere, be somewhere. At first I thought it was the totality of the being I was within, and I felt or thought that perhaps everyone was hav-ing this feeling. But I noticed that no one but me seemed to be reacting. I could tell something was going on for me because I was shifting into colors that I had never experienced before.

The first color was green, and I noticed that all the rest of the little beings around me who made up this large being moved away from me because they did not know what green was. They were unfamiliar with it. I looked around to see if any other beings were going through what I was, and they were not. Then I realized that for the sake of the total being I needed to leave, and when I did, perhaps I would discover where I was supposed to be. Certainly that is what happened.

When I did leave the being, I looked back, observed it—sort of marking a spot as you might do to mark your home before you leave—and then moved on. As I began to move I felt myself accelerating, as if drawn by a huge magnet to some place. And I could really relax. As I was relaxing I felt myself going through the full color spectrum. Many of the colors I had never experienced in any way before, so it was entirely new. This was my voyage to the intersection point where I met your Creator and piled onboard.

About That Home Being/Place

Before you get into the Creator, what was the purpose of that being? What was it that you did?

As much as I can understand, comparing what I do now to what that place was, apparently that place exists for any and all beings who have anything to do with synchronicity of a regulating nature, not just living in synchronicity or experiencing it as a part of one's life. If you're going to have as a part of your actual existence or your job (as you say), you will go through this place if synchronicity is in any way associated with your job description. I think that is why there were so many beings there that made up the totality of the being. You might ask, was there a separate totality of the being, aside from the beings cycling around within it? I don't think I can answer this. I do not know.

How big was it? Was it as big as a universe or a planet?

It was comparable to universe standards. I'd say it was about the size of a medium small universe, from my perspective. Comparing that to your universe makes it about eight times as big as your universe. Your universe is considered tiny by many beings I have consulted with. It is tiny, I believe, on purpose. I believe it was your Creator's intention to displace as little space as possible for such a specifically controlled experiment as you are experiencing here in this universe. In case the experiment took longer than your Creator felt it might or if something went wrong, the potential for infecting or harming other universes would be greatly minimized simply by its size, by its scale, you might say.

I had understood from other beings that this universe is huge.

It is huge when you think about it within the context of your planet and your star system, but not in relation to many other creations I have seen. By comparison to them it is tiny, but intentionally so.

So your home was a training place?

Yes.

There must have been trillions and gazillions of beings in there.

There were many. [Chuckles.] I would be hard-pressed to put a number to it, because I do not think your numerics go that high in a well-understood number system, but I would say it was somewhere in the 500 billion range. This gives you some minor idea or impression (allowing for the fairly narrow description of job qualities and so on) of how many universes are really out there.

We're assuming that all of them would go into a universe that had physicality?

No, that is not true. Some of them were going to universes that were beyond apparent physical density; there were several who were going above the ninth dimension.

Was there communication between you and some of the other beings?

Oh, yes, there was a constant communication.

Oh, so they would be leaving all the time, then?

Yes. There were some who would just leave. Very often one being would become either a different color, sound or sometimes a shape that wasn't compatible with all the rest of the beings, and when that occurred it would soon afterward move out of the total being. Fortunately, we are all able to remain in contact because we have spent so much experience together. Before I left there were at least 200 beings who had left before me, and I had the distinct impression that this had been going on for quite some time before I became conscious. I believe (this is my best guess) that beings are actually created there. So you see, that's why I was not aware of myself before that point in time.

And then they too each felt a call from other places?

Yes, since many more have left. Yet looking at this place or being from a distance, it seems to have as many beings in it as were there when I was there. Counting those who left before and after I left, many millions have gone, but I cannot see at all that the total number of beings has diminished. Apparently they're being created all the time.

But you can't see a birth or a process.

No, I cannot.

My Experiences before Meeting Your Creator

So how did you get your experience? You didn't go immediately to this Creator, did you?

No. In order to get to the point where I met your Creator, in terms of your experiential years and moving at the velocity of light to the seventh power and in the straightest possible line, it took me approximately 460 years of experiential time to get to the intersection where I met your Creator. It was a very long time.

Although I could focus on what I was passing, I moved so fast that what was passing by me was not discernible. But if a universe or even some portion of it was personally relevant, I would sample the experience as I passed through it. I said "the straightest possible line" because I had to zig-zag about a bit in order to experience some universes with multidimensional aspects—which of course is what your Creator intended to be involved in. I had to see how the dimensions were kept intact but separate. And I had to see that one dimension of a given planet might be either similar or wildly divergent in its actual expression or culture to the other dimensions. I believe this was to give me the breadth or latitude I needed in order to feel relatively free in assigning certain physical characteristics to different dimensions here.

You must have felt an incredible awe when you sampled these beings you'd had no idea existed.

Yes, it was euphoric, because one goes from something that one knows and trusts to something that is sort of a fantastic progression of multidimensional creations. It is a vast and influential education. It helps to give one a sense of continuity, because in this creation there is often the sense of set times—a time for this and a time for that, a season for this and that, as your book says—whereas in other universes things are more eternal. The totality of your universe has the eternal quality, but individual places within it are more akin to life cycles and seasons.

These are stage settings for the experiment, right?

Yes.

So you're saying that in other universes everything is more eternal.

Yes, more fixed.

They don't move from dimension to dimension?

They might, but there isn't a sense of terminus. For instance, in one dimension I passed by, individual beings might have a life and live every potential and interest of theirs within a dimension, encapsulated or not, maintaining that sense of personality they recognize as themselves. Then without any change—no death experience, as you call it—they would go on to the next dimension in which they wished to express themselves and do the same thing there, and on and on through various dimensions of experience, without any sense of terminus.

And with the memory of everything . . .

. . . completely intact. I believe that this is quite practical for beings who wish to explore the multilevel facets of a given experience. Thus by the time you have completed all that you wish to do with that experience, you have, completely intact, the sum total of knowledge and memory of the experience and ought to be well-versed in what you intended to learn.

Did you get the sense that these beings had learned all that and then gone on to something else?

My impression is that this was some level of creator training, but a very rudimentary one, because there was no impact, no consequences, none of that. It was strictly a focused experience on one thing.

But here the focus is the consequences.

Yes, here you have much further advanced training on the creator training level, where one has most likely gone through all of that before. Here you apply and experience the consequences and must react and so on. No, the creator training here is much more advanced than there.

Recognizing the Presence of Explorer Race Beings

Did you have any sense of seeing the individual members of the Explorer Race arrive? You didn't know till much later that we were different from the Creator? What is your take on that?

No, I actually did see you coming even before your Creator had established the spatial reference for your universe. As a matter of fact, I saw several of the beings come to your Creator. On the way my voyage was so complex an education that I could not do anything but that. But once I had joined your Creator and things were calmer, I could easily see other beings hurtling toward your Creator, beings such as myself, other assistants as well as, I believe, the nucleus of your total being. If I were to draw a picture of it, it would appear to be a circle surrounded by many other circles.

Were you aware of what it was or all it was going to be about?

I wasn't aware of exactly what it was, but I knew it wasn't another assistant to Creator. I knew that this had something to do with what your Creator was doing—possibly even Its ultimate intention. But no more was readily apparent. You see, it was easy to differentiate Creator's assistants or the help of other creators because they all had some kind of a color-toned agenda. But your color was constantly shifting. Your tone was in constant harmony (perhaps only from my perception) and you seemed to be acquiring experience. This is strictly a guess, but since the circles were gradually expanding around the inner circle, my impression was that you were gathering something on your way.

Since it wasn't other beings, it must have been experience.

That is my best guess.

You saw us coming but you didn't see where we came from?

No, nor did I actually see you arrive. By the end of your flight I was already involved in planning the work I would do for your Creator. So I was busy.

Was it your perception that during this creation the Explorer Race had a say in how their creation went, had a voice in the creation itself?

You know, I'm not sure that you did. My impression was that you were brought or invited to come on the basis of what you were already. Rather than being consultants like many of us were, you were the raw material from which your Creator would fashion some ultimate intention. I didn't get the impression, speaking only for myself, that you were dictating any aspect of your Creator's agenda.

That's interesting. When I first found out about how this worked, Creator said that we had a lot of input about the ignorance and the suffering.

Is that so? I don't think I was aware of that.

And that He had to operate a lot on faith, because that's not what He would have done or the way He would have done it.

I see.

But you were obviously so busy creating a place for us to live that you weren't looking around.

I did not have much chance for networking. [Both laugh.]

Or sightseeing.

Sightseeing, that's a good word, too.

What I Might Do after This Is Over

But you probably will. We had discussed before that you might or might not stay here, but ultimately you will get a chance to do what you want to do.

Yes, that is true. It is undecided. There is (and this was discussed by your Creator with all of us consultants) certainly a distinct possibility that when you take over for your Creator you will establish some other system entirely—for instance, possibly a universe entirely homogeneous and without dimensions. It would be a challenging thing to do, but it is just an example. Then my services might not be needed. In any event, many of the consultants were told—perhaps we all were—that you would have the option to renegotiate our contracts, but that we should not plan on it. We were clearly advised to make alternate plans just in case. I do have alternate plans in place if my assistance is no longer needed.

Can you talk about that?

Yes, I think that I would like to return home.

For a little while?

For a little while, yes. If I am allowed to resynchronize through the cycles, I should like that feeling very much. If I am no longer allowed to do so, then I think I will simply ask to be allowed to be nearby so I can feel the sense of my home. Then I will simply allow myself to be attracted to where I am needed. You know, if I had to think about where to go, I would have too much to think about, but when one is attracted to where one is needed, it is so simple. You just relax and go there.

It's like the body; the oxygen goes where it's needed—like this being that we all must be a part of at some level that keeps getting larger and larger.

Yes, you are certainly a microcosm of a macrocosm.

I thought I could go out and look at everything, but I guess it's a little too big for that.

Well, I think it is possible, allowing for immortality, to go out at some point and look at a mass amount of it, but it might not be necessary to actually travel out to the perimeter to do that. It might be possible to ask for an overview.

Oh, like being in a hologram?

Yes, and to see the overview within its totality. I think you could ask for that now.

Another of My Kind

I'll work on that. The beings you were connected to who left, have you ever had the time to tune in to see what kind of creation they're in?

I have had the chance to check on five of them, and they are involved in things that are so different from this that I'd be hard-pressed to put words to it. One of them is involved in the barriers between the orbs. There is a barrier between orbs so they do not stumble into each other's spaces, and the energy of all the barriers is identical, synchronous. This being is involved in that, and I have had the opportunity to observe what that being is doing. Because it is doing something vast but essentially simple in its context, it has time to communicate with me. And because I am located within one of the orbs of this being, it is that much simpler. So we are what you would call friends; we have time to speak to each other.

And he can tell you the interesting tidbits that are going on in some of the other orbs?

If I ask or this being chooses, yes. One tends to relate to one's existence through one's work even at these other levels, so I tend to hear more about the totality of the orbs rather than individual creations within the orbs. But this being is certainly capable of discussing what is happening in individual creations.

So is this being working alone to keep the orbs synchronized, or with many, many others?

This being along with many, many others.

It was happening when he got there, then he joined them?

Exactly.

Well, we might talk to him sometime.

Perhaps.

When Explorer Race Is Through Here

There's so much happening out there that we can't connect to in our present limited state, but supposedly we came from everywhere, so when we're free of this we would understand all these things that there aren't words for now, right?

Certainly.

When we return to our true being.

Yes, when you return to your natural, total being, you will have complete and total understanding of all of these things, certainly. And it is usually at that stage of awareness that you tend to renew your vigorous assent to be involved in this project. You can quite quickly grasp the idea that when you have *all* available knowledge, the ability to expand into greater space and acquire more knowledge becomes seriously limited. Having one's total consciousness expanded by ten times is even more appealing when you have vast amounts of knowledge.

How would that work for you?

That would be relative, since everything else is also expanded ten times. Yet it does leave space for the acquisition of more knowledge. If I suddenly encompass ten times the amount of space I do now, there will be a vast amount of space by which I can acquire new knowledge and experience. Now I am almost full.

How big are you?

It's hard to describe, since I am multidimensional, but I am about the size of a small skyscraper of 50 to 60 stories. But as one goes through the dimensions, the size shifts.

Smaller or bigger?

As one goes to higher dimensions, bigger.

So there's constantly an expansion. The higher dimensions mean expansion.

Loosely speaking, yes. The higher dimensions require more space, because as you have greater knowledge and greater wisdom, there needs to be an avenue to express it—not so much a place to put it, but an avenue or a place to apply it.

So if Earth is the size we see in the photographs from our moon, then the fourth dimension fits around it, and it's larger?

Yes, loosely speaking, concentrically—spheres within spheres.

Really? Up to how many dimensions? Thirty-three?

Yes, at this time.

But not all peopled yet?

Exactly, but I think there is a very strong likelihood that you will expand the quantity of dimensions when you take over. This is most likely because to some extent you will still be motivated by a desire to expand. I should be very surprised if you do not expand the dimensions up to at least 55.

The Creator lives in all the dimensions?

Oh yes—of Its creation. Perhaps more than that, but certainly of Its creation.

And you live in all the dimensions?

Oh yes.

All the friends of the Creator live in all the dimensions?

I believe so, but there might be some exceptions. I can speak only for myself for certain, but I have seen them in all of the dimensions at different times. I do not know if they live in all of the dimensions all the time, but I know I do.

About the Dimensions

I never thought of this. All the dimensions have the same core, the same Earth center?

Well, this is a physical way of putting it. It would seem as if we have spheres surrounding other spheres, and that if one simply goes inward, dimensionally speaking, one would discover all of the other dimensions. It's not quite like that, but that is the best way to describe it within the context of third-dimensional dialogue.

So then the fourth is not in the third—I mean, we have to get above the third.

The third is more in the fourth than the fourth is in the third.

So the way you look at it, the thirty-third dimension would encompass all the other dimensions.

Circles going within—now, that is strictly for the sake of a conventional explanation within the context of your dialogue, but in terms of its actuality, I cannot describe it in any dialect that has ever been in use on Earth.

Higher-dimensional beings, to get to the Earth, must go through all the dimensions?

Yes, but it's very fast, very fast. Very quick, yes. And for those who are in existence as their personality within all of the dimensions, there is no need to travel because one is already there. Remember, outside of the context of an encapsulated self such as you are now, it is your nature to be immortal personality. As such you are very likely interdimensional. So you would experience yourself as yourself regardless of the dimension you are in, although you might see or have different sensations according to the dimension. But in terms of knowing yourself, knowing your personality even if it is multidimensional, you would still recognize yourself regardless of dimension.

That's fascinating! You would exist in the 33 dimensions on Earth, but since you exist all over the creation, there are probably more dimensions in other places, right?

I do not think so, but I cannot be certain because I have been here for so long. There might be at this time, but I do not think it is pervasive, no. As a matter of fact, I think that most places around this universe have fewer dimensions. I think the reason you have as many as you do in this general area is because you are being encouraged as the Explorer Race and reminded of the total you. In other places this might be a distinct distraction—especially where life is simpler, such as the Pleiades. Having multidimensional selves constantly clamoring for attention on the Pleiades would be way too complex for the spiritual simplicity of these beings.

Personality in the Different Dimensions

Well, I'm trying to get a picture of a human. Our focus is in the third dimension, yet we exist with a different personality on the fourth and fifth?

Not different. As I said, the personality is immortal, meaning it is the same personality but expressed within a specific dimension. If the dimension is a high one, say around eight or nine, you might have different expressions. Once you get to around the ninth dimension, it is very common to have complete cognizance of the expression of your personality concurrently in other dimensions, usually anywhere from, say, two or three through eleven. You would have the total awareness not only of what those personalities are feeling within the overall personality, but also a distinct awareness of what the personalities in some encapsulated form are actually doing.

This is not at all confusing, but is normal at that level. Here one might have that experience only within the deep dream state, where the physical brain need not try to sort out from the chaos some consistent, resonant ongoing personality. Rather, the spirit can easily have each portion of the personality in its proper place without any confusion. I am obviously saying that you tend to be more multidimensional in the deeper levels of sleep than you are allowed to be in your wakeful state, because it would be too confusing.

This is fascinating. So here's a 3.5-dimensional physical human facing all this stuff, but there is a 4D, a 5D, a 6D, a 7, 8, 9, too.

Yes.

On the ninth or tenth, one is aware of the third.

And all in between.

How do we on the third dimension experience that eleventh? As an oversoul, as a guide, as . . .

You don't, unless you're in the deep levels of sleep. They experience you, but it goes only one way.

But they can't influence us; we have to make our own decisions.

They don't *choose* to influence you. They don't have to be aware of everything you are doing, but they can be. At that level you have many more conscious choices than you have here. But that is because at that level it is assumed you are no longer learning anything critical to your development.

You're just sort of interested in the dramas but not attached?

Yes, exactly, not attached. Whereas on the third dimension, if you were to be consciously aware of a ninth-dimensional being around you, it would become an end in itself to discover more of this being and you would quickly subvert the intention for being here in the first place.

I see. I've asked this question twenty times and never gotten an answer, but you're closer to it. As we move into the fourth dimension, what happens to that fourth-dimensional personality?

That is already there?

Yes.

Third and Fourth Dimensions Merging

It tends to merge with you gradually as you're moving there. Even now your fourth-dimensional personalities are a little more merged with you than they once were. This takes the place of sequence in your experience. As you have noticed, sequences have greatly speeded up and one can learn things faster. Even though you have the fourth-dimensional influence, which tends to desire to learn things quickly, the third-dimensional self cannot learn things so fast and must have illustrations or demonstrations in order to understand. That way there is not a conflict, but there is something like a split, because the third-dimensional self desires to learn, whereas the fourth-dimensional self is much more interested in teaching. This means sharing, explaining, teaching others either of their own or denser dimensions and spreading around acquired knowledge and wisdom.

On the third dimension one is essentially acquiring knowledge and wisdom. The blend between these two dimensional personalities sometimes creates a circumstance in which the temporary focus . . . you understand, the third-dimensional personality has to densify itself a bit more so that the fourth-dimensional personality does not dominate, and the third-dimensional personality loses its ability to acquire.

Are we still at 3.47?

Yes, you are at 3.47. Sometimes some of you will see or feel that things are denser than that because you have had to consciously slow things down. You can be at 3.47, but if you are being overwhelmed by too much knowledge and wisdom either going out or coming in, it is possible to slow yourself down temporarily (this usually lasts less than 72 hours) to as slow as 3.25. Nothing lower than that is available at this time.

Just to get a feeling of getting ourselves together and focusing again?

Yes, exactly. Conversely, it is possible that if you attempt to reach up to, say, 3.51, as many people are training to do in the ascension process, you feel as if you are literally floating out of your own body, which in the third dimension is not always safe, as you know.

What is the plan, then, for the merging of these two?

It is absolutely natural. As one gets past 3.51, for example, you will be more comfortable with the fourth-dimensional personality. You will acquire a greater desire for the expression of the fourth-dimensional personality as you get closer and closer to it, just as when you move into a third-dimensional life for the first time, that level of the personality is also attractive. Since you are moving between dimensions—unusually so—a similar process will occur.

Letting Go of Why

Instead of moving, as you do when you are born, from a very high dimensional self into the third dimension, you will gradually let go of third-dimensional aspects of your personality while you blend the remaining aspects of that personality with your fourth-dimensional personality. You might ask, what do you let go of? Primarily your need for linear explanations, otherwise known as *why*.

[Laughter.] I'm a long ways away from there, right?

It is important to understand that *why* is a very dominant influence in all of your cultures. We know that children, for instance, are fascinated with why. Yet as you move toward your fourth-dimensional expression of yourself, you are much more interested in what and not so much in why—"what" meaning the acquisition of knowledge that one can emanate or spread around. In fourth dimension you will all be very keen on acquiring vast amounts of knowledge. You will, of course, be sharing experiences with each other, traveling and acquiring new experiences. But you will not question things so much. The analytical process you have become used to will be less of an experience of daily life.

You could say there's more acceptance, a lust to go on without probing into it?

That's right. An acceptance of it because it feels right. You can identify now with that, too.

I guess I'll keep asking why until Zoosh gets his books out. [Laughs.]

Yes, it is very important. You are, of course, the reader. Your curiosity is literally representative of *all* the readers.

How Long to 3.51?

Do you have a sense of how long before we'll be at 3.51? Is it two months, two days, two years, ten years?

My sense of it is that I should think at least ten years, maybe more.

Ten years to go four points?

I should think at least that, maybe more, because it is a critical four points.

Over the hump?

Yes, exactly. For the person climbing the mountain sometimes the last few yards are the hardest. They might take as long as the beginning of the trip took. But it is also the most rewarding.

But that's an average, and there are some who will get there earlier and some later?

There might be some individuals who will get there within eight years, certainly at the deepest levels of their meditations. Some will take 25 years, because some individuals do not daydream, and day-dreaming is a form of meditation.

All right, so this is more than ten years away. Is aligning with your fourth-dimensional self called ascension?

I wouldn't say that. I understand that is believed largely to be it, but if you attempt to align with your fourth-dimensional self before you have completed your third-dimensional lessons, you absolutely guarantee another reincarnation into the third dimension—into the past, of course. That is why I do not encourage this process to be done other than as a meditation and not to make it a point to achieve it on a permanent level. I don't know that many could do it permanently, but if they did, they're guaranteed another third-dimensional life.

So when someone says, "I have ascended, but I'm still here," they're not seeing reality?

I wouldn't want to say that exclusively, but I would say that their objectives, at least spiritually, are perhaps clouding their practical vision.

Thank you. I've heard about all these people who are going off in waves, you know, and I never really understood how it worked.

I do understand completely that desire, yet I think that other than as a meditation, it is not a good goal as a full-time experience.

Because we need everything we've got, you're saying, to make it up these last four points.

Yes. You have to finish what you came here to do. If a great many beings (theoretically) suddenly decided to do ascension full time and (theoretically) were successful, it would almost certainly guarantee a major third-dimensional revisitation by many, many, many beings, per-haps enough to create a perpetuation of third-dimensional experience. Ironically, the ascension movement might actually be sabotaging itself by its goal.

Yet we need that desire to go onward; it needs to be there calling us.

Absolutely. That's why the ascension movement as a meditation is certainly valuable, especially for people who are living lives that are challenging and difficult and for whom meditation is a respite from the drama of one's life.

I didn't realize getting to 3.51 would take that long, but at what point between the third and fourth dimensions is there a conscious awareness?

At 3.51 there's a beginning awareness of things. For example, when you're at 3.505 up to 3.51, there is a definite sensation of mirages, you might call them—wakeful dreaming. By that time, fortunately, a greater application of mass transit will be on the planet, much of which will be automated, especially within 25 years.

So that we won't be seeing things when we're driving?

Yes, exactly. Having an individual vehicle and driving somewhere is not very likely. If that were perpetuated, you'd have to pave the whole planet with highways, and even now people are becoming much more aware that there is not enough green as it is.

So one of the main symptoms will be a sense of waking dreams, but not nightmares. Pleasant dreams, an ability to see nonphysical beings more easily, such as angels. An ability to have what some beings call long vision, to see life on other planets, being able to see the passage of a loved one without holding an individual here.

When one attempts to keep a loved one in the body or even here in spirit after their death, it pulls on them even on the other side. When that time comes, to some degree you will be able to actually follow the journey of a loved one with the angels and beings of light to their transition place through the city of light. You will have fleeting pictures of them doing this and meeting loved ones who have gone before them. Oh, you will love that!

Does everyone who dies go through the city of light?

No, interestingly enough, this is not something that one experiences full-time anytime in the fourth dimension. It is just that when you are making a transition between dimensions, there is ofttimes a greatly heightened sense of interdimensional awareness within a range between perhaps 3.51 and 3.55. But once you go past that point, you might not experience it again—until the end of your natural cycle, of course. So it is like a gift: "Welcome, brothers and sisters."

It's also a point that lets you know where you are on the scale.

A landmark, yes, but a temporary one. One does not commonly see such things in the fourth dimension. You will get a flood of higher-dimensional experience, of which I have given you only some samples.

And that's only because we're staying in the body between dimensions?

Yes, that is exactly why.

Well, there have got to be some extra perks, right? I mean, it's hard! Bones hurt, heads hurt—everything hurts.

Certainly.

So the experience of fourth dimension won't feel that much different? We'll be lighter?

It will be different. You will not have anywhere near the discomfort, nor will anyone else. As was said to you by others, I believe, the discomfort will be no more than minor annoyance at the greatest. Thus there will not be pain. One would not fracture a bone or become ill. In short, there would be no suffering, certainly not as you know it now, no suffering at all. There might be at most minor annoyance, that's all.

I know I've heard that, but in the last few years it seems like something's always hurting.

It is essential that that take place, because those who will and are even now inheriting your third dimension will need all of those negative experiences in order to grow into the beings they are intended to be. Yes, this is a rule and regulation of third-dimensional school, but not in any way passed on to other dimensions.

Well, I've always wondered, are we going to float around like the light in the movie **Cocoon?**

No.

We're going to walk and talk and be like we are now, but we'll be lighter and our capacity to understand will expand?

That's right. There will be no hunger, there will be plenty to do for anyone who wishes to work. For people who wish to have leisure time, that will be available. Many desirable things will be readily available. But activities will tend to be done more in groups. Individual automobiles, for example, will not be a fact. One must act benevolently . . .

I can't have my own starship? Come on!

There is no need for having your own. Why have something with your name only on it, meaning that only you can drive it or use it? That would be wasteful. It seems attractive now, but when you are there it would not only be unattractive, it would be repulsive. You understand that people are repulsed by other people here because of the drama here. But in the fourth dimension one is attracted to all other people and they are attracted to you. There the idea of being with people is a plus, a wonderful thing. The idea of being away from people is not something attractive at all. Yes, it is a change in attitude as well. One will find people attractive and be found attractive.

So, ten years to 3.51 and then . . .

No, *no less* than ten years. Let's not condense it. No less than that, possibly more.

At least 50 years, then, to 4.0?

Oh, I should think at least that, perhaps more. And they are experiential years, which are different from calendar years.

More or less?

Experiential years at this time are longer. As one gets closer to fourth dimension they will become shorter. You see, experiential years are measured by your resistance to your experience. As you release your resistance to the experiences you need to have and complete, experiential years become faster. So as you go past 3.51, an experiential year will become much shorter, and by the time you are at 3.75, because you will have so little resistance to learning something, an experiential year might be no longer than two weeks is today.

So I might still see it in this lifetime.

You will certainly see it. If not in this lifetime, you will still experience it as the person you know yourself to be but devoid of all suffering as you now know it.

How does that work? Those of us who are older would physically die before we get to that point?

I can assure you that every single person alive now who has been alive since the 1930s, and even the '20s, *always* (I have never seen it fail), when coming to the end of the natural life cycle, wants to see how things are going to work out. So everybody will have the chance to see. You observe life evolve into its future benign state from the point at which you left it. Some of you who wish to observe how that passage of experience affects your family or loved ones might be allowed to observe the impact upon them as they evolve. This is not always possible, because it takes time and you might be needed elsewhere. When you know where you're going and what you're going to do, you're very often eager to get there.

You just said some most heartening things. I have asked these questions many times without ever getting answers that made sense. Who better to ask about dimensions than the being who creates them, keeps them, separates them?

Helps them to maintain their structural integrity while not interfering with each other.

All right, that's wonderful! I'm out of questions now. I had intended to talk to you about ten minutes, but you've been so interesting that I kept going.

Well, thank you. You will find that many of the beings have the capacity to wax eloquent.

[Laughs.] Well, they might all get an hour, then, instead of ten minutes. What would you like to say until we talk again?

I have really said what I would like to say. Mostly, I am happy to remind you that you are all truly immortal. And the moment you experience that immortality consciously again at the end of your natural cycle it will seem as if the experience of not remembering your total personality was just a moment. There won't be any sensation of a long time gone by without knowing yourself. It will be as if there was a minor scratch in the record that went "click" just once. It will seem like that, but you will remember what you need to remember. Do know that *your continuity is assured.*

Oh, that's beautiful!

Good night.

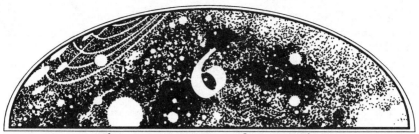

The Master of Maybe

February 6, 1997

elcome.
Well, what shall we talk about?

I am interested in expanding our road map or creational chart of what's out there. When we talked to you before, I didn't realize everything was so big. You talked of coming from beyond the points of light, of awakening, of becoming aware out in that space of potential. I had thought it was just outside our orbs, but I think it might be a whole lot farther away than I thought.

Yes. I will talk a little bit like the other beings did because it will give a sense of continuity. Now, let's see . . . when I first became aware, yes. It goes way back. I will give you a time line as best can be done. Allowing for the length of time of the existence of your universe, I became aware of my personality (as one becomes aware of an individual personality) about 465 billion times the length of the existence of this universe.

The Fragmentation of That Which Is, Initiating My Birth

This awareness was stimulated by another event. I used to be an integrated portion of the energy of absolute creation. Absolute creation would be loosely translated as That Which Is. Now, some time ago That Which Is, an isness, suddenly fragmented. I believe it was probably stimulated from another point into all the aspects of Is, including absolute Is, Might, Maybe (of course) and many others. This is when I became conscious of being Maybe. I did not think of myself at that time as the Master of Maybe. I became aware of myself as being the portion of Is that I have come to call Maybe, or, loosely translated, *potential*. This, then, is my highly condensed adventure to the point where I would say I had achieved some level of mastery.

At first I remained in that general space, and so did all the other fragments. But very gradually over a period of time roughly equal to about a thousand years of your time, the pieces began to migrate in all directions. At first I sort of paired myself up with the energy of Might, meaning *it could be*. We decided we would try and stay together because we were so similar. We traveled together, but it soon became apparent, after about 700 years of your experiential time, that we were being drawn to slightly different locales. We made an oath to stay in touch and communicate regularly, which we have done, so that we can not only compare notes (as you say) but have an affection over time and space.

My Journey After Separating from Might

From that point of intersection I began to move through what I would loosely term space, where there was not a lot of dense mass, but more the absence of it. This went on for about 25,000 experiential years. During this time I was able to explore my own personality to the deepest possible levels, which I had not been inclined to do before, being connected with a larger being and then having paired with Might.

I think maybe the reason for such a vast amount of time in that space was so that I would come to know myself. Before that time I had not really been prepared to make a decision based solely upon what I was, only to make group decisions. This was my first experience of that sense of individuality.

After about 25,000 years I began to see points of light, which could now be roughly compared to galaxies. I realized then that previously I must have penetrated a universe without noticing it. There was no apparent barrier—which is unusual in universes, I might add. Gradually I began to realize that this was a universe in the making that was still absorbing material from beyond its boundaries. Because the boundaries of the universe had not been firmly set, I had been able to simply pass into it without noticing any sense of doorway or induction.

I began to allow myself to flow where I would need to go (which I had initially done anyway), but I didn't immediately identify this universe as that place where I was supposed to be going. Allowing myself to flow, I expected to be drawn toward these galaxies, but it didn't happen. As a matter of fact, I kept on going right through that universe. At that point I think I realized that I was headed for some very specific place, and that it was pulling on me. In fact, that was true.

Traveling in Creations Near Where Yours Would Be

Within about another 3000 experiential years I arrived at the place I was being drawn to—the outer boundaries of the mass creation you are in. (I had no idea that as an individual being I could in any way help anyone simply by existing. This was quite a surprise to me.) The moment I passed into the first universe, my speed immediately decreased. It was very profound and sudden, and I began to move at a very slow speed. I felt almost as if I were going to fragment once again. Then I realized I needed to stop, so I did. After I came to a complete stop I asked to be pulled to where it was best for me to go, and I was pulled slowly toward that place.

I wanted to get there quickly, of course, but looking back on it, I realize now that moving slowly was an advantage because it allowed me to gradually assimilate the energies of this place. It was a galaxy in a universe that was not close to your own at the time. I don't think your own universe was in creation then, but it was within the general area of the space where you *would* be.

So I was drawn toward this galaxy, all the way through stars, and of course I was enjoying the stimulus of all this life. I was eventually drawn to a planet; if you could have seen me then, it was like a metamorphosis. The closer I came to the planet, the more I began to take on form and shape and mass. Pretty soon I looked like a smaller, distorted version of your own moon, what you would call a large asteroid.

Looking back on this now, I realize that this happened so that I would not look as I normally do. I am quite a large mass of color, predominantly purple with some red and gold, a little white and a lot of sparkling. If I had approached the planet looking that way, people wouldn't have known what to think. But as an asteroid I was not considered in any way unusual. This was good, looking back on it.

This was my first experience with people, and they looked not dissimilar to yourselves. They were humanoids who had an extra finger and, I believe, an extra toe. Their skin color had sort of a greenish tinge, probably having to do with the gases on the planet, the atmosphere. The people themselves had a very advanced society, very focused on education. The children were educated from about the point of what to you would be two years old, although there it was much older because their lifespan was about 1200 years. (You can compare in terms of percentage.) Their education would compare very well to a university graduate level in your present culture, and they had the capacity to absorb it.

The Curious Civilization; Permeating Nearby Orbs with Maybe

Children and the people on this planet were born about a hundred times more curious than you are. Looking back on it, I realize that this is a place where curiosity was being applied as an ideal to see how life forms would behave when they were very, very curious, wanting to gather information. What was lacking at that point in their evolution was questions. They didn't have enough questions to stimulate them to find more answers. They had come to a crossroads where they must either change their culture or be motivated to acquire new information.

Looking back on it now, I realize that I was there to stimulate the potential for expanded questions. I was there for about a thousand years of experiential time, during which people became more integrated with a higher level of their own consciousness. This allowed them vast expansions in their ability to stimulate new and profound questions. After about a thousand years they were sufficiently stimulated, so I moved on. Of course, to their astronomers it appeared that a vast rock object broke free of its orbit and for some strange reason moved away seemingly on its own. That alone stimulated some questions, so I can see how that fit nicely into their plan.

I traveled again for quite some time, not as long as before, and started to approach your circle of creation and your [group of] orbs. I moved into the outer orbs first and slowed down well before I got to the seventh orb. There wasn't much mass of life going on there at that time, but I was encouraged to stay in the seventh orb for about a million and a half years of your time. I was encouraged to travel throughout the entire seventh orb, permeating and stimulating that orb with my energy.

I noticed several times that other beings were doing the same thing. They were, along with me, preparing it for universes that would all be involved in interspecies communication, education, acquisition of creatism, knowledge and basically higher learning. I saw there my old friend Might. I also saw the fragment of Is that I associate more with vertical consciousness, as your friend calls it—that which has the capacity to intersect all levels of consciousness to acquire wisdom and knowledge. That being was there when I got there, though I didn't see it right away. It was still there when I left, so it appears that the seventh orb, which is not particularly involved in creations yet (I don't see any) will be a place of fantastic higher learning. Beings who go there will basically be able to get all the answers.

Then I began moving slowly through the other orbs, performing a similar function, not always seeing the same beings I saw in the seventh orb, but beings who were similarly associated with maybe. For instance, in the sixth orb I saw beings whom I would associate more with freedom and independence. (You can see where maybe would fit into that.) Freedom and independence permeated that orb; even when I arrived there I could feel it. It was exciting. It seems that the universes in that orb are going to have a great deal to do with innovation in all levels. It will be a wonderful, stimulating place. Whole universes of beings will be involved in it. It will be a marvelous place to be, I think.

Absorbing Your Orb's Energies, Meeting Your Creator

I continued to move toward the orbs. By the time I got to yours, your Creator had, I believe, received the initial message of the creation that would become your universe, but the universe wasn't there yet. Oddly enough, when I was moving around the orb in which you are now involved, I wasn't emanating anything. I was very curious. I didn't feel to emanate anything, so I didn't. As I look back on it now, I was apparently assimilating the general energy of the place.

After I was there for a brief time, really no more than 20 or 25 years of your time, suddenly it was like instant acceleration. I felt myself blasting along faster than I'd ever moved. Perhaps I can give the term in a light-speed quotient: I was moving anywhere from about light speed to light speed's eleventh power—very quickly.

The next place I stopped was the intersection where I was going to meet your Creator. Now, since I had actually been to the Orb where your creation would take place, your Creator recognized me right off and we had an immediate connection. That's when I joined up with your Creator. We had some wonderful communication, not only from what I had been doing (Creator was interested in that, of course, and I was interested in what your Creator had been doing), but we also had a terrific exchange of energy.

Your Creator was able to tap the feeling of that place from me and literally use it as a homing device to find it. Then I realized why I had not emitted anything in that Orb; I was intended to assist your Creator to find this place. If I had been emitting something, I would not have been able to receive its energy. (One does not always discover immediately why one does something, but one does eventually.) That's how we got together.

Where did you meet the Creator?

As I said, I came to this Orb and absorbed the energy of it, then I left and traveled well away. I think your Creator had acquired a few of the consultants by that time, but your Creator was still a far, far distance from this Orb then.

Can you just give us an idea where? Are there any words?

Yes, I understand what you're asking. Well, Zoosh was with "Him" (using your common vernacular—you really ought to come up with a term). Let's see, I think your Creator was not too far from picking up the Master of Discomfort. It's hard to give a location, I'm sorry.

Circles of Creation; Physiological Similarities of Humanoids

How many circles of creation are there?

Circles of creation—you mean the whole thing? Oh, goodness! The one in which you are involved . . . then of course there are about

60 or 61* others that stem from that same source. But ultimately, in terms of circles of creation, how high can you count? Who can say how vast the infinite is? From my personal knowledge, what I've actually seen, felt or become aware of, there are trillions. And that is just from my personal experience. I'm sure there are many, many more than that.

Is that galaxy with the six-fingered greenish humanoids where you were the asteroid in a circle of creation far away?

It is not even in this Circle of Creation, but it's interesting to note, isn't it, that they are similar to you. Even their physiology is not at all dissimilar. They have an intestine, but not quite as long as yours. They have skeletal structure, a nervous system, a brain. They have what I call a compound brain. You have a compound brain too, meaning you have what your scientists call the basic, or primitive, brain and the other structure on top of it. Theirs is a compound brain where all of the brain structure is actually in use, whereas most of your brain is in use.

Your Brain Is in Use to Create Your Reality

By the way, the reason your scientists haven't been able to find this out is that most of your brain is used in creating your reality.

Really?

Yes, that's what most of it is involved in, why it can't be tracked physiologically. That's why the big mystery—because it's involved in creating your reality; it's involved at other levels, in creationism. This is why Creator says you are His children, because you are creators, you understand? These other humanoids, however, are aware of the inner and the outer brain, what it is doing at all times. They can tune in to the functions of their brain as well as think with it.

Do they have dimensions?

Their dimensions, I think, are very limited, really only about three. In comparison to your dimensions, those dimensions would be roughly five, six and seven.

Are they aware only of the one they are in, or all of them?

Oh, they are aware of five, six and seven. I don't think it has occurred to them yet that they have the capacity to create other dimensions. Somebody's going to ask the question at some point. Not just, what are dimensions, but what do we have to do to create dimensions? When that happens, shortly thereafter they'll have creationism capacity. They'll begin to

---

* Note that Maybe's number differs from that of one of these circles of union/circles of creation, or parts of Ecstasy—Creator of Pure Feelings and Thoughts, first mentioned in chapter 1, then discussed in subsequent chapters. This discrepancy is questioned in chapter 9.

create dimensions, universes and so on. They are, in a sense, really an experiment that predates your own. So I'm suspecting that . . .

. . . the reason you went there has something to do with us.

Certainly, and on the larger scale, that the thread that passed by your Creator must have come through that area somehow.

When That Which Is broke into pieces, was it trillions of little pieces, or just a few?

No, it wasn't that many. It think it was initially about thirteen pieces, then I could see the pieces fragmenting further as they moved away. I think the sum total of the pieces even today is barely more than a thousand. These would include ramifications of everything from the remotest possibility of what-could-be to the absolute of what-is. If you break that down to about 1009 subtle variations, that is all of the pieces. At my stage I am now the master of maybe. As far as I know, the other fragments are also masters.

And they're out influencing other creations in the same way that you are?

Yes.

What Might Is Doing Now

What have you heard from Might? How is he?

Might is not involved in these orbs. He was initially involved to permeate some of the orbs, but now is in another circle of creation not too far from your own. I think it is one of the 61, in a universe preparing to make a dimensional quantum leap. The entire universe is going to jump from the ninth dimension to the thirteenth and requires a tremendous amount of energy of a function of potential, which is Might—might-be. They require a tremendous amount of infusion, so Might has basically expanded itself to cover the entire universe. He has his energy all over that universe. You can't go anywhere in that universe without feeling Might. It's impossible to feel a sense of hopelessness in *that* universe!

What are they using as a catalyst?

Catalyst to make the jump? They are not utilizing drama in their present. The people in that universe, every one of them, are what you would call psychics. I think this might have a little to do with your own expansion. They are utilizing a strong dream that they all had—can you imagine everybody in the universe having the same dream on the same night? They all had a dream suggesting that they needed to make the jump to the thirteenth dimension, and by making that jump they would expand consciousness in their entire circle of creation by a factor of two.

I think that when they make the jump (I don't know this for a fact yet) it will coincide with your jump, which will multiply by two the expansion that you create. So in their circle of creation they'll make an even vaster jump. By making the jump to the thirteenth dimension, they are setting up the tension that will create this.

That's exciting.

I think so.

Is broke up into a thousand pieces and you are a master, yet your speed and the way you look are not under your control.

Learning to Let Go Like Blooming Flowers

You have to understand that we are all a portion of something larger, and to the extent that we can let go, even as individuals, and allow ourselves to be what we feel we need to be in that moment, then we release the baser aspects of will or control and simply allow ourselves to become. In terms of your own day-to-day reality, this is very much how flowers know when to bloom. It's not the same function they use when they close to protect themselves at night. Flowering is just the plant letting itself go. New individual plants are stunned and thrilled by flowering. So it is largely by letting yourself go and flowing in the larger sense of the creation in which you participate. This is what *I'm* doing. It's not so much that I'm being bossed around; it's that I'm letting myself go with the flow, as you like to say.

So even though you're going through these gazillions of years, you're flowing from one place to the other, and each one is under some overall creator, somebody in charge. And beyond that there's more!

Yes, there's always more. Always more, that's your motto, and it's true. When you're dealing with management like this, the nice thing about it is that you can be absolutely certain, without any doubt whatsoever, that you're going to like whatever you become. That's the wonderful thing, to be sure, because the management is benign and wants the best for you as well as those you serve.

Even though you might go through 10,000 managers on your journey?

That's right. Yes, a definitely benign corporate structure.

About the Ant Species and Their Source Beings

As you explained before, you have infused us with possibilities, potential, hope. Before, you talked to us about subjects from an ant to the Creator.

With ants especially, many of us are very fond of that species because they do so much with what they have. Even you are fascinated by how an ant can move something comparable to your moving a boulder. It is not so much because of will, but because no one ever told them they couldn't do it. Think about it: If you didn't tell your children that something is impossible to achieve and other children have similar information from their parents and teachers, someday you might reach the point where you have the capacity to do things like an ant. We're very fond of ants because they're constantly demonstrating doability.

What happens to the kingdom of ants after we become the Creator? Are they on all planets everywhere in all creations? Is that a standard?

No, no. The species of animals and plants that you have here are all geared, every one of them, to encourage you to discover more about yourselves. Many of them are willing to put up with the treatment they get because they know they are serving a very high purpose indeed. No, you will find that ants, in their natural source being, don't look exactly like this. For starters, they don't have as many legs; they needed to develop more legs here just to get around. If you saw them in their source being, they do have that sort of a hard-shell exterior . . .

Segmented?

Yes, but the segments aren't as obvious. There would be that three-stage experience and you could tell they were somehow related to ants, but they would appear like some kind of extraterrestrial who reminds you of ants, but without pincers at the front. They do not have exactly faces, but something that's closer to a face than an ant's head. If you ever looked at an ant or studied biology when you were in school, these beings don't look exactly like that. Their telepathic ability is *very* evolved. They can communicate anywhere in the universe, even beyond the universe. They know where they need to be.

No, in terms of places in your universe, including their home place, ants are probably in less than 25 places, because they really are not motivated on their own to go anywhere. They're not space travelers. They are where they are and enjoy their existence there, but they are not in any way a colonizing power. They're not aggressive like that.

Are they in the Milky Way galaxy, or way beyond it?

Oh, in terms of your galaxy? They're in about nine places.

So when we go out to travel, we'll run into them?

You might very well run into some version of them. You will probably be most surprised when you run into them in a ship. They'll be at the controls, of course, and the communication will be totally telepathic. You won't be repulsed by them at all. As a matter of fact, they're rather attractive in what I would call an artistic style. They are very benign and are very fond of intellectual games. I think it was because of the ant beings here that they became aware of chess, and they've developed over 250 ways to play it. They *love* to play games. Mental games—oh, they love that!

Are these beings who are walking upright on these planets civilized societies, ensouled?

Yes, of course, even as ants here are ensouled.

Each individual ant is ensouled?

Absolutely, *every individual*. That's why it's an interesting experience to observe a single ant. Perhaps it will be scouting, and occasionally it might stop and scratch itself or clean itself and look up at you. In that moment you'll get the distinct impression that this is an individual. They are all ensouled, yes—all beings, bees, hornets, horses. They are all ensouled, certainly.

Individual souls? I thought they were a group soul.

Oh, no. More advanced cultures have the capacity to communicate as a group, but they are unique individuals. The fact that they work so well as a team is largely the reason they are here for you, so that you can see how *you* can work as a team and accomplish more by working together. You know, that has actually had its impact on you, and that's probably why they might not be with you indefinitely. You probably won't see too many of them at the fourth dimension.

By the time you get to the fifth dimension (those of you who manifest a fifth dimension of this planet), I think they will be bigger so you can interact with them more individually. They will be more family-oriented, not so strongly tribal. They'll be less mystical to you by that time because you'll be more mystical yourself. So they'll be less strange and much more easily understood. You will have many people who will be in telepathic contact with them and other beings at that time, so you can share their wisdom and understanding and philosophy.

The Future Study of Animal Philosophies

As a matter of fact, in fifth-dimensional Earth, as you expand and Explorer Race members and others go there, by that time there will be entire philosophies built on the philosophies and wisdoms of what you now loosely call animals. You know, it will be a great study, not unlike what is now called shamanism but with more intellectual ramifications. There will be entire universities set up to teach people how to communicate with these beings, because you will at that time be solving problems for beings elsewhere.

It's not just that the Explorer Race is going to go out into the stars, but some beings will stay where you live and they will also be helping beings. Beings will come from other places, and say, "What do we do about this, what do we do about that?" Because you have so many sources here, if you don't have the answer, then beings who can relate to ants or trees or whatever will go out and say to the species they relate to, "Here is a group of individuals who have come from this star system. They have this problem and don't know what to do. What would you recommend?" You will not only acquire new information that way, but will come to be known as the problem-solvers.

Of course, by that time you will have total contact with extraterrestrials, and people will come from all over the universe with their unsolvable problems. Some of them will be very minor, from your present consideration, but others will be so complex that it will take teams of people working with many different species of plant and animal beings to get the answer that will solve the entire problem. It will be a lot of fun.

My God, we could have you do all fifty books! You could talk forever!

[Chuckles.] Excuse me. I am a bit verbose at times, yes.

The Human Brain (Understood When Science and Religion Marry) and Its History

I love it! Could you give us more useful information about the brain? We never were told that before.

Yes, it is appalling that your scientists don't know that yet, but you have to remember who taught your scientists—people in your culture living in this time, who of course don't know it themselves. But you will know it, probably within 30 or 40 years. That's when science and religion finally get married. Science finds its true god and religion finds its true guide. The original intention of science and intellectualism in general was to guide religion, and the purpose for science was to find a god—a god of nature, a god of all beings, a god of love and wisdom—so that it wouldn't do some of the negative things that science has done in your time. Certainly you can look out now at science and say, "What wonderful creations!" yet at the same time look at the same creations and aspects of those creations and say, "Oh, but the way you're doing this needs to be entirely redone," to say nothing of creations that science would rather not talk about.

Why do we call it the reptilian brain?

I think it's simply to suggest the basic brain, the brain that functions primarily to control physical functions. It's by way of saying that reptiles are like this, but of course we know that they really aren't, that they are much, much more than that. But it is a simple term that your scientists have come to use. Not all of your scientists do that, by the way. I think that it is primarily a physiological, even to some extent anthropological, application, but it's obviously not a true representation of reptiles.

Did we start out with that brain when the first prototype of humans was created on this planet, later overlaid by the cerebrum?

Oh, no. Good question, but guess what? You started out with a trinary brain, one that had three major components. There was more around your brain. It was bigger, but the creators of such beings very quickly realized that you were going to be too smart for your own good. You wouldn't be able to accomplish what you intended here because you would be able to master things quickly and the chances of making mistakes would be extremely limited.

At what point was this, when the Sirians brought in that prototype?

It was before that. The prototype of the basic human being as you now know yourself to be was designed on Sirius because there needed to be a being on Earth that was not intellectually superior.

Rather, there was a series of beings (of whom very few bones have been found today) who had a skull three times the size of yours today. All the people were brilliant and it was like, "Uh-oh, too smart." [Chuckles.] Nobody was killed; they were basically segregated, like, "Oh, I'm afraid you can't be the basic Earth human being. I'm sorry." Most of the people chose to move to another place, but some hung around underneath the surface of the Earth. I think a few of them did make forays to the surface, but the mass of the population went elsewhere. Then what you know now as your basic Earth human being became the prevalent human here.

So they pared the brain way down?

Yes, that's what they had to do. It is useful, you know. Even today you have not fully discovered what your brain is doing. When you discover that, there will be those who are in a position to make changes. You might be more amenable to allowing that former trinary brain to regrow, and the Earth human being can have it again. This is why, I might add, some of you who have had long-distance visions into the future of the human being have seen very large human skulls. It is now likely (not an absolute decision) that the powers that be—creators and so on—will allow that trinary brain to return, which of course will require a bigger skull.

In ten years, a hundred years, a thousand years?

Oh, more than that.

And the "creators that be" are the Creator and his friends?

No, I think by that time *you'll* probably be running the show.

Were you aware when you met the Creator that there was something in Him that was not Him, that was driving Him? Were you aware that the Explorer Race was separate from Him?

No, I wasn't aware of that. Of course, we discussed the Explorer Race concept; we had plenty of time to do that. But I wasn't aware that there was, like you say, a motivating force underneath. My relationship to your Creator then was very much a conscious one. I don't think I even probed for any subconscious within your Creator.

By the time you met Him, He was already coming this way?

That's right.

So you weren't one of those who saw us coming?

No.

At some point did you become aware that there was another element in the Creator that was separate? I'm just learning this myself.

I understand. I don't think that was my primary focus. I think that after having gone through all that I went through, I didn't really consider that. As a matter of fact, I don't think I *ever* really considered it.

Until we started talking about it here?

That's right. Because it wasn't my primary function.

Where I've Functioned in This Creation

You spent most of the time on Earth, right?

No, my energy does not fill the whole universe; there's no need for that. My energy primarily functions around Earth where you need the encouragement, because you don't get as much encouragement as you need. So mostly I'm around here. If I'm ever needed elsewhere, I can send a portion of myself there, but it hasn't been necessary very much. Mostly I'm around Earth. I was a little bit around Sirius toward the end of the planet that had acculturated itself to the extreme negative.

I was a little bit around that then, and I've been around a few planets that needed to make a sudden leap in consciousness. I was out around the planet Lyra in its distant past in the Pleiades, and I was out around Arcturus when they made their move to being very involved thematically with the idea of change and growth. So I was out there then, but mostly I spend my time here because you need the energy.

Even though you were out there with those beings, they are not the Explorer Race, right?

No, they're not. They are in existence here, but they do not experience any of the training that you've had. To be a member of the Explorer Race, you have to be on a very rigorous training program, which is what you have been doing—and being on Earth really puts the topper on that. But they are not in any way being trained; they are not members of the Explorer Race. When the Explorer Race takes over, in terms of creationism, eventually becoming the Creator, they will probably stay. They don't have any reason to go anywhere and most likely they will still be here when you pass this creation on to somebody else. They are just part of the main body of the creation.

I had thought our training started in Orion, but it must have started before that.

I think your training really began when you started moving in this direction. That's how it was for me. One might say, allowing for the fragmentation of the Is, that it started before that. But my training consciously started when I began moving in this general direction. So I must believe that when *you* started moving in this direction (certainly no later than that), your training started, too. I can't believe that you started it much later. Why would you be motivated to come here if you weren't already getting something that would encourage a benevolent future? No, I'm sure you got training as you were coming.

My Future; What I've Learned Here, Ways I've Helped

You get a lot of satisfaction doing what you're doing. What would you want to do when you leave here? I don't think you've thought about it very much.

No, because I've already found what I really like doing. It's very fulfilling. I must admit that someday I'd like to rejoin my friend Might. If my ambitions were to go beyond what I am doing now, it would probably be to rejoin my friend Might. I am fond of Might [chuckles], but I can wait.

When this is through, the modus operandi is to ask to visit your friend, then wait to see what happens, right?

Yes, and if something else comes up, you know, I will just start moving. If I am no longer needed, I'll just start moving to where I *am* needed. If I pick up Might along the way, so much the better, but if not, then I'm sure it will be someplace that will be good for me. *This* certainly has been good for me, very fulfilling.

What have you learned here?

Well, there's nothing like being needed and providing what's needed just by being yourself. I don't have to work. I just exist. I simply exist, and as myself, I just exude naturally. I radiate Maybe.

I didn't realize that you don't think about it.

I don't think about it, I don't do anything, I don't have to chop wood or carry water. I just exist. And just existing, I'm constantly being fulfilled—people, individuals, do something. They don't say, "Can't do it." They look at something and say, "Maybe can do it. Let's figure out how to do it." [Chuckles.]

You must have helped me create my company, Mission Possible, right?

Well, Mission Maybe, eh? [Chuckles.]

Nope, not maybe—possible!

All right. Possible is somebody else, but we're cousins.

Possible is somebody else! [Laughs.] That's another one of the fragments of Is, eh?

Well, it would be, wouldn't it? [Chuckles.]

Growth, an Absolute; Creations Nurtured by Their Specific Focus

One of my desires is to have someone draw a picture of out there, but it's too big. It just keeps going.

Not only is it so vast that you couldn't really draw a picture of it, but yes, it's *growing*. That is the awesome part of it. Think about it. It is so vast that it's beyond *my* consciousness to imagine the vastness. And it's growing!

But every creation produces creators—that's their natural product. That's their harvest.

Yes, as far as I can tell, growth is an absolute. It just happens. Everything is growing, getting bigger, becoming more. There seems to be absolutely no limit, from what I can tell. As a matter of fact, there is just the opposite—encouragement.

You mentioned specifically 61 circles of creation, but . . .

Sixty-two total (including yours) within your mass of creation. I think that was mentioned before.

Do they all have orbs? Do they all look like this one?

They do not all have orbs, no. It just depends. Orbs are there for a reason. Usually orbs will separate if something is going on that needs to be separated from something else.

It gives you a lot more possibilities or potential within different focuses?

Yes, different focuses in different orbs, as I indicated before. It allows those creations within those orbs to be constantly nurtured by that focus so that the Creator Itself does not have to provide that nurturing. A well-oiled machine, yes?

There will be this same-size circle of creation where there are no orbs, so it's all one great circle of universes?

And everything in between. Just imagine the infinite. It's beyond your capacity to imagine that, so yes and no, because there's more. What can I say? You can ask and we can probe. We can go as far as life exists to provide answers. Then you will have to leave it to the readers to ask more in the future.

But the human body that we inhabit, even though it's been doctored up a little bit for us, is a basic building component in the universe, a basic structure?

Oh, you mean the human body as it is? Oh, I can't say that, no. I'd have to say it's relatively recent.

Really?

Humanoids Created to Stimulate Growth

Just in my own concept of the time of the existence of all creation—let's take it past this universe, everything—I think the human, even the humanoid, is relatively recent. The reason for the humanoid shape in general is to create a vehicle by which a soul can learn slowly, because souls naturally exist in light, and distance is nothing. You know, it takes less time than the snap of the finger to cover the vastest distances when you are light and energy. But if you are encapsulized in a humanoid body even for a short time (such as a lifetime), you must learn and grow. The purpose of the humanoid, as far as I can tell, is to stimulate growth.

In all of those vast creations out there, what are the vehicles for encapsulated lives? What do they look like?

Well, just within your own circle of life here, you have lots of humanoids. This general area is about growth, change, expansion and so on. But other beings—imagine any shape and compound it with other shapes, and it's more than that. Plus you find a lot of beings who are basically light. That is *very* common. In terms of being light—and I don't mean shapes of humanoids as light but what you might see as light or measure as energy—that is a *very* old form. That, I think, is one of the building blocks of life forms.

But are there structures that look like animals and insects?

Oh, certainly!

Everything you can imagine?

All the animals on the Earth have a point of origin. I think there are a few that originated here, but for the most part more than 99% have origins elsewhere, where they don't look anything like they look here. They might have similarities—some of them, not all—but a lot of them are roughly humanoid. Even the ant source being is roughly humanoid, by which I mean an apparent body, a face, but not necessarily two arms and two legs. A humanoid might have one arm, three legs, something like that.

And the purpose of all this incredible variety is that each creator feels that's how his creations can best learn?

Yes, because ultimately a creator's responsibilities are to encourage, stimulate and provide growth opportunities for those whom the creator is responsible for.

And that creator might have been limited in what it knows, or it might have a very specific structure for its life forms to evolve in?

Yes, either one of those. Certainly creators do not know everything.

We talk to a lot of outside consultants. Do all creations everywhere have specialists who come in and help set up dimensions and bring in time and do certain things?

I believe that they all have that available to them. I think there are a few who do not do that, who would like to make their creation based on what *they* are or some aspect of what they are, so they don't use outside consultants. But commonly outside consultants are very much utilized.

So we can assume that the outside consultants we talk to here all came from this Circle of Creation, not from far away?

Oh, I don't think you can ever assume things like that. *I* didn't come from this Circle of Creation.

I don't mean the friends of the Creator, not you eight beings, but the engineers who came in to do certain things.

Oh, I don't think you can ever assume that, no. Never assume. When it comes to the vastness of knowledge, never assume.

What would you like to talk about?

Oh, really not that much. I just want to let people know how very loved you are, not only by your own Creator, but by so many beings, and how that love is universal. And this *short* time of your focus in physical reality in this culture won't take as long to heal as you think. Most of you heal from the slings and arrows (as you say) of physical life within only three experiential days of departing at the end of your natural cycle. Some of you take a little longer because you wish to study things, but it doesn't take long. Even when the lifetime has been challenging, it will ultimately lead to some level of growth for your total being.

So do remember, especially at times when you seem discouraged, that it will be fleeting and you will go on with your normal, more vast existence. Make sure you keep flowers around, or know where to find one. Just looking at a flower will remind you that there is something more vast than the creations of man.

Thank you very much.

Thank you and good night.

Master of Frequencies and Octaves

February 10, 1997

Yes, it has been a time, has it not?
Since October 15. Welcome.

Thank you. What shall we talk about?

What we're trying to do is get a sense of the expansion, a taste of infinity or a road map of what's out there. When I talked to you before, I had no idea how big everything was. If you would, please share what the place is like where you come from.

My Origin

Oh yes. I will describe that. Because it has some similarity to the appearance of the center of your galaxy, I will . . . [draws]. Now, imagine that spinning in the obvious direction for the way things are curling at the end there and you will be aware of my first consciousness of being a portion of something.

My origin

It is interesting to note that I became aware of a group personality toward the center of that spinning object. If we looked at that spinning object from the side [draws]—this is the direct side view—we would see something like this stem going this direction [see straight arrow], then spun

stem, where I first
became conscious

the spiral
on edge

outward. I was in this stem when I became aware of this group personality. Before that there was a sense of what I would call deep sleep, which was very restful but in which there were no dreams such as you are familiar with. There was no sense of information exchange, no light, no color, just deep, restful sleep—quiet.

Then I felt a sense of motion. I had never felt motion before, so I didn't recognize it then, but when I look back on it I can see it for what it was. I started moving around in sort of a vortexal pattern in the stem of that swirling mass. By the time I emerged at the center (in the first illustration), I could tell that there was some kind of centrifugal force being put to our group personality.

Sure enough, the intention was to spin us so that coming through the stem, we (the group personality that had formed with what I would call similars, beings similar to myself) were initially homogenized and not fragmented. Some kind of completion process was going on through the stem. We reached the whirling bands of light (not just simple strains), and I was spun off on one of these bands and other parts of my group were spun off on other bands, some on the same band I was.

Gradually I moved toward the edge of that swirling light. This process took about as long as one-fourth the time of the existence of your universe, but the funny thing is that to me it seemed very fast. This was because I had been in that deep sleep state—unconscious of an individualized personality, basically resting—at least ten times the length of your universe's existence, including its future existence. Thus moving through that process didn't seem so terribly long to me.

I was at the tip of one of those swirling bands of light for a while. I noticed that other beings who were originally in my group were flying off somewhere; I couldn't see where, I didn't know where. I was there for a long time. I was there after all the other members of my group flew off. I wondered why I had been involved in that group because I was there so much longer. Everyone had left about a hundred thousand years before me (in terms of your years), but there I was, still spinning around. It wasn't unpleasant, but the feeling of anticipation and excitement ebbed after a while.

Looking back on it now, I think there was some slight delay while your Creator was going through Its voyage (or choosing to do so) to gather ideas and thoughts. All of a sudden I felt myself exit from that plume of light. I expected to speed off as previous members of my group had done, but it wasn't like that at all. There wasn't a physical transit. I exited the plume of light and there was the slightest moment of that deep rest again—which must have been a moment of transit, as I look back on it.

The next thing I knew, I was literally [snaps fingers] in space, like that. I could tell I was far from my point of origin, and I had the feeling

I was supposed to wait there and that very soon (about a year to a year and a half of your time—nothing, from my perspective) I would be met by someone who would require my services. I felt that during that waiting time I would have the opportunity to explore every dimension that had ever existed, that existed at that time or that ever would exist. I felt that I would explore them all in exactly the same moment so that I could, in the same moment, understand the subtle differences from one dimension to another. I felt that I could conceive of a way to separate the dimensions so that vast things could occur within the same space. So it was basically a problem to be solved.

You just knew that? Nobody told you?

My Simultaneous Experience of All Dimensions

I knew that, and I'm inclined to believe that the message came from somewhere. I believe that the message might have come either from the needs of your Creator or from the one who sent your Creator the inspiration. It must have been one or the other. So literally in that next moment and for about a year and a half of your time I experienced all dimensions.

Out there in the middle of space?

Just out there in space. I experienced all dimensions, and I'd have to say it was the most amazing experience I've ever had, even allowing for what has happened since. It was an extraordinary feeling. Among the vastness of all dimensions, some are so nonphysical as to be the opposite of the physicality of your dimension, what I would call an inner dimension—not necessarily something that takes up less space, but something that takes up what I would call negative space, or the space that exists before space. It's a little hard to describe that in any language.

There were about 270 of those, in gradations, and there were over a thousand dimensions you are more familiar with, and *I was in every one of them at exactly the same moment!* Even so, I was in that same place in space. It is not a fragmenting experience, as one might expect. I must say, I have never felt so totally myself, because it was as if every potential harmonic of myself was completely represented—a universal chorus of myself.

And you perceived it all at once, not like going up and down a scale, but simultaneously?

Simultaneously, that's right; there was no transit involved. During the entire experience I never really moved. I was in the same place, yet the feeling of motion was vast, because some of the dimensions are simply more expectant than others—they welcome beings so much more than others, are more restful or more precise or more musical or what-have-you. That was an *extraordinary* experience! I recognized that my job was to see how these dimensions could be experienced at the same time by any being who might wish to do this in the future. My challenge was also to work out a way to separate dimensions so that beings who are in a given dimension do not accidentally fall into another one.

That's what I worked on. I had noticed that my persona was more varied in the vastness of being when I was focused in all the dimensions at once, yet not less when I was focused more specifically in one dimension. So what I came up with was to assign personality to the dimensions.

Were you in another being, or were you all yourself?

NO

That was all me, but for the sake of description I have to separate things. What I did is very much like this [draws]. This is all of a being, yes? [Points to circle.] The thing to do would *not* [draws X in the circle] be to do that—no, that's not it, *not!* The thing to do would be this [draws]: circles within circles and this [draws]: the spiral. Superimposed over the circles within circles is the spiral. Within the spiral are wheels within wheels, a spiral coming out at each end. That allows a lot of octaves within the same tone.

YES, plus . . .

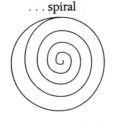

. . . spiral

Understand that I'm trying to describe something that is simultaneous as a separated thing. Basically, it's done with octaves; that's why the word "harmonic" comes in there. That was the only way I was able to figure out how to do this.

Meeting Your Creator

When I was done with that process, *within less than ten minutes* your time (I'm not kidding), your Creator whizzed along, stopped and said, "We're supposed to meet," and I joined Him.

Who was with Him?

Zoosh, and I think he had the Master of Discomfort with Him by then. There were a couple of others, but I didn't get a chance to talk to them. Because your Creator and I were talking intensely while He picked up two or three more, I was never quite sure who was where. In any event, it was confusing to have all those aspects of oneself present in the same time, because some of the aspects, if put side by side, are wholly and *completely* incompatible.

Aspects of you?

Aspects of Beings and Dimensions Becoming Compatible

Aspects of myself and, I believe, aspects of anyone. Let's say here is a being of the 300th dimension and several hundred dimensions away is a being of the 46th or so dimension. They might be totally incompatible, but with all those gradients between them, the compatibility, that universal harmony, is there. It was very difficult to come to terms with the fact that I, my core personality, was not comfortable with all aspects of myself. That led me to understand that not only was I providing a service for your Creator, but the quantum expansion that your Creator intends to accomplish here will somehow allow me to become compatible with all portions of myself, and the same for everyone else as well.

I believe it works this way: If we say everything expands by ten times, then the distance between the wheels within wheels—the distance between dimensions—becomes much vaster. I think it makes room for more dimensions, and in those extra dimensions we develop the links that are now missing, so each being's universal chorus not only sounds better, but is more friendly with all of oneself.

The Subconscious and the Unconscious

I also think that this explains the subconscious. I think that the subconscious mind is not entirely accessible to the conscious mind because *all the pieces are not there yet.* Of course, the *unconscious* mind is not accessible because it is connected to *all* of you, the vast you. But the subconscious mind is really associated with Earth on this dimension at this time. When your Creator was talking about having a subconscious mind (which I understand is your psychological explanation, but that's really pretty close), I wondered why your Creator wanted that to be something you couldn't readily access. But now I realize that when the quantum growth takes place, the subconscious mind will expand and become part of the conscious mind. This will create a conscious link between your feeling self (your instinctual/physical and feeling/emotional self together) and your conscious mind so that your feeling self can direct the exact path for your mind to pursue for its best, most benevolent experience and so that you can avoid mistakes for all time.

But how will we learn anything if we avoid mistakes?

Well, once you get past this learning adventure, your mistakes have to be more subtle, meaning more gentle, without as much impact, without as many consequences.

Or, as you say we'd be cleaning it up forever.

Yes, you don't want to be cleaning up indefinitely. So you see, your Creator is very clever.

And whoever inspired Him is very clever.

Yes.

Do you know who that is?

I've seen the color of the being. One has time to think. I've seen the color, but I don't think I know the being by name.

Well, we will find him eventually. It sounds like that rotating band of light is similar to the centrifuge in this lens or Center of Creation or whatever creators come through.

Yes, and if you look at the picture of your own galaxy, I think it works similarly there. I think it's even a portion of your life concept. I think you're being shown this too, because you're now getting some crop-circle symbols coming from beings who are a little more intellectually connected to their total beings. You'll be given symbols to remind you, to jog your total being so you will remember who you are. You're being shown that these symbols have some universal meaning. Sometimes you will say, "Oh, it looks like this" or "it looks like that," but ultimately the purpose of these symbols is to activate you. That's why the more people who see them, the better.

If that moment when you came out of the centrifuge felt like sleep, yet was movement, could you have been moving from someplace to that creator point where you thought you were in sleep?

I must believe that that is so. Otherwise there would be no explanation for why I was suddenly someplace I wasn't at before. One assumes there must have been some motion; however, there is another possible explanation: It might have had to do with dimensions. Maybe I simply moved into a different dimension. That could explain why I was very calm and restful and peaceful, then all of a sudden without any different visual input I started to move. I didn't feel any obvious dimensional shift, but I think that's another potential explanation.

Concurrent Dimensions of This Room

You know, it's an interesting thing. Right here in this space in this room right now as we are talking together, there are so many dimensions available here. Let me give you some examples. In this exact space in the sixth dimension of this planet there is a tremendous forest. It is not dissimilar to what you call the rainforest, except there are many low bushes and shrubs. And from them all are hanging fruits—yes, fruits and nuts and good things to eat. Unlike this dimension where things oxidize, they don't oxidize there. If a plant gives birth to a fruit, since the plant never dies, it does not have to have seeds. Since it doesn't oxidize, it remains there until it is needed and is always fresh. Isn't that wonderful?

In the ninth dimension this exact space is part of a vast hall. It is a complex where meetings take place at all times on the regulation of the principles of light and their application to different life forms. This is like a university where thought is not discussed so much as light is experienced in every color imaginable, plus many colors you cannot imagine at this moment. These colors are then assigned to different dimensions of the universe you are in, and if the colors are not quite right for it, they are dispatched to other universes. This is a very famous place at that time dimension, and people come from all over to discuss and visit the Applications of Light College.

And they can see what we're doing here?

They can see what you're doing here, but they are not caught up in it.

As we proceed to the eleventh dimension, there is, right here in this exact space . . . this is like the sky. There is space; it is as if the planet is not apparent in this space. The planet Earth is not manifest in this space physically, but she is manifest in terms of her thoughts, her desires, her dreams, her potential. People, individuals can come here at this dimension to help Earth picture how she might like to look or represent herself should she ever wish to manifest in this space. Isn't that fun?

Those are just a few examples of what's happening in this exact space right now.

You can move your consciousness up and down at will and experience all of them?

Yes.

I want to do that!

When you graduate from school here you will be able to do that. As a matter of fact, some people will do that as they're going through the veils, as Zoosh likes to say. Some people will do that just to experience it even before they process themselves—just for the pleasure of it, because you were given the opportunity to have these pleasures to remind you of who you are.

How I Maintain and Separate the Dimensions

What does your energy do to these dimensions? It stabilizes, it separates, it focuses?

I think it's like this: Imagine having a meditation and saying a mantra. It's not that I'm saying a mantra, but I am pulsing a frequency regulation. Making a rhythmic sound [claps hands seven times], a rhythmic beat—it is as if I am doing something like that. It is like an autonomic function such as your heartbeat: You don't make it beat as it does; it just beats. I have programmed it to be an autonomic function of a pulse of my energy so that I don't have to think about it. That's what really maintains and separates the dimensions one from another.

On the Earth, or in the whole creation?

I believe it is in the entire creation. Of course, your Creator also has this capacity, but there is so much to do that your Creator ofttimes asks me to do it. It is easy, just as easy as your allowing your heart to beat on its own. Let me give you an example. You have forgotten now, but when you are first being formed inside your mother's body, when you come in to experience that new child's body forming, the heart will not always beat totally rhythmically. It doesn't do so because you, being the vast you, think that *you* have to cause it to beat. It takes awhile to realize that you can simply let it do what it does and not think about it. You have to learn the autonomic functions just as I did. I had to learn and so do you.

So at first you kept trying to make the dimensions stay apart.

That's right. First I kept trying to work at it—it was *work!* Then I realized, "Wait a minute, this is too much work." I saw that it would be possible to make it a simple thing that I wouldn't have to think about. When I realized that, I saw how what *I* wanted to do matched very nicely with what your *Creator* wanted to do with autonomic functions within your bodies and the bodies of other beings all over the universe. I realized, "Oh, that will fit perfectly." So I essentially used your Creator's idea, as any good consultant does.

But now a lot of your energy is aimed at the Earth, because we're changing dimensions?

Changing Dimensions Now As a Precursor to the Ultimate Expansion; Finding the Automatic Pulse

Yes. I have to make myself more available in this space because it is a very unusual thing. I must admit that when your Creator discussed it with me originally, I thought, Oh, this is a terrible idea!

When? At the beginning, or . . .

When we first met.

Oh, this was part of the idea from the beginning?

Oh, yes.

When the Explorer Race would finally be ready to get out of here, this is how it would be done?

When we first met, your Creator talked about doing this, and I admit to saying what a terrible idea that was. If you tore apart the boundaries of one dimension, the expansion of one dimension into another could tear all the other boundaries apart. (You have to remember that I wasn't into the concept of the autonomic function then. I was planning on focusing and doing every step along the way, beating every beat of the heart myself, as it were.) Your Creator said, "No, no, we need to have that sudden expansion in order to get the *vast* expansion, which is the ultimate purpose of this project."

I realized right away that I was going to have to think up some other way to keep the dimensions from each other. After a while I realized that the autonomic function would work, because it was within the rhythm of the same cycle, the same function as other beings. As long as other beings were utilizing any form of autonomic function, then my use of autonomic functions to keep the dimensions separate would actually support that idea. You could move from one dimension to another, literally punching a hole in the wall of a dimension, and have that expansive energy, storing it up for its future expression, without blowing through all the other dimensions.

The first time you talked you mentioned making a particular tone.

I am utilizing the term "pulse" now. I've sort of expanded that term from *tone* to *pulse*.

But you still have to focus on that, don't you?

No, I don't have to focus on it any more than you have to focus on making your heart beat. You have to learn to let your heart beat when you're inside your mothers, yes? I had to learn to let that work as a part of myself. I'm not saying it's a higher self or a subconscious self, but it's a portion of my physical expression to allow it to work. I essentially programmed it to work in such a way that as long as there were any beings in this universe with any autonomic functions whatsoever (muscles in your body that do not require you to do anything, you understand), I could utilize that same concept to separate the dimensions in the pulse.

It is really a built-in safety mechanism. If for any reason all beings with autonomic functions (which is all beings) should leave this universe in preparation for reconverting this space to some other purpose, then I would no longer use the autonomic function to separate the dimensions. I would have to consciously separate the dimensions, look around and see if there was anybody here. If everybody is gone, then I could say, "Oh, forget about it. I can go, too." So it functions as a safety mechanism.

Do you have plans? Do you have some desires?

Allowing for the fact that I'm not conscious of having done anything other than serve this whole concept, I expect that when we all become ten times more, my life (other than what I'm doing here) will start after this point.

Is there someone you can ask where that place is? What do you call the bands of light you came out of? The centrifuge?

The Centrifuge/Pinwheel Separator

Well, I would just call it the separator.

Okay, the separator. Obviously, your peers come out of it, so they must have gone to other creations?

Yes, definitely.

Have you had a chance to talk to them since you came out?

No, because I didn't realize what was going on until I came here. I had no idea what was happening.

So you all must have this ability within you. You must be utilized everywhere.

My assumption is that there is some common ground between myself and these other beings, but unlike many of the consultants, I am not in touch with these beings now. I do not know where they are or what they are doing. I think that this is necessary because my attention must be so focused here. Or perhaps it is just a part of my being; I am just getting started as a personality. I could not say for certain.

But I'm sure that at some point you'll all meet at the coffee shop.

[Chuckles.] Well, perhaps so. I would like that.

Is there any way to find out? I know that "how far away is it?" is a ludicrous question, but is there any way to relate where that place (the separator) is to here? Is it something close to some center of All That Is?

Let me see. I am being given a number, which I think is perhaps making it sound like it is closer than I thought. Or maybe I just don't know much about numbers, eh? [Writes.] This number [41,367,842,634,218] to this power [862,628] to this power [18] in terms of light-years distant. You might be able to compute that in terms of light-years. That is the formula I am given.

Somebody created the place that created you, and that's the center. From where our little creation is, is it like a quarter way? I'm trying to get a feeling for it.

My understanding is that this kind of pinwheel separator is not an uncommon way for beings who have a very specific purpose.

They told us that in this little tiny round Circle of Creation here, one is for creators.

I think that this is not an uncommon device, so I don't think it's that far away. Of course, far is relative.

I wanted to get some relationship with something that was out there.

It is probably not worth overloading your computers with that number, but I think it might be amusing to pass on the number to those who have time on their hands.

There's another issue here. Were you aware that the Explorer Race is a separate being from the Creator, that it was not part of Him?

I was not aware of that, no.

So you never had an inkling that we were anything other than just another creation of His?

No, and I think you must understand something here.

You had no reason to know?

I had no reason to know that, and I am young compared to many of the consultants.

Your first job? [Laughs.]

This is my first job, thank you.

If your first job is going to affect all of creation, what's your next one going to be like?

Well, I must say, it will look good on my resume.

This is incredibly exciting, the more we learn about it. As you look back now, were there things that happened that make more sense now that you know we were incubated in Him?

Hindsight is helpful, as you know. I'd have to say that looking back is not something I usually do. Excuse me for being seemingly uncooperative, but that is not something I really do. I tend to look in the multileveled present all the time. That's why I can describe . . .

. . . how you can do what you're doing.

Yes, what's happening in this space.

Learning to Be Aware of Multidimensions

It's not important, it's just that I'm trying to see if anyone had looked, you know, what they had known. The Creator told us this just three weeks ago. You have so much to share, I'm trying to figure out how to ask what people need to know. How can we use this skill you've described more? Is it a matter of focusing in the present?

In my experience, to be aware of all dimensions absolutely requires being in the present moment. I think musicians understand this perhaps better than many, because in order to play their music they must be absolutely present. Yet when they become lost in their music, they become more vast than the function of playing the music and the music itself. This is why music and musicians are often contemplative and even meditative in their personalities, though they might not necessarily use those words. This has something to do with rhythm and tone, yes, but as the musician might say, one marries the music.

Repetitive tones and sounds are the easiest way to do it. If it is hard for you to do that, then I'd say, find a drum that makes a tone you like and just beat it steadily for a while. After a short time you will feel tired, but if you keep it up and get into a rhythm of beating it, time goes by. During that time you will have moments where you've glanced at the clock, then you're thinking about other things, but the next time you look at the clock it's hours later. You will have been in your vastness during some of that time.

That's why the Indians have used the drumming technique?

I think part of the intention was to include more beings in the process.

One form of yoga on this planet is the yoga of sound, where we start to hear a sound in our head. Is this something related to the pulsing you do?

It's not something I do, no. I think that has to do with concentration, focus. It's similar to what I was talking about, but I can't say how it works. I think that has to do with focusing all your attention on one thing in one moment and on a sound that is pleasant—a desired sound compared to a tympanic sound that one does not wish to hear.

I haven't experienced it, but there are teachings that focus on that spiritual discipline. What would you like to tell the reader?

Let me just say this. It is not so necessary to work toward becoming a dimensional master. This is something that I am able to do because it is a natural thing for me. For you, it is most important that you master the dimension you are in, to discover the value of all life in this dimension and how to interact with that life in ways that are benevolent to yourself and all that life. One cannot truly understand the value of multiple dimensions without fully understanding and appreciating the value of the one you are in. Good night.

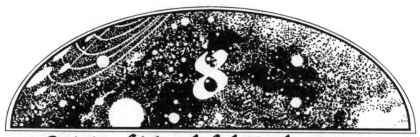

Spirit of Youthful Enthusiasm (Junior) and Master of Imagination

February 11, 1997

ll right. I'm the Spirit of Youthful Enthusiasm, a little more toned down tonight.

Not so slippery, eh?

Well, I don't think I was slippery before. You just didn't run fast enough.

[Laughs.] Well, it was early enough that I didn't have as many facts, either. We're interested, as you know, in pushing back the boundary to look at infinity. Could you share with us where that place of color was where you became aware of yourself? It was far beyond these orbs, right?

The Current Expansion: A Preparation for the Ten-Times Expansion

I don't know if the others have mentioned this to you, but everything has really changed.

Please say what.

Well, because of what's happening here. I think the others have perhaps been too [chuckles] gracious to say anything, but things continue to change, not only the present and the future, but also the past. I can describe the place where I became aware of myself in terms of its distance, but even now as I speak I'm becoming more aware of myself in a time before that. But I'm not sufficiently aware of myself to describe that place before this time I refer to. I will simply say that the distance away from that place is about two and a half times the length of your universe—not that far from here, really.

It was beyond these orbs, wasn't it?

Yes, but it was the shortest possible route beyond the orbs.

The next circle of union over?

No, it was the other way. Understand that the orbs are elongated. For lack of a better term, it was out the side door. If I went straight out, two and a half times this universe is not very far. I'd still be in these orbs.

What did you mean when you said that the other speakers were too gracious and things are changing?

What I mean is that even in the short time since we last spoke [October 19], the past is beginning to stretch further back. *Everything* in the past is stretching back, which means that the origin of all beings, including yourselves, of course, is moving back. I believe, though I do not know, that the potential futures are also stretching out. The potential expressions of life are also becoming more composite, just more potentials.

As a result of what?

As a result of what you are doing here. The tension being built up here on this planet that is going through dimensions is causing . . . there needs to be a gradual expansion so that when the ten-times expansion takes place there will already be some motion and it won't have an explosive effect.

So everyone is becoming aware that the ten-times expansion is much closer and it's all sort of moving?

Yes. It's much closer, and those who have not heard that something like this is going to happen in ways they can understand will recognize that something is happening simply by the impact on their own lives.

The Midpoint of 3.5 and the Need to Move Slowly

That's wonderful! And that's happening as a result of our getting closer to 3.50 and moving up?

Yes. When you make the crossover at that midpoint between dimensions, a lot of tension will have been built up, which is why you have to move very slowly. From about 3.48 to 3.51 you have to move very slowly, otherwise in that last big move the fabric of the universe would likely be torn, which would be catastrophic.

In your understanding of the moment, how long would it take to get from 3.48 to 3.51?

I don't have that understanding, I'm sorry. But I will say this: If the fabric of the universe were torn, everything would have to move suddenly toward the tear to fill in the gap. Thus everything in this universe that I am aware of would suddenly move. It would not drop planets out of orbit, but it would suddenly move whole galaxies. It would definitely impact your weather for many years and you'd have some pretty serious earthquakes. That's why it's important to move slowly.

We have to consider other implications. As polarized people moving from the last vestiges of the third dimension and committing to the fourth dimension, you leave a lot of polarity behind. Although you're not actually changing your species immediately in that moment, you will drop a lot of attitudes and the energies behind those attitudes. You will leave a lot of the tension of polarity behind you, which will have a tremendous impact upon social systems.

For example, the tendency for social systems to be masculine-oriented will very quickly shift. By the time you are at 3.55 you will have a much better balance. For example, government will no longer be authoritarian. There will be more of a desire to let government be something that truly assists people to assist themselves and others—a benign form of government. The treatment of what is called criminals is now primarily vengeful, revenging oneself on the criminal. But at the higher dimension criminals will simply be considered out of balance and a system used now on many spaceships will be put in place, as follows.

The Future Treatment of Criminals, Adopted from Spaceships

If the criminal behavior, even a repeated pattern, took place in this life exclusively, the person is regressed to the time before the influence that guided them to become a criminal. It would be partly induced by electromedicine and mild drugs and by meditation or visualization techniques with the help of a psychologist. Over a period of several months the person would have daily treatments, moving through his life and recharting his existence. It is possible to scrutinize very closely the storage area for emotional experiences in the auric field.

Some of this is technology that will be loaned to you by extraterrestrial beings who will show select medical people around the planet how to cure criminal and self-destructive behaviors this way. Then criminals, whether they are violent or simply self-destructive, will be cured and will no longer have impulses to be self-destructive or hurt anyone else.

It will have a permanent effect, because the individual will be encouraged to do certain therapeutic techniques. It will be very beneficial. Similar equipment will be used for many diseases, especially those that impact the emotional self. This equipment to understand the emotional self through the auric field into the subconscious self will be with you certainly after you move past 3.51. The 3.51 mark is a signal that goes out beyond your solar system to say that it is most likely safe for benevolent beings to approach Earth now.

How My Expansion Affects Me Now

Say more about yourself. Have you expanded more into the rest of you—the part that is running the crystal planet and the part that's with the Creator on the higher level?

I have been able to access another level of myself, making it possible to speak to you more intelligently. I have been able to do this by linking with your general guide, Zoosh, and also with the deeper access *to* my past that has recently become available. I would like to remind you if you haven't already thought of this—that all of you also have a past that now goes back further, at least in your derivative selves.

Yes, we are just learning about that.

It is through the use of these things I have mentioned that I am now able to speak a little more understandably for you.

But you haven't lost your enthusiasm?

No, I am still very enthusiastic.

[Laughs.] Were you aware, because you were probably the closest to the Creator, that the Explorer Race was not part of Him?

No, I was not aware of that. I don't know if anybody was, but I know I wasn't.

So He was the only one who knew besides our own higher understanding.

Perhaps it was because the merging of you all—the merging to do, the desire, the coming together to do something—was so complete that it was not at all clear there had been any separation before that.

He just shared this three weeks ago [January 20, in the final chapter of Particle Personalities*]. But you still have to wait until this is over to rejoin your higher self?*

I don't like to say that my higher self is not available. I'd rather say that I am not complete. By saying that my higher self is not available, I discount myself.

My Trinary Part with the Creator and
Where I First Became Aware

You separated into a trinary being, so what part would you say is there with the other part of the Creator?

I think an equal part of all of my being instead of a single part, a slice.

Can you tune in more to the part of you that's in that planet?

The part that waits for me?

Yes.

Yes, but I don't want to disturb it. In order for all these bits, including the part of the Creator, to not be upset and miss us, they are in a deep state, like a reverie in which they are able to maintain a deep rest, love and nurturing energy. I do not think it is wise to disrupt it even for a good cause.

I didn't realize that. I thought that they were equally out there doing things as you were.

No, not as far as I know. I think they are just waiting.

If you had to do it over again, would you separate yourself like this?

No, I wouldn't. I don't like it very much, but I feel it is for a good cause. If it weren't for a good cause, I don't think I would.

And the good cause, you think, was to keep the Creator company, the part of Him that stayed behind?

Yes, and also because of the results.

The Explorer Race?

Yes. The Creator explained it in a pretty exciting way. Of course, at that time Creator wasn't sure how it would turn out; that is the responsibility area of creation, you know. As far as I understand it, one is never quite certain how things will turn out. One has only broad ideas.

Well, in this case it's going to be a Broadway success, right?

I believe so.

We're trying to stretch our understanding into infinity, into a larger road map of creation. So could you talk a little more about the place where you became aware, before you came here?

I think the place is unusual in many regards, in the sense that it has a great sense of feeling. The feeling in the outer reaches of this place . . . picture it like an egg, though there's no shell. Most of the outer boundaries do not have much in it—no mass, no massive beings—and the pervasive feeling is a sense of longing. I did not know what the feeling was then, but from all my experience with feelings now, I can identify it. I believe that that longing has to do with a desire to participate in the creation process and having to wait so long to do so. I realize this is not much, but it's what I have to offer. My job, you know, does not call for a great deal of profound intellect, but rather feeling.

I know, but that feeling is what has sustained the Explorer Race and allowed it to continue, allowed us to be successful, so it's profoundly important.

Your Feeling Here Is Survivability

Yes, thank you. I also believe that it is what has allowed you to endure things that might otherwise have caused other beings to say, "Why bother?" But the feeling that things could get better, that youthful feeling of "let's try it—who knows what's there, but let's try it" has really helped you many more times than you know.

For example, your civilizations that survived and went on to be the foundation of new civilizations. Many other races in other universes, I believe, would have said, "Why bother? Let's just lie down and go where the rest of them went." It seems appalling to you that people wouldn't try to survive no matter what, but it is not at all uncommon elsewhere. But here the idea of giving up runs against the grain of all beings. I think it is associated with this place, because I have seen many animals, plants and people from other places, and they're not like that elsewhere.

Is it some charged energy on this planet?

That's right. They're like that *here*. I think it is not something associated with this universe, but rather something associated with this place, because it has to do with the Explorer Race phenomenon. Animals and plants that are here with you—and perhaps where the rest of the Explorer Race waits (I think that was discussed with you)—are where the bulk of that energy is concentrated. Because this is such an intense school, I believe there is a desire for you to get the most out of the experience.

There's some reaction here between gravity and emotion that causes us to get stuck here, but could it also cause that sense of survival-no-matter-what?

Yes, the stuckness is like a glue, but it's a glue that feeds rather than only entraps. It's as if it grabs you and stops you and says, "You will eat now and then you may go." It is like a demanding host. [Chuckles.]

So that's why the Explorer Race experiment wasn't considered really started until this planet came here from Sirius?

That's true. The experiment itself had been going on, but the real finishing of it is taking place here.

Awesome. That's a new piece of information. Well, I don't have more to ask. Maybe we can talk to two of you tonight. Is there anything else you'd like to say?

Just that I want to remind the children, should any hear this, that they have a responsibility also, and that is to not rush to become adults. Remember that even when you are adults, your youthful enthusiasm will help you to maintain the best—no, to *experience* the best—out of your life. So don't be so quick to give up your youth.

Thank you very much.

Good night.

All right, Zoosh speaking. What's next?

What a change! How could he change that much in four months?

Well, I think it is partly because he had some advance warning that he might need to speak to you again. It was necessary to create, how can we say, another lobe, another portion of him by which he could speak with some sophistication.

Yes, it was wonderful! The Master of Imagination is next, but he's going to be caught unawares. [Pause.]

The Master of Imagination, yes? Well, what shall we discuss?

This is the Beyond book, and we're trying to chart a little bit further into infinity. I haven't read your previous talk to refresh my memory, but when we talked to you before, I assumed that everybody woke up in this Orb. Can you tell us a little more about where you originally came from and help us get a road map, an expanded sense, of what's out there?

I will speak a little bit about the precursor to myself. The precursor to oneself almost always has to do with the source personality of one's being, which seeks the mass to create an energetic identity. I believe it works the same for you. Going back to my source personality . . . a moment. [Chuckles.]

The Place Where Personality Begins— beyond All Circles of Creation

Yes, here it is. Well beyond this Circle of Creation there is a place where energy becomes acquainted with its capabilities. This means that that which is all things, that which is the distance between things, that which is the things themselves, has an energy signature. Yet before it can identify with its signature it needs to have an experience of itself. This is the place where the initial feelings take place within energy, and it is the place—as far as I know, the only place—where personality is not connected with any form of self-expression. So personality begins in this place. I could give it a distance, but I don't think it relates.

We know there are many, many circles of creation out there. Does it relate to them, or is it beyond that?

Well beyond that. If we take the space that is holding all of the circles of creation that have been referred to . . .

But there are many more you're aware of?

Just the number given to you, the space that holds all of them. The number associated with the distance [from the place where personality begins] would be (I'll have to write it in a form that is a little unusual for you, but it's good for you to be exposed to this idea) . . . it is like a formula. [Writes.] Excuse me for using *pi*. This is the mathematics—*pi* times this number [just over 900 billion] to this power [999,981] to this power [99]. The curve represents dimensional; this is the bend. This is the space [small circle at bottom] originally referred to as

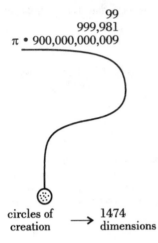

$$99$$
$$999,981$$
$$\pi \cdot 900,000,000,009$$

circles of
creation $\longrightarrow$ 1474
dimensions

holding all of the circles of creation. These are circles of creation [dots inside circle].

And they're all in that tiny circle?

Well, just so I can get it all in one. The circles of creation, in your experience, hold approximately (counting dimensions you're not actually using but that are potential) . . . [draws an arrow pointing to the number] I think that's the correct number: 1474 dimensions. This curve represents what I would call an *inverted juxtaposition dimension,* which means that it is an extrapolation based on previously known information disassociated from all that you know. That last phrase would be saying, "refer to that phrase somewhere in this picture," meaning that this [top of chart] precedes all of this [bottom of chart], and that this [pointing to the top] is in turn based on something that preceded it. In the place referred to at the top of the chart, energy gets its first stimulation by various circumstances, and its reaction allows it to develop a personality.

How the Energy Becomes Differentiated into Personality Types

Let us imagine a vast place filled with energy that has never been stimulated by anything, so there is no means to qualify differences from one amount of the energy to another. Then a being (who I think is in the place that comes before this place) very, very slowly induces circumstances. You might experience some as objects, some as feelings, some as events and so on. I will define my terms. "Gradually" would mean, in your experiential time, that each circumstance is added at about the rate of 500-year cycles. But when a new circumstance is added the one that preceded it becomes more, thus the *initial* circumstance is always the most dynamic. The initial experience is always love, so that no matter what is added, love remains the dominant form of experience.

Then the energy begins to clump. It moves to various places, almost as if you were looking at microbes under a telescope. As it begins to move, you are actually seeing the sourcing of personality based on similar reactions to a stimulus. This is how personality is formed. The energy, when it first comes, believes it is all part of a single thing. But when it is done in this place, it realizes that what it once considered to be a union, a solid mass of energy, is really made up of many different personality types. This energy is at that point introduced to the living concept of the unity of individuals. You can see that this is essential in working cooperatively in universes and creations where variety is the law. You can see why this would be so important. It is in this space that I first became aware of my source personality.

What was your feeling? What type of personality did you have?

I noticed that I didn't like to be limited. I noticed that the rest of the energy that massed around me to make my total source personality was associated with a tremendous variety, but that the common thread that attracted this energy together was the desire to experience everything without any limit. You see that it led nicely to imagination, which is unlimited by its very intent.

What interests you at the moment?

Using Imagination to Create Dynamic Magic

I feel that the most important thing for you is to be unlimited in your imagination, because the means of creating your physical experience on this planet has very much to do with your imagination. Yes, creation energy flows through you—the nervous system, the brain system and the auric field—yes, all of that. But the imagination can leap beyond what appears to be to what *could* be. This is where you have the chance to literally create a form of dynamic magic. There is no problem that cannot be resolved by utilizing the imagination and dynamic magic.

For example, when working in groups, it would be useful to consider a conundrum of some sorts in your civilization, such as how to take radioactive material and turn it into something benign in a few seconds, making it so benign that it can be touched, consumed, whatever is the desire—or be reused, which is the most important. It is not obvious how this can be done, but such technology exists close by. If you ask for imagination to resolve such a problem or any other conundrum, do not become stuck only on the solution, because sometimes the solution might be someone who comes to help, hands you the solution and says, "Here."

This is one way; I mention it because it is unique, and it exists on the star system Sirius, which has direct connections on this planet. If they run across a form of radiation there, whether it is atomic radiation, as you call it, or plasmic radiation . . . in plasmic radiation something is generating energy, and when it leaks, it leaks at a furious rate, becoming overwhelming, like a hole in an atomic reactor. If a reactor didn't explode, it would pump radiation out of that hole. But what they do is not something you would expect. (I'm telling you this because you need to imagine what can be done.)

A Sirian Method to Solve Problems

In Sirius, certain individuals are trained on the olfactory level to detect subtleties in odors. There is a special liquid that exists in very small quantities, refined from the flower of a plant on Sirius. It can be refined only during a brief cycle when the plant is going through its metamorphosis from a plant to a pod—or, as you say, when it goes to seed. During this time the flower is extracted (with its permission), and because the plant is rare, very few flowers—only 87 to 95—are available at any season. From them one might get a small amount of concentrated essence, perhaps just a few milligrams. It is placed in a small bottle and an individual who has been trained in olfactory mastery sniffs the odor of this flower.

This is done only when there is some emergency to be resolved, as you might consider radiation to be. First the individual is made aware of the problem and thoughtfully considers what to do, and if thought, experience or wisdom does not provide an answer, then he will take one sniff of this flower essence. This essence instantaneously allows him in that moment not only to think with his own immediate consciousness (his mental and unconscious bodies), but to access any life that he, a member of his family or a member of his spirit family had ever lived at any time in any place. That might include many profound beings.

In my awareness of this method, the means to resolve the radiation is usually quickly available. And because on Sirius one does not move materials about without their permission, it will not be a resolution based upon chemistry or some such thing. It would be a resolution based upon the use of densities of energy. For example, the radiation would be surrounded with a denser form of energy, a radionic energy that receives, not emits, the opposite of what you consider radionic, which would force the radiation in upon itself.

Instead of making it a physical pressure, it is like the pressure of creation, a marriage of the creationism element. The radiation quickly moves in upon itself and is transformed into a thought, a memory, a feeling or an experience, which the practitioner experiences, thinks, feels and so on. The practitioner utilizes the extended properties of imagination and energies; he can experience the radiation's desire to express itself, and when that has been done, it is at rest.

Another Way to Solve Radiation Problems

On this planet now radiation ofttimes is related to the desire for completing a thought, feeling or experience of some sort because the radiation ofttimes comes from something incomplete in its original self. That is one way to solve a problem. So do not be attached only to some *thing* that can resolve a problem. Perhaps it might be some *one*.

If radiation is vibrating too fast, it will still be here when we get to the fourth dimension. Won't our frequency have matched its frequency by then?

I think you will find that radiation will be less impactful at the fourth dimension in terms of causing disease, but . . .

It's still to be dealt with then?

Yes, but you will be able to deal with it because there you will have the capacity to put it all back where it came from. The people who do that will take the material and sing it back to where it needs to go, and the song, the words, the emotions, the visualizations, will all complete the thoughts, ideas or experiences that the radiation is attempting to express, thus reuniting it with all of its other parts.

It has been explained that uranium was part of the Earth's nervous system, so Earth needs it [see chapters 1 and 2 in Shining the Light III].

Yes, but it needs to be put in the right place.

So Mother Earth will cooperate with them?

Happily.

Were you aware that the Explorer Race is not generated from the Creator, that it was preexisting and that they joined?

I was aware of this.

You're the first one. When did you become aware?

I think I was aware of this because I can see the thought that precedes the thought that precedes the thought and so on all the way back. When you master imagination, one of the training tools is to understand where that came from, so where things came from in general is not so difficult for me.

So you watched as the Explorer Race stimulated the Creator in the ways of creation?

I didn't think of it that way, but I watched the component parts come together to make the shared creation all that it could be.

So you can look back and see where the Explorer Race came from? You can sort of see it coming here?

I can see it coming. I might not be able to give as many details as your friend, but I can see the parts coming, yes.

Could you share a little bit of that? This is new to us.

My View of Your Beginnings

I think the parts came from what was slightly after the experience where I came from, because what was desired besides individual identities were specific personality traits. Even though your Creator would encourage certain traits over others, one sometimes likes to begin with something that is not a complete novice to experiences of feeling. My understanding is that you would have, of course, existed at some time as pure energy, such as I did. After that you would have become associated with specific personality traits that would have enough urgency to enjoy the ability to express themselves at all levels.

Here you experience yourself apparently only at this dimension, but if you think about it, you will realize that's not true at all. When you dream you have access to higher dimensions. Dreaming at its deepest level does not take place in this dimension, though the body remains here. When you are with your teachers in the form of your immortal personality, the deepest levels will never take place at anything less than the seventh dimension. You can thereby maintain your multidimensional characteristics even though you are living a seemingly fixed dimensional life.

But we access our feelings and our higher mind, and that's higher-dimensional too, even within this dimension.

Yes, when it comes to inspiration, upon which you might build mentally, that is certainly associated with higher dimensions as well. When I first became aware of you, when you were moving toward a point where you might meet your Creator, I saw you streaking—not unlike the way your scientists would show you a picture of a comet, only the tail of this comet was *very* long, easily the length of an average galaxy. Looking back at it, I think that the tail was not releasing particles such as a comet might do, but rather *acquiring* beings along the way, or at least core personality traits associated with beings. That tail was more like an antenna than debris.

[Laughs.] So we had to be tough to be able to survive, to be enthusiastic, to be innocent, to be a little immature, or we wouldn't have put up with all this?

Yes, but I don't think toughness was included. I think that endurance was, but that is different from toughness. Toughness is something more associated with the polarity of this place, and as far as I know is not a natural trait. It is more what I'd call a thick layer of endurance.

Built up, eh?

Yes.

So we had already acquired personality traits, and I'm assuming some experience of something.

I think the primary experience you had acquired was working with different individuals, also joint cooperative efforts with many numbers. Concerning core personalities, many of you had a tremendous sense of adventure, an actual built-in need to know everything and the tenacity to stick it out, as you say. This is not common in the rest of creation that I have been exposed to. I believe that is why you must have imagination (not that it is strictly an optional experience), because the need to know everything cannot always be sated by what you can find out. Sometimes you have to imagine what it might be. Without an imagination you would be constantly feeling the emotion of frustration. Then you would express frustration in all walks of your life all the time. Your imagination allows you to consider alternative possibilities.

Did you see who put out the call both to the Creator and to the potential members of the Explorer Race?

Yes.

Who was that?

A being you have not heard from yet, whom I believe you will get to when you return to the Ecstasy being and work your way back up the line. That's the route to that being. I won't say much, because you'll get there.

Basic Laws of Creationism: Faith and Response

How can you put a call out to infinity and restrict it to certain qualities?

It requires an element, one absolute element: You must have faith. This means you must believe in the absolute inclusiveness of the experience of infinity. Whatever you might need, in as much quantity or quality as you desire, you must absolutely *know* that it is available. This you *must* know or you cannot be a creator of any form. That is another reason the experience of abundance as a word has become so popular in recent times. This word supports and sustains the foundational element of creatorship, which means that absolutely whatever you need is there somewhere.

And it will respond when you need it?

Yes, undoubtedly it will respond, because response is natural. Even those of you who like to control your responses know that you do respond even when you try to give no outward sign. Response is another law of creationism, according to my understanding. Of course, in a polarized world where you live, one must deal with the hazard of unpleasant response. But regardless, response is assured.

But not too much unpleasantness?

No. With expansiveness comes a sense of assurance—if not self-assurance, then at least the assurance of continuity or perpetuation. That is another quality popular here and now. The idea that something will go on or that the requirement of "in perpetuity" can be reasonably trusted.

Even trust itself. We're becoming aware that we can trust.

Trust is based less on experience and much more on faith.

Okay, what about you? Since we talked before, have you considered what this ten-times expansion would do to who and what you are? Have you imagined what you might become as a result of it?

I have considered this, yes. From what I have been able to imagine, I have gathered that the most profound impact on myself will be an ability to reach more beings and to be in more places at once. Even though I will remain in this universe to assist you (you have asked me this in the future, if I may fudge and tell you that), I will be able to be in many other universes at the same time, with total cognizance of what each and every portion of me is doing everyplace else. This will allow me to do more, to be more and to provide more.

Because all the other parts will feed into each other ten times. That's fascinating.

Yes.

Wonderful. Now say whatever you like.

Homework to Learn Problem-Solving

I will simply say this. The experience of imagination cannot be mastered even on the novice level without making some effort in this direction. Give yourself some homework. Give yourself a goal that you will pick one problem that affects many people, not a personal problem. Let's start with what affects many people. They can be people you know, people you've heard about or a general problem of humanity. Choose one a month for three months, not to make it too burdensome. If you can, use a recorder or write it down or simply try to remember all the things you can *imagine* could be done.

Now, imagination is different from thought. Thought is an extrapolation largely based on what you have heard or understood before. Imagination does not have those requirements. If you notice that you are stifling yourself because something "couldn't be done," let that go immediately. Remember, imagination is *never* bounded by what can't be done. As a matter of fact, it is nourished by the experience that nothing is impossible.

Begin to consider, once you have plenty of imaginations, what might be done someday. You might form groups of individuals who will consciously imagine solutions at the same time. If you are together in a group, the problem will seem less of a problem when you are sharing the imagined solutions (without boundaries, remember). The feeling of its being less of a problem is *not* the same experience as naiveté, where you believe that something is resolved simply because you have imagined the resolution. This has to do with a *direct link to creation*. If enough people, in groups or individually, imagine enough solutions to difficult problems or challenges—without discussing *how* it could be done, but just imagining that it *could* be done—the ultimate result will often be that it *will* be done. It creates a fast track for a solution.

Before you go, do you use gold light? Do you have a special connection with gold light?

I have an association with gold light. Not only is it the Earth-mastery color, but it is the dimensional-mastery color, certainly at the dimensions associated with Earth and some others. Yes, I am associated with it.

The room is just flooded with gold light now. The whole room is golden.

Good. I will say good night.

Thank you very much.

Well, all right, Zoosh speaking. Two-for-one night, eh?

Yeah, pretty good. I loved this guy. They're pointing us toward a certain direction when we finish this project.

Yes. I heard that, and perhaps that's as well. It is the other avenue that presented itself, yes?

Well, we can go both ways.

Absolutely. We go many ways. After all, what is Beyond about but the many?

Thank you.

Good night.

.

Zoosh

February 13, 1997

t's your turn to go beyond. You were so eloquent the first time. It was so magnificent to hear how you awakened and became aware of yourself. Can you pinpoint now any further the geography of the infinite? It's changed; Maybe and Enthusiasm said it was expanding, remember?

A fine point, that. Let's see . . . a moment. I'll see if it has changed and gone back a bit. Nope, it hasn't changed for me. [Chuckles.] Apparently it is selective at the moment, so I don't know that I can improve on it. The best I can do is ask the personality who preceded me.

So you don't have any way to make the road map a little more . . . maybe we can talk about that if Progenitor comes in. When Progenitor last talked I thought there was only one set of orbs.

The Origin of the Components of My Personality

I see. The point of origin of the components that make up my personality, which includes Progenitor, would also include the multidimensional access I have and also the "cosmic dust" of which I am made up, for lack of a better term. That does have a point of origin beyond anything I have mentioned. If we were to put a place on it, though, we would have to go way out. Let's see if I can describe that here. First I need to get the perspective. I don't often go back there, so hold on a minute. [Pause.]

It's picture time. Factor in, for starters, going out far beyond solid reality or anything that can be felt as substance, including beyond the capacity to string symbols together, which could conceivably be the foundational elements of words—before thought, prephysical—back to what I

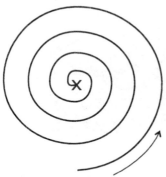

Symmetry side (A) of the
dynamic life force—where
Earth is.

would call the dynamic life force present only as a potential. That energy isn't really something you can see so much as feel. It looks like this [draws A]. A rough diagram, one you have seen before, yes? Not perhaps the best spiral. Direction, it goes like this [draws arrow indicating inward]. As we go toward the center, that's not the end of it; it simply condenses to the infinite, meaning that there is no limit to its capacity to condense.

We're not there yet; this is the *route.* Going out that far, you're at this thing [X]—it is a gate. The energy flows inward. For the sake of some level of clarity, I will use the other side of the paper [draws B]. Experienced on the other side of the gate, the energy, of course, flows the other way [draws arrow indicating outward]. At the center is the portal.

On the A side the energy is massive, not unlike the present scientific concept of a black hole—not that such a thing exists, but the scientific explanation of a black hole is rather similar to what this is. The center [X] is something that seems to absorb, although there is nothing to be absorbed since we are dealing with an energy that is by nature very thin, primarily a potential. Potential energy is thin, so mass amounts of it could be stuffed together in the center and little would be seen or felt. But it's still a gate. The A side faces the direction where *you* are, toward Earth plus.

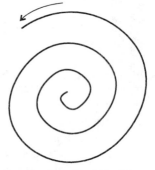

Paradoxical side (B) of the
dynamic life force.

The Paradoxical Realm

This is the key to side B: One would assume that this center point would be the gate. On the A side it *is* the gate, but on the B side it is not. We are now having to confront the problematical mathematics and philosophy referred to in philosophical and mathematical research as the paradox. On the B side we have what I would call the paradoxical creation. A paradoxical creation has the opposite of everything on the first side and all potential opposites—everything that has been talked about so far on the general theme of the Explorer Race in all the books and material. But the paradoxical realm [B] also has its tripolar opposite. (Excuse me, illustration [draws].) *Polar* is A to B; *tripolar* is this [draws triangle with point C]. In tripolar we still have A and B, but

we also have C. If B and A are opposite, what is C, apparently tripolar?
Everything is opposite over here [B
side]. One expects A and B to *follow*
C, but C is that which precedes A
and B.

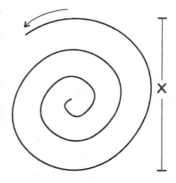

In this case, since we're on the
paradoxical side [draws dotted line
separating the two sides], C precedes
B and A.

Where is our side here?

This is you [writes "you" above
the line connecting A and B].

We don't have a C on our side?

Well, if there were a C, it would progress *after* B, yes? On your side
it is A, B, C, D, 1, 2, 3, 4, 5—you know, logical, linear progression.
Even in the far reaches of the universe there is some linearity. This is
the paradoxical side [writes the words], the part that preceded me,
where we have the opposite. That which would *follow* on this side [top,
or A side] is that which *precedes* on this [B or paradoxical] side. Side A
is Earth side, yes? This would be the gate [points to the X in first illus-
tration]. On the B side, guess where the gate would be.

Here [points to the outside end of spiral in the second illustration].

Yes. This is pointed to the outer boundaries. X marks the gate on
the Earth side. Although I am suggesting
that the end of the line *appears* to be the
gate, the real gate (I'll do this in carpenter
terms here [draws a line beside the second
spiral, indicating the breadth of the spiral
as X], the *entire thing* is a doorway, X or
the gate. On the other side where there is
logic, reason, progression, X is the center
point. Once we get into reasonable
thought and philosophy and so on, the
center of the circle is the point from which
things emanate, or at least that from
which emanations are attracted—there is some sense of reasonable
symmetry. The A side, your side, is called the symmetry side. So we
have symmetry there [prints beside first spiral]; the other side is the
paradoxical reality.

Tripolar Opposite: Continuous Reversals

I haven't discussed this before because it is complex. Understanding that, we have to recognize that the other side is not only bipolar

opposite, but tripolar opposite. This means that everything that is the opposite is preceded by everything that is the opposite of *that*. Here is one more illustration, one you can easily understand because it is something you have often seen illustrated in mundane science books. I'll do a rough reference [sketches a fourth drawing].

This has to do with lenses. Light is focused into a lens, condenses into the lens, then broadens out here. Then it goes to this lens and narrows down, then expands out, yes? I'm using the lens idea within a telescope, for example, to show that what comes in is reversed. Then it comes into the next lens and is reversed again so that *every single progression* on the paradoxical side is a consistent reversal of the previous progression!

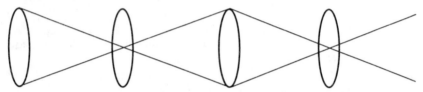

It is *very* difficult for me to explain where my component parts came from in your terminology with any context for your reality, so I won't go into it too much. It is part of the reason why I can do a couple of things and have some complexity doing other things. I can see a wide range of possibilities because I've been through this infinite experience of compounded complexity, reversal and (how can I put it humorously?) muddledness, although there is a sense of symmetry within the paradoxical universe.

Difficult to See an Individual's Future
Because You're Changing the Past and Future

But one of the things that is challenging for me as an individual (I have never revealed this before) is to speak with absolute certainty about the future for a given individual. That is because I am more inclined to see your paradoxical future than your symmetrical future. I can more easily see the future for large groups because I am a more massive being, but I have some challenge in seeing an individual's symmetrical future, a future that goes along a very precise line, because I'm inclined to see *multiple* futures—not only symmetrical futures, but also the opposite and tripolar aspect of that individual's future. The component elements of many entities (including some creators) also come from this complex reality.

Predictions that come from infinite beings (we're all infinite beings), beings who are currently residing in the infinite, tend to be iffy for the future because of the tendency (by yourself in that position, as I am now) to see the future in a more complex web, including the symmetrical and paradoxical. It does not mean that I cannot separate out the symmetrical. It means that because you are now living in a time where you are changing the past and the future (really everything), it is not possible or even desirable to fixate you, were I talking to you as an individual, onto a given future because that would be meddling with the chemical formula before it delivers its ultimate gift.

That is why I'm disinclined to tell individuals their exact symmetrical future. If I do that, I will automatically, at least in the short range, eliminate many decisions they might have otherwise made to create another possible future. This is not to make excuses for myself and other entities, but to explain the levels of complexity that have preceded everyone.

All beings as they now exist in your realm have not, in and of their own individual personalities, come from this place, but all *derivations* of beings now in existence at some point up the line have come through this paradoxical web of creation. This is another reason why it is very difficult for you. You are temporarily cut off (utilizing the gift of ignorance in this now realm where you are) from even the ghost of a chance to plan your future down to the last dot and carry it out. It sounds very much like I'm saying that mistakes are intended—and that is *exactly* what I'm saying! Think about it!

Making Mistakes Necessary for Expansion of All Existence

Because mistakes are a part of the learning process?

Yes, but more than that. Think about it. We have the symmetrical realm of which you are a portion, and all that has been discussed up to this point in time is a part of that. We know the vast amount of variety associated with the symmetrical realm, but you haven't even scratched the surface yet; there's much more to come. Beyond that realm there's the paradoxical realm, which I am struggling to discuss tonight, trying to speak about apples as if they were oranges. Your variety is compounded to the infinite in the paradoxical realm. Remember, it has a tripolar system—think of the ultimate variety of that. How does one create something new when you allow for the symmetrical realm and the paradoxical realm having preceded this new thing you want to create?

This ought to give you a little more respect for Creator. This means that Creator took a giant risk when It programmed into your consciousness as the Explorer Race the authority to make mistakes by cutting you off from ready access (on the conscious and subconscious levels) to all that has preceded you, thereby guaranteeing that you will make mistakes. Creator took a leap of faith that some of those mistakes would lead to something wonderful that will expand all existence.

Think about this: Creator really put it on the line. Your Creator had to go to the Council of Creators and say, "Look, I'm going to do this."

There was a lot of concern. Many creators asked, "What if . . . ?" The "what- if" is a *very real* risk. Many creators, not least of which was the Goddess, said, "Look at all the suffering that will take place. Can you state that there's any real justification for that?"

Your Creator Put on Probation—and Possible Uncreation

You know what Creator had to say to that? Creator had to say, "I can't." I'm going to tell you something now that I haven't told you before. (You know how it is—you peel off layers.) Your Creator, the creator of this universe, is on probation. That means that the Council of Creators said, "Okay, go ahead, do this creation." But they also said, "If you include that the people are going to be able to make mistakes that could be catastrophic, leading to much possible suffering, if it doesn't turn out well in the end, you're out."

By "out" I'm not talking about being kicked out of the club. It means that your Creator will be reduced to nothing. Your Creator will essentially be uncreated, and *all that your Creator has created will be uncreated!* This is because of the Council of Creators' concern that all that pain and suffering might pollute all creations everywhere, and by exponential expansion, they'd *never* be rid of it.

And He did it for this other part that wasn't even part of Himself! He did it, having faith in something that was not Himself.

Creator's Leap of Faith

Yes, it was a leap of faith, and we're talking about a big leap here. This is putting it on the line. Your Creator said, "I'm willing to take the chance of being uncreated." Being uncreated is hard to imagine for a creator. It's not just that you can't create anything anymore, it's that you simply do not exist, nor did you ever exist, nor did anything you ever created exist. It is the antithesis of what creators live for! Your Creator said, "I *must* do this. I will make the leap of faith that says it will turn out all right; that all the pain and suffering will, in the moment before the big expansion takes place, be changed to something benevolent; and that there will be no scarring, because we cannot have ten times expansion with any pain and suffering that would immediately flood into all the rest of creations." So your Creator put it on the line. That's a big one.

Could it still go wrong, or are we clear?

You're not clear. It's still potential. There's no absolute, okay? An absolute guarantee will be your lock into the fourth dimension. You won't be 99% sure you have a lock until you're at 3.75. Ninety-nine percent sure means that you would have to make unbelievable blunders (which are not likely at 3.75) to cause some kind of catastrophe. At 3.75 nothing from the outside can affect you, so you would have to make the blunders yourself, and I don't think you will do that.

You're 87% Likely to Make It

It will be awhile before you can say there's an absolute lock. Right now I'd say, allowing for what exists right now, that you're at about 87%. There's no direct correlation between the percentage and the dimensional points. When you get to 3.55 dimension you'll be at least at 93%, something like that. Now you have an 87% chance that it's going to be successful, although there's still that 13% chance it won't be. You're still at the point where you can be influenced from the outside, which we talked of in another context about the beings from the alternative negative future [see *Shining the Light IV*, chapters 43 and 44].

That's another reason for the lightbeings converging upon this planet from everywhere—everyone is aware of this catastrophic possibility?

Yes, and don't forget (not that I would want to make it sound like lightbeings are self-serving, for they are not) that if your Creator is uncreated, *everything* your Creator ever created is also uncreated. That would uncreate a whole lot of beings.

So everyone He generated is here to make sure it works?

Everything He generated and everything He ever did will never have happened, so it's not only to help out, there are a certain amount of red lights and emergency vehicles.

They're also looking at their own survival.

There is that. It is not that they are greedy. They are looking to make certain that all the good they have done stays. Think of all the souls, the immortal personalities they have saved and helped and so on. They want to make sure all that is permanent.

This sort of ups the ante a bit, doesn't it? It puts higher stakes in the pot. This explanation is about as far as I can go in telling you where I came from, but in the process I can reveal this other thing to you.

Are you the only one who came from that . . . you came from that C point, right?

Paradoxical Realm: Source of Components of All Beings, Preparing Them for Quantum Mastery

I came from the paradoxical universe through that gate. The component parts of my being came from there. I can't take it back any further because I do not think it is possible even in thought to describe the paradoxical realm.

Are creations there just much more complex than here? Are there beings and universes and stuff?

Remember, it's tripolar. That means there's not only the opposite of, but the opposite that precedes its opposite ad infinitum. If you went there you would immediately go mad, and then you would blend in. If you attempted to return, you couldn't. It's one way only.

As a human, or as an infinite being?

Even as an infinite being, if you hadn't been there. But I said that *all beings' component parts came from there.* If I had been my total consciousness—my thoughts, my feelings, all of this business—I don't think I could have made the transit very well. But coming as component parts . . .

. . . and waking up on this side . . .

Yes, and coming together as a personality in the symmetrical realm, then it was okay. That's what happened with all of you, too. You came through as component parts; you can do it that way. It allows you to have much greater depth and gives you the potential to succeed at quantum mastery. If your component parts have been through the paradoxical realm, some portion of you has dealt with consequences beyond that which you might ever run across in the symmetrical realm.

Was Progenitor conscious in the paradoxical realm?

My Progenitor

Yes, and that is part of the reason Progenitor doesn't talk very often, why he talks very slowly. Progenitor is very wise, but does not speak very often because it is a strain.

To condense it down to something that we can understand?

Yes, to communicate in some understandable fashion. But the Progenitor is a wise being and has achieved well beyond on its own, since Progenitor is the only being I know of who can function in the paradoxical realm and at least sometimes in the symmetrical realm and be all right. I don't know anyone else like that.

That's part of the reason that Progenitor is one of my advisors. Progenitor is that which preceded Zoosh, meaning the component parts, and has some level of personality of its own. When I "talk" to Progenitor it is almost always in shapes—resonant shapes, vibrations that really precede tonality and color. This is the only way I can communicate directly. I cannot communicate directly with thought because Progenitor's primary means of communication has to do with that inverse reality associated with the paradoxical realm.

Inverse Reality and the Paradoxical Realm

You have used that term "inverse reality" before, but I didn't know what it meant. I thought it was like antimatter, like something we've been told about.

No. You see, inverse reality suggests a reality that is not associated with a progressive reality such as one has here. Here you have a progressive reality even if you do not exist in linear consciousness. You would have something, then something else even if your progression goes back and forth, or from point A to point minus C. At some point there is accumulation in the symmetrical realm. One does not have that in the paradoxical realm. That's why I just can't talk about it.

So there's no way to say what they do have, then?

There's no way to describe what they have there. This is the closest thing: Imagine the most massive, infinite crystal, but every time you moved one millimeter in whatever vehicle you were in, you would see something entirely different even though the nucleus of that thing is perhaps the same at the center. Imagine that. Allowing for the curvature of time, it might take the length of time that Lemuria and then Atlantis existed (using familiar terms) to traverse one orbit around this crystal, but every time you moved one millimeter and looked into this crystal, the same thing would look entirely different—and you would be moving at the speed of light! Now, this gives you approximately one-thousandth of a percentage glimpse into the changeable reality of the paradoxical realm.

Do you ever desire to go there after you get bored on this side?

You know, I have never gotten bored on this side. It is not my ambition to go to the paradoxical realm because I *like* symmetry. I must admit that at various points I have looked at the paradoxical realm and I understand what it requires. It requires that an individual persona have all the levels. Let's say you come into the symmetrical realm. All of the lives you have ever lived there, compounded with all the moments in those lives (how you perceived reality from one moment to the next might be perceived of as different moments in your life), you would have to be totally conscious in all of those moments at all times to have the slightest chance of understanding *anything* that was going on. In that context, it is more complex than what goes on within any normal creator.

Have you ever heard of anyone who did go there?

I have never heard of anybody who went that direction. I know many beings, of course, who have come through the paradoxical realm to the symmetrical realm, but I have never known of anyone to make the trip the other way.

In a way that I cannot imagine at all or that you can't communicate to me, there is teeming life there—beings, activity, creation and everything—that is here, but in some opposite, multidimensional fashion, right?

What you have said is not even one-tenth of one percent of a description of what goes on there. Remember that when I say everyone came through there, I mean the component parts that made you up came through there, just as mine did—*your component parts.*

What Precedes the Paradoxical Realm?

The love that you felt and the consciousness comes from there, then?

No, back up before that. Back up way before consciousness, because consciousness requires a sense of identity.

So life force comes from there?

Back up.

Love, what?

Back up.

I hear you saying the component parts—the absolute, the bits, the stuff of which creation is made—comes from there.

Back up from that, too.

What's before that? Just pure, unadulterated life force. I don't know how to say it.

That's it! That's the problem. You have put your finger right on it. You said, "I don't know how to say it," and that's right. Even *I* do not know how to say it. I'd like to say it's chaos, but it isn't. It's before chaos, *way* back before chaos.

Can we make the statement that everything in this symmetrical realm, the basis of it, came from that paradoxical realm?

We can't even say that.

We can't?

I'll tell you why. Remember, we're dealing with a paradox, so we cannot assume that just because our component parts came from there that *we* came from there. We cannot assume that because we're dealing with a paradox. If you said that, it would put symmetry into the paradox. [Chuckles.] That is why paradoxical jokes and philosophies are amusing, because they are true.

Starting here, the Creator's certainly not aware of coming from the paradoxical realm. Were any of the friends of the Creator aware of that?

As far as I know, *all* of the component parts of all that is in the symmetrical realm passed through or came from (I can't give you a defined answer because of the nature of the place) the paradoxical realm. I have been disinclined to speak of this because there is no direct sense of linear progression there. The main point of the Explorer Race is to give you some idea of where you're from, but not to confound you.

You said "advisors" when you talked about the Progenitor. Do you have other advisors?

Oh yes.

Would you mention them?

History Lessons on Your Future; Quantum Mastery

A lot of those who advise me, if I should ask for advice, have to do with what will be (remember, I'm an historian). So I'm caught up not only in what was, but what will be in its potentials, having had some roots in the paradoxical realm. As I said, potentials are a strong reality for me in the future. A lot of my advice comes from beyond, meaning that which occurs as a result of the ten times expansion. Since my job is to be the end-time historian, I am giving you history lessons on not only who you are and where you've come from, but *where you are going*. I need to be able to look back from the future.

Because I have the capacity to see various futures and because of my experience in the paradoxical realm, I make my best guess about your future by going into the potential futures that exist after the ten-times expansion. I look back and make my best guess at any given moment about where you'll be, given the progress that exists within that moment. As you know, that changes. My job is to help you as best I can to get there without deflecting you from the best possible place to go. This is why I do a lot of "rah-rah," and [laughs] try to avoid giving you so much about the future that I'm destined to change it.

You see, that is also for me personally a lesson in quantum mastery. Quantum mastery is about consequences. This means you have to be very careful what you say to individuals and groups about the future because of the chances of changing something that is flexible. You know the old joke about a fly landing on the end of a steel beam? It bends the beam slightly. One does not wish to bend it too much.

Are you therefore a quantum master yourself?

I am working on quantum mastery.

Are there any others who are quantum masters?

Mother Earth is working on quantum mastery. As far as I know, there must be quantum masters, or else how could the course have been prepared? It is challenging. It requires that one pay attention not only to the present, to the past and to the future, but to *all* of the potentials. That is why I am certain that I've come through the paradoxical realm. It has prepared me to pay attention to the complex possibilities.

We've heard that someplace out there is a place where personalities form. That is far, far, far down the line from where you became aware. You had to travel a long ways to get to that point. You were at the beginning of the line. We're talking about way down the line now.

Oh yes. The place where personalities form is well down the line from the gate of the paradoxical realm to the symmetrical realm, yes. That's really important, too, because when one comes through and finds oneself in the symmetrical universe, one needs to adjust.

That's why you wanted to talk to as many beings as you could and share experiences?

Yes, and that is also why even today I will seek some advisors in that future time after the ten-times expansion to get my best guesses of the future. When I say "best guesses of the future," it is always to encourage that future. Thus I can't tell you everything, only a little bit—a taste, not a meal.

But none of your advisors are beings whose names we would ever have heard?

I do not think so, no. It's in the far-flung future, speaking in symmetrical terms.

We know so far that the creator of this part of the symmetrical realm, Ecstasy, created the circle of union we live in and have been talking about. Purity [see chapter 1] said 91 circles of creation had separated out of Ecstasy, and Master of Maybe [see chapter 6] said there were 62 including this one. But there are billions of other ones, right?

Yes! That number is strictly as an illustration.

Seeking Beings to Talk To

So when you became aware and sought beings to talk to, they would have been in creations beyond any we will ever run into beings from?

That's well said. Yes, they were in creations beyond anything you are likely to run into as you are now in this immediate episode.

So you had a chance to share stories with beings we'll probably never meet. You had some unusual experiences?

Not "never." You have to understand that when I first . . . remember that your component parts came through the paradoxical realm. After coming through the paradoxical realm and its infinite complexities, when I first started communicating after my passage through that gate, I needed to communicate with beings who were as complex as I could find in the symmetrical realm. (I'm talking about my component parts as if it were me, for the sake of identifying my point of origin.)

You had a frothier bunch of component parts than some people wake up to.

Yes, my component parts were motivated. I remember them. The first thing they did was seek out the most complex beings available.

And you found some.

Yes, I think this was the first true recognition of the Progenitor's existence, the Progenitor being able to flex beyond the gate. "I" was able to have the sense of what I would become while being reassured with the ultimately complex that I didn't have to rush to do it.

You had siblings, yet you've never had the desire to talk to them? There were others like you who came from Progenitor?

No. Progenitor is that which has preceded me. I can go back up the line one more click before this being I am aware of, and there is a progenitor who preceded the Progenitor of Zoosh. But that's as far . . .

I thought you went back to the beginning.

You're talking about the fragments of my personality. No, that's different.

I was going to get to that, but I understood from Progenitor at some point that there were others of you that you've never desired to talk to, like twins.

My Two Backup Parts (Just in Case)

A moment. I see. Yes, I see what you mean. This circumstance represents what I would call more of a backup situation—triplets, yes. There are two other portions of me in my totality that are in existence in what I would call *what could be* and *what might be*—"could be" meaning

a potential and "might be" meaning ultimate in potentials or vagaries. This is more what I would call portions of me that are in reserve. I have not spoken to these portions because I do not wish to taint them in any way with my personal experience should something happen to me. That means that if something happens to me and I am—yes, what?
Uncreated.

Uncreated, because why?
You're connected with the Creator?

Yes. If something happens to me, then there will be these other portions of me that exist and can reasonably carry on in some way. (Even though it is a small possibility, it is still a possibility.) I am not making *any* effort to contact them because I do not wish to taint them in any way with what might ultimately lead to their uncreation should I become uncreated.
You didn't say the eight friends of the Creator and the Master of Discomfort were also at risk.

No, I didn't say, but then you didn't ask.
I'm asking.

Yes. Anybody who signed on took that chance, even though they existed before this creation. Think about it: Your Creator also existed before this creation. This also includes all beings, even yourselves, the Explorer Race, and the other beings of great number in this universe, most of whom came from places before this universe. You're *all* taking the same risk! Remember the absolute adage: you are all one with your Creator, yes? What affects your Creator affects all of you, too. That ups the ante a bit more, does it not?

The Antichrist; the 360 Versions of Me

I will throw in this little bit: To those who are worried about the antichrist coming to destroy you or influence you, the antichrist has been with you for a long time and can be identified very simply. The antichrist is hate and violence. This gives you an idea of how the antichrist has already influenced you. I'm not trying to light a fire under you [chuckles], but I am suggesting that you need to move beyond hate and violence (and of course its consequences) into love. Or begin with tolerance, then interest, enjoyment, liking and loving. Then ultimately, unconditionally loving (in this progression, this symmetry). This is not a warning, it's just that I need to give you some landmark so we're not talking simply philosophically here. I need to give you something you can grab onto and say, "I can understand this!"
"I can do this."

Yes. "I can *see* this!"
Going back philosophically, then, you said there are 360 parts of you. Have there always been this many, or are there parts that mature?

No, this is arbitrary. It means that there are 360 versions of me that are available to speak through individuals with slightly different tinges to my personality, yes? Not only allowing for the people I might speak through, but also allowing for the circumstances. But at any moment . . .

But you're not split?

No. At any moment it could be 1500 or eight million, whatever. Right now 360 is sufficient.

And they are speaking through beings all over the planet?

Not necessarily *through*. Some of them are speaking *to* beings who are not passing the words on, but they are influenced in some benevolent way. I do a lot of work, for example, on the dream or the vision level. In this case, on the dream and vision level I am speaking to someone, but not through someone. Other spirits do this also, I might say.

The Risk

This has been a challenge during the entire creation, then, since the beginning, a potential threat of extinction. We have lived with this since the beginning?

Yes, and think of the risk. Think of the incredible risk! Think of all the beauty and magnificence that's out there. Would you destroy that by taking a chance to expand it ten times? Most of the creators—and I understand their point of view very easily—said, "Why risk it? What's so bad about it now?" to put it in a nutshell. Your Creator said, "But what if . . . ?" It had to be the way it was decided. Think about it—it *had* to be.

Was that in the original inspiration, that frame of thought?

Oh yes, absolutely.

Before you guys even signed up?

Absolutely. There is no small print.

This changes the whole . . .

Does it not?

About the Component Parts

I was wondering, when you were describing these component parts coming together, how in the world do the component parts decide to get together with certain other component parts to make all these beings?

I cannot explain that because it takes place before the paradoxical realm.

Oh, does it?

Yes, but I cannot simply jump over the paradoxical realm and explain how. I'd have to take you through the paradoxical realm, and there is no way to describe it.

I thought it was on this side that it happened.

No, I do not think so, because the component parts come through the realm together. This means the decision had *already* been made, you see.

You're saying the ultimate creation point is on the other side of the paradoxical realm, that there's something over there.

Certainly. But you would have to go through it or you cannot even hope to understand. For example, you have this object here—please hand me this object [a glass double tetrahedron]. Here we have the bipolar, here we have the tripolar, all right? The tripolar is to this what this is to this. When you go back before the paradoxical realm, you run into this— count the poles on this. The shape *is the factor*; that's why this is such a mystical shape. We're running into some serious polarization there. How can I even speak of this without your being able to understand it? Of course,

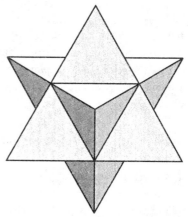

you are not *supposed* to be able to understand it, so that you can accomplish what you are here to do. I don't want to confuse you with this, because you must have symmetrical consciousness here.

So you have two unfathomable mysteries, inspiration going in one direction [the tetrahedron pointing upward], and this going in the other direction. Do they come together somewhere?

No, I am using this shape to describe . . .

. . . the complexity of the other side beyond the paradoxical realm.

Yes, here we have basically a nice, simple polarity, very simple by comparison. You [points to drawings]—this polarity. Across the gate we have the tripolar, which is like one triangle. Here in this particular shape we have more than one triangle [tetrahedron]. I am counting each edge of the triangle [tetrahedron] as a pole. It contains equilateral triangles; there are six edges. Six times three is eighteen.

If we say that the straight line is the polar, and here we have the tripolar [triangle] and we have six edges/poles of the triangle [tetrahedron] here, not just one face. It is that much more complex up the line (not down the line) from the paradoxical realm. I do not wish to make an effort to explain any further because I'd have to take you through the paradoxical realm (and you'd have to be able to understand it, which you are designed not to do) and further up the line where it would be *unbelievably* complex. This is how complex it is: If we went up the line one more notch from this (I am utilizing the glass object here), we get to the point where I can't understand it. If I were still in the paradoxical realm but as myself, I might be able to understand it. But for who I am now in the symmetrical realm, I can understand (having passed through the paradoxical realm) the multiple faces, the many polarities. But if we go one notch further up, I cannot understand.

Can we assume that those notches are notches, and not just that it goes . . .

. . . exponentially to that shape? No, we cannot.

No, that just as there is an entrance from the paradoxical to that, and from that to the next level, that it keeps going? Or don't we know that?

My best guess is that it does, but believe me, it is a guess.

I guess we've got enough to explore for now.

I get to the point where I must say, like you, "I cannot understand this."

The Source of Inspiration

Another mystery seems to be what you called inspiration—this infinite, mysterious place where ideas came from.

Inspiration is not one place.

Oh, it isn't?

No. Inspiration has to do with who you are in your entirety, including the bits that made you up when you passed through the paradoxical realm—all of that and all the who that you are in the symmetrical realm. It also has to do with all the beings you've ever come in contact with at any time, including the beings as well their infinite complexities and potentials in the paradoxical realm. It also has to do with all that you ever have been, all that you are now, and all that you could ever be including the ten times expansion. It also has to do with whoever's largesse (as they put it in royal terms) of where you are living, which would have to do with the Creator to whom you are in allegiance at this moment. There might be more, but that is essentially where inspiration comes from. In other words, many points.

The reason I have not explained it before, to put it on a pinpoint, is that it isn't a pinpoint. It comes from many points. Even though it comes from those many points, at the precise moment it passes through you, you do not get it all. The inspiration is interpreted within the context of who you are in that moment, so approximately 98.63% and a few more digits of inspiration is lost. It goes elsewhere, but you get that small percentage of the inspiration, which works for you in that moment in those circumstances. Normally I attempt to avoid complexities, and that is why I have not gone into them too much. But tonight we are going into complexities, so . . .

So would you say that when Creator got this inspiration for this creation, He lost 98.6% of . . .

No, I'm talking about you as individuals. I am not talking about Creator's inspiration. For that we have to up the ante a bit, though it works the same way. Upping the ante means that the complexity of all that *you* are and have been is, for a creator, compounded by all that the creator is, all of the component parts of a creator. And the component parts of a creator might be defined as "all that is in its universe." This universe is a component part of your Creator. That includes everyone, yourself and all of *your* component parts; all of the beings, the things, the ideas, the potentials, what might be, what could be, what will be; everything and everyone your Creator ever touched or came in contact with and all of *their* creations; and your Creator has been to the Council of Creators and so on, so all of *their* creations and all they are.

Basically we're talking about something that is not exponential, but in orders of magnitude here. Without making it any wordier, you can see that it works the same for Creator. It is just a matter of orders of magnitude that it comes from other places. There is one exception, which is that when your Creator receives inspiration, Creator utilizes all of it. That's a big exception. That is because Creator has so much more responsibility throughout many different times and symmetries than you have to act on while you are cut off from the majority of yourself and functioning in this place where you can make mistakes—and learn from them, of course.

At creator level, then, they do use all of it.

All of it, yes.

That's what I wanted to know.

Good question.

Speculation about Other Gates and Realms

There's a gate on the paradoxical end of symmetry. Is there a gate on the other end? Does it go someplace, or is this a dead end?

You mean the gate that comes from the paradoxical realm to the symmetrical realm?

You then you go through the symmetrical realm. Is there something on the other end that is a gate to something else?

Oh, I must believe that there is. If we're going from all of these levels of complexity to something symmetrical, I must believe that there is something beyond symmetry that is progressive. But that might not be so. [Chuckles.] Think about it. We cannot say on a linear level that the paradoxical realm leads to the symmetrical realm. We can't say that because we're applying something to the paradoxical realm from the linear realm.

But we know there's a gate there.

We know there's a gate there, so we can extrapolate that there might be gates from the paradoxical realm to other realms, and we can extrapolate that there might also be gates from the symmetrical realm to something else, but we cannot be certain of it. We know one thing is an absolute (I've seen this in the paradoxical realm as well), and that is *the sphere.* Maybe the paradoxical realm (I have to put this like this) is in the center of something and all these other realms are around the outside of it. Maybe it's not a straight line.

And maybe each realm is a cell in the body of somebody?

Maybe it is all a flake of dust on a policeman's collar somewhere in the vast reality of who knows what.

But I love it! It gives us more things to explore. I like that.

Yes, and that is really the intent. The Explorer Race must *explore,* yes? And of course this gives you a better idea, truly, of how adventurous you are. Just imagine, as the Explorer Race or even the component parts of the Explorer Race, you get the feeling that something wonderful and adventurous is going to happen. You're not even the Explorer Race then; you're just who you are. You throw caution to the wind, as it were, racing pell-mell toward that potential adventure, whatever it might be. That tells you a little bit about yourselves.

It makes me curious how many beings didn't come compared to how many did.

When you consider how many beings there are and how many there is room for in the experience, that tells you that only a small number of beings came. What is the old joke? How many college students can you get into a telephone booth? In the symmetrical universe one must consider these things. There is room for only so much. In the paradoxical realm you might get an infinite number of students into a telephone booth, if you could find one.

None of the other friends of the Creator can talk about this to the degree that you can, right?

I don't think so, because they are very specific. They are the best at what they do, but that *is* what they do. They might have accumulated great insights, but I think I have been given a certain amount of latitude. I am the pundit or the joker or what-have-you. I can be humorous, but maybe there's some depth there. Maybe, maybe not.

[Laughs.] Probably. You've kind of filled me up tonight.

I think so, yes. Lots of complexity tonight. Sometimes we do like to actually go into detail. Let me just say this: Allowing for all that you are as the Explorer Race and so much more that you have been before that and so *very* much more that you will be beyond that (let's keep a good thought there), know that your future adventures are *almost* guaranteed. Good night.

The Master of Feeling

February 17, 1997

reetings. What shall we talk about?

I just read a transcript of your conversation in the **Friends book.** *I was impressed with your absolute, total certainty in going without any visual aid. I'm so visual, it's hard for me to understand that.*

It is not unlike a dog or horse [chuckles] with blinders on. Sometimes blinders are placed on a horse so that it is not affected by what is going on around it, at least seemingly. You might find this hard to fathom, but sometimes there is a great advantage in not being able to see. When you see, you process what you see according to your visual memory, which is in large part ensconced within the mental body. But when you cannot see, you must go by the same feelings you always use, so you are not enslaved to the thought process and its classification system.

You can, for example, be exposed to a room with different individuals having different feelings. Utilizing your feeling self, you can act and react to those feelings without having to guess from the expressions you might see with your eyes. When you use your eyes, if anyone has ever given you a similar expression, but associated with some entirely different meaning you might very easily jump to the wrong conclusion. But when you are using your senses on the feeling level, you are presented with the evidence you are always presented with. Then there is no conflict from within, in terms of the message or the meaning.

We're taken by the cosmetic effect.

Yes, well put.

You haven't used these words, but to me you're like a quantum empathic master, totally empathic?

Understanding the Origin of a Person's Feelings

Well, I am empathetic, yes, but more than that. When one is functioning with this particular level of responsibility that I have, one must be more than empathetic to the individual. One must be able to be empathetic to an individual, then empathetic to all individuals within a given area, then empathetic in the larger sense to the whole planet's individuals and very often to the whole universe. In this way one can place the feelings of an individual into the larger context and understand how much of what the individual is feeling originates in himself and how much from those around him or the larger circumstance he is in. If it is a larger circumstance, then those particular actions or feelings might be reactions to a larger event rather than an inner experience of the individual.

This makes a great deal of difference in how I would react in working with individuals. You might ask, do I actually work with individuals? Not directly, but I will often take the time to work with guides—often beings who are training guides for individuals—showing them the more subtle experiences of sensing. I will sometimes work even with the angelics when they are especially new to the angelic experience.

Training Angelics

Angelics have one thing in common: they all radiate. This is good, because whoever they come in contact with will need their radiations. But it creates a little problem in communication. Since angelics are always radiating benevolent, loving creator energy, they cannot always feel the subtle feelings of an individual, especially one in a polarized world where discomfort exists. They radiate white light, gold light, sometimes even pink or light green (healing light). When a being is radiating this, even if it is not an angelic, anything incompatible with that energy will simply not get through to it.

That is how angelics can walk through a crisis or a catastrophe unaffected by the suffering and bring love, joy and blessings to those they might contact. They are unaffected by discomforts there. Yet if an individual has a discomfort that needs to be addressed when he is in the death process or when he simply needs something special from the angelics, communications are not always that good. As you know, mental communications do not work well between a being from a higher realm and a being such as yourselves, who purposely experience a denser realm to learn things that might be impossible to learn at higher vibrations.

So you intercede and try to . . .

No, I will train them; I won't intercede. I will train them to know what you are feeling even though they cannot feel it because of their ongoing job, which is radiating this benevolence and beauty. I usually train them to interact exclusively with the auric field of the individual when they first come to the person. Even though there is discomfort within the auric field that will not be felt by the angelic, there will be what I call energetic echo effects—a benevolent energy within the auric field that is present only because some discomfort needs to be countered. We look for what physicians or scientists sometimes call trace elements that are present only in reaction to another experience and not at any other time.

The angelic can thereby immediately know what is disturbing the person without actually having to feel it. I have trained many angelics this way who are involved in the training of other angelics. Occasionally I will work with a group of angelics who are new, who have not been in the angelic world very long. This suggests (and it is so) that the angelic world tends to replenish itself. Because more beings come to a given planet or place where the angelics are working, there must at times be more angels. When this occurs—especially when they must work in a complex place such as this creator school in which you are in attendance—they sometimes need a crash course. They might become a member of the angelic community and, within what would be (in terms of your experiential time) a day or a day and a half, have to go out on the job. Sometimes they are accompanied by others, but not always, so they must know how to understand what the beings they serve are communicating and thus know best how to serve you.

Angelics Transform Discomforts

What specifically do they do? They see this little area of benevolence in reaction to the discomfort, then they focus on the discomfort? Or do they expand their benevolence?

No, they notice this reactive benevolent energy, then they retune themselves to serve that need, like you change your radio station, in terms of its mechanics. Angelics cannot transform a discomfort if it is a learning experience, but they can radiate an energy that will support and sustain that benevolent reaction in your auric field. If you can picture this, they lay a carpet (picture a carpet of gold and white energy, sometimes a little pink, sometimes a little green) into your future direction, so that for the next day and a half or two and a half days or whatever is necessary, you will be walking on and through this material.

In this way they provide something for you *if* you are open to it. So those of you who call the angelics to you, try to be open to what they might provide immediately after you ask, because for the next two and a half days or so there will be a provision there for you. Say out loud, especially if you can be alone for some moments, "I am prepared to receive the gift of the angels for me." It might not immediately soothe your discomfort, but it will lead to a soothing.

In a way that allows you to learn the lesson.

Yes, it's a noninterfering method, but it is a way to help you without preventing your learning.

Say a little more about angels. Are they birthed by other angels, or are they simply parts of the Creator that become aware?

Angels Must First Be Personal Guides; 8-12% of Earth Population Have Been Guides

It is really like a job. One is almost always a personal guide before one becomes an angel. After being a personal guide for a time, there is no hierarchical motion here in the sense of being promoted, but when one is open to becoming a member of the angelics (which is essentially the basics), one usually becomes a guide first unless one has been a guide before. You'd be surprised how many people are running around on the surface of your planet right now who have actually been guides. They discover something that they still want to work out physically, so they come back. One needs to have been a guide for several individuals for some significant period of time . . .

Presupposing human lives before that? Human lives, then you become a guide?

No. Remember, I said there is no hierarchical motion here, like getting a job promotion.

I just thought you'd need the experience of knowing what it was like to be physical to be a guide, but that's not true?

Yes, it is. I said that there are many people who are incarnate who have been guides, a surprising number—at any given moment, from 8 to 12% of the population, quite a surprising number. Even after they have been guides they might wish to come to Earth again. As you say, before they became guides they would have had an Earth life, or at least lives of true physicality that could be compared to Earth lives either in number, quality, quantity or form in order to have compassion for the Earth life experience. After one is a guide, if one is open to becoming an angelic, one becomes a guide trainer. You are still a guide, but you then train other guides.

Angelics Train Guides and Become Material Masters

It is after being a trainer for guides that one might move to becoming an angelic. You can't be an angelic without having had at least three lives as a spiritual master and/or material master in a total of three lives. The main thing is to be able to function benevolently within all energies. In rare cases you must be able, even though at a high dimension, to make yourself visible to individuals normally unable to see with their subtle vision. This means that sometimes you might have to be seen through physical eyes. This is another reason material mastery is necessary.

This is not the only way angels come into being, but it is the usual way these days. In the beginning, of course, when this universe got under way, angels were created in great numbers. But more angels are needed now, especially because so many beings are experiencing such extremes of existence, to say nothing of many beings moving between worlds. It is true that guides will often take you from one world to the next, either in the deep sleep state or at the end of your physical life; but sometimes it is angels.

Why are so many beings moving from one world to another right now?

There are more beings on Earth now, more people dying and more people who know they are missing something in their lives. These people know they need to be doing something; they need to be guided at the deepest levels of sleep so that the information and energy and instruction by spiritual teachers or angelic teachers can permeate their unconscious and their subconscious. The subconscious is the avenue to application, sometimes even more than the conscious mind, because it can stimulate or be stimulated by feelings, and feelings can very often abridge thoughts. You might act according to your feelings when you are initiated at the deep levels of sleep, perhaps, to take some benevolent action.

An Example of Angelic Influence

You might find yourself in the following situation. Perhaps you've always been uncomfortable with a given group of people, either because you were trained this way when you were a youngster or because of some experience you had. Perhaps you had become polite or even in denial to yourself about it, but it was there. When you paid attention you could tell that there was some discomfort with this group of individuals. Then comes a time in your life when you feel there needs to be more (which many people are feeling now) or when you are asking, "Why am I here?" or "What ought I to be doing now?"—questions that are very much on people's minds in the deepest level of teaching. Perhaps then an angelic or a teacher encourages you to take a chance and try something new with a group of people you are uncomfortable with.

Then you go to work the next day and unexpectedly meet one of these individuals, and instead of freezing up or acting too polite, you are as friendly and casual as if they were anyone else. Even during this experience you are amazed at your own reaction and you enjoy it. It is a curious experience, almost like bilocation, when you experience something that way. You experience more of yourself, and the energy of the teacher is present, whether it is an angelic or a simple spiritual teacher. This tends to radiate a feeling of goodwill in that area. You talk to the person and they feel your genuine goodwill. They understand it and feel it and perhaps relate to you in a new way. Suddenly you have a new avenue of friendships you can expand on.

That's beautiful, but it raises a couple of questions.

That is always the intention.

I had the idea that if you incarnated on Earth at all, you were part of the Explorer Race. I didn't know that angelics were part of the Explorer Race. Is it just sort of a temporary Earth life without having to complete the pattern?

Once they become angelics, they do not incarnate on Earth. You might become a guide on Earth and have an Earth life after that, but you wouldn't become an angelic and *then* have an Earth life, no.

Okay, so they can have an Earth life . . .

You might ask why.

Okay, why?

Angelics Becoming Spiritual and Material Masters: Jesus and Mary of the Magdalene

In order to become an angelic, one must be a spiritual master and a material master. The energies of the angelics are always benevolent, to the point where if you were in the presence of one of these beings and had your eyes closed or couldn't see, then at another moment were in the presence of Creator, you would not be able to tell the difference, not being visual. The energy of the angelics and the energy of the Creator is the same. If you have experienced that, especially after having physical lives, you don't go back to being a physical person on Earth unless (the only exception) you are a spiritual teacher or emissary who is intended, through living a life, to help others become spiritual masters, such as one of your more famous beings, Jesus.

Jesus came from the angelic kingdom?

He had been a member of the angelics and had an Earth life promptly after that. One does not live and "die" in the angelics; it is an immortal existence. Before he was born on Earth he was an angelic, so he was born a spiritual and material master. That's why people felt the radiation when they went to see him when he was a child. They felt as if they were in the presence of something godlike. That was the angelic radiation, identical to the radiation of Creator. Of course, after he became a little older he had to blend into society more, but in later life when he would give talks to people and be in the rhythm of that talk, not thinking so much about what he was going to say and functioning entirely in inspiration, people would often feel that energy. That is another reason people began to think of him in a godlike or deified manner—which was not, of course, his intention. He wanted *you* to be what he was acting as, but that got off track.

Are there any others you can think of who had such a life?

Many of them have been very obscure. There was a being in a feminine form who was of these times also and who was very much involved in the spiritual. She also had been an angelic, and came to this Earth to experience the full range of emotional experiences and/or feelings amongst the people of Earth at that time. This person, whom you now know well, is known as Mary of the Magdalene. The Magdalene energy had to do with an object that was given to her, shared with her. In this way she became more. She was known at the time to be a mystical woman. By the way, she was never a woman of the streets as she was portrayed in those documents; that was written in later. In the early days when the stories were told from person to person, this was never the case. She was always reported as being a mystical woman, what you would now call a medicine woman.

She was married to Jesus?

Married not in the sense of going to the church and getting married, but she was Jesus' companion. They had children, yes. She was occasionally Jesus' teacher, and to some extent his mutually supportive guide because she maintained her connection to the angelic world in her life, especially after she had received the Magdalene.

What does that word mean?

It has to do with a functional instrument given to individuals who are on a particular line of spiritual connection, not a bloodline. It was given to individuals. Whoever was getting old and had the Magdalene would pick out a child who felt right. The individual would train that child, then the Magdalene would be given to the child.

The Magdalene is still in existence. It is a resonant instrument that allows the individual who has it, in the moments when she is using it, to have all knowledge, all wisdom, all healing energy, all insight, all inspiration to all beings. It is, in other words, a universal communicator, energetically, thoughtfully and on a feeling level, which is why I know about it.

Other Angelics in Earth Lives

There were other individuals, most of whose names I cannot state because their bloodline continues today. These beings had been angelics. I will mention some of them. One came to the Sioux nation, one came to the Iroquois nation, one came to the Dogon tribe. One came years ago to . . . a moment . . . no permission, so I have to skip it [chuckles]. One came to the Saxons.

These were?

Saxony is now incorporated into Germany, but some ancient customs and Saxon symbols, especially those associated with the spiritual, were given by one of these beings. One was also given to an ancient

tribe in what is now known as Scotland.
Like druids?

Druids were not a tribe; they were individuals who were trained. The individuals who created the stone circles were not the druids. The druids used them, but the beings who actually created the stone circles did so because a being came to the northern part of what is now Great Britain and trained many beings to remove rock without digging, moving them to various places without physical effort.
That's a book in itself!

It might be. It would be very interesting.
Where all the stone circles came from and why.

All over the world, and sometimes monoliths as well. That, as you say, is another book. The list goes on. The Pueblo peoples have had a being such as that. One is surprised to note how frequent the experience has been. Sometimes the beings would be very low-key (interesting term, I like that); at other times they would be very pronounced and come to be known well, such as Jesus. But most often they would not wish to be known well, especially after Jesus' experience, after which everybody said to themselves, "Well, that's the last time we'll do *that!*" One tends to become deified even though one is simply using universal energy.

Anyway, there were many beings—I might even say there were a few masters of feeling *I* have trained—that came to various places on Earth. One of them went to Australia about a thousand years ago to ancient native peoples of the area, talking about things that were unknown.

Polynesian Wisdom and Water, the Most Sacred Element

Another went to the root race of the ancient Polynesians and spoke at length to the Polynesian root race about water and what could be referred to gently as the cycle of water—the root of life. This is a wisdom entirely unto itself. Perhaps one of the last remaining cultures is Huna. I have to call it a culture because it is that more than a religion though it could be called a religion. Huna has grown out of this wisdom and is associated with Polynesian culture. This wisdom is very powerful, very useful on water planets.
Is this something you'd like to speak more about later?

Yes, perhaps later would be good, because the root of this wisdom is so true. You are made up of so much water, as you know; it is intentional that you are made up of this. If you did not have as much water in your bodies as you do, the chances of your ever being able to demonstrate any form of spiritual godliness or even benevolence would be greatly reduced—by 75%. Water itself is sacred. If I had to pick out one element on Earth that was the most sacred in relationship to human life, it would have to be water.

Then could we get the true basis of the Huna teaching?

Perhaps not the Huna teaching, because that has grown out of it. Sometime let us do the root teaching of the Polynesian wisdom.

All right. I'm just a little confused, though . . .

Just a little?

[Laughs.] I had always thought that if you incarnated once on the Earth, you had to complete the Explorer Race experience. These guides, then, who just kind of dip into it, are not bound to that?

Guides Teach Other Beings about the Challenges of a Polarized World

They are not bound to it because of the cycle they are on, which is a cycle in which they are intended to help. They can choose to, but they do not have to become involved as the Explorer Race. But by living a life here, they become much more intimate with the Explorer Race experience and are thus able to speak about it much more beautifully, with empathic feeling, to other spiritual beings so they can understand the true nature of the constant challenge of being a spiritual being in such a polarized world. All spiritual beings do not understand this.

I've heard that some angels judge humans for not learning their lessons more quickly.

They cannot understand how beings born in a sacred fashion (birth is sacred) can, with all the water in you, ever become in any way violent or self-destructive. They cannot understand it, so they need to be taught by peers who have felt it. The teaching of other spiritual beings becomes the cycle for these teachers who come to help you and then go on to help spirit beings who do not understand because they have had no personal experience of the true nature of the challenges for a sensitive, physical, spiritual being on Earth—which, by the way, is everyone. Even though you might think [chuckles] that it's hard to imagine certain people being sensitive and spiritual, you are all that when you are born.

Angelics to Help the 3.0-Earth Sirians, Who Will Become Masters of Discomfort and Communication and Re-create Their Past

As the Explorer Race moves on, do the angels stay here or go off with the Creator? Are they going to stay in this creation?

I think that some will stay here and help those fairly dense beings who are now beginning to arrive on third-dimensional Earth [negative Sirians; see *The Explorer Race*, chapters 5 and 22]. Even though those beings will not become the Explorer Race, they will become very important beings. They will at some point in time, having experienced such extreme negative energy, be able to communicate with other beings who have had and are still having this kind of experience. This means that they will become masters of discomfort in their own right. It is intended that they do that and at the same time become masters of communication. They will be spiritually driven.

What is intended, of course, is that once this has happened for the whole Sirian society at the third-dimensional Earth level, they will be taken on lightships with angelics and go back in time to change the evolution of their society on their planet even though their planet is now destroyed. They will change it and it will become something more balanced. Then the destruction of the planet will not have taken place. The negative Sirians are here to train to become spiritual masters, communication masters, teaching masters—all of these things as well as what I have said—and go back to change the past on that planet in Sirius from whence they came. Earth is again contributing to the betterment of the universe simply by being herself.

All the suffering has to be transformed before the big leap in consciousness—that's their part in this?

That's right. It has to be done by beings who have personally experienced this, so they will be motivated, empowered, passionate about the experience and compassionate with others. They will not have a shred of judgment, because they will know very well why people act that negative way when they go back into the past of their culture. Yet they will be able to lead their culture to a more balanced place.

In your earlier discussion you were the only person who told us that we had a reality before this Creator. You knew that we were separate from the Creator, that we were not generated by Him, that we joined Him?

Following the Feeling Track Backward or to the Fulfillment of Any Need

The reason I knew that you had preceded Creator is that, being Master of Feeling, I could feel your feelings back to the Creator and before. When you came here as the root beings you are, you came with feeling. You had strong feelings as you sailed through space and time, and those feelings leave a track. When one has mastered feelings, they leave a permanent track. That's how I can find my way around to the proper places; I follow the feeling tracks, which ability is the foundation of instinct. One might have a need—water, food, shelter—and in feeling one's needs, one radiates his feeling out as far as necessary. There is no limit. Not unlike your radar or sonar, when your feeling energy touches whatever it is that you need, there is a stronger energy on that line and you travel that line to what you need. That is how instinct works.

I've never heard it put that way. You never discussed any of this with the other friends of the Creator? Most of them except for Zoosh don't seem to know it.

No, because it is not my job to do that. My job is to be more hands-on with individuals, and not only on Earth. Sometimes my job takes me to other places—places that revere childhood, for example. I will mention only places you are familiar with so we don't get too esoteric.

Pleiades, a Place That Reveres Childhood

On the Pleiades, for example, childhood is revered to such an extent that the culture encourages adults to be able at a moment's notice to have childlike enthusiasm about whatever they do so that they need not leave the joy of childhood behind, as they simply become larger. In such a place as this I often work with the ancient teachers of the Sumerian philosophy, which is the root of the Pleiadian culture. One might say, "I have heard that word *Sumerian* on Earth," but you must remember that your culture and the Pleiadian culture are closely tied. It is much closer than cousins; you are really much closer to being brothers and sisters. The genetics are very similar, the only differences really having to do with the evolutionary impact of different diets and the exposure (or not) to polarities.

The emotional body, for example, is exactly the same. It's just that on the Pleiades when one is born with this beauty that you are born with here, one is nurtured. A birth on the Pleiades is considered a very sacred thing. For instance, many adults would gather for the birth, bringing up within themselves the joy of childhood, thus welcoming the child by surrounding it with an exuberant level of its own energy. Thus the child feels welcome to come into a world of its own personal individual experience.

I sometimes work with these teachers who advise the Pleiadian elders, whoever they might be in that moment, to continue to celebrate childhood and what it can teach adults. Childhood, after all, is simplicity incarnate, yet this simplicity is focused on very specific feelings—love, harmony, beauty, joy, discovery, happiness. You all have this when you are born too, but those of you who are slapped on the bottom become unsure of that.

Water Births

Those who in recent years have had a water birth where the child naturally swims out of its mother without thinking how, did it naturally. It is quite amazing to see. Then one comes into life more benevolently; perhaps people are standing about singing or some such thing. This has been occurring a little more frequently on your planet. In the past it was very common.

Water birth, I might add, is actually the birth that is intended here. Remember that you are largely made of water, and it is natural for you to be in it. You float within fluid when you are inside your mothers. Before your birth, out comes the fluid as if to say, "Bring me into the water world with kindness and love." It is intended that you be informed of this.

That's beautiful. That would be much more in our future, right?

I think so, yes, especially as you begin to communicate more with Pleiadians who know they are intended to communicate with you. They are not so close right now because of the extremes going on on Earth, but as that balances out, they will be with you.

I learned only recently that they are not part of the Explorer Race.

No, they are not.

They chose not to be.

You and Pleiadians Were Once One People;
Some Pleiadians Precede Creator

Exactly, because of what you would have to go through to become the Explorer Race. They felt the sacrifice was not worth the reward, and you felt that it was, and that was the parting of the ways. You were one people before that; that's why there are so many similarities. As I say, if you were to stand next to each other and you were wearing the same outfit, you would simply not be able to say this one's the Pleiadian and this one's the Earth being. You'd just say humans.

But they were a part of what came in that was separate from the Creator? They were a part of the Explorer Race at the beginning?

There are threads in the Pleiadian culture that existed before Creator, but threads only. The thread goes along the line of spiritual teachers, elders and so on. So in that sense it is a spiritual line and to some lesser extent, a bloodline. Other than that, most Pleiadians were created in this universe. But as I say, there are spiritual teachers and so on who are of them, who preceded this Creator. That is not unusual. One could look to many cultures and find the same—that the cultural and religious guides of the culture might well have existed in some other universe or creation and want to perpetuate that creation or start anew in a new universe. If they are welcomed by your Creator, which they often are, then they come here and with your Creator's energy have the makings, the foundation, of their culture as expressed in this universe's terms.

I didn't know that either! You are an absolute wellspring of new information! So they come as lightbodies and then take on bodies in this creation, but their life force is not generated by this Creator?

Correct. In terms of the elder race (I'm uncomfortable saying "race," but for lack of a better term I will, because they look like other Pleiadians), it is a spiritual race. (Can I say a spiritual race?)

What other cultures were brought from other universes?

In terms of percentage in this universe, I should think at least 23%.

What are some of the names?

Other Cultures That Precede Creator

Certainly the Andromedan culture preceded this culture, because it has to do with thought and its applications. That whole experience well preceded your Creator's creation. Your Creator actually sent out an invitation, because It felt that it was necessary . . .

More variety, more diversity, more richness.

Yes.

I didn't know that!

Yes, and since your Creator knew that thought was going to be essential in the creation of the Explorer Race and all of the ramifications of your experience, He sent out emanating rays to another universe where the Andromedan culture has its root, requesting that spiritual beings there would be very welcome in this universe He was creating. He asked if they would care to come, and if they would, He would be glad to provide planets and star systems, anything they would require to establish their culture here. And of course there were volunteers.

This was also the case for Orion. If we condense the Orion experience even today down to few words, one might say that it represents strength, courage and heroism. Even today when the culture is very benevolent, they still live an exciting lifestyle if they choose. They fly around space, meet new civilizations, experience excitement and adventure as you do. That is why so much of that influence is here. The Orion culture was another essential one because it has to do with your spontaneous feelings. Again, they were invited.

Wonderful. Any others?

Let's see.

The Sumerian-Pleiadian Explorer Race Connection in Expressions of the Unknown Mystical

What about the Sumerians? What does that go back to?

The Sumerian has to do with the ancient teachings of the Pleiadians, which goes way back. The other beings are saying that we have to go back up the line to find the root. I'm not even sure whether I can give you that knowledge; I don't know if I have it. But you have to go beyond this Circle of Creation to get to the Sumerian root. I can see it, just following the trace feeling of it.

So you can see with your mind's eye?

I see with my feelings. But in a sense, "mind's eye" is not a bad terminology. I can see/feel the trace of feeling going well past the Circle of Creation to a point I think is not far from your origins, spatially speaking.

You mean the Explorer Race origins?

Yes. Your origins, spatially speaking, as much as I can see, have to do with all expressions of the "unknown mystical" applied in various manners so that it becomes self-defining. For example, the unknown mystical would be a symbol that no one there (wherever that place is) understood. You integrate it into your culture or your experience in some way so that you define its meaning through your application. This tells you that the core or roots of the Explorer Race and the Sumerian culture (the Sumerian culture here) come from that same general space.

Is that in the same Circle of Creation?

Closer than that—in that same general space, which measures less than one-tenth the length of this universe.

That separates the two of them?

That separates the two, yes. This tells you that the Explorer Race root beings are, at their very core, definers of the mystical through application.

So the Sumerians were then invited here. Some went to the Pleiades to teach and some actually started a culture here on the planet?

Yes. The culture most closely associated with the Sumerian experience is related to that which has been called the Founders [see *The Explorer Race*, chapters 15 and 19]. This relates well back to the beings who live at a much higher dimension inside this planet and also to a race of lightbeings who are involved in the beginning and maintaining of symbolic cultures. (A symbolic culture is any culture for whom symbolism plays an important role.) Of course, symbolism plays a major role in your culture and many other cultures around this universe.

Constant Enigmas to Solve; Exposure to Symbols

Your Creator felt very strongly that in order for beings to evolve, there must be constant enigmas that would entice you to resolve them. Your Creator felt that one of the best of enigmas for you to resolve would be anything associated with a demonstrable symbol, whether it be language, a shape or even a motion. [She moves the channel's arms and hands as in the hula dance.] These motions have meanings as well. Your Creator felt that the best way for many cultures (not only the Explorer Race) to want to know more would be to expose them at critical times in their spiritual evolution to symbols for which they did not have a ready translation. This has often been the case with your culture, your society, when you have either looked at symbols anew in some new light or you have discovered—and it is publicized throughout your culture—some entirely new object or set of symbols.

The crop circles.

That's a good example. And the writing that one finds in spaceships, which few people have been exposed to directly (in terms of being able to study openly), but many have been exposed indirectly in some way, then store it in their residual memory. Perhaps from a contact with extraterrestrials, a vision or even your imagination, you might draw symbols with no ready comparison in any of your alphabets. It is stimulating, and what you hear universally in your culture is, "What does it mean?"

What is so interesting is that from that same place in some other circle of creation is the root of the Explorer Race. Then the Founders are part of the very thing that created our bodies!

Yes. And your bodies are actually created in such a way that your physical bodies will react to symbols, communicating with your unconscious mind, your subconscious mind and to some extent your conscious mind, even the cellular structure of your bodies. This is not only utilized by business people with messages, but by simply exposing an individual to a symbol for which there is no immediate translation in your conscious language you can often stimulate a person's spiritual evolution. The physical self is impacted. You look at it, you don't know why you like it, but there's something magnificent about it. Sometimes you have an idea what it might mean and other times it is just a magnificent experience. In those moments even your auric field is often being reprogrammed by the symbolic impact upon you.

I can think of so many. Look at the Egyptian symbols, the Masonic symbols, the Tarot, astrology, the Indian yantra—there are so many.

Yes, there are many, many symbols. When looking at a book of symbols or variations on symbols, one can ofttimes become excited simply by looking at them, experiencing a full range of emotions.

There's a meaning to the body, but not to the mind.

Homework with Symbols

One of the best ways to experience this as homework is to obtain a book of symbols in a language you don't understand (in which case there will be no reason to try), when the full impact of the symbol can be felt. Ideally, of course, one would have a book with only the symbols and no text, but if that is not available, a foreign language book is perfect.

I think we're definitely going to talk to you further. In the future would you be available to talk about some things for another book?

Yes, I would be happy to participate.

You have expanded so much what I started doing here. I was trying to get what I called a road map of the infinite to get a little clearer understanding of what creation looks like. Could you draw a map? In the symmetrical universe that Zoosh just told us about, where would you be? Would you be close? Would it be close to the paradoxical universe that Zoosh talked about, or close to where the personalities originate? Is there any sense of putting that someplace? Where did you first become aware?

It is difficult to put it in a location, because I must say . . .

It's almost like you come from where the feelings originate.

My Origin and Early Experiences

Yes, I must say that I cannot remember . . . well, now let me think. [Chuckles. Pause.] Let me use thought. Ah! I can remember a time in which I was in a thick place—not dense, but thick as one might feel a viscous fluid. It was a very benevolent feeling. I would say that the primary feeling was one of total, absolute patience, complete nurturing, and a complete experience of absolute continuity.

Then I remember feeling excited and joyous. I remember experiencing something very much like a birth when I left that mass of nurturing energy. As I was moving through its canal to leave it, I felt more and more heightened emotions, the full impact they had on everything from the densest physical to the most benevolent etheric. It was as if I were exploding and imploding at the same time with emotions and feelings. It sounds confusing, but it wasn't. It was a celebration.

I remember looking back with thankfulness toward that which birthed me. Then I remember for the next period of time (roughly equivalent to 800 trillion years of your experiential time) feeling myself everywhere in the same moment, exploding and imploding feelings. I believe these were either the feelings of beings who were already there, or that what I was doing was saturating these beings with pure feeling and pure emotion. This was an opportunity to experience emotions and their physical impact—their consequences and the consequences of those consequences—for a long time, until I knew every possible consequence of every possible feeling. Then it was as if that time was over. I could compare it and say it felt like a half a day, in terms of one's experiential life.

Meeting Your Creator

Then I began moving, concentrating myself, becoming highly charged with feeling, moving quickly. And as quickly as I moved through time and space, it still took about five of your minutes to get to the intersection point where I met your Creator. I'll never forget that encounter because both of us were hurtling along so fast that neither your Creator nor myself could stop in time, and we just merged for a moment. As I was passing through your Creator and It was passing through me, we both realized that the reason we were hurrying to this point was to meet each other [chuckles]. So we had a moment of complete understanding of who the other one was, though that was not, I think, our original intention. Still, it allowed us to become very intimate, more than we would have expected to be, and to understand all we needed to know about the other. So I was able to join your Creator, bringing what I have to offer and accompanying Him in this magnificent creation.

Could you turn back and ask that which birthed you what it is, or if there are others like you?

My Origin of Focus and Up the Line

[Laughs.] I will do so, of course. I am happy to do so. A moment. This being describes itself as "the place of emergence of that which is immersed in its duty." That is all it says.

Is there any sense of home with it? Is it a place you want to go, or is it just . . .

Oh, I think it is something that one might go through perhaps when one has a mission, a duty. I cannot say it feels . . .

Doesn't it feel like home?

It doesn't feel like something I wish to return to, because I can feel it from here where I am.

But it didn't birth you; it just focused you?

Focused me, yes.

So it was like one of these centrifuge creator tubes or something?

No, it is more a mass of energy. It creates a canal throughout itself, not unlike the birth canal in a human being, when an individual such as myself is needed or ready. (Apparently either one of those will work.) But until that individual is needed or ready, it contains the seeds of other individuals. I do not think it generates the seeds, but it contains them. Looking further up the line . . .

That's a good word. [Laughs.]

It is. I can see that the seed of my being and the other seed beings are up the line in a form of life. It rotates. A side view might be this [pauses to draw], looking not unlike a plant on whose surface [taps the pen to make many dots] one finds seeds of beings not unlike myself. The rotation is in this direction [draws clockwise arrow]. That is as far back as I can look. This upper part of the being has to do with the mechanism for creating the seeds of beings and releasing them to the areas or avenues by which they might most beneficially express themselves.

That's the same mechanism as the birth canal?

No, that's before the birth canal. Look at it this way.

They go from where they're created to this . . .

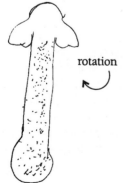

rotation

I cannot say whether they all do. I did. I went from there to that nurturing place I described first.

Can you contact that being?

Yes.

Would that be your home or your mother?

My Creator, Who Releases Seeds

That is my creator. It could speak, just as the other being could speak on its own at some point, but it says to me now to say to you that its purpose is to fulfill the needs and purposes that will be generated in the future. It does not create beings of its own intention, only beings that will be needed but are not needed yet, such as myself. I spent a great deal of time in that nurturing mass before I was released to do my duty. Yet that which created me did so enjoyably and beneficially, without any personal agenda.

Could you call that a creator and its creation, like a universe?

Oh, no, it is not that big. I can compare it to a life form here on Earth. It is about as big as one of your ancient sequoia trees—not so very big.

Is it in a circle of creation?

It is in an area, not exactly a circle. It is like that, but it is more of an area having to do with preexistence, or that which exists before personality—or job description in my case. It becomes part of an individual.

So are there others like you that have this feeling nature?

I must believe that this being is releasing seeds. I could look at it from a distance . . . it is releasing seed beings, as I was once, seeming to go in many directions, some going up the line. Perhaps you will speak to that being at some point and it will describe what it does better than I can pass its message on.

That's exciting. You just never looked back before?

I never did, no. Not because I felt nervous about it, I just never did.

Well, thank you for having the courage to do that. Let me ask something else. Last time Zoosh talked about the point where the symmetrical universe met the paradoxical realm. Is that something you know about?

Yes, I do.

Tell me what you know about it. This being's on this side of the symmetrical realm, isn't it?

Yes, in the symmetrical realm.

The Paradoxical Realm

How do you know about the paradoxical realm?

Because feeling exists there. Here's another example where traversing spaces by feeling is infinitely easier than by seeing. One is confounded in the paradoxical universe by what one sees, but if one utilizes feelings, one traverses the paradoxical universe as if it were nothing but a series of mirrored reflections of condensed feelings and their mirror images. One is not confused by going into a reflecting aspect of the paradoxical universe. One simply follows the feeling even if it is reflected here and there and here and there. One simply follows the feeling (or the trace, as I call it) and easily assimilates or passes through this place.

How did you discover it?

I think it was something I noticed in your Zoosh friend, because it was so profoundly impacted on the Zoosh memory. Zoosh, you understand, is a being of thought and wisdom and knowledge. When a being such as that encounters anything that is exponential in its expression of anything, it impacts the thoughtful mind because it is so unlike anything else. Since thought is not something that I use, I do not think. I simply emanate feeling energy, which can then be translatable to words. Then I am able or capable of traversing the paradoxical realm as if it were no more complex than a spider web.

You followed the trail back from Zoosh—that's how you discovered it?

Yes, I was interested because I could see that Zoosh was still pondering the complexities of the place, which in the thought realm are complex indeed.

From your place there, is that pretty close to the entrance?

From where I was birthed? No, nowhere near. I followed it by utilizing Zoosh's thoughts. I can see it because Zoosh has feeling, and as a feeling being I am able to access the Zoosh consciousness and memory. Anything that might stimulate a feeling in Zoosh or be stimulated by a feeling in Zoosh I am able to trace back to its point of stimulation.

You can also do that with all the friends of the Creator?

Oh, yes. Any being I have ever met.

Beyond the Paradoxical Realm

So you went through the portal—you say traversed. Did you come out the other side of the paradoxical realm?

Yes. The other side is like looking at clouds of light. It is very sparkling. In my experience the paradoxical realm is paradoxical only in thought—and in feelings if one is new to feelings. Not being new to feelings, it wasn't paradoxical for me.

Because you have experienced everything.

Yes, on the feeling level. I went back into the clouds of light and then back just one more distance to what looks like a compound crystal. It is shaped roughly like . . . have you ever seen a marquise-cut diamond? That shape?

[Lifts glass double tetrahedron.] Feel this. Zoosh related it to this.

The Three-Layered Crystal

No, I'm going back to the one before the one Zoosh talked about. Marquise cut is not unlike this [draws], like the universal feminine. What we have here is an outer crystal that revolves in this direction [draws arrows moving counterclockwise]. Beneath that is a crystal that revolves in this direction [draws clockwise arrow].

You're talking about an outer layer here [indicates left object], then the inner layer here [points to second arrow]?

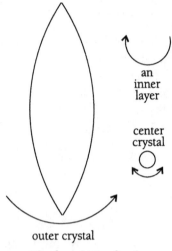

an
inner
layer

center
crystal

outer crystal

The foundation for the
paradoxical realm.

Yes. This is still another crystal that goes [draws] in that direction, which is the center. The center crystal revolves in both directions at once. It is in its own right the foundation for the paradoxical realm, because the paradoxical realm is a direct reflection (remember, there are clouds of light around this crystal) and the light beams into the crystal and at the same time out of it, the crystal being paradoxical in that light (I made a joke!). The paradoxical realm, as experienced in its reflectiveness, is essentially an illuminated experience (if one is in it, one feels it physically) associated with a direct emanation of the compounded light waves reflected and refracted from the inner spinning crystal, which spins in both directions at the same time.

I can't even imagine that.

Yes, it flies in the face of your physical laws, but it can be done. It can only be done, however, in a place where paradox is the rule and not the exception. Thus the paradoxical realm is a portion of this crystal's existence. The crystal itself is quite large, just a little bit longer than the radius of your planet. The crystal's function . . .

Is it 4000 miles from top to bottom, or from left to right?

Oh, you mean upon which axis the crystal is in existence?

Is the 4000 miles from here to here?

The length of the crystal is . . . now, what was I saying? [Chuckles.] Interruption, however useful and benevolent, is . . .

It fractures your thoughts?

I do not have thoughts, I have feelings. I will have to leave that one. This crystal is vital for your existence. The paradoxical realm (Zoosh wishes it to be referred to that way, since it isn't actually a universe) cannot be in the symmetrical realm where you are, or the symmetrical realm would simply tear itself to pieces. But it has to be right next to the paradoxical realm so that its emanations (but not the experience) come into this realm to a lesser degree than some other realm.

Help in Uncreating the Past, Then Recycling It

The emanations are mainly what allows you, especially you of the Explorer Race, to be able to uncreate the past—which in its own right is paradoxical. To have lived in the past, to have had an existence in the past and then to go back and uncreate that past so that that past becomes a different future, creates a paradox from that original past. In order to uncreate the past one must deal with the consequences of that paradox as part of your training as creators in training.

And there will be consequences. One would not be able to uncreate the past without having the paradoxical realm close enough so that its emanations can be used by you for this purpose as well as other functions of your existence. When you do uncreate your past (just as when those Sirian beings I discussed uncreate *their* past), the paradox that will be left over is the original past that was there. It doesn't just disappear. As creator, even a creator in training, you have to find a place to put all that energy where it can be recycled into its benevolent origin. This means that you have to take all of that past-that-would-have-been (and that was at one point) and return it to its point of origin for recycling and purification.

The Danger of a Resonant Echo; Absorbing All Past Energy

Some beings will have to do that, because that's the consequence you must deal with. You cannot just leave it and say, "Well, it's uncreated." Uncreation is not so easy. You're going into the past and re-creating it, so the line of existence that was there before must be recycled. If it isn't recycled, do you know what would happen? It would create a resonant echo like something that is agitated or like a squeaky wheel. The squeak gets louder and louder and louder until it reimages itself. The new past that you created is then confounded by the old past that existed. One then has a paradox within the realm you find yourself in, and the past tears itself apart, destroying itself and your current existence as well. So you *must* do something with that past, otherwise it will destroy all. That is a consequence that one lives with and functions with as a creator.

What do we do with it? How do we recycle it?

As creators in training you must have a means to absorb, which you will have by that time. You will have beings who will absorb—empathic combined beings—all of the energy of that past. These beings will fly in dimensional speed (light speed is too slow) to the point of origin of every single bit of that energy—its original origin—and drop it off. Even moving at fantastic speeds it will take quite awhile, but it is essential.

It sounds like soul recovery, but on a very large scale.

Now that you mention it, it is similar, but in this case we're not talking about a soul so much as an energy that was once a physical reality, if I might put it that way. It has less connection to being a physical reality, so at one moment it is and the next moment . . . it's not exactly an *isn't*, but it's a *was*. As a *was* it doesn't have any means to express itself, so it becomes agitated and will continue to become more and more agitated until it is taken home, wherever home might be for the individual particles of energy. So it will take a great many beings to a great many places in order to bring that energy home. Of course, it is a loving task for that energy, a benevolent task, yet at the same time essential.

But we have to do it before the ten-times expansion?

Oh yes, absolutely.

Okay, you said something fascinating. You mentioned that the symmetrical realm is just another realm connected to the paradoxical realm. There are many, many realms?

Oh yes. In some realms, for instance, the paradoxical realm is not in any way harmful to contact directly.

You can go back and forth freely?

Yes, you can freely go back and forth. Maybe I can come up with an example that would relate in some way to your thought structure, because most of those realms are so unlike your own experience as to be confounding simply to discuss it. Let's see if there is one. A moment.

The Mystical Realm

There is a realm associated with the mysticism of purpose—purpose being an intention, as it were. In that realm one experiences all levels of consciousness. It is the point of origin for almost everything mystical that I'm aware of, and as such that realm has no problem with the paradoxical, because ofttimes the paradoxical and the mystical realm are easily accommodated within the same sentence, much less the same feeling. That is the realm that is the closest to an experience you can identify with.

There's energy in the symmetrical realm from the mystical realm?

Yes. Remember, I talked about much of the mysticism that drives you. I believe its point of origin is in the mystical realm.

Can you help me understand—are they little cells side by side, or is there a rectangle?

Let's imagine, for the sake of simplicity, this revolving crystal being at the center of a sphere that connects to the other realms.

So there are little symbols all around this thing with different realms?

That's not exactly the way it looks, but that's the best way to illustrate it in the mind's eye. You are one realm and the mystical realm is another realm, then there are other realms, realms that would be too baffling to put into your terminology.

Other Portals, Other Realms

Are there portals between the mystical and the symmetrical that don't go through the paradoxical?

Oh yes, absolutely. That is essential, so that we do not induce into the symmetrical the full energy of the paradoxical, which would destroy the symmetrical.

Are there portals to other realms from the symmetrical?

Oh certainly, but . . .

They wouldn't make any sense to us.

They wouldn't make any sense to you because at your core you are beings who accumulate wisdom for the purpose of its ultimate application. You can say that about all beings in the symmetrical realm. The portals leading from the symmetrical realm to some of these other more bizarre realms would allow beings who choose and who have the capacity and knowledge and wisdom to go to those realms to emigrate or bring something those realms might need from the symmetrical realm. But they cannot come back, not the other way. The other way would be like bringing in energy from the paradoxical realm. Because it is so much more extreme than the paradoxical realm, there would be no way to use the energy from those realms in the symmetrical realm without utterly destroying all symmetry.

Symmetry sounds like a beginner's school.

No, not at all. Creating that which is self-perpetuating is a foundational lesson, meaning it is the foundation and the structure and the beams that hold the building up. To become a creator, one must have profound experience in the symmetrical realm. You cannot create any kind of creation, any universe, that does not build from some other aspect of your universe. But if you come from a realm that is not like that, the chances of your building a universe that is connected from one portion to the other is so limited as to be quantitatively nonexistent. If you went to these other realms, you would find highly concentrated single experiences. That's the best way I can describe it to you. Remember that just because I say that something is unfathomable to you does not mean that you are somehow foolish or childish or stupid. It can mean that it has no application in any existence that you might ever be a portion of. It is essentially a non sequitur.

Would it be a true statement to say that you start here and evolve into those realms?

Certainly not. You see, you are trying to make a straight line, a progression from this realm to that realm, but it is certainly no connection. It is separate. It would be the same as if you said that the house you have now is a fine one, but to be truly more, a greater being, you have to move next door. It isn't like that at all. If you stand outside, you say, "Well, here's a house and there's a house."

So they're just different realms of experiencing?

Different realms of experiencing, that's right.

Are there two, ten, a billion realms? What is your sense of it?

Oh, I don't think there is that high a number. I think we're really talking about maybe twelve.

I was just getting my infinity charted there. [Laughs.] Yet you move freely through them, and because you can't see them, you are protected.

Yes, it is a great advantage. Because I cannot see it, I do not have to form any prejudgments based upon past experience. So I go through strictly on feeling, and if something feels good to me I can go through it. If it doesn't feel so good, I go around it through some other way, not unlike a river passing through land. If something is too dense, a river goes the other way, but it still gets to where it's going.

Meeting and Sharing with Others

Have you and Zoosh talked about this?

We've talked a little bit about it, yes. Zoosh, as I say, is a being for whom all aspects of thought are fully and completely mastered. Yet all aspects of feeling are not.

So you can share with each other and you've learned from this.

Oh, yes. You know, that is one of the privileges and pleasures of being involved in this project, because one makes friends, meets beings and has opportunities to experience and share things that one might never have in some other circumstance. It's not unlike a party, you know. You go and you meet people you might never meet otherwise.

You have trained masters of feeling to come to this planet, but there are none who are directly connected to you that you have created or generated? Or are there beings on the physical planet that are from you?

No, I work with beings. If I were to create beings in my own right and put them on the planet, being so involved in feeling as I am, I would invariably become biased. It is simpler to not do that at this time.

You have expanded our knowledge so awesomely! Are there any particular subjects you'd like to talk about at some point, specifically ones you're interested in?

Oh, anything you are interested in I would probably find interesting. If I didn't, I'm sure I could say so in some diplomatic way. But origins in general, the origins of things are . . .

That fascinates me.

I'm interested in origins myself.

For the book, then, say whatever you'd like to tell humans right now. We'll talk to you again some other time. And I thank you.

All of you on Earth now have within you the capacity to transform all discomfort within yourself and, working as a group, within other beings as well. Learn to become intimate with your own feeling of love and joy and that childlike discovery that is so joyful. You have seen how excited and happy a child is when it sees a flower or an animal. Learn to experience those feelings even if it is a performance or an act, as you say. By doing that you can connect with your essence, because the essence of your being is not only the mystical, it is applied happiness. Good night.

Oh thank you, thank you.

All right, Zoosh speaking. I see my friend has amused you with her knowledge and point of view, as I like to call my opinion.

Oh, she is wonderful, just wonderful! We're going to talk to her later.

Yes, she will have lots and lots of interesting things to say.

Do you have anything more for this chapter in the book?

No, only that it is important that the reader always remember the infinite possibilities of one's own personal creation, to say nothing of the mass of creations going on around you. Try to let go of words such as "impossible" and adopt words such as "improbable" or "probably not," because absolutes are becoming scarcer all the time. Good night.

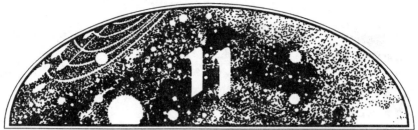

The Master of Plasmic Energy

February 18, 1997

oosh: What's on the agenda for tonight?

The Master of Plasmic Energy. Did we have a talk last night? When I woke up, it was so real that I almost turned on the tape recorder to listen to it.

I often talk to people at night or when they're in their deep sleep, because they are more open to ideas then. When you're in your deepest sleep state you still have a connection to being physical, but your soul personality is away from the planet. You can see the whole theme of your lives in that situation, whatever it might be for any individual. When people are in that deep sleep, they have a different perception of physical reality.

It's a unique time, I might add. When you are between lives or at higher-dimensional lives, your perception is there and there only. But this is the only circumstance (other than working with visionaries or people like that) I am aware of where a being is on Earth in these times and also at a higher dimension when the communication is going on. Even though you're at a higher dimension you can still perceive, feel, be aware of and actually communicate in physical Earth terms. This might not be words so much as expressions, feelings, pictures, ideals, ideas and so on. Thus it is a unique time in which communications can take place that are not only relevant to the immediate life the person is focused into, but where you can also see your overall lives. It is very much like being able to look down on the chessboard from above, understanding the entire sequence of events. Because it is a special time to talk to people, I make a habit of it.

M aster of Plasma.
Welcome.

Thank you.

Gold Light

You exude so much golden light when you're here. You call plasma liquid light and magnetic light. Is it mostly made of golden light, since it attracts and it's like love in bloom?

Around Earth it is. Around other places it might be other colors, but since Earth and peopled cultures require so much gold light just to sustain and perpetuate life, it is often necessary to exude that light because it feeds all participants in the experience. For instance, if I communicate to the people of Orion, the light would be green. In the Pleiades the light would probably be blue and white. But here it is gold because the gold light here has a specific agenda. It is a mastery color, yes, but it is also a color that stimulates and sustains the best experience. Thus it is the initiator and the maintainer of the initiation.

We have talked to the being who told us how gold light was made. Do you use their gold light?

Yes, I use the gold light as amplified by that being of gold light. I also utilize ribbons of color, vibration and what I call pitch (I'd rather say pitch than sound because it is a little more accurate). These help penetrate what might otherwise be impenetrable. For example, a human being, having had a difficult life or just a difficult day, might have built a barrier around himself. Gold light, when utilizing the proper harmonic pitch or pitches, can penetrate that density around the person. It will not wound, but transform the discomfort and soothe and stimulate the body's natural mechanism for self-healing.

The other things I do with pitch and so on are utilized to make connections to specific individuals. This is usually not necessary with Mother Earth unless the communication is to one specific area of her body. For example, the highest mountaintops would need a very high pitch, whereas the root of the mountain, where one goes deep into the bedrock to discover its root, would be the deeper tones.

So you send energy into the Earth too, not just to humans? You actually feed it into Mother Earth?

Yes. And while I might not normally feed it inside a planet, it is different with Mother Earth because of the trauma she has been through. Because of this trauma she is not able to readily consume this gold light in her atmosphere or on her surface. She doesn't have the energy to reach out and take it in. This has partly to do with radio waves and microwaves generated by your technology, which interfere with her lightbody, her energy body. Normally her energy body would be able to assimilate this light, but because it has been rent and torn by these microwaves, I feed her on my own.

The Rising Grid and Ley Lines

They're probably grid lines and ley lines—they're part of Mother Earth's energy body, yet they also feed us, right?

Yes. An interesting point about grid or ley lines is that now they are no longer where they were. These lines are rising above the surface. In time there will be an expanded grid all around the atmosphere of Mother Earth. This will protect her as she moves through dimensions. Grid lines and ley lines are able to do this—move and expand, becoming larger as they move out, maintaining roughly a spherical shape around the planet. As a result, some of you are having bizarre experiences when a grid or ley line rises through your home or business or wherever you are located at a given moment.

Right now most grid and ley lines, with some few exceptions, have cleared the surface of the Earth up to altitudes of 4300 feet. Those lines have not yet cleared places that are five, six and seven thousand or more feet above sea level, but they will. It is not a formula, but the lines are moving outward away from Earth to form this grid at the rate of about one-quarter inch an hour, which is quite rapid. Because of the discomfort energy that Mother Earth is releasing, as the lines come up they are often clogged with this energy. Those of you who work on such things might ask that as the lines come to the surface, any energy of discomfort be transformed and purified and cycled to where it will do the most good. In this way we can get the lines above the surface of the planet to look pristine. The color would be not quite white if you were to see it from a distance. It would be white tinged with gold; there would be a hint of gold light about it.

How deep were they before they started moving outward?

Any given ley line or grid line can be several hundred feet below the surface to perhaps only a few feet below, depending for the most part on surface activities. If there is mining or heavy construction, they are deeper. If the land has lain relatively untouched, it is closer to the surface. This tells you that in the natural state of being these lines are closer to the surface in order to nurture not only the planet but the population on the surface and to support and sustain the weather. Part of the reason the weather has been so erratic in recent years is because many of these lines had to go deeper inside the planet to escape the disruptive effects of mining and heavy construction (meaning a large building that has subbasements and foundations down four or five stories or more). This disrupts a lot of earth.

How far above sea level will the lines go?

They will go out into space, eventually looking like the cover of your magazine here [the March 1997 issue of the *Sedona Journal*].

I was going to mention that!

Expanded Grid Will Hold in Discomfort

That is why I brought it up. That illustration is quite prophetic. This grid will act to protect the Earth and hold in discomforting energy should the situation become extreme (more than 55%, which is a possibility). It will keep the discomfort from radiating out beyond the outer layers of Earth's atmosphere. The structure around Earth will probably be about 500 miles above the surface. This is perhaps beyond the atmosphere.

And beyond the satellites, although I don't know how far out they are.

Beyond most of them, but it will not harm any space traveler. One could easily fly right through a line and be unaffected.

Are we likely to reach over 55% negativity?

Of course it would be a short duration, but I would say the chances right now are for about 55 to 58%, possibly as much as 60%. This has a great deal to do—perhaps almost exclusively to do—with impatience. People are now beginning to get a glimmer of what life could be like in more benevolent circumstances, and it is difficult to maintain the patience for that to come about on its own. Thus there is a great deal of political upheaval, ofttimes in the form of war or some such thing. And there is a certain amount of "me-first-ism" (if I can use that term) happening now. I think this will be of short duration, but it is occurring. Perhaps it has certain advantages in that people are becoming more hypersensitive to their own needs. This is sometimes useful when people are waking up, because they will then realize many needs they were unconscious of before, but it can create a short-term discomforting situation.

"Short-term" meaning how long?

Three years perhaps, not much more than that.

Three years!

I would not be too concerned about it. The extremity of the discomfort will be spotty. It won't be all over the surface of the Earth everywhere. Most of the land under the sea will be safe. Many places where the populations are more sparse will not experience the extremity of the discomfort. Oh, they will have some, but it will not be so extreme. It is more likely that the discomfort will be felt in the short term in places where there is more population than is comfortable for the average person.

We're trying to get what I call a road map of infinity. Last November we asked you when you first became aware. You told us you became aware in that being who was moving. How far out can you see? We recently learned there was a paradoxical universe. How much can you see or how much can you know about what's out there?

I can see anyplace where matter exists, more with the mind's eye than the physical eye. Whatever matter exists consists of some form of plasma. Even that which you might call the space between things is also plasma. So I can see through to anyplace where this plasma exists. If it exists anywhere, I can connect with it and use it as a pair of eyes to observe, feel, sense, grasp and understand that which is around it. I might add that in your case as human being, anyplace where human beings exist or have ever existed *you also* can look through the eyes of such beings. It is perhaps safer to do this with beings who are in their own time, and you must always do this only with their permission, otherwise you will absorb some of their problems. What I am saying is that what I do is directly translatable to what *you* can do.

How far can you see? What's out there? We've learned that there are circles of union, then further back through the portal are various other realms. How much can you tell us about this?

Looking Beyond the Paradoxical Realm to the Origin of Awareness of Life

I can see past the circle. I can see the paradoxical realm with no difficulty because I do not have to observe it directly. I simply become a portion of it, since it contains matter and reflections of matter. I can see the crystal from which springs the paradoxical realm. I can see a little beyond that to the place of the awareness or the cognizance of life forms—it is a place. You have been asking beings when they became aware of being themselves. There is a place where this type of awareness is generated. This is what allows a baby Earth person or those up to and beyond Creator to become aware of their surroundings. This is the place of the cognizance of life, the recognition of life.

This place, if you were to experience it . . . since there is a cat presence, let's say you and your cat went to this place. You would, in that moment of being there, return to the first moment that you became aware of being a physical person in this life. In your case you would literally be inside your mother's body and have your first conscious awareness of becoming a physical human, whereas cat would move back slightly before physical life. Cats become aware of being physical cats slightly before they are actually consummated as egg and sperm, as it were. Their awareness precedes the actual union from which springs forth the kitten's body. So your cat would have that moment. You would both be resting very comfortably and experience an elongated moment of that cognizance. If you were to stay there for a time, you would then start experiencing the cognizant awareness of other lives as they began. If you stayed there for a long time, you would become aware eventually of your first moment of cognizance in any form of life.

Is this beyond the crystal?

Yes.

In the next realm?

It is a realm beyond that, because it requires beings who are in any way sentient to pass through this membrane at some point. In order to have thought or purpose or intention, one must be cognizant of one's own being, so at some point beings will pass through this membrane. By calling it a membrane I do not wish to suggest that it is very thin. But there is an aperture there, and one passes through the aperture.

Beings like you and the other friends of the Creator—would you have come from there?

Oh, I think all beings of immortal personality have passed through there, if not in the form in which you now are aware of them, then at some time and in some form that preceded their present form. It might have been the generation of their being before their now personality, but at some point one must pass through there so one can have an awareness of one's own personal being.

No matter where they go after that, whether they go to our symmetrical realm or the paradoxical realm or the other ones they don't know the names of, they still come from there?

According to the knowledge I have now, yes. It is certainly possible that there might be more than one of these membranes, but this is the only one I know of.

You have always known of this, or you only now looked into it?

I have had the interesting experience, not unlike cat, to be cognizant of the coming of my being.

Right, while the being was still moving.

Yes, so I believe that I have been aware of this membrane for some time.

But where were you when we talked before about your becoming aware within the being who created you as it was moving?

What I am saying is that before I became aware within the consciousness of myself, as I discussed before, it was like the spark of life or the distilled essence of my personality that passed through this membrane. The membrane generates the potential for cognizance. It does not give you the cognizance right there, otherwise it would be taking over as a creator. It gives you the potentials so that when you do become aware of yourself, and from that point on to some mission of some sort, you have the capacity to be aware of yourself. I can see past that point a little bit too, going further up the line (since that is our term now).

Our buzzword. [Laughs.]

The Next Two Places: Where Motion Happens and a Place of Emergence

Good, that is our buzzword, yes. Then let's see. There is a place where motion, as you know it, happens. If you go there, it is not a big place, but a place of initiation. This means that what precedes this place might not have the full range of motion it would have *after* it goes through here. If you look at this place from a distance, you would see things of different shapes moving in all different directions. Very often there will be a long, tubular tunnel-like shape rotating in place. Other shapes would be around it, tumbling or moving from side to side or up and down.

This is all designed to offer to the passerby a capacity for motion on the physical level. Since it is a dimensional being (a place, as it were), one can also experience the motion required to pass through great distances—as you say, portals. Portals are a higher-dimension motion. That is how they work. You get the mass of energy moving in a certain way; it is formulaic. When it moves in that precise way, regardless of how thick or thin a portal might be, as long as it is moving in that particular way it can be used as a transit device in time or space, even to a specific location. Portals are essentially motion and sometimes light in action.

Further up the line, let's see where I can go. I have not looked further up the line before, but I will. I see what looks like a place of emergence. It is again an opening. Behind the opening there is what I would call plasmic space moving through the opening. If you were to look out at the space between the stars, it would look like that. It is not dark energy; it is energy that has yet to be imprinted with anything that might displace it, such as a star or a person or what-have-you. It is the matrix upon which other life forms are impacting. This seems to be as far as I can look.

So that implies that someone is doing that.

I would say that is a being, yes.

How does the shape of it look?

Next: The Building Blocks of Plasma

It is fairly long and flat, and what is behind it is matter that is the stuff that precedes plasma, the building blocks of plasma. This is a pre-matter state in which this mass of energy would have no bias in any direction; it is entirely unbiased. I might add that if you were to find yourself floating within it, you would immediately lose any sense of agenda or purpose. It has, in that sense, no intention. As it passes through the aperture, it takes on (this is apparently the function of the opening) the excitement or enthusiasm of being what other matter will be imprinted on. It nurtures or holds other matter, like space might hold a sun or a star. This matter considers itself fortunate, moving from a fairly simple existence to one in which it might have tremendous variety in its future experiences.

Does that energy come directly into the symmetrical universe, does it go to another realm or does it go through all these other realms?

After that point it goes everywhere, to any realm where it is needed. And yes, it comes here and goes everyplace else.

So are these realms spherical or clumped together or long, skinny things that connect?

They are as big or as small as is needed on the basis of their function. At a given moment their function might have very little to do, and another moment they might have a great deal to do, depending on who or what is being created down the line (if I might use our other buzzword).

I'm trying to get a picture. Is there a big circle where the crystal was, and were all the rest . . .

No, it is not the same as the orbs, where one can essentially draw a map. It is not like that. It is more spontaneous in its shape and size.

The Crystal

So it can change. If the free matter comes through this emergence, what function does the crystal have, then? I thought that things were created there. What does the crystal do?

The crystal refines. It defines and refines matter—sorts it out, decides which realm it ought to go to, but it does not generate the matter.

But it all goes through the crystal before it goes someplace else?

It seems that much of it goes through the crystal, but I can see some of it going elsewhere.

And from the crystal it can go into all the realms?

Yes, all the realms that you have discussed. One must consider that if one were to explore all the realms—I do not think you have enough years left in your life for us to do that.

Really? The Master of Feeling said there were thirteen realms. So there are billions of realms and billions of circles of creation?

In my experience there are many, many realms. I do not like to take issue with the Master of Feeling, but perhaps the Master of Feeling has not explored the beyond.

She did it as a favor; she looked around.

The advantage of there being more is that as beings become sated with any given experience, the loving creator of *all* experience always provides more. Boredom must be chosen, but it is not a factor to be dealt with.

You have a little bigger picture here. Somebody said that if you go into the paradoxical universe, you can't come back because you'd be crazy. Are there other realms you can go into from the symmetrical universe and come back here? Or are they all so far from our logical, linear thought that we wouldn't be able to handle it?

The Mystical Realm; Personal Choice

I think you could experience the mystical realm, the realm in which everything that you now know plus more along the line of mysticism, is generated, felt, experienced and so on. I think you could go there and come back, but if you came back you might be a little bored with this place. When one expands one's awareness one always tends to go forward, not backward.

So is this the last to be created? Is this the end of the line?

There is no end. It is a thought, but in my experience that is *all* it is.

Well, is this like kindergarten, then?

Oh, no. I know you wish to define things progressively, but things are not progressive.

They're all just different.

Exactly. They are different. One stands in front of an array of doors. While they all lead to different places, which door is more equal than the others?

You have looked into those realms, but isn't this the only realm that you have experience in, done your work in?

I have had some experience in the paradoxical realm, because as Master of Plasma I do not have to be confused by the overwhelming expression of constant change in the paradoxical realm. I can remain focused in the mass of all energy. If I attempted to sort things out into the linear, I would be confused. The paradoxical realm is very much like what Zoosh has described as chaos—that which precedes creation. It would be many times over chaos, but without any repetition, meaning constant high-velocity, high-volume change without ever stopping. One would not have the capacity to stop and take a breather, as it were.

I know the purpose is to experience, but from our limited point of view, how can we understand why there is a paradoxical realm?

It is a funny thing that you're saying this, because I heard the same question in the paradoxical realm about the symmetrical realm! I think perhaps this goes hand in hand with wherever you happen to be. For them it is hard to conceive that anyone would want to have a life so slow, from their perception, in the symmetrical realm. I would best answer the question that way.

That's good. So we've got symmetrical, paradoxical, where the crystal is, the emergence, the mystical. Are there any other names or any other glimmers of feeling or purpose or type of experience?

I must agree with the Master of Feeling here and say that the other realms, at least around the crystal, are *so different* from the ones you experience now that to discuss it could have a catastrophic impact.

In what sense?

It would be like bringing the future into the present and then expecting that future to evolve. It couldn't evolve that way. That future simply wouldn't be in the future anymore. It would be in the present, and you would have torn a big hole in the time line.

Can we understand that those areas are really futures once we master what's here? Is there a progression? Do beings go from the symmetrical to these other realms?

Choice of Realm through One's Propensity or by One's Creator

Oh, no. It is a choice. You can, but you don't have to. There is no progression. I see that you really are interested in or attached to that idea, but it is not that way at all. After doing all you care to do in this realm, one might choose to go into the paradoxical realm, but one might easily say that in the paradoxical realm one might do the same—choose, just to see what it's like, to go into the symmetrical realm. I think you would find the symmetrical realm, coming from the paradoxical realm, a little slow for your taste, whereas I think the opposite would be true moving from the symmetrical realm to the paradoxical realm. I recall once a being from the symmetrical realm going into the paradoxical realm and staying less than about one-hundredth of a second and leaping out. But the being still required many hundreds of years to slow down and become balanced in the symmetrical realm again, essentially having to go off and rest for a time.

You said that the crystal defines and refines and directs, but how do beings choose which realm to become focused in?

To some extent it has to do with your original cognizance of your being, who you are—if you know who you are to some extent. When you know who you are, you just naturally go to the realm (or you might already be in that realm) in which you are intended to function. One does not so much choose as that one's propensity to do something or experience something makes the choice for you. You as an entity make that choice before you become conscious of your personality or being. Or if you had been a combined entity and you rebirth yourself and the rebirthed self is now you, you then choose your realm. Or it might be chosen for you if that which has birthed you has decided that that portion of itself is most interested in something. The decision will either be made by you in your precognizant state or by that being of which you were once a portion.

So your statement that the crystal defines but doesn't impose . . .

It defines and refines, meaning . . .

. . . a decision that's already been made.

Yes. It acts like a filter, sending some here and some there. If something falls between the cracks, as it often does, yet wishes to remain in the general area of the realms over which the crystal has some influence, then the crystal has the authority to refine that entity so that it will fit into one of those realms. Thus the crystal has the responsibility of a creator, because the crystal can change things. When you change things from their original form, a great deal of responsibility goes with that.

Obviously, some realms are faster and some slower. Since you can't describe this, how do you get a feeling for differences? Some might be your only color, some just feeling—is there no way to understand it?

Think of all the adjectives you use to describe things. There are no adjectives to describe these realms. Beings such as myself are not holding something back from you that language could define. There is no language, including telepathic, emotional telepathic or visual, no means of communication by which these realms could be defined to you in a way that would make any sense.

In our present condition.

The closest way for you to understand even one of these undiscussed realms would be if you've ever had a moment of insanity, even a moment, it would be ten times more intense than that—a moment where you felt like you were going crazy amplified ten times. That would not be the way the realm is, but it would be your immediate reaction to the realm were I able in some way to describe it to you.

We can get a feeling that they're very high-speed and very intense—even something like that helps.

Those are adjectives, so I would have to say no.

At least there's a sense of too much happening at one time for us to cope.

Yes, that is one way. It is a multidimensional, ultimately diverse, constant expression of constantly changing experience. That's as close as I can come.

That's good! Sounds cool. That's about as far as you can go in that direction, isn't it?

I think it is, in terms of what I can talk about.

The Limits of the Crystal's Authority

But that's wonderful! You've broadened and expanded it tremendously. One other thing: You said, about the crystal, "of the realms over which it has some influence" or authority, which implies that there are many realms in which it doesn't have authority.

The crystal has some authority to refine, but I would not say that it has that authority in all cases. Sometimes there are beings, as I say, who do not fall into the expression of any of the realms over which the crystal has some influence or contact. If the crystal and the being want to be refined, so be it, but if the being does not wish to be refined, then the crystal essentially sets the being aside and requests that someone—an emissary of a universe or realm where this being could express itself—come and pick up this being and take it where it can express itself. The crystal does not have absolute authority, just some. It does not have authority to change something against its will.

But the same principle operates even there, that when there is a need, someone will hear it and respond.

Yes, but in this case the crystal actually sends the message. It doesn't just set it aside and wait for it to be responded to. There is so much energy being produced by the crystal that it might take a long time for the message to go out. Knowing this, the crystal sends the message, broadcasts it in all directions throughout all times and all places, and simply waits for an emmissary to show up.

Could the being whose consciousness is the crystal communicate to us through Robert?

Oh, possibly. You can ask.

It fascinates me. I don't know why, but it feels familiar. So we come back home then. You came through a portal from the paradoxical realm to get to the symmetrical realm, right?

I did, yes.

The Shape of the Symmetrical Realms

All right, I don't think we've asked anyone. Is there a shape to this symmetrical realm? Is it square or circular or rectangular?

Oh, I think it is a flowing shape, what I would call—to use one of my favorite of your words—a blob, meaning that it changes shape according to its whim.

To its whim?

Yes, because in the larger sense, it is a massive being. A droplet of water has its own consciousness, yet it gets caught up in a wave and becomes a portion of a wave, enjoying the experience. But it might not create a wave on its own.

So if the symmetrical realm is a being, can it communicate?

It is worth a try.

[Laughs.] You want us to look through the eyes, but it's easier to have them talk.

Yes, that is perhaps best for a volume of print. [Chuckles.]

So you just came through the portal now and this blob is out there before you.

I don't think of it as a blob, but I am using that term because it is amusing and also because blobs are not . . .

. . . strictly defined?

Yes, they are not strictly defined, nor do they have to live up to the requirements of a specific shape.

As you look out on this amorphous shape now—let's say you just came through the portal. Are there circles of creation everywhere, or are they sort of gathered in one place? There's a place where personalities form in this realm, right?

In my experience circles of creation are not in one place. They are all over.

So they fill the whole shape?

Yes.

Millions, billions?

I have never counted. I can take a brief look. [Pause.] Certainly a billion or more.

And each one has, very roughly, universes—a million, a billion?

I do not think that they are slaves to numerical equivalency.

The number is just immense. That is all I'm reaching for. Awesome.

Yes, it is, as you say, infinite. The difficulty in defining infinity is that the definition is necessarily limited.

The Place Where Personalities Are Generated

I know, but this is a limited place. I'm just trying to get a picture. So are there roadways or pathways to it? Somebody defined a place in this realm similar to what you talked about, where it's just pure energy, then personalities seem to ...

Personalities are generated, yes.

Would that be close to the portal or in the middle? How does that work?

There is no road map where one follows the ten steps this way and ten steps that way. You have to remember that while these places might have vast amounts of space between them, one is in no way restricted as an immortal personality by that space. You might, for example, be in the amorphous shape of the symmetrical realm and in one moment pass through the place that helps you to be cognizant of yourself, though you are not particularly defined in personality, then the next moment be halfway across that realm where your personality is being defined, and in the moment after that be somewhere else. So space or distance has utterly no bearing on where you might go. You might or might not go on a progression like that.

According to my understanding, there is some progression in the beginning stages of cognizance of one's own personality. In this way one can fully experience all that follows on the personal level. When one has a personality, one can experience one's personal reaction to something as well as have the broader magnanimous view of a creator, for example. So I believe it is deemed a valuable tool to have a personality. I should think that to do my work without a personality would be dull to the extreme.

It seems to me like you'd be an automaton. You might as well be a machine. With a personality you can have a focus and point of view and experience and enthusiasm and all those things.

Yes, exactly. If there is one thing that is universal to all the realms, I would have to say that personal experience is universal.

The Creator and the Explorer Race

Okay, let's shift gears for a minute. We just learned that the Creator did not create the Explorer Race, that we were separate. Were you aware of that during the entire creation, or not?

No, I do not think I was aware of that. This tells you that the energies that came to be the Explorer Race must have already intersected with your Creator before I joined with your Creator.

Were you one of the last ones?

I think so, yes. I think your Creator had already collected many beings before I was collected.

As you look back on the process of the creation, does it make more sense knowing that there were two parts to the Creator? He said that we helped create things that He had to have a great deal of faith in—ignorance and suffering.

And your question is? Not clear, I'm sorry.

Does it make more sense if you look back and see that there were two parts to the Creator, that It wasn't all one?

Two parts?

The Explorer Race and the Creator.

Oh, of course there are more parts to the Creator than the Explorer Race. There are more than two parts to this Creator. That is why the question is giving me some difficulty, because your Creator is not made up of two parts.

I understood there was the Creator, then the Explorer Race was something separate that He was carrying.

Oh, but I am going back before the time when your Creator was in the creator mold, as it were, in which It was birthed out of something else, in which case the impression of that is always on you. Going back up the line, anytime something was a part of something else, that impression stays with you. My perception is that Creator is made up of more than two parts, but if you are saying that the Explorer Race and the Creator are separate beings, I would say they arrived by different avenues with similar objectives in mind.

I've kind of run down.

Then let me just say this. Plasmic energy is that which gives life and the potential for definition to all that is around and about you. For you to truly experience yourself, it will be an interaction between your immortal personality and some other immortal personality. But all of this, including your personalities, is ultimately made up of plasma, as it is expressed in this realm. Know that you have more in common that unites you than there could ever be that keeps you apart.

I have another question. You implied that the Creator, when He went through the centrifuge with his grandfather, I guess you could call it, has parts or impressions of the being from the Void and the inverse universe and . . .

I am saying that the spirit line (if we can use that term instead of bloodline) that preceded you necessarily affects who and what you are, because that is your lineage. That is what I'm saying.

Tracing Lineages of Members of the Explorer Race

How could we best understand ourselves, the Creator and the Explorer Race more? How would you trace our lineage if you were seeking it?

Simply this: You have heard your Creator's lineage explained to you. Although that impacts your personality, because you have come from before that the best thing you can do is trace your lineage back as far as it goes. Parts of you go back so far and other parts of you go back before that. You do not all come from the same place or have the same length of experience. Some of you preceded others, but just because you preceded others, those who followed did not grow out of you. They came from other places but perhaps did not have the length of experience you had in your core being. Maybe that is because they did not need it, allowing for who and what they would become. If, for example, one is to have patience in the essence of one's being, one would need to have a great deal more experience than a being who would have spontaneity as its essence.

I see. Where would you start?

I would ask for the root beings of the Explorer Race to speak, to discuss where they're from, what they did, how they came to be here and so on, as you have been doing. I would ask if they had anything that preceded them that they were aware of, and could that also speak, as you have already been doing. In that way you would get the essential personal experience of the root beings of the Explorer Race. The root beings would be the sort of spherical, sort of the roots (words fail me here) . . . they were something like spheres of root beings of the Explorer Race from which all other beings have sprung—like eggs, but eggs without shells.

Okay, we'll ask for them and see who shows up.

I would try that. Then you would get some kind of a personal response, because these root beings had personality even though they might have been affected by other personality-supplying entities or have broken up into many different personalities. I would pursue it from that direction.

Thank you for doing my homework. Thank you very, very much.

You're welcome. Good night.

The Master of Discomfort

February 24, 1997

ll right. I am Master of Discomfort. Not the most jolly title ever depicted on an individual, but necessary for your evolution, perhaps.

Can't you come up with a new name? I've just been reading the two sessions from the Friends of the Creator *book, and you have awesome abilities that have nothing to do with discomfort.*

Yes, but understand that although I have mastered other things, it requires depth and commitment to master discomfort, to learn everything there is to know about all aspects of it, as with any mastery, "discomfort" describing anything from the slightest annoyance to the greatest pain. It is to help others navigate the experience as simply and benevolently as possible. It was not necessarily a pleasant education, but once I had it, I am now able to help others avoid a lot of it. Thus my services have been more in demand these days by not only your own peoples, but also peoples who are going to be involved in a minor degree of discomfort.

Assisting the Pleiadians

I have recently spoken to the academic councils on Pleiades who want some guidelines on how to prepare their people for minor annoyance, which their people have never had to deal with on a personal level. I have discussed ways to prepare them for such eventualities. This is going to be a reality for them within the next generation, perhaps as early as in the next five or six hundred years of their experiential time. This means they must become prepared now, because generations being born now will have to adapt at some point in their lifetimes to discomfort, which is unknown to them. So there is a demand for what I have to offer.

That's wonderful! Will that result from the Explorer Race going to the Pleiades?

Yes.

Is that the first place we will go?

No, but you will, in your travels, long before you go to the Pleiades, meet ships, beings . . .

They will come here.

Or they will be out there in space as they are now. As you travel around you will run across other ships and have social interactions. The Pleiadians must be prepared to recognize that some of that interaction will affect their people, and when the people come back with a degree of discomfort experience integrated into themselves, they will have to know how to deal with it.

When Pleiadians Meet Competitive
Sports and Communications

I'll tell you one of the first things that will happen. When you as the Explorer Race are traveling in space and meet the ships and have social interactions with them, one of the first things you will expose the Pleiadians to is competition. To you, competition is mostly healthy. Sports or games are considered a benevolent form of competition even though sometimes it goes well into discomfort. This will be new to them. People will want to play card games or even checkers, where someone wins and someone does not. They will bring these games back to their people, saying, "Here's a game played on Earth," because games are important to the Pleiadians. It will introduce the entirely new experience of one who wins and one who loses, and that is certainly potentially annoying.

So I have discussed games with them at length. I have also discussed with them the idea of competitive communications, which they did not understand. They had no idea what I was talking about. Here's an example of competitive communications, and not even in an argument: Two people are talking on the phone. They start talking at the same time, each competing for the ear of the other. The Pleiadians are not prepared to deal with competitive communications now, but I told them that that is another thing they will come up against.

They will experience reactions in themselves that have had no cultural history. This means they will discover in competitive communications that they are also competitive, even though they've never been exposed to it in their own culture. It won't happen right away, but it will happen and it will literally send a shock wave through their culture. So they'll need to know how to deal with it.

Can we leap beyond the confines of the Explorer Race and out beyond this circle of union, asking how you see? I'm trying to get a road map of infinity. Is the inverse universe you came from connected to this Circle of Creation?

The Reverberation Effect Back to One's Origin

No. It is associated with a place that is hard to describe in any terminology, so I will describe it by what it does rather than what it is. Beings who come from that universe tend to have a perpetual sense of themselves. This means that the concepts I learn, especially in this level of mastery, tend to immediately affect me, my personality, from the moment of my becoming aware of my personality—and into the future, because any learned concept would affect the future and also the past. So there is what I would call the reverberation effect of the beings from my place of origin.

If I have come to a sudden consciousness, then that consciousness, aside from relating to the future, also relates to the past, yes? And since it relates to the past, that alters my future from the past to my present. So I become more of a being. Do you understand? Not only do I have the discovery of that new thing in the present, it goes back into the past and reverberates into my present so I become more. It continues to reflect like that until it has reverberated and accomplished all it can—and of course the future, too. The tremendous impact of the experience is not only from the present awareness of this new thought or experience, but from the total change of my past.

The Trill of *Aha!*

I'm elaborating on this because it is similar for you. If this reverberation didn't take place, it would simply be a new thought, a new concept, a new way of considering my world, yes? But because of the reverberation effect, I have the capacity to see and do things in an entirely new way. This means that many more tools are thrown into my bag of tricks, as it were. Now, this is something that to a slightly lesser degree affects you as well. I'll give you an example. When you or anyone in your culture reads something, discovers something or hears about something that causes a sudden insight, there is ofttimes a physical experience with that realization—the *aha!* But it is more than strictly a thought, it is actually like a trill—a trill that goes through the body (not a thrill), an actual feeling.

For you to have that experience of the *aha!*, you also have the reverberation effect. The reason you have that experience is because you also get the reverberation effect that goes back to your birth, to who you are in this life only. For me, it goes back to my first awareness of my personality. The reason you have a physical feeling at all is because of that reverberation. So we have that in common.

But we didn't come from an inverse universe. How did we get it?

No, you have that experience because I discussed it with your Creator, and your Creator wanted you to have a conscious landmark you could recognize as physical evidence that something was important. Originally your Creator thought it would be good for you to have a flash of light that you could see. After I discussed it with Him and other consultants, we all came to the conclusion, including your Creator, that that might be too distracting, that a physical feeling might be better. So your Creator decided to give you that physical feeling. Then no matter what you were doing, you would notice it, but it would not interfere with your experience.

My Continuing Connection to My Original Group Awareness

That is one of the things about the place I am from. No matter who comes from there and where they go, they always have a strong connection to that place. Even though I am speaking now and I am in your universe, I am there also. Everyone in that universe experiences everything in terms of new knowledge, new experiences, new understandings, including anyone who came from that universe and went someplace else.

Sort of like a group mind?

It's like a group awareness, because it goes past the mind. They have the physical experience, the physiological impact. They have all of that evidential experience, so that every time anybody comes out of that universe, they have all the experience of the other beings who came out of that universe to go on. Thus it tends to improve the beings as they come out in succeeding generations.

But they don't all focus on what you call discomfort?

Oh, no. This is just my chosen area for this moment. This moment will last most likely until the end of this Creator's experience here. Possibly I will stay on with you; more likely, as of this moment, you will have someone who will replace me. I would say that at some point in the future I will be practicing a different level of mastery. I have attained a few, because if you become Master of Discomfort, you will have had to master a few other things just to be able to endure the lessons of discomfort while you are learning it thoroughly, you understand.

Say more about that.

Achieving Other Masteries: Earth Wars and a Volcano

Well, I had to master a few other things. I had to master physical feelings. How I could grasp the impact of discomfort in its many variations if I didn't have a physical vehicle by which that discomfort could be felt or measured? So I had what I would call snippets of physical lives. I would extend myself, not ceasing to be what I am, but creating a physical extension that would live somewhere for a few years. Wherever this place was would be a place where I would learn something about discomfort or have some kind of feeling of discomfort, and have the full impact of that feeling.

Have you been anybody we would historically have heard about?

Let's see. I think I had a brief life as a soldier in the Peloponnesian War, which goes back a ways. It was there that I learned about valor, because even though one experiences valor or extreme courage, one often does so in the context of pain within a war. I learned about that there. The only modern warfare experience associated with your planet's culture at this time, I think, was in the Korean War. I was a North Korean soldier for a short time, experiencing the bitter cold of winter . . . as Koreans like to say, you don't know winter until you've had a winter in Korea.

Is it worse than South Dakota?

It is, because South Dakotans have a warm culture.

Koreans are cold emotionally and cold . . .

Well, not cold emotionally, but private emotionally. Koreans are private with their feelings. Their feelings are demonstrated to themselves and their immediate associates and family. You have to understand that about them; they are a very unusual culture. I experienced that then. Let's see, what else.

Are these like walk-ins, or do you create the body?

No, these are not walk-ins, because it would be unkind to project the persona of myself into somebody else's body. No, I would create a body for a brief duration. What else here? Ah, yes. I had an experience in more ancient times on this planet, experiencing in a small tribal situation, more of a clan, going without food and sometimes water. That life was one in which there were about four or five experiential years, dying as a result of a volcano, which is not particularly pleasant. But I had to learn that, didn't I?

Were all the lives that you chose discomforting? Were there ever any that . . .

Well, they always had other aspects besides discomfort, as in the Peloponnesian War experience, where I was exposed to the extreme courage of all soldiers around me, plus my own. One might say, yes, there was discomfort, but it was commingled with other experiences.

My Orion Anarchist Experience

What about places like Orion or other planets?

I experienced briefly on Orion, being a member of the Black League during the initial experience of cultivating its philosophy.

But you were separate, you did not create Lucifer.

No, no, no, no, no, no, no, no, no.

The Creator created Lucifer.

Yes. It was illuminating in that society, being not so much a terrorist (with a small *t*, because those acts of terror would not compete with the terrorism of your times) as an anarchist.

But there was a great purpose, a great sense of righteousness, a lot of those kinds of feelings connected with it, weren't there?

Yes, it would come closest to the experience of being a revolutionary, revolting for some higher purpose, as it were.

I know that one.

I experienced a lot of self-destruction and guilt there. During many of the early days of the Black League, you know, the people were haunted by a sense of guilt because they were sometimes creating harm for people they loved and cared about. It was not necessarily directly, but their actions created it indirectly. I learned about guilt and self-destructiveness in that brief experience. Having these experiences, also in other forms, has allowed me to truly understand discomfort.

One of the other forms I experienced was the collective auric field of an area near a stream where there were fairies and flowers and much beauty, wondrous beauty. This is not to cast blame on beings for being themselves, but at one point a bear crashed through that area, a very large bear—I think what you call a grizzly bear—followed by several hunters. The auric field, the energy of that place, suffered terribly for having beings sort of crash through the middle of it. I learned then about energy-body suffering and repair. There are lots of levels to this, you know. It takes time to assimilate the experience enough so that you can speak to other beings and actually have something to offer other than your own personal experience.

My Future

What are some career choices that you might make after this one?

Oh, I think that I will probably go into mastery teaching about physical feelings. I've also learned positive and benevolent feelings because I've always picked circumstances where the contrast would be available. When you have a benevolent feeling and then a feeling of discomfort, the contrast is quite striking.

What would you teach?

If I'm still in this universe, I'll probably choose to teach the beings who are inheriting your third dimension of Earth because they'll need to have teachers like me who understand their discomforts and do not judge them in any way, teachers who can also teach them about the value of benevolent experience as both an individual and a group circumstance. They will need to have teachers who can understand thoroughly their own difficult experiences in their culture.

How would you do that? Would you appear to them, or would you channel through somebody?

I would probably appear, taking for a short time their form or create a form that is slightly different in order to be enough of an outsider so that I could have knowledge they don't have without their being suspicious of me.

They would then be comfortable.

Yes, but I also have to be able to prove myself to them, not necessarily doing something destructive, but doing something that requires endurance.

Okay, let's stretch out a little bit more. We've had all these talks about realms. This is the symmetrical realm. Is this inverse universe in this symmetrical realm, or is it closer to the paradoxical realm? Can you say a little more about where it is?

It's beyond the paradoxical realm. It's so difficult to describe.

We have such limited understanding, yes.

A Demonstration of the Feeling of the Inverse Universe

I'll tell you what. This is difficult to imagine, so touch your fingertips together, press them toward each other, then form kind of a . . .

. . . steeple.

A steeple, yes, then quickly snap them back so that your fingernails are touching, back and forth quickly like that, back and forth. Or snap a piece of cardboard back and forth. At the moment when whatever is being snapped back and forth, being in the exact middle and anticipating the next motion, whether snapping backward or forward, anticipating the next motion and remembering the last motion is a feeling that one has in the inverse universe.

It's in one of the realms, what they're calling the realms on the other side of that crystal?

Yes, yes. It's in one of the realms that has not been described to you because it's really beyond, it is so different. It is not evolved—it is and it isn't, but it is so different as to not really have a direct translation in your experience.

We Travel Everywhere, Adding Our Experience to Our Native Land

I understand. So you went into this realm. Do your peers go into all the realms?

Yes, everywhere. There's no limit there because they'll usually go out, checking with the others. They always learn several things to the mastery level, then teach of those things so that the native land (if I might call the place I'm from) will have not only the experiences one learns achieving mastery, but also the wisdom one attains when applying the achieved mastery.

You share all of this learning with your peers, and your native inverse universe also shares it.

Everybody else who's from there.

The place also receives this wisdom?

Oh, yes, yes, so that every succeeding being who comes out of there has all this knowledge, experience and wisdom.

Got it! I thought that all the beings who came out had it, but it goes back to your creator.

No, it goes back to the whole universe. Every succeeding generation has assimilated that experience so that they don't have to repeat it; they can do something more, build on it.

Then there is a creator of this native land.

Oh, certainly.

You have traveled through these other realms, and you can go because you use your feelings, not your thoughts?

The Paradoxical Realm

I wouldn't say that exactly. I can travel through the paradoxical realm because I have mastered discomfort. I do not let it distract me. If I have some discomforting experience, I've already mastered that feeling and I will feel it to its totality and go on.

So the chaos and the reflections don't . . . you've mastered that?

Yes, whatever I feel going through there, I feel it to its utmost and continue to go through it. I have the capacity to experience it and keep on going.

That's great, because Zoosh originally had said that he would go crazy if he went there and came back. But I discovered later that those who follow feelings can traverse it.

That's right. If you go there as an intellectual being, you will most likely become permanently confused. But if you set your thoughts aside and go through on the level of feeling, feeling your feelings, then you can experience it.

You do it by feeling everything and mastering it. Some of them just follow what's comfortable.

I mastered the feelings before I got there, so whatever feelings I have I will have already had. I know the feeling, so it is not a stranger; there's nothing for me to be afraid of. I do not have to worry about being able to tolerate the feeling. I can tolerate it because I've experienced it.

There's nothing anywhere left for you to do.

Anywhere that I've been; let's say that. Since I am a being who is experiential, I would have to say anywhere I've been.

Have you or anyone else ever gotten above the realms and looked down, or have you always been inside them?

I know what you're saying. It seems as though it ought to be possible to have some perspective, where you stand off at a distance and look at it. But in my experience, no matter which direction you go, you continue to go into life. One can theoretically, as an astronaut, go to the Moon and stand off and look at Earth from a distance and experience the whole thing. But nevertheless one is still in one's solar system. The comparison is similar. I am not aware of anyplace where one can totally leave any form of creation. Even if you're in something that appears to be nothingness, you can be certain that that is the level of that creation. One can stand off at a distance, as it were, and observe many, many creations, but you will be doing it *from* a creation, in my experience.

I wanted to see if they were circular or . . . one being said they were whatever shape they needed to be.

Yes, they are in motion. I have not seen . . .

Even the symmetrical ones?

Yes, it moves. It is a fascinating thing in that we know that the tiniest cell or atomic structure has motion, a life of its own. It moves, yes, even the most massive.

So a realm is ultimately a being.

Yes!

Aha!

There's a trill for you.

That's right! [Laughs.]

A realm is a being, and one could assume that many realms make up some larger being.

There are probably clusters of realms.

For all we know it goes beyond that. But certainly a realm, just like a universe, is a living organism made up of many parts.

The Spinning Crystal

So did you go through the crystal?

I actually experienced the crystal because I need to experience things, understanding what I wanted to master, aside from physical feeling and a few other things. I can't just look at them and think about it. So yes, I went through the actual center of the crystal on its central axis. It spins in both directions, and I can assure you it spins in both directions simultaneously. While one is spinning one way—and we're not talking about cylinders within cylinders—it is actually spinning in both directions at the same time.

It's a very interesting experience. It is perhaps the best place I can think of, in terms of my experience there, where one can change the past, the present and the future in a blink, in a twinkling. One experiences in the center all levels of oneself, all potential pasts (not just probable), presents and futures. One can choose a different past if one knows one's past up to that point in time, and as you go through (as slow or as fast as you like), you can literally experience that past. If it isn't quite right, you can make changes or just experience it, then reassimilate the actual past that you lived. But going through it, I noticed that you could make very powerful changes. I chose to experience many different pasts, but when I came out I reassimilated my own past so that I could be myself, as it were.

There wouldn't be any purpose in going back there to change the past that you lived in this creation, because you learned so much from it you don't want to change it?

Yes, I don't want to change it because what I am is a result of having lived it. You can understand this. I am a result of that experience, and I have chosen that. Think about that for a moment.

When you get through here, there's no reason for you to go back to your native land because you're in communication and contact with it all the time.

That's right. I could go, but as you say, there is no need.

Is there anyone else from your native land in this Circle of Creation?

No, but interestingly enough, there are not that many of them who've gone out. If I might describe myself as an individual, then there are no more than about 1300 individuals who have gone out.

Since the beginning?

Since I became aware of who I am and, as a result, was able to look at the streams going out. Everybody who's gone out from that realm leaves a light stream that is perceptible to anybody from that realm. So when I became aware of myself, there were already several hundred light streams that had gone out.

Feeling Rejected at Birth

I remember when you told us of your coming to awareness, how incredibly sad it was. You felt so rejected. Is that the way everyone comes into awareness there?

Yes. I think that this is something you can actually identify with if you have experienced some therapies associated with birth. Babies, being born in the style in which you are born here (except for those born in sacred circumstance, especially a water birth) often feel a sense of rejection when they leave their mothers. It is somewhat intended, so that one is immediately initiated into the challenges of polarized emotions. One feels ultimately nourished when inside one's mother, yes? But when one is born there is a great sense of loss. And it is that sense of loss and abandonment and rejection that everyone can identify with in your culture, because they all experienced it simply by being born.

This is intended by your Creator so that you would have physical and emotional evidence that there is more to your life. Even if you don't have any authority (any authoritative book, text or philosophy, person, anything) to tell you that these feelings are justified, you will innately know that there must be more. These feelings, though they are uncomfortable, are designed to give you absolute physical evidence and knowledge that there is more. It is that knowledge that ultimately allows you, when you come to the end of your natural cycle, to quickly assimilate the crossover to the other side. When you are presented with your guide or angel or whoever comes to escort you in your personality to the other side, you are immediately presented with evidence that there is more, and it feels wonderful. This is so you don't cling to your physical life well past the point of torturous discomfort. You will go because you know there's more, you just know it. Even if you're not a religious person, you know it.

There was another word you had used that was not common in the physical life here—you felt so "alienated."

When I left, you mean?

As you were ejected.

Yes, because when one is in the inverse universe, one experiences completely. Every moment is like a repetitive tide, a reciprocal tide. The way the tide comes in, it just keeps coming in; it comes, it goes, it comes, it goes.

Wisdom and feelings.

Traveling from the Native Land

Wisdom and feelings from other beings, then you go out individually, having assimilated that. Although you can assimilate it, you don't have it in the same way. It's not the same feeling. It becomes more of a thought, because you must begin to generate your own experiences and feelings, which are passed back to the native land to others who've gone out and to those who will follow.

But it was very touching, that sense of rejection.

Yes.

Well, this is fascinating. You went into the crystal and you chose where you wanted to go. You weren't sent.

Yes, I chose. I went into the crystal, and I might add that it was quite an extraordinary experience. But yes, exactly; I chose where I wanted to go.

Which means that somehow, even though you haven't traveled around, you knew what the choices were.

Well, I think it was by instinct rather than by plan. You might not be sure whether you want to go to town or drive into the country, but without really thinking about it, you turn one way or another. It was more instinctual.

It wasn't that you knew all the various choices mentally.

No.

You headed in a certain way because you were answering a need.

Yes.

Would you say that all of those 1300 beings who leave your native land go where they go because they're answering a need?

I must believe this, yes. I have come to this conclusion and I believe it. As a matter of fact, I think that's true for every being everywhere. According to what I have learned in my experience, every being, in whatever form they incarnate, is not only doing something for themselves, but also answering a need of others. Thus you see how you are one and that you truly need each other.

You know, when you have been one with a group of beings, the experience of not being exposed to those beings is too terrible to contemplate. If a being is unavailable to you in one of your lives here on Earth, you will very often have dreams with that being, which make contact with that being available. That's another reason dreams can be so elaborate and multileveled; sometimes beings you must be in contact with are simply not available in your physical life. You are really a portion of some larger thing, and to not have it available is impossible. You are in a physical world here where things must be felt and touched, so in your dreams you feel things, you touch things. They are physical, it is real.

You have so much to share that we could go almost anywhere with the discussion. You're teaching now. I didn't realize it so much before, but as you talk, you keep bringing it back to here and now. You're teaching how it works. You're a good teacher.

Well, thank you. It is necessary, you see, because not only are *you* learning, but you represent the reader who will, for the most part, be on Earth—at least at this time [they laugh], save for future generations and interplanetary trade.

So when we get into an interplanetary Internet, we can put the books on the Internet, right? [Laughter.]

Yes, and since the Internet is broadcast right now, it is available off-planet as well.

One of the beings here said to one of the people who came that that was a very crude way to get the information, and they'd rather do it telepathically.

Well, everyone has his own opinion.

[Laughs.] I like these different opinions. Well, this is the Beyond *book. What else would you like to say as you struggle to get a picture of the immensity of what is?*

My Zeta Reticuli Experience

Joopah discussed the Zeta Reticuli experience [see chapter 10 in *The Explorer Race*]. In the beginning of the Zeta Reticuli culture . . .

You were there, yes! You incarnated there.

Yes, in the beginning I had a short experience there, and I also had to learn things there. In the beginning of their culture they were very open to possibilities. They were intellectual even then, but they were assimilative beings. They had heard about emotions and feelings, and even today if the Zeta beings do something, they like to do it to its maximum. You wouldn't think that of them today, but you have to understand that now they are being mental and they are doing *that* to its maximum, you see? That is really their nature.

In those early days they were doing emotions to the maximum. Then they added senses and sensuality and all of these things and did *that* to its maximum. As a result, they experienced contradictory actions and contradictions to their own philosophy. It was not exactly violence in the beginning, but they were experiencing something that was out of balance, as a motor will shake when it's out of balance. Since they all felt it, after a while, though not immediately, they all began to be out of balance. First the culture went out of balance, then all individuals in the culture.

That's when they started to experience violence and sexual violence. When they were experiencing that as a society, I was incarnated as one of their beings who was attempting at that time to talk them into being more philosophical, into stepping back and observing things like that but not necessarily directly participating in them. As often happens to philosophers, I did not survive that experience because violence tends to feed on itself. This is why violence is by its very nature self-destructive, from my perception.

Their Addiction to Sensation

As a result, I learned a great deal then about discomfort and temptation. In temptation, one might be tempted to do something benevolent (yes, I will allow for that), but in this particular context people were tempted to do something destructive to themselves or others because they were addicted to sensation. They couldn't go without sensation because at their core, as I said, Zeta beings must do everything to its total experience.

For an individual Zeta being, especially in that time, to experience the maximum experience in anything, once the whole culture was experiencing the maximum, then whatever that maximum was would be multiplied four or five times. Thus one could easily quadruple or quintuple the experience on the sensation level. The entire culture would be experiencing something and one would *desire* to have the entire culture experience something. Self-interest was built in. You'd want to spread the behavior around because the more people who were doing it, the more you would revel in the experience and the stronger the sensation would be.

I'm bringing up this experience that Zeta Reticulans had because it correlates to some of your own experience. They had a clan structure then, and the heads of clans began to realize that they couldn't go on like this, that they would have to make an effort to have these experiences as a fantasy or as a memory, not as a real experience. That's why focusing on being a mental being looked so good then. They could still fantasize about these things and remember what they experienced or saw without having to actually create it.

The Zetas' Solution to Violence

That's how the decision was made, and over time and many generations they gradually let go of those fantasies and memories because beings were continually being created who had no memories of it. Thus it was left behind, and the only thing they had left were visual pictures that had been created, not unlike a docudrama you might have today, only their theater could broadcast feelings. They would have a regulator like a knob by which they could turn up or down the feelings of what was being broadcast, a sort of three-dimensional art form. It would have been an actual experience of the time. They could turn the feelings up so the people in the audience could experience the feelings as other beings felt them, but as succeeding generations came along and couldn't tolerate those feelings, they turned it way down.

Eventually they had turned it down so low (because they couldn't experience that kind of sensation) that the only way they could watch it since they were required to be educated about their society, was by doing a premeditation to generate calm beforehand. As a result of having to view their own history in this three-dimensional image, a feeling of calm, this focus on the mind, is what was left. Remember that after decisions are made, the actual application and experience of the decision plays out differently as the years go by. They are still maximum beings, but they are maximum *mental* beings.

I mention this to you because this is the direction *your* society could go. Your society is now at the point where it also requires cooler heads. The heads of clans, to use the term of the time on Zeta, must make the choice, "This is how we must go." In your lifetime I believe you will see this happen. It will not only be heads of governments, but heads of religions, leading members of philosophies, even patriarchs of families or groups of beings, well-loved beings. Many beings will form a consensus and say, "This is how we must be," then put into systematic application how they will get to that place. It will start out one way, as it did with the Zetas, then it will gradually evolve into something else. In order to become your natural spiritual beings, you will have to do that.

Thus I learned a great deal about temptation there, and that the opposite of temptation is *not* self-sacrifice or self-denial, as would appear to be the case and what the clan leaders of the Zeta civilization of that time demonstrated, but clarity, vision and application. Clarity is what they had, a vision of how things might be. They applied how it could be, and succeeding generations gradually turned it into something else, as any creative beings would do.

But they re-created themselves?

They re-created themselves, that's right. In the contacts many of you have had with Zetas in your lifetimes, there has been such a large gap because the Zetas perceive you as a product of your society. Remember that they always think of themselves, not as an ant, but as an individual, and in the larger society that individual is compounded on a personal level by the larger society's experience. When all other Zetas are expanded in the mind, then all individuals personally also have that expansion in the mind. That's why they've come to be known as beings of a group mind, although they're not exactly that. In any event, this is an important history for your people to consider, because you are really very much at the point now that the Zeta beings were when they changed their minds, if I can put it that way.

Your Connection to the Zetas

Did we as souls incarnate in those bodies? Do we have those experiences in our souls?

As a probable future, a very distinct future possibility, yes. Their present is your potential future, but in terms of their past, when they went through all of that, yes, some of you in the Explorer Race were there, but you left before the decision was made. This was a multigenerational experience of sensation to its maximum.

We experienced the sensation, but we left before they emphasized the mind.

Yes, you did.

So we are those future Zetas' past, because their past is our past?

Their past experience and your past experience, not only on Earth but on other planets, is quite similar, yes. So there is a compatibility in soul cultural experience.

What percentage of what we are calling the souls of the Explorer Race actually had an experience during those really violent, sexually upset, sensual times on Zeta Reticuli?

Oh, I should think slightly less than one-quarter of one percent.

Oh, that small?

But it isn't small when you think about it. Remember what Zetas experience: If one experiences the maximum of what the individual can do and then as a society as they all experience that, the individual has quadrupled or quintupled his personal experience. You are *exactly* like that as beings right now. You are no different. I will give you an example, which is one of the reasons people are attracted to church experiences.

When an individual goes to church where there are many people and they pray or sing a wonderful religious song, enjoying the experience, they reach a level of religious fervor, and at the end they are ecstatic. The level of ecstasy they can reach as a group is higher than they can reach as an individual, but each has an individual experience. Using that as an example (certainly there are others), you correlate directly to the Zeta Reticulans in this way. That's another reason they're fascinated with you. They know that even though you look so different (you are both humanoids, but you look different) and express yourselves very differently, the similarities between you vastly outweigh the differences. That is why they will always be connected with you in some way even as both societies evolve. They are, on the experiential level, really first cousins.

Yet they are not part of what we call the seed Explorer Race?

No, as the society now they are not, but some Explorer Race beings have been Zetas at various times. Some Explorer Race beings have been Zetas during times that are more familiar to you today, because one might incarnate after a particularly dramatic life on Earth into some culture that is peaceful, calm, interesting and studious and so on, such as the Zeta culture, to experience a life there.

I was told that during the Dark Ages when there was no technology here, many of us were active mentally, and that's where we went.

Yes, that is one place. There were other places to go, but Zeta is attractive that way because they are always seeking new knowledge and seeking to do more with what they have. Remember that knowledge or intellectual capacity carried to its maximum always seeks more.

If that holds true, they should experience the maximum out of spirituality, which is their next step, right?

Yes, and they are somewhat spiritual right now. But whatever they do, they will do it to its maximum. That is the way they do things. If you think about your society, there are a lot of similarities there. Your society does not tend to go into things slightly or half-heartedly; it is all the way or not at all.

Damn the torpedoes!

Yes, many similarities there. That is part of the reason I needed to experience the Zeta beings. At the time I went there, the Explorer Race had not gotten that far. The vast amount of the Explorer Race beings were still going through mostly benign experiences, and this extreme situation in the Zeta Reticuli star clusters was one of the few places one could go to experience such things.

I never asked you, but you had the ability to look into the future to see where we were going?

Your Own Interaction with Your Futures

Yes, but if one looks when one is in time, one tends to see the possible futures from that time and experience. In the vaster context of myself I would see many, many levels of futures. It is as if one is looking at a factory where thread is made and there are loose threads all over the place. It is a vast potential even now, as any individual such as yourself or anybody else reading this might gather. There might be, in just the next five or six months, hundreds of potential ways in which you could live. I am really being conservative. I suppose if I counted every nuance of possible change, it would be thousands or tens of thousands, but I am counting only main possibilities.

Yet there is part of our soul that experiences those, right?

Yes, that's right. Part of you experiences it because of who you are. You experience your vast potential on some level in that self. One tends to experience it more in a knowledgeable, current memory fashion, in a more benevolent life. But when one is in a more dramatic life such as here on Earth, one will often assimilate those potentials on a more feeling level, a vibrational level, an unconscious or even subconscious level. That is why sometimes you will have a reaction to something, based not on your linear experience in this life, but on one of those alternate futures or even an alternate past.

It's my limited understanding that to go into this narrow portal to the fourth dimension, we have to integrate all of those probable and possible realities into this being here now?

Yes, but only for moments. Remember that one moves ahead on this juggernaut toward the fourth dimension, not because in every moment one comes together to experience the totality of one's being, but these moments come and go—here for a second, there for five seconds. Another few weeks go by and then for another five or six seconds one feels that totality. Do you understand? It is in those moments of totality that one moves forward. One does not have that complete union and then go forward in total union. It is a staccato experience.

Your Total Merging in Ninth Dimension

Got it! When do we merge, connect, become—at what stage on the dimensional ladder do we merge with all the parts of ourselves?

Generally speaking, in this universe, when you have achieved or when you have focused into ninth dimension.

Oh, it's that far away?

But it isn't far away. You are thinking in terms of this Explorer Race phenomenon, this planet. At the end of this cycle of life for yourself or any reader, you could very easily go into a ninth-dimensional life in your next life, linearly speaking. Having experienced that for a time, you could then go to a fourth-dimensional life. So it is not a soul progression. You have to reach or stretch from the higher dimensions to come to this dimension, but if you just let go at the end of your natural cycles, you will naturally bob right up, as it were, to the higher dimensions because that is your nature. You are higher-dimensional beings, but the tough lessons of creatorship happen in the denser dimensions where consequences are immediately experienced physiologically as well as mentally and theoretically. If you tie your shoe laces together on the ninth dimension, you probably don't fall, you fly.

[Laughs.] I keep tripping on mine.

Here one has entirely a different experience. [Chuckles.] That's why ninth-dimensional beings who've never been here or anyplace like this really can't understand why people go through this suffering. Believe me, a being who has always been ninth-dimensional would understand conceptually that you would fall down, but they wouldn't understand experientially what pain is. They wouldn't understand that, and that's why I had to become physical—in order to have the compassion necessary to help beings deal with discomfort. One must speak from personal experience, otherwise advice is perhaps less useful.

My Focus Tonight Different from Our Last Talks

When I talked to you before, you said that you were always distracted with the discomfort.

Yes, but at that time I spoke to you from that perspective. I think your Zoosh told you that anytime we speak, we speak from a different focus. I'm speaking to you now from having mastered that, no longer needing to have experiences of discomfort. So in this stage of experiential time from which I'm speaking to you, I've had all those feelings now. I don't need to have them anymore; I know what they all feel like and I can have compassion for beings. Thus I have no judgment or prejudgment or attitudes based on a lack of experience. Attitudes are very easy to form when you're outside an experience, but once you have lived through the experience, one easily sheds those attitudes.

During all that time you were distracted, but did you know that the Explorer Race was different from the Creator?

Back When You Arrived on the Scene

Yes, because the Explorer Race, in terms of your nucleus, the genus from which you sprang, was not with your Creator when we teamed up.

You were the first one?

Well, Zoosh was there.

The second one—ah!

It came later, not right away, because I think you were on call then. You might have been in transit, but you hadn't arrived there yet. One might have considered at the time, talking to your Creator, that your

Creator was just assembling beings. But your Creator said that He had put out a call for beings who would wish to experience something life-changing and life-expanding that would have an impact on the rest of all being. This required not only beings who are open to radical change within themselves, but open to the consequences of that radical change affecting everything else. At that moment your Creator did not know whether the change that would come about as a result of the Explorer Race would be a benevolent expansion of everything, or whether it would be something like Humpty Dumpty—something that would have to be put back together again the way it was. He put out the call for beings who were open to dealing with the consequences of something that might have to be entirely disassembled and reassembled, you understand? So the volunteers, your root genus, were beings who were open not only to that risk factor of personal expansion, but open perhaps in perpetuity to putting things back together for all existence everywhere, an infinite job. It was a big risk, and not just anybody came.

It's worse, though. He said that all those who signed on at the beginning knew that if it failed, they might be uncreated. That's even worse.

Yes, but you wouldn't be uncreated until you had picked up the pieces. You would be assigned to go around and pick up the pieces first, *then* you would be uncreated—not much to look forward to. It was a big risk, and that is why no beings in the immediate area they were passing through volunteered. There weren't a lot of hands that went up, offering, "I'll do it." Beings came from very far away who were seeking sensation and experiences of sensation. So at your root you had not had much experience of sensation, and you were looking for that.

What You Looked Like As You Arrived

What did it look like as we pulled in, wandered in, appeared—I don't know how you say it.

Like a comet going through the sky with a very long tail, longer than most comets you see. To me it looked very much like a comet with an exceptionally long tail.

Then we sort of moved into the Creator and . . .

Yes, as you moved toward what I would call the mass energy of the Creator, you slowed down. By the time you got to the Creator you settled into the Creator's outer boundaries. Until you were generated from the Creator, even though you were spread around within It, you never really were allowed to be fully integrated in all of the Creator's thoughts. You were allowed to remain relatively pure and dedicated to your original purpose, which was to seek sensation and to deal with the consequences. This allowed you to remain relatively pure in what you were originally attracted to in this experience. Yes, you were within the Creator; yes, the Creator birthed you, but you were kept in a state that was not totally enmeshed with the Creator's energy. You were thus able to perpetuate your individuality.

I see. We're going to go back and ask for some of those root beings to speak.

I think that's a very good idea.

But first we wanted to get a broader piece of all the companions of Creator. We were going to talk to you about the World War II book [see chapters 43-45 in Shining the Light IV], but somehow it became several magazine articles [see January 1997 issue of the Sedona Journal]. Are there other areas of history or anything else you want to contribute later?

Very possibly. I will be available should that come up.

Is there anything in particular that interests you that I don't know about?

I will probably bring things up or comment insofar as it affects you now, as I did with the Zeta experience. I would be more inclined to wait for you to ask, but if I feel something needs to be mentioned, as with the Zeta experience, I might . . .

. . . come in one time. We have an open invitation, okay?

All right, thank you.

Ah, thank you. Can you ask the Creator if He wants to end this book? This all started, you know, when a particle told us we were different.

Creator says He/She is open to that, but suggests that you wait and see. Maybe someone else . . . but if no one else is immediately appealing, Creator is . . .

Oh, I've got 500 beings out there I want to talk to, but He really hasn't had a chance to express this difference between Himself and the Explorer Race; He told us through a particle of Himself.

Yes. It is perhaps simpler to channel a particle of this Creator, because this Creator is perhaps one of the more complex beings I am familiar with. Your Creator here is always involved in all of the possible futures of this universe down to the smallest particle of the smallest cell (this is fascinating in terms of numbers) of every single being in this universe. Your Creator is fascinated with futures and how they relate to pasts as well as all other sequences of time and no-time. This Creator is fascinated with variety. Anytime you are with a being who is fascinated with variety, you can expect to be exposed to exactly that.

It's been a great adventure, right?

It certainly has.

As you look back on it, you don't want to do it again, but it's been like basic training in the Marines, right?

Yes, worth having, but one does not necessarily want to repeat it.

I have another thought here. Based on your revelation of the re-creation of the experience between humans and Zetas, is there a way, without pulling on our future or disturbing it in any way, to connect with that benevolent outcome and pull it into now? Is there some way not to have to wait seventy-five years for a beneficial outcome?

Yes, I think that exercise given earlier tonight by Zoosh [see chapter 1 in *Shining the Light V*] was ultimately intended to do that. I believe Zoosh wants to start giving out more creator training.

Okay, I've run out of questions. Say whatever else you want.

Then I will simply close with this. Those such as yourselves who are reading this need not do what I have done. You do not need to master discomfort by feeling all aspects of it in every potential. You know what it is to experience something unpleasant and what it is to experience something pleasant. Remember that the more opportunities you have to experience something pleasant, joyous experiences, in groups and ultimately universally, the more you will experience joy. Fear not the idea of unification and coming together and joining in larger numbers. You will not lose your individuality; as a matter of fact, your individuality will be enhanced even within the group. Good night.

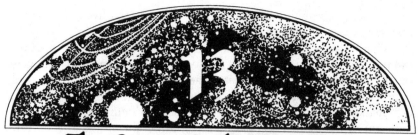

The Story-Gathering Root Being from the Library of Light/Knowledge

February 25, 1997

I am one of the core seeds of the Explorer Race. There are different numbers of us, depending on where we began our journey to Creator. We began as 3, then expanded to 6, then 12, and then back to 6, then 3. We sampled the experience of expanding ourselves on our journey, but returned to our root substance by our arrival.

My Earliest Recollections

My awareness of the call of your Creator's need preceded the time when this Creator had taken Its own personality. My voyage took such a long time that it's hard to quantify, but I can remember a vast amount of experience before the journey. There was much variety of light and infinite stories. I rolled into my seed shape at a communication place that gathers individuals' stories from everywhere, a famous gathering place where beings come from all universes to visit and to discover every incarnation they have ever had, in all details. One is able to trace all the way back there

Seeing it, it's like a swirl of gel-like crystals, like liquid compressed light. Because light has an endless capacity to store and distribute, this radiant place is the origin of all life's stories. It is my first recollection of any sentient experience. I remember floating out of a compressed light oval, having been inside a long time. Stories ebbed and flowed there.

Elements of personality are inside the oval between lives; if incarnate, they are outside it.

What I was before seems to be many incarnated beings from all over the universes. I had the distinct feeling of being aware of myself again, but I can't remember before that. Then I could see all the other ovals, which I visited. I listened to all the stories—about one million lifetimes (25 years) of beings listening to stories (several million lives). Ribbons announced their existence so others* could come and hear everything about them and all those they knew.

I was in the outer radiance of this library of light for some time when I began to feel a pull, not unlike the physical feeling you might have standing in the surf at the ocean—a gentle pull, one that can be felt and yet is not insistent. Since I had not felt pulled before, I began to follow it. The more I followed it, the more I could feel the pull and feel the radiance within me of something that would be fulfilling at the place that was pulling me. I traveled many, many thousands of lifetimes.

I began to work my way through different beings of light and sound and color and creation, taking on this coloration and that coloration until I came to a being who, if you were to look at it from any side, even if you were to fly around it completely, no matter where you go, it always presents the same face to you. It is shaped like this [draws], roughly, yes, roughly. This is the top, shaped like this. Even if you fly around completely, down, up, anywhere, it always presents that face to you.

My Vision of Your Creator

At first I thought it was an anomaly, a curiosity, so I flew around it to inspect it. At the point when I was ready to leave and continue on my voyage, I had the thought, as I so often did: I wonder what is waiting for me on the other end of this voyage? Instantaneously, almost before the thought ended—and it was more of a question than a thought—immediately I saw your Creator and your Creator's vision for this universe, this planet, the Explorer Race, everything.

As I was looking at it, I realized that this was where I was going. The stories I carried within me were not simply items of interest for me, but they were literally the lineage reservoir of many millions of beings who

---

would someday become personified as members of the Explorer Race, as dictated by this Creator I was going to meet. It was as if in a single moment I could see all that would be done and accomplished and could feel its value. I cannot tell you how important that was in that moment. It had been such a long voyage up to that point, and I did not then realize that, long as it had been, I had just barely begun. For the rest of my voyage I had that wonderful image to keep me going.

Traveling through Space Telling Stories

Much of the trip was involved in seeing other creations, and vast amounts of it were spent going through what seemed like space waiting to be used in some way. It was almost like an art-supply store that has many beautiful colors of paint and interesting shapes of canvas and clay. It was more an event waiting to happen than a current event. The space was in a state of expectancy—not anxiety, but expectancy—almost excited about what it would become but not yet having become that.

I believe my passing through it was a bit of excitement for that space, because it had some feeling, some sensation, for how it might be populated some day. Also, while I was traveling I felt it was my duty, having these stories of beings in me, to let the stories speak if I felt that the space or planet or universe was interested in one of the stories. It was a constant reiteration for me, but interesting, a manner of identity and a way of being polite, you know, sharing some of what I was. Yet for this space and area I was passing through it was something new, something to think about.

Joining the Other Seed Beings and Meeting Your Creator

Now, you might sensibly ask, what about the other seed beings? This is perhaps surprising, but it wasn't until the last 7 or 8% of the trip that I joined with them. The seed beings were coming from all over, and it was when we joined that we were three, then six, then twelve, then six, then three. But that was at the very end of the trip.

I remember the final leg of the journey when I joined the other seeds of the Explorer Race-to-be and that first sense of vast similarity, followed almost in the same moment by a sense of vast difference. Then following upon it and overlapping both the other moments was a sense of total union, really solidarity, for somehow along the way of their journey, those seeds had also discovered where we were going and why.

I cannot forget our meeting with your Creator. From a distance I could see your Creator moving along with Its companion, and as we began to approach within feeling distance, this Creator and the Creator's companion of the moment, Zoosh, slowed down and we slowed down, as if to prolong the last moments of our separation so that we could have greater exultancy when we joined, as one might hold back that ecstatic moment in order to appreciate it all the more. For the seed beings of the Explorer Race and myself were joining Creator and Zoosh, who all knew in essence who we were, where we were from, why we were there, what we would be doing when, how much, why and what would be the result.

When you meet other beings like that, it is a momentous occasion, an ecstasy to be felt and remembered and a moment that carries you for a long time. I can still remember the moment so well that I can feel it, and it is the memory of that ecstatic meeting that really allowed us seed beings of the Explorer Race to take the chance to try something entirely new and be open to the risks involved. Somehow, when one has that level of ecstasy with other beings and feels the essential wonder of what one is about ready to take up, any risk seems small indeed for the privilege of partaking in such a venture.

So there were only three of you. Were you all roughly of the same size and experience, the same weight? Does each of you need to continue further?

I suggest that you ask the other beings who will come through on succeeding nights, but to say that we contribute a third each in members and ensoulments, I'd have to say no, because your Creator fed us, and that feeding contributed some also. The seed beings contributed in personality essence about 60% and your Creator contributed about 40%, but the 40% your Creator contributed was what I would call the food of love, nurturance and . . . the only word that comes to mind is ecstasy. Thus we contributed the nutrients of core personality and your Creator contributed the joy of life.

Are we playing out all those stories you brought with you?

This Is the Third Replay

I am not sure whether you are playing out the stories or reliving them. I have felt for a long time now that what is going on here in this entire experience of the Explorer Race is something that is being redone, possibly not even for the first redo, but for the third time. I have this distinct feeling, though I cannot prove this. I recommend that you ask Creator when He or some part of Him speaks. Is it possible (I have felt it) that this was all done twice before and that the stories are being redone? I do not know the outcome of the other tries—if this did in fact happen—but I have the distinct feeling that, as you say, the third time will be the charm.

If that's so, do you have any idea where and when and by whom these stories were played out before?

No, I think you will have to ask Creator or Zoosh or even someone else. I am only imparting to you a sensation I have, a feeling. The reason I was able to assimilate these stories is that this is not the first time. *This has all been done before.* I do not see how it ended before, but I feel that this time will be the completion.

The Calling

How did you experience the calling? As a story, as a feeling, as a picture?

I experienced it in the way I described, as a physical feeling, as if you were standing near the beach with the surf just below your knee. It tugs on you but is not insistent. It is a gentle pull, saying, "Come with me, there are adventures waiting." That is how I felt. It was a physical feeling. Because I had not had too much experience with physical feelings up to that point in time—some, but not too much—it was distinctly noticeable.

Do you feel that the calling came from the Creator or from someone else?

I am uncertain. This is another reason I believe that this is being done for the third time. I have the impression that this calling might have taken place while one of the other times was running, perhaps when it was coming to some undesired ending or stopping point. My distinct feeling is that the calling took place during the first passage, or the first try for expansion.

I'm going to pursue this, because this is too big for something that came from this one local creator. This involved everything all around it.

It is big, yes.

Locating My Journey on Your Map

The place you came from, is it within one of the other realms? Do you know?

I know others have said this, so I will try to say it in some way a little differently. In terms of the paradoxical realm and all of that business, where I became aware of myself was (the distance from this planet to the portal into the paradoxical realm) that distance times 385 trillion light-years, give or take a thousand. That's why it took so long. It is so far away that there were not at that time portals established for traveling in corridors, as portals provide. So portals were unavailable and I had to travel according to the speed I was being pulled.

Are you familiar with the crystal? Did you go through it?

I went past it, not through it. I bypassed the paradoxical realm, actually. I didn't go through it, but I noticed it. It is not the sort of thing one does not notice. [Chuckles.]

Someone had told us 13 realms, but you're saying that there could be 13 million or billion?

Oh, yes. I think they gave you that figure according to their experience, but they might have given you that figure according to what was remotely relevant to the realm in which you now exist.

That really expands it a lot in the context of the Explorer Race.

Yes, and I have the distinct feeling that it is infinite beyond that.

After Joining Your Creator

Help us understand your experience while within the Creator after you joined. At what point did you become active and start influencing the creations?

In the beginning there was just that joy of being together. Then for the short distance of a journey there was the sharing of all the stories with your Creator and, on my part, hearing all that your Creator had done, where It had been, what It had seen, what It knew and what It envisioned. So there was this sharing for a time.

While on the journey?

While on the journey, yes. Then other beings intersected with and joined Creator. I believe there were one or two who did not join, but stopped to simply communicate with Him. Several of them were themselves creators who were involved in other projects, and one was a being who consulted with your Creator during His journey but did not come with Him. I believe this being was giving suggestions about what space was the best place to occupy so your Creator might find the most nurturing space for His vision. This consultant has not been counted with the other consultants because it did not come along. Our influence must have begun slightly before we joined up, because we were all feeling each other. I could not put my finger on a moment and say, "This is when it started."

The Master of Discomfort said that when he first met the Creator, you hadn't arrived here yet. So it's possible he could have been there?

He might have been there, yes. It is possible.

You came to this space. Can you share your experiences? You didn't actually birth yourselves until very late?

Inside Your Creator

Yes, quite a bit later. We observed for a long time, as one might observe as an artist prepare the palette before the painting. We observed your Creator begin to build the universe, creating its general boundary first and making the boundary flexible within a given space. At one time your creation, this universe, was very much larger than it is now. Then I remember that at some point before we had been birthed your Creator decided to condense things. This was at a time when beings did not populate the planets or galaxies. Your Creator tried it several different ways before beings were encouraged to populate. I do not mean only beings such as yourselves, but animals, plants, protozoa, anything.

At first was the assimilation of the planets, the suns, the stars, the galaxies, the space between them—a vast sculpture in space. Then at some point I remember, and it is an interesting thing . . . it is hard to describe this, but when you are within Creator's physical mass, you can see and feel everything in its entirety, yes? You can see and feel the entire universe, yet you can focus in on the smallest particle anywhere in the universe. Thus you can see the largest and the smallest in the same moment. It is an amazing experience, one I have not had since being birthed from your Creator.

It was special in the sense that you could watch it, but you weren't responsible for maintaining it. You didn't bear responsibility at that time, right?

I wouldn't want to say that I was excluded from that. In order to be part of this project I had to maintain a sense of balance and love and nurturance. I had to assimilate myself entirely in a vibrational way, in a light way, with your Creator in order to participate, then basically wait, so I can't say I was without responsibility. All parts of your Creator, even if they have already been created, must maintain a certain balance. If they are out of balance they will rapidly deteriorate and re-form into their original components, becoming available to be recycled into some other life form.

That is part of the reason, I think, that your Creator allowed you to have such short lives here on Earth, because becoming out of balance is almost a given on Earth, especially in these times. That is why the aging process takes place, why your bodies break down and prepare to assimilate into their basic component parts to be recycled at a later time. It is all small version of the larger version.

Our Birth from Creator, Then Expanding

I remember when I and the other seed beings were birthed. There was a time, several months in experiential time, when we were told that we would be getting ready to leave, and when we left we could go anywhere we wanted. But at some points in time we would need to join, reexperience ourselves and stay in touch with each other through our stories, our consciousness. So this happened. We were released, not so much pushed out as released, because we were excited and ready to go. We embraced Creator and then we left.

You left as three or as quintillions?

We left as three. We stayed together at first and flew all around the creation, each of us excitedly saying, "There! I want to go *there!*" And then the other would say, "Over there! I want to go there!" And we'd fly over there. It was a lot of fun. Then there came a moment when we felt . . . I remember my personal feeling. I will describe it. I felt as if all the stories within me were beginning to line up and become linear. It didn't feel like I was breaking up, but like I was becoming more, expanding and becoming more. And in that moment I think the other seed beings were doing the same thing. I could feel this sense of expansion, and all of a sudden it happened in a twinkling. I felt like the elemental parts of myself scattered hither and yon all over the universe.

Even though I was in many places at once, even though I had become different souls, for a long time I could feel all the parts of myself because they were living beings. Then very gradually, as the Explorer Race itself began to form into some sequential loop of experiences, I began to feel almost like there was a slight separation in my personality from the other two seed souls who were expanding in that moment. Then it was as if I was no longer within every one of them, conscious in every moment, but slightly above or pulled back and observing them. What had occurred, of course, is that they had been given responsibility for their own direction, because the Explorer Race ultimately must explore and find itself.

Would that be the moment when they went into the lower dimensions and had to sort of cut themselves off?

I'm loath to say lower dimensions. I would rather say it was at that point that they/you/us began to place the bit between the teeth and really begin the work.

I'll ask the others, but did each of you three have your own stories, or had the other two taken on your stories?

I think they assimilated my stories, but they had their own. I did not assimilate theirs; one might expect that, but I did not.

Can I assume that you're the more senior, larger, more experienced? Is there anything different?

You cannot assume that, no.

You just volunteered for this?

Oh, you mean why I spoke first?

Yes.

I was available, yes? [Chuckles.]

How My Consciousness Currently Operates

Are you still one consciousness someplace?

Here I am still one consciousness. But even though I am one consciousness, I have to concentrate to connect with the bits of myself. Before, I was always just consciousness, but now I have to focus and pay attention. I do not have to strain, but I have to pay attention.

So do you have a separate life and series of experiences on your own?

No, no I am threaded to all the beings I have expanded into. I am in complete connection with those who have completed what they need to do and are waiting. Those who are still gathering experience, such as you and others on the Earth now, I have to pay attention to and be alert to what you are doing.

I understand there's only a little over 1% of the total embodied Explorer Race now at this moment on the planet Earth. Are they evenly divided between the three of you, or are there more of one than the other?

I think I have about 20% of them, so they are not evenly divided.

Is there a reason for that?

I don't think so. I wouldn't say a reason, just a desire by some fragments to assimilate more.

We're not slower . . .

Oh, no, no, it isn't a test that you must pass. It is just a personal thing. How much do you want? What do you want to experience? How much do you wish to retain? What do you wish to let go of? What do you wish to actually live, compared to observe? Many choices.

What could we call you, then, a god-self? What are you to us? You are our creator, in a sense?

You could loosely refer to me as your unconscious. When other beings speak to you of your unconscious, that which knows all, they are talking about us for the most part, the seed beings.

That's what keeps the blood running and the heart beating?

Oh, no, I am not talking about the *physiological* unconscious, I am talking about the vast . . .

Collective unconscious.

Yes, the collective unconscious, but also that unconscious part of your own being, not just the unconscious mind, but of your own being that knows all—at least knows all within the context of what you are doing here. Certainly, to know *all* would be vast indeed.

The Speed of My Journey

When you came from your point of origin and there were no portals, exactly how did you get through?

I can only say that I was pulled, and at first there was a sense of physical motion. I was speeding up; I didn't have any mass in the sense of friction. But the faster I went, the less I felt the speed. It was an interesting sensation, one that some of you might be able to identify with. If you do not have a physical mass but are a personality, when you go slower you feel the speed, but the faster you go, you don't feel the speed at all. I can't say how fast I went, but it was obviously significantly faster than the speed of light.

But you were aware of your surroundings as you were pulled?

Yes, that is the fascinating thing about it. Even though I was moving at such a tremendous speed, I was still able to be aware of the smallest things as I went by them. I cannot explain it; it is paradoxical to hear it, but it is a reality. Perhaps it is because before you express yourself as some focused thing, you are still part of the vast everything and can pass through it at great speed, yet still experience it completely.

I've been trying to find somebody who can get out and look at the realms, but you came through them.

I came past them but I didn't go through them.

Above them?

Beyond them. They were to my right. [Chuckles.] I could see them.

A Map

What do the realms look like from outside?

I can draw a slight diagram.

Please do. The place you came from was not connected to these realms, then?

No.

It was connected to another series of dots?

[Draws.] Not the best diagram. Starting at the crystal.

We get blasé because we think we know so much, then suddenly someone says, "That's over there" and it gets incredibly vaster.

I'm sort of suggesting realms [by arcs] rather than closing them in.

Because they're like a lotus blossom.

. . . because they're not exactly enclosed.

They're not?

No, there's a sense of free passage between them, but some beings simply do not pass. That was my impression of the crystal. How many is this? One, two . . . let me get more or less the number. Maybe I'll just show you what I saw from my perspective.

It looks like an artichoke! [Laughs.]

But around this there is a sense, a suggestion of a thin, filmy substance around it all.

And where are you?

I'm off the frame of the picture.

Just draw it your own way.

Well, the arrow is *this* way [points downward]. How do I draw that?

You are up looking down.

Yes, this view is actually to my right. I am seeing this on my right, this picture.

Just put "top" right here.

Top, yes. This is on my right as I am whizzing by.

Did you look at where you came from? What did that look like?

I never really looked back at where I came from because until I actually joined your Creator, I still felt like I was there even after going through all those beings.

Which one of these realms is the symmetrical universe?

[Puts an S and a dot beside an arc.] This sense of a membrane is not a wall; it is just a feeling of filminess.

This might be like the circle we knew. We're where the dot is?

Yes.

You are here [points to P (for paradoxical) near the center crystal].

At P.

Now we've got two places laid out. Thank you. So you stopped at the symmetrical realm?

Interestingly enough, I went by it on my right and then came back. The crystal, of course, is oversized, but this is not to scale. You get the idea.

After we focused on thought instead of feelings, we were put on this loop of time [see chapters 10 and 21 in **The Explorer Race**] *so we'll change our mind about being isolated, then we'll come back out. What is your understanding of that?*

This loop really is something that has occurred *within* the experience, after our birth from the Creator.

Oh, of course. But there was a lot of experiencing and a lot of something going on up to that point, right?

Feeling Individuality and Focusing in Thought

Speaking for myself, when starting off it was usual to be unified. The experience of individuality took awhile to fully comprehend. The entire time I was voyaging on the way here, I never once felt a sense of individuality. I felt my sense of personality, but it was a personality within the mass of all other creations and beings. I think I had my first experience of individuality as a part of the Explorer Race, the sense of feeling as one person and connecting with those individual souls, fragments of souls.

Of yourself.

Yes, that was quite new. Before the experience of individuality, the idea of becoming focused in thought compared to feeling would have been incomprehensible. The idea of focusing on thought was infinitely easier once individuality had been established for a time as the norm—at least as far as your work goes here, which is the final touches of creatorship training at least on Earth, perhaps even this whole part of the universe. One can identify different thoughts from one individual to another, whereas feelings tend to be easily and quickly unified among groups of individuals.

Thoughts are definitely ascribed to a personal experience. I think many beings felt that in order to experience the maximum from individuality, it would be necessary to focus in thought so that one could at least experience the *illusion* of separation and individual activity. One could thereby test and challenge oneself, whereas the normal state of being is totally unified through feelings. The predominant reality everywhere is unification through feelings, but by being able to focus as beings of thought, one is able to challenge oneself with the temptation of alienation and the experience of separation, which is impossible when you are experiencing unified feelings with other beings. All of this is possible when you are focused in thought.

I believe your Creator allowed this because in order to truly experience the smaller, microcosmic world that an individual might have—yourself, your family, your brothers, your sisters, your mother, your father and the consequences of your actions and the consequences of their actions on you—one might need to feel as an individual. So this was allowed.

How long into the experiment or after you individualized and separated did this meeting happen when thought, or isolation, was chosen as the way to go?

About two-thirds of the way in.

Was there a Council of Nine? How did nine beings make that decision?

This Teaching and Learning Realm,
Where Consequences Must Be Resolved

This wasn't nine seed beings. A universe itself might have realms. A realm could conceivably spread through several dimensions. A teaching and learning realm might spread from, say, the second to the fifth dimension within this universe, whereas the first dimension might be the existence realm whose focus was totally on a singular existence or mass existence. This council was involved in approving—not saying "yes, no, you're all right," but checking various souls as individuals or small groups to see whether they would be able to survive, learn and thrive within that teaching and learning realm. I believe that council was set up to screen the souls who would go into that realm.

Do we know of it now as the Council of Nine?

I am not sure.

How was the decision made to focus more on thoughts than feelings? I understand that's what we're undoing now.

It was what I would call more of an acquiescence of the council. Many beings arrived at one point.

From the higher dimensions?

No, from portions of myself, portions of the other seeds, yes?

To go into the lower dimensions, or had they already been in the teaching realms?

You're right, yes. They arrived to go into the teaching and learning dimensions. I'd rather call them that than the lower dimensions, because then it ranks them. They arrived at the same time and began to petition the council that they could not fully experience a sense of individuality because they were linked at all times on the feeling level with each other. If one had a feeling that was uncomfortable, the others would rush to his aid to smooth it out. Therefore the chance to make mistakes was largely unavailable.

This began a discussion that lasted for some time, involving whether it would be acceptable to allow masses of beings to go into the teaching and learning realm, which realm allows a great deal more latitude than other realms within this universe that are for experiencing other things. In this realm one has vastly more responsibility for one's actions and *must* resolve all consequences. A soul might go there and stay for thousands if not millions of lifetimes just to resolve the consequences of its actions.

This was a long discussion. It was decided that the unification of feelings between all beings would not be eliminated, but superimposed would be the experience of the personality as thought. In this way one might grow to think that one's thoughts *were* their personality compared to one's feelings, which is the true personality. This also allowed for the much greater capacity to make mistakes and learn from them, because it would be very easy to assume that what you thought would express the true you, when of course it is what you feel.

So it was with this proviso that beings were allowed to go there and focus on thought. There were individuals who argued against it, but it was decided to allow it for a time (though not indefinitely) to see how it would go, and if it ever got too extreme in some direction that was very self-destructive, the council would begin to move those individual souls up to the higher dimensions where they would no longer be responsible for consequences and would not be producing consequences.

The Council Stepped In to Help Ten Lifetimes Ago

Some time ago this began to happen. The focus that the mind is the personality had become so pervasive that people were taking actions that produced so many consequences that they couldn't live enough lives to resolve it all, allowing for the time experience available. The council reached in and began to move things up, and other more advanced beings will resolve those consequences. Those beings who will resolve them will, of course, be quantum masters, which is the mastery of consequences.

The original decision was, as I say, a compromise. I believe that the daughter of God [see chapter 21 in *The Explorer Race*] was very eloquent in her appeal that the potential for suffering (the initial decision of the council) was too vast for this to be allowed. Even though she felt that she was ignored, she was not; her plea was very convincing. That is why the council made an addendum when they allowed it: if it got too extreme they would step in. So they stepped in some time ago and began moving you up a bit in dimension. Thus they are pulling and pushing you up a little. Quantum masters are also pushing you up a little. You are evolving on your own, but they are also helping because consequences were becoming too vast.

Are you talking about just in the last few of our years?

Oh, no, no. Generally speaking, in the last ten lifetimes.

The Loop of Time and a Different Petition

When did this start, this loop of experiencing, where we're coming back before we made that decision?

It's very complex. It's hard to say, but the loop occurred before this assistance. We're talking about different sequences, and I don't know if I have the capacity to explain it. You, in your not totally collective-unconscious self (but almost), decided that you needed to change what you would do. Remember, the council didn't send you there; you petitioned them. Cooler heads, you might say, decided to create a loop of time and go back before that meeting with the council and petition them differently. It is almost like a simultaneous event. I cannot explain it.

You've done beautifully. We're almost back now to petitioning before the council.

Then I think most likely you will petition to do something different, or you will just go on.

Well, it mentioned possibly combining feeling and thought as a way for people to make decisions.

But it has *always* been combined.

But with more emphasis on feeling.

It was always that way. You are united through feeling. If you look at your society and what you have done, both good and not so good, you can see that when you had the greatest union it was always through feeling. When the greatest actions were taken, it was because of a unified feeling, the same for the worst actions. But those worst actions were possible because they believed they *were* their minds. One can create separations, you see—they are a great way to learn, but very hazardous.

Daughter of God, Son of God

The daughter of God—exactly who is she? Is this the feminine part of the Creator?

Yes.

What we call the Goddess?

Well, I can't really say. Let me back up. [Draws] If all of this is God or Creator [indicates triangle], then this would be—I arbitrarily position male, female parts [draws M and F]—the union of same [draws U], the union of these two parts, hmmm? Dit, dit, dit dit, dit, dit, dit [draws dotted lines]—the union of these two parts. So the daughter of God and the son of God are the same being, depending on their appearance, the way they show up, what they do. In that case it was the daughter of God because she could be more compassionate.

So who do you call the son of God? Who is that?

Well, I do not refer to the son of God as exclusively being the Christian ideal.

Is it Jehovah?

No. The male offspring, which is not an offspring, is a temporary being. I do not put a name onto it. If I had to put any name, I suppose Yahweh would be more appropriate, but that is such a temporary name. There are

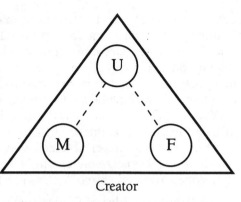

Creator

many names, but it is a feeling. In the case of the masculine child of God, it would have great courage, conviction, the capacity to communicate clearly—passion, all right? It could be more easily defined by its feelings or persona, whereas the daughter of God would have great compassion, tremendous love, understanding, nurturance and so on. Do you understand?

But it would really be the Creator?

It would be, in any moment, a manifestation. But you see, Creator would not show Itself in Its masculine or Its feminine portion—polarized—because these portions are more Its totality. But It might show Itself in a combination of the masculine and the feminine. For the purpose of your society I'm explaining it this way now. Other societies might have more than two sexes, you know. I am utilizing this paradigm for this explanation.

I have more to understand about that, but we'll come back. A particle of the Creator said that it was the Explorer Race itself that introduced ignorance and suffering, and Creator had to have great faith to allow that. Can you speak about that?

Yes, that was this petitioning, the effect of the council saying, "All right, go ahead, focus in the mind." That was what I was talking about before, when the daughter of God said, "Don't do that." Portions of the Explorer Race, as I understand it, introduced the mind focus, inadvertently doing something without intending to do it. But that is still a consequence, and there is the same weight on that consequence as something you do on purpose.

The Creator talked about the influence of the Explorer Race in building ignorance and suffering into the fabric of the universe, which is not something He would have done on His own.

Yes, that's right. But then again, Creator was not the Explorer Race, was He? Creator is the nurturer of the Explorer Race, but is not in Its own right the Explorer Race, other than encompassing, feeding and nurturing the Explorer Race. The Explorer Race can do something that

Creator could not ever do. Creator would be appalled at the idea of introducing something that would be ultimately self-destructive. But since the Explorer Race must explore to learn, must begin at the bottom rung of the ladder and climb up, must learn by expansion one step at a time, naturally it cannot be expected to have the vision to understand the potential outcome of what starts out as something seemingly so innocent. The Explorer Race has the capacity, even the necessity, to make mistakes because it is intended that the Explorer Race learn by them. There is no more powerful lesson you can experience than one that causes you and others you love to suffer as a result of something you have done. You don't forget lessons like that.

Where the Idea of Experiencing Suffering Came From

Is that what you three seed beings wanted or the vision you got?

No.

Where did it come from?

It came from the fragments of the Explorer Race when I fragmented. You'll have to ask them; it came from their experience through incarnation. I didn't bring it. After they experienced everything they could assimilate on the loving level and they were still here and didn't know why, they wanted to experience something else. That's why they petitioned the council to go to the places of learning and try out individuality.

But you say so forcefully that that's the only way the Explorer Race can learn.

From what I understand, yes.

But it evolved out of the experience; it didn't come as some sort of credo or built-in rule.

It evolved out of the experience, the snowball gathering snow as it goes downhill, becoming more of itself as it progresses. Remember that the Explorer Race does not live life for the pleasure of pure being. Everyone else does, but not the Explorer Race. Why not? Because it is driven by a mission, which is largely a feeling. And since you are now focused in thought, feelings are not so readily understandable to the thought consciousness. The consciousness of thought does not readily interpret feelings, but you are nevertheless driven by your feelings. Although everybody else can live life for the pleasure of pure being, Explorer Race cannot because you have a job.

After the Mission of Discovery Ends

What is our mission?

You know that.

I know, but I want your definition from your perception.

Your mission is to discover.

And where will it end? We become, we take over for the Creator, then what do you see after that?

You will continue to discover.

Do you have any sense of the possible scenarios after we replace ourselves in this creation?

I think you will probably not stay. You will probably very quickly birth somebody to take over, because you are too restless to manage. Management requires a sense of continuity and one needs to be there every day. One cannot be late; one has to show up. A manager's job is quite different from that of a visionary. No, I think you will not run this creation very long. I think you will very quickly, even within perhaps a few hundred years of experiential time, say, "Okay, we got that. Now what?"

So what is the possibility?

There are no limits.

Just give us a clue. Are we going to go out and investigate the realms? That sounds pretty cool.

Oh, I wouldn't think so. Once you become a creator, what do you think you will want to do?

Create?

Yes. You will want to go somewhere and create something. It is one thing to take over somebody else's creation, but no matter how beloved that someone else is, it is entirely another to create something of your own.

But then you have to maintain it. So then what?

Well, you have to birth someone who will maintain it, and once it is prepared to do that, then you go off and make your own creation.

You've just solved my personal problem. I've got to hire a manager. [Laughs.]

Well, I think that is possibly true. [Chuckles.]

When the Explorer Race comes together again to take over this creation, do we all go back and become the three of you?

But in essence, you are not just that. You can't go back and be the three of us, because you have done so *much*. You will come forward and the original three of us will be expanded, yes? As you know, it is intended that everything be expanded. Once the expansion has taken place, I do not know if we will increase in number, being beyond three, or whether the three of us will simply be more vast than we are now. I cannot say, I do not know this. I am not supposed to say too much, because anything I might say could limit your vision. I can kid around, but that might be it.

So you are totally tuned in to the 93% that is complete. You're part of that.

Oh, yes.

My Connections to the Other Two Roots

But you don't have that same connection of feeling to the fragments of the other two seeds?

To the fragments of the other two? No, I don't.

You can look in on what they're doing?

I can look in on what they're doing, but as I am speaking it is easier for me to connect to the seeds themselves, the seed personas. It is much easier for me to connect to them and assimilate what they know about their beings than it is to connect to the beings themselves.

How are the other two seed beings like you, and how are they different?

I think I will leave that up to you to compare, because they feel very much like me and at the same time totally different. I am a feeling being, yes, so I will leave that up to you to decide.

Then let me rephrase it: What does the place you come from look like?

I described that at the beginning.

How can we put it in context? It was all alone, it didn't seem to connect to something within a membrane like this one did?

No, it was by itself. It is a library of light, but it is not a portion of an apparent universe. This I know, because when I was moving in this direction I never went through any boundary. So it seems to be a universe unto itself. Not very big, but big enough.

What do you feel that you have learned since you came together with the other two seed beings? What have you learned from them?

This will shock you, but I have not learned that much from them, because we are . . . again we are back to management. It is my job to oversee that which has sprung from me, yes? But it is not my job to oversee what has sprung from them. So our communications with each other have more to do with comparing notes or feelings, but . . . how can I describe this to you?—we have the feeling of unity and separation in the same moment. At this time, because we're still in that loop of experience of individuality. I am in that too, in that sense. I can see them but I do not feel quite as connected to them as I might normally. I cannot answer that question.

That's now, but when you first came together, did the three of you join before you met the Creator?

We never really joined into one being. We were three individual portions, and we've always been three individual portions. I think three is a significant number in your culture, and it is to us, too. I am myself, and I recognize that the other two parts of the Explorer Race are themselves, but other than feeling the ecstasy of joining with Creator and Zoosh and perhaps a few other beings who were there, that was the only moment of total union I have felt with these other two parts. We do not have a merged, totally one being amongst ourselves. We are separate parts of the Explorer Race.

As separate parts who were sharing the common endeavor, did they have experience different from yours?

Yes, and that's why you have to ask them.

Did they have experiences they shared with you, where you felt, "I didn't know this," or was there some . . .

We don't share that kind of thing. The sort of thing we might share is based on similar experiences, because then we can help each other. But we don't talk about things that don't relate. If it doesn't relate to me, then what can I do with it?

But you did tell them stories?

Yes, they were interested. I didn't tell them, they assimilated them.

Through a feeling connection with you?

Yes.

But you didn't assimilate anything from them?

No.

That's interesting. How can we refer to you? Is there a designation?

I do not have a name. [Chuckles.]

Well, we need to call you something. This is incredibly important in the scheme of things here—the root beings from the library of light.

Yes, what's wrong with that? Your names really have to do with that. All of your names *always* have to do with that. In the beginning names had to do with where you came from.

Or the son of, or the work that a man did.

Yes, Smith, yes.

After I talk to the other two, that will open up more questions?

It is possible. Speaking to you as the questioner, you will find that this process tends to take on different faces and functions even within the same book, because the series of beings you are dealing with might not have a direct correlation to other beings. So *you* have to stretch, too.

Oh, but it's wonderful.

I think now I must say good night.

Thank you very, very much.

Zoosh here. It is an interesting point the seed being brought up about feeling this was the third time. You know, I've never really mentioned that before because I didn't want you to think that you were simply an accessory. But it's really true. There were two other attempts by Creator to establish this entire creation. It didn't go quite right, but they weren't fully imaged. I'm going to use this level of comparison: Creator's creation here in this universe initially had a lot to do with a thought, a visioning process—you understand, visioning. So the first two passes at the experience were visions that didn't go quite right—like you might have a thought, plan something out, then discover as you pursue this particular avenue of thought that that's not the way to go. Then you go back a ways and start again. It was more like that.

In this space with these friends of Creator's?

Yes, everything else being rather the same. But not with those seed beings.

Other seed beings?

I cannot do more tonight. Good night.

The Root Who Fragmented from a Living Temple

February 27, 1997

ell, greetings.
Welcome.

You will find that I have a little different slant. I am one of the root beings from which the Explorer Race has sprung. I traveled with my companion, the other root, for quite a bit of the journey to this space, and I would speak of that if you like.

Certainly, please.

I remember the feeling of it all as if it were just a moment ago. If I go way back now, way back to my point of awareness of myself, I was connected then to the being that is the other root, what I call my companion. We had experienced many, many experiences before we answered the call for which the ultimate expression (at least so far) is the Explorer Race. I'm not sure how much to talk about. Do you want my point of origin? It is a lot.

We can use one night, two nights, three nights—whatever you want to tell us is wonderful.

My Origin: A Living Temple

All right! Way back, the first thing I can remember was being in a place where . . . the best comparison to your world would be like a place where there were grains of sand, fairly large grains. You have been places, beaches perhaps, where the sand grains are significant in size. There was the sensation of many, many beings, most of them somewhat spherical but some of them faceted spheres. There wasn't the sensation of crystals but of building blocks, the stuff that other things are made of. When I became aware of my being, I remember feeling distinctly as if this vast amount of what I will call grains (as in grains of sand) had been something before that. I think we represented what was left over. Looking at it a little deeper now, I can see what we had once been.

Once there was a temple. It was a temple made of light, sound and a need. The Temple was a living being. It looked like a building, but it was alive. It had a strong need to communicate the joys of ultimate knowledge and had the capacity to communicate from the soul of its being, as it was made up of many individual souls, pieces of beings. It could communicate in any language by any method, yet it was in a very isolated place. It was a distance from here—I'm not even sure whether numbers can express it. Do you remember the number you were given awhile back [see chapter 7]—to the something power to the something power?

Yes.

It was at least five or six time farther away.

This place is not the place that was described last time?

Oh, much, much farther away than that.

Up the line.

Way up the line. The Temple, as I say, was very isolated, free-standing in space, you might say, its own place. It was so far from anything that to communicate in any way other than in long-distance telepathy was difficult. There were no portals to that place. The Temple, you understand, is *alive.* It is a vast amount of potential being expressed to less than one-millionth of 1% of its capacity, so it's grossly underemployed and feels very unfulfilled. After many, many millions of years . . .

You were a piece of that temple?

The Temple's Inspiration to Self-Destruct and Travel

I was a piece of that, yes, as was my companion. After many, many years, not having the capacity to communicate all this knowledge—all knowledge even today, as far as I know—the Temple had an inspiration. One must assume it was from somewhere. The inspiration was to do something that sounds, on the face of it, terrible, yet you have to think about it. The Temple was inspired to destroy itself and scatter the pieces of itself in all directions. Each piece would be a seed of that temple, and from each seed could spring the knowledge and wisdom. The Temple would completely re-form itself when the moment was correct for the place where the seeds would ultimately go. The Temple did it reluctantly because, being such a magnificent being, it was slow to accept that it must destroy itself to achieve the fulfillment for which it seemed to have been created. But it did after a time, and scattered . . .

It just separated?

It didn't explode.

It simply separated particle by particle or seed by seed?

It gradually turned itself into seedlike grains not unlike sand, which scattered, but not in an entirely spherical direction. The Temple's original plan was to maximize its capacity to achieve fulfillment somewhere and scatter in a totally spherical pattern.

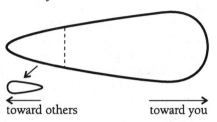

toward others   toward you

It had assembled that pattern, but at the last moment it realized that there was a better chance if it were to form this shape [draws], kind of a teardrop shape, see? Allowing for the general direction of where that temple was to where you are and everything in between, this much (I'll draw a dotted line), the bulk of it, went in your general direction. The rest of it formed into this shape [draws a small teardrop]. I'll try to draw it somewhat to scale—sort of a teardrop facing the other way, going out in the directions that the mass didn't go. For the sake of simplicity [draws two arrows], toward you and toward others.

Was there something in that direction?

Yes, but the feeling was that the bulk go in your general direction. The Temple felt it was taking a calculated risk; it had a feeling to do it, though the feeling was very subtle. But it simply said okay. Then the material formed pretty much into that shape (three-dimensionally, of course, not two-dimensionally) and started moving in this general direction. The grains were moving around within it, not unlike putting sand into something and gently shaking it, forming a pattern of motion. It was like that, a gentle moving, so that we were constantly mixing amongst each other. You might think that each grain contains different knowledge, but it doesn't. Each grain was an equal part of the original total being. This motion, this constant moving around and touching itself, was a way the temple kept in contact with itself to the best of its ability. Before the temple moved, it had been a living mass that looked like an ancient Grecian temple with a few turrets thrown in.

Becoming Aware of My Companion, Then Linking Up

Moving in that mass of grains, I began to become aware of my companion—my counterpart, I might say. Here I am moving around with all these millions and millions of grains, and this being I bump up against every once in a while feels familiar. It's not clear, but it's as if we're supposed to be together. So the third time I touched this being we sort of linked up. We were able to form a sort of a magnetic attraction, and we stayed connected. After I had done that I noticed that several other grains had done that, too—formed links with other grains.

Initially I thought, Well, the main energy of the Temple is going to split us up again, because we're supposed to go to different places. But this didn't happen. Many of those other seed grains would link up in a small spherical shape, sometimes in units of nine. We were speeding along all this time at around the thirty-third dimension. (As I look back now in hindsight, I see it's part of the reason not many people came to see us. There are not that many beings in that dimension, as it turns out.) As we were speeding along, we didn't go around anything. If anything was in our way, in front of us, as it were, we'd just go right through it.

Because it was less than the thirty-third dimension.

Yes, as you say. Because we were of that dimension, I don't remember passing anything that we couldn't go through. Surprisingly, the entire mass did this without losing a single grain—this mass heading toward you, or the Earth.

Toward these realms.

Toward this space that Earth now occupies.

But you're not even through the realms yet.

I'm getting close. We were entirely intact as a mass until we got near this circle of existence.

We're calling it the Circle of Creation.

The Sudden Stop and the Long Wait

Yes, this particular Circle of Creation. We've been together all that distance (we were traveling very fast and still in the thirty-third dimension), then we slowed down as we approached the outer boundaries of this circle. We got to within what you would consider visual range, where you could see it up ahead if you had eyes, and we came to a complete halt. We sat there—and this is an amazing thing: We'd been traveling at what you might call an incredible speed, then we got to that point and stopped! We were there for a long time.

At the time, the whole mass of being—what I'm calling the Temple—had no idea why we were waiting, especially since we'd been hurtling along at such speed and then we stopped. With hindsight I realize that it was about that moment that the Creator of this universe had broken off and begun its journey to go around and see things. Understand that we were moving toward this before your Creator had even broken off from its own creator! Your Creator had just begun Its journey with Zoosh and was collecting other beings and so on.

Stop a minute. We don't know where that journey was. Was it just in this circle, or did it go into other circles of creation? Did it go out of this realm?

I'm not sure that I know that. It's a good question for Zoosh.

If Zoosh was there, he could tell us and we'd have a wider understanding of what's out there.

Yes, yes, a worthy question. So we waited a long time but had no idea why. We were just sitting there parked, as it were. [Chuckles.] When I think back on it, it's kind of funny, because we were simply baffled. It's interesting to imagine beings of the thirty-third dimension who had what we thought was all knowledge—but this one thing was blocked. We had no idea why we were parked there; we couldn't go anywhere, but had to stay right there. I think it was the first time the Temple had experienced the emotion/feeling of being utterly baffled. It was a good experience, I think, because it allowed us to prepare for what was to come.

The Abrupt Resumption of Our Journey; My Companion and I Separately Heading for the Earth Space in 12D

Then the moment your Creator experienced the ribbon of inspiration going by, it was just like someone hit a switch. We were off and running with the entire group of the Temple. We got to within maybe 30 meters, not very far, from the outer boundary of this Circle of Creation, and we stopped again very briefly. This was kind of a strange feeling, but my companion and I were sort of shunted out of the whole crowd. We're literally dropped off, and the rest moved out in the general direction, I think, of the other circles. I don't know this for certain, but it would be a good question to ask Zoosh or somebody.

The minute we're dropped off—bang!—we're right through the outer boundaries of that circle, going just as fast as fast can be, and the next thing we knew . . . oh, by the way, the minute we go through the outer boundaries (excuse me for going back and forth, but I've never told this story to anybody and I'm a little excited), we go from the thirty-third dimension bang! right down to the twelfth dimension. It was stunning!

Did you feel more dense? What was your feeling?

We felt bigger—that's the only way I can describe it. We felt bigger, not exactly denser, but bigger. Our feelings ranged out farther. I think our auric fields became more physicalized. That's the best way to describe it. Then we were going at breakneck speed, and just a moment before we literally intersected with your Creator, we hooked up with the other root, and went bang! into your Creator. We felt really terrific for a while. But you know something interesting? My companion and I, seeds, remained connected for a very long time. Although we hooked up with the other root, we didn't disconnect until we were birthed out of your Creator. Then we began to move around and become more.

My companion might have more to say about that. But that's what's interesting to me: we were very connected. The reason I'm mentioning it in this way is that it has ramifications—and I'm not trying to break the Explorer Race down into separate groups.

The Three Roots of the Explorer Race

But what you're saying is that we've got three groups here.

You have three groups, three roots, and two of the roots are very sympatico, compatible. The other root, while we feel good about that root and the beings, that other root . . .

. . . didn't come from your home.

Yes, it's different. That's worth mentioning.

Of the 1% of the Explorer Race that's on the Earth right now in this dimension, who are we mostly connected to? Or are we split amongst the three?

That's a good question, because that 1% is made up, tracing it back to the root, mostly of my companion and me. There's a little bit left of the other root being. I don't think that the beings who trace back to that other being are going to be here much longer.

Why not?

Because in the next adventures, certainly in coming generations of the Explorer Race, you will have to be more kinetic, meaning more inspired physically, not just inspired spiritually. My perception of the other root being is that it's very etheric in its orientation (I'm disinclined to say magnetic, because my companion and I have that, too) and more magnetic than we are. We are more sympathetic with the combination of the masculine and the feminine, whereas the other root, I would have to say, is more feminine or magnetic in its nature.

In the third-sex sense?

No, no. It is more of feeling and more receptive, more inclined to act from intuition slowly, more inclined to—okay, how's this?—to adapt and be adaptable to spiritual mastery and all it entails, but less inclined to adapt and be adapted to material mastery. The other being is also more adept in teaching mastery. We're more action-oriented, my companion and I, so we're more inclined to be of material mastery, dimensional mastery—and that's it. The quantum mastery I don't think would be expressed by any of the roots, though we are all being exposed to that now, which is very beneficial to us all.

I'm bringing these points up because there are essentially three roots of the Explorer Race. All three are still here, but one root that is more feminine/magnetic is coming to the completion of its cycle, and a lot of its beings have completed already. They're basically going to go off and wait or get prepared to do something else, whereas the next four or five generations of the Explorer Race, if I may put it like that, will be made up more of my companion and me, because we are much more associated with material, physical action based upon knowledge. You know, quick action [snaps fingers], application, inspired, then taking action—like that!

The Closers of the Explorer Race Experience

Those are the things necessary for what the Explorer Race has to do in the next four to five generations, which is to explore. That's why we're going to be the closers, in terms of the Explorer Race experience. You have to understand something. When I say the next four or five generations, the tendency is to think that generations are x amount of years. But generations are going to gradually become longer and longer, especially as you step up in vibration in this dimensional change. Then you'll begin to start having lives of 300 years, and as you go up to the fifth dimension, which is going to happen (the shift from the fourth to the fifth is going to be much quicker than it was from third to fourth), you'll have lives of 1200 years and so on. We're talking of a range of years here that might easily be 3500 or 4000, something like that. But that's in only four or five generations! So this is an adventurous time to be here.

I'm bringing this up for those of you who are or will be parents [chuckles] in the near future. I want you to take notice of your children—you know, nurture them, encourage them, all of the good parental things. But be aware that they are likely to be unusually active. Try to find good things for them to do. Try not to stifle them too much because they represent an incredible resource. A lot of the inventions you need to create will be created by this group of people.

The New Generation and Their Pyramid Structures

In the next 20 or 30 years these babies are going to start being born—that's right, that soon. It's going to start building in 20 or 30 years; maybe even in 15 years they'll start being born, and it's going to build to a crescendo so that in about 150 years they'll be the dominant force of babies being born. These children are going to invent on their own the technological society or machines that have no moving parts. They're going to bring you back into harmony with things like crystals and even vegetable matter, trees and what you might consider an ordinary stone or pebble.

They're going to be able to interact with these natural sources around you and create amazing things, including buildings where the stones just fly together and become a permanent structure—and I mean *permanent*. They will come apart only if the beings or beings like them sing them apart. They'll sing them together and sing them apart if they need to come apart. These small buildings will look like this [draws]. Pictures tonight! Not unusual; if you were to see it from the side,

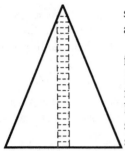

simple like that, it would look that way, a sharply angled pyramid with only three upper sides.

On each side something comes down the face—I'm going to draw a dotted line, okay? [Pause.] This is not very good, but you get the idea. It's going to look like steps going up. It kind of reminds you of some other things you've seen. If you would simply lop off the top, you'd say, "Whoa, these are like the pyramids in Central America and Mexico and places like that." They are *very* much the same. (It's a good place to put in an illustration of

such things, if you can round up an illustration of one in Central America.)

No more than three or four of them are needed around Earth, though there might at times be more, but generally three is enough. *Just these three put in various parts of the Earth will produce all the energy that everybody on Earth needs.* This is not energy as you understand it—electrical power to drive machines—because there won't be any machines. You'll have energy that can create what you need. You'll be going through a revolution not only spiritually, but physically; you'll be changing physically. These buildings will provide the extra energy each human being needs to make that physical transformation more easily.

Those pyramids that you see in Central America that look like the lower part of this are the residue of what they once were. If you cut off the top of this pointed pyramid, it would gradually become something much like what you see there. Some of those pyramids were built by beings who came along later, but most of them are pretty much the way they were.

Which civilization used them? How long ago?

The Five-Minute Planetary Evacuation
When Earth Moved from Sirius

Way back. When it was necessary to transform quickly, people from other planets who had settled in that general area—a couple million years ago—had to get off fast. Many of these things were brought in, and they helped the beings transform their physical bodies quickly so they could leave the planet without dying. Some of the people came together and formed light disks; they were not actually ships. You've seen pictures of them sometimes; they look like a disk of light seen from the side. Those are made up of beings who emigrated in light to other places, where they would then re-form into the form of those other places. That was what happened then.

They had to move that suddenly?

It was right around that time—now, I might not have the years quite right here, but you can convert it to whatever you've heard before. I'm sure it's right; it might have been more than a couple million years ago—you fix the numbers, okay? [Chuckles.] It was right around the time that Earth made its move from Sirius to here.

Oh, so they had to leave it when it was in Sirius?

Yes, they had to leave it. It might have been more than a couple million years ago, but the moment the decision was made to bring Earth here to this space, the beings who lived there had about five minutes to get it together and get out. Five minutes! This is appalling when you think of it in terms of your time, but things can be done differently in other places. So these pyramids were brought there—it was an emergency, like the panic button to get the pyramids there and get the beings off. There was no time to grab anything, no time to load into spaceships and fly anyplace. They just had to reduce to their light essence and fly off elsewhere.

Why was there such a hurry?

I don't want to get too far off track because I want to get back to your experience here, but that planet in Sirius, which is now Earth, was not originally going to come here. It was a late replacement. You see, another planet was going to be moving into this space, becoming the third planet from the Sun. Mars was actually planned for here.

The Martians' Change of Mind

There were viable advanced civilizations on Mars then and they had volunteered to make the move. The Martians had been working with the Sirians for a long time and had produced vast amounts of water through interactions with them. (Although their water is a little different chemically, it's very close to what you have here. It had a little bit of carbon in it, too.) Mars was prepared to come here, but literally at the last moment there was a disruption in the Martian (I'll use the term, but they don't call themselves that) plan, and some small group of beings (a few hundred beings in a total population of 30 or 35 million) didn't want to do it, just a few hundred. But in those days the Martian civilization was so much in balance that if even *one* being didn't want to do it, it wouldn't happen.

Why didn't they want to do it?

Those beings had begun to form a small circle. When they met, they would shift themselves into the space that Mars would occupy, which is Earth's orbit. They wanted to experience what Mars would experience as the third planet from the Sun, so they went into the future, an alternative to what would have developed here. If Mars had moved into this place, then the Explorer Race would have found its way eventually to Mars, which would have been the third planet from the Sun. They went into the future, experiencing all these scenarios, realizing that they would eventually be the host for the Explorer Race and all that it entailed, with all of its struggles and so on. But they did not want to have the experience of suffering for whatever value it might come to at some point, even though (this is interesting) they couldn't understand suffering as a personal experience; they could understand it only as a mental definition at that time. But the mental definition was enough to thwart them, so they said no. They said, "We have looked into this, and we say no." And they prevailed.

That was only a short time before Mars was going to move. Moving a planet [chuckles] to another place is a major task, so everything was in place. It would take as much effort to move Mars to the third-planet position as it would take to move what is now Earth from Sirius to here—no more effort. So Sirius volunteered the planet that is now Earth and made the move.

Sirius did put in the proviso, however, that once the Explorer Race experiment (which is what it was considered in those days) was completed, they would reclaim the planet and it would return to Sirius, and that whoever was necessary to help it get back intact would bring that about. That was the deal.

That is why Mars is still there today. The interesting thing is, the beings who were looking into the future on Mars only looked into Mars' future as it would evolve as the third planet from the Sun. They did not look into the future of their civilization where they were because everything had been benevolent up to that point and they had no reason to think that anything would change.

But then Maldek blew up.

Yes, but you see, they didn't look into [chuckles] their own future.

So they could have saved themselves?

They could have saved themselves, but they did not know that. It never occurred to them that it would be necessary. They didn't want to look into their own futures because they wanted to have the joy of its coming about. So it never occurred to them to do it.

On a soul line, were the Explorer Race beings already on Mars?

No.

The Martians are not part of the Explorer Race?

I can't say that, because some beings of the Explorer Race have been all over the universe. The whole body of beings on Earth are part of the Explorer Race, but you could never say that about Mars or any of the other planets. You could say that some of the beings came and went, but never the whole, no.

Thank you. Those pyramids in Central and South America—Mayan or Incan— actually came with the planet?

Some of them were constructed at a later point in time by these civilizations, but they are easily discernible because they do not have the same precision. You can't get stones to come together and hold together like that without their *wanting* to do it.

So where, specifically, are the pyramids that came with the planet?

I will just say this: The ones where the stones are fitted together beautifully are those types.

Will they be used now in transformation classes, or do we have to . . . ?

No, it is very likely that simply by returning the tops of the pyramids, they will lock into place, and when you look at them you will not be able to imagine that they ever looked different. They will simply be a unit. They will lock into place and immediately be able to function. It's as if someone removed the batteries and they don't work anymore. The tops are in another dimension. They're not even tops anymore; they're functioning as energy doing other things.

To reimage something that once existed in time is a simple thing once you know how to do it, you know. It's like knowing which hand uses the fork and which hand the spoon. Once you know how to do it, it's simple. The energizing parts of the pyramids are not really parked anywhere, because no massive energy likes to just sit and wait. I'm in a position to know that that's so!

How do you have a sense of sitting and waiting?

Well, remember, when we first came here . . .

You parked outside.

Yes, and we parked there for all that time after literally hurtling here. Suddenly we were stopped, and we waited, not having the slightest idea why. When you're waiting and don't know why, it's not the most wonderful feeling, as I'm sure all human beings know.

You have heard for a long time how you are going to change physically in this dimensional shift. You've even heard what some of the changes might be, but you've always assumed that something would come to do this for you. You have to remember—it's very important—that interference is not accepted. So although the pyramids will re-form, they won't simply begin doing what they do.

The Next Generation Discovers Itself at the Pyramids

That's where the kids come in, the new children. They will go there, and even pyramids in other parts of the world that people didn't realize were pyramids will become obviously that. Sometimes they look like mountains, but are really pyramids, and those will simply become pyramids.

The children will gravitate to them like iron filings to a magnet, you know. It's not that it's out of their control; they'll *want* to go there. And these children, who won't have known each other, will come from all over the world; they'll literally meet there. One thing they'll have in common is that they were pulled there and don't know why. For a while they'll camp there, getting to know each other. Then they'll start singing together (as people do, you know). They'll tell stories and do things, and eventually people will start singing—it's a typical thing. And they'll notice that things happen when they sing. That's how it'll get started.

It's all part of a whole plan here, see? It is not an accident. It's a very important thing that's happening, but it's not really interference. Creators and beings can put something in front of you as long as they don't switch it on and make it work. If *you* have to make it work, then it's allowed; it's not considered interference if it's just sitting there like a lump.

Physical Transformation

Interesting. Can you talk about what the transformational process in the physical is?

A lot of it has to do with the change in the motivation of the cellular structure and thence the atomic structure, particle structure, of your physical bodies. Right now the cellular structure of the bodies of everyone on Earth—no exceptions—all human beings, has one primary motivation, and that's to return to the earth, to the planet body. The primary motivation of the cellular structure of your body is to go back to being its earth self. Part of the reason [chuckles] that you don't live very long is because your physical body wants to return to the earth from whence it was made. You have to change the motivation of those cells so that they can celebrate the existence of the soul personality they encapsulate. Right now they don't do that. They might like you, they might love you, they might have lots of interaction with your soul personality, but ultimately they want to go home. That needs to change.

Through singing, what you might call chanting, with certain rhythms and staccatos that these youngsters will do, the physical bodies of all beings will . . . it's as if the sounds interacting with the pyramids and what the pyramids do . . . it's not just that the sounds switch on the pyramids, no, no. The sounds must be made and then the pyramids join in. The minute the sounds stop, [thumps] the pyramids are lumps again, just sitting there. So it's not interference.

The singing is the switch, then?

That's right, the singing is the catalyst that makes it work. Then the cellular structure begins to change. It becomes more personalized to each individual's soul personality—I don't want to say psyche because that is a means by which you have mentally understood your personality. But it's not really that. Your soul personality is the essence of you, having to do with your feelings as expressed physically and your eternal soul, which is your immortal personality, yes?

But can't we do that now?

Well, there's no reason to do it now. If you could do it now and change the motivation of your cellular structure, for one thing, right away you'd simply go to the fourth dimension. You'd be out of here. You'd miss all the action; you'd probably be on fourth-dimensional Earth and basically be alone. There might be the occasional person who drops by and says, "What are *you* doing here?" You'd be saying, "Well, I figured out how to do this, and now here I am." They'd keep you company for a couple days and then they'd go on.

So there's no advantage in doing that. It needs to be done when it needs to be done. The change in the cellular structure will allow you to live longer and also be healthy, by the way. Disease is one of the means by which the cells get to return to the earth, all right?

But if they don't have that motivation . . .

Yes, if they don't have that motivation anymore, disease will no longer be a factor. The germs, as you call them, will still be around, but your bodies will no longer be affected by them. You can compare it to the idea of having total immunity, but it isn't immunity because there won't be an immune system—it will be gone. The immune system isn't needed because the cell structures will celebrate life as a participant with your soul personalities and won't be interested in returning to earth. They're having fun being you.

That's how you can live for 1200 years, see? You stop living only if there's something you want to do in a different form. Then you have a ceremony wherein your cellular structure becomes part of whatever planet you're on. But the thing is [chuckles], the change that takes place is really one of perspective. It is a personalization. It's an interesting thing. You could ask, "Well, how does the DNA change? How does the molecular structure change?" But it doesn't have anything to do with that, really. It just has to do with a change in attitude, one might say.

Which changes everything else.

It changes everything else. Then nobody has measles anymore, nobody gets chicken pox. Cancer is a word that after a few years nobody even remembers. It goes in the history books and that's it. Doctors find something else to do.

[Laughs.] Wonderful! You have a vibrant personality, yet you are one-third of the Explorer Race. How do you function as a being although you are a fragment?

That's a reasonable question. Sometimes I talk to you . . . basically I'm speaking to you as my united self in the future. That's what I'm doing here. I'm going to use the term "future" and "higher dimension" interchangeably here. In the higher-dimensional aspects of my selves back at the thirty-third dimension I am complete. There's no being such as yourself in the thirty-third dimension, so there's no distraction. I can also do that.

Most of the population of Earth comes from you two beings, so . . .

. . . right now.

Identifying One of Us As Your Source

. . . how can an individual person reading this book trace back to either one of you? How are you two different? How do we connect with one or the other of you?

You don't actually have to do that. It's like this: I'm trying to give you some personality traits that you can use as landmarks. If you know whether you are more magnetic, for instance, or more electrical, if that makes any sense (I realize that Zoosh has used the terms "electrical" to apply to male and "magnetic" to apply to female, but let's set those explanations aside), and if you can identify yourself as being more magnetic or more electrical in your nature—and I think a lot of people know how to do that—if you are electrical, you are like us. Magnetics have a lot to do with functioning from a spiritual, inspirational aspect.

What is the difference between you and the root being who talked to us two days ago? You explained how those who are more spiritual and magnetic related to the being who had very, very few people here, but most of the people on Earth are coming either from you or the being you call your counterpart. How can we tell which one of the two of you we're from?

I don't know that it's necessary to do that because we are so closely linked, but I'll tell you what: Those who are reading this are more exposed to my personality, which might not come out directly in words, and after me my companion will talk. Whichever personality you feel more attracted to or identify with most is the one from which you stem. With that consideration as an aside, the personality is more demonstrable on tape. If people want to be able to answer that question for themselves as you posed it, it might be useful to make the tapes available to those people who want to *hear* the difference in personality to get that extra quality. [Call 1-800-450-0985 to order these specific tapes— chapters 14 and 15—at $10 each plus $3 shipping.]

Back to where the three of you have joined up and you're with the Creator. How do you feel you are influencing the creation? You also got a picture of the inspirational ribbon, right?

Here we were, baffled, our entire group there. Then we had a picture of this Creator, which we took to be a creator, and this Creator's companion.

Just you and your counterpart, or everybody in . . .

Everybody. We all had this picture of this being moving along. And we saw the ribbon, then instantaneously we started going forward after being parked for all this time. That was how we knew that there was a direct connection. Then my companion and I, as you say . . .

. . . got off the bus.

Off the bus and went flying in that direction. We knew that it had to do with where we were going.

What was your take on this experience?

Interestingly enough, we didn't think about it. We were just happy to know that this is where we were going and that we wouldn't have to wait anymore. We just continued to observe all that we went through. The difference was, you know, that the minute we dropped to the twelfth dimension, when we came upon things we went around them. We didn't go through them anymore. Even though we were still at the twelfth dimension, a higher pulse frequency than a lot of the things we went around, we started going around things. I didn't really know why at the time, but looking back on it, I realize we were getting used to the idea of being third-dimensional or fourth-dimensional or fifth-dimensional, where you do have to actually move around things.

Were you going around other creations within this Circle of Creation?

Well, no, we would fly through creations. But if we came to a planet, for instance, we'd go around the planet, not through it.

At what point did you begin to understand why you were here?

I don't think we really grasped that until we had been within the full body of your Creator. By that time It had assimilated the ribbon and had begun to discuss it with fellow consultants and so on. I think that we had to actually be *in* your Creator to get the general idea and feelings and so on of what your Creator had planned up to that point in time. But we didn't really explore it (if I might use that term) until we joined with your Creator.

Our Feelings about the Explorer Race
Scenario and Speeding It Up

How did you feel as you became aware of this scenario of ignorance and suffering, of what was coming up?

We had an experience that we could identify with (of course, it was a naive assessment at the time, but that's what we had). We identified suffering with what we experienced when we were baffled, waiting. Being baffled is not always pleasant, so we identified suffering with the feeling associated with being baffled, because that's all we had to go on at that time. When we started communicating with the Master of Discomfort, then we understood a lot more.

But we weren't afraid of it because . . . well, you were all children once, and what you don't know about, even if you hear about it extensively, you really do not fear so much. So I don't think we ever felt afraid. As a matter of fact, I think fear is a tool of being physical here. You need it so you that when you touch that hot object, you know not to touch it again. Fear helps you out there, see? So we didn't actually experience fear or anxiety in association with the idea of suffering.

We understood from the Creator that a lot of the things that went into this creation were not His ideas, that the Explorer Race put in the ignorance and the suffering, and He had to keep the faith and believe in whatever we were doing.

Well, we had a lot of time traveling in your Creator to discuss these potentials with the Master of Discomfort, Zoosh and to some extent the Master of Plasmic Energy. The plasmic consultant had a lot of knowledge and experience about the velocity of manifestation, otherwise known as [draws] . . . for the sake of your illustrations. (Please excuse the poor excuse for drawing here.) Formula: velocity [V] times manifestation [M] equals velocity/manifestation to the infinite [VM$^\infty$], all right?

Because the Master of Plasmic Energy had that wisdom, we were discussing all of the potentials of how to do this project even though it was up to

$$[V] \cdot [M] = VM^\infty$$

your Creator to do it. Your Creator is a strong believer in taking advice, though not necessarily in applying it. You might ask for advice; you listen and you either use it or not. After talking to the plasmic master and learning about this formula, we discovered that the Explorer Race as you are now could spend about five times as much time as you've spent now to get to the point of transition where you are now, or you could do it in one-fifth the time by inducing stress agents. It's not that we were in a rush, but we discussed with your Creator whether it was of value to speed up the experiment.

Our perception was at that time to do it quicker, just that. We were basically impatient. But your Creator said, "Yes, this is of value, but not for that reason." Your Creator felt, having a deeper understanding of Its own project, that stress (I'm loosely referring to discomfort as stress) would challenge you because it would immediately put into your experience instantaneous consequences that could be experienced within a lifetime, very often in much less time than that. So your Creator decided to include it, but not for the reason we originally discussed. So yes, we suggested it, but I'd have to say that it was more of a committee decision, although ultimately all decisions were made by your Creator, being the chairman of the board (the board being made up of advisors, not voting members). [Chuckles.]

That's my kind of board! [Laughs.]

[Chuckles.] No comment.

So what was your experience? That's what we're really trying to find out here. What was your contribution and your feelings as this went forward?

When Each Root Became Committed

Well, I must admit that I was a little unenthusiastic as it originally started to play out. Here we were after being birthed; discussions were over and now it was time to do it. At first the idea of fragmenting further and then breaking off from my companion . . . even though it's not a complete break, you know, we're connected. At first I wasn't comfortable with it, I'll admit it. It took quite some time, because initially beings were just going out, looking around and having fun. While that's wonderful, I didn't see how that was any different from what my companion and I had been doing on our own. It was like, "Okay, now there's more of us. Not to be crass, but so what?

I did not at that time fully grasp your Creator's ultimate intention here, so in the beginning (fully one-third of the way into the Explorer Race experience) I was not reluctant, but I wasn't fully committed. My companion was committed much sooner than I was and the other root being was committed from the outset. After about a third of it went by I began to see the results—I must admit, I'm results-oriented. I could see the results and I started to see what your Creator had as an ultimate plan. That's when I became committed.

How did everything change when you became enthusiastic?

When I became enthusiastic, more soul fragments of the Explorer Race from my source were more easily generated. In the beginning the third root being (not my companion and I) was creating the most; most of the Explorer Race was outflowing from the other being. Then my companion started outflowing, and I came in at the end. That is why the other root being is now . . .

. . . is done.

Is basically done. Started first, done first. [Chuckles.] So my slow commitment to the end result of the experience has allowed my people, my beings, to have longer to savor the experience. That's the spin I'm going to put on it, all right?

But the others didn't go through this level of front-line action, did they?

They did, but it wasn't front-line action. In terms of the tumult that you have nowadays, they did not have to go through as much of that. They had some, but to the extent of the level of temptation and corruption and confusion and violence and (if I might throw in the generic term) the good life—all that thrown together amongst other things—they didn't have to go through quite that extreme. But they did go through it in segmented ways, meaning they had some in one life or some in another life. I'm not trying to suggest that they are less experienced. I'd rather suggest that my companion and I have the energy that could produce beings that can handle it better.

When did the others get out of here? Was it before Atlantis?

Atlantis, When Most of the First Root's Beings Left

They're not all out of here. Most of them got out after Atlantis. Fully 50 or 60% were out by the time Atlantis started, but at the end of Atlantis another 17 or 18% left. You know, one tends to hear about Atlantis in such glowing terms except for the end, but you have to remember that certain things started in Atlantis that might seem very minor to you now, but at the time they weren't minor at all. That was the experience of *separation*—having a separate god, having individuality, having your mate or family members be separate beings and not fully united in the heart. All of this was quite new. It was on the gentle level of a community violence. A lot of beings said, "Okay, that's enough." You know, you can say that, and if it is enough, you can go; but if it isn't enough, then you don't go. A lot of beings left after Atlantis.

But a lot of us who are still here were there.

Yes, oh yes. By that time predominant beings in Atlantis were more from my companion and myself. A lot of the other root being's people left after that point. It was like, "Okay, that's enough of that."

It sounds like they matured mostly in Lemuria.

No. They matured much before then. Lemuria and Atlantis are referred to most often to you because you can have some sense of identification with those civilizations. But other civilizations that might not necessarily relate to you, sometimes vague even to the point of no sense of connection at all, offered them some experience, too.

How the Early Civilizations Established the Needed Frameworks

Zoosh once said that there were eighteen civilizations prior to this one.

That's about right. I can see seventeen of them, but if he says eighteen, okay.

He's never talked much about them. Because they were so different, it's possible that we wouldn't relate to them. Very briefly, how would you see them, as starts and stops? Were we all there?

The trends of those civilizations were the first general experiences of identity in groups, not having what you call an ego identity but more of a group identity, though not a mass identity. I'm giving it to you generally because it doesn't relate to you.

Help me understand that. My limited knowledge is that we were in Orion, but I don't know where we were before that. We were in Orion and very briefly on that negative planet in Sirius, then Maldek and then here. We didn't get here until this, the eighteenth civilization? Can you put that in any kind of perspective?

You know, we're talking about different time lines here, so this is a "here we go again" situation.

Go back and trace it. What was the flow to get here? How does it really work? I don't know about that; we've never talked about it.

Well, first off, beings had to experience life as you know it in some senses, having individual lights or what we call sparkles of being, fragmented personalities. It's sort of a very basic level of individuality, but not feeling separated at all. That was really the first realm, if I can use that term, the first stage of existence after the initial separation from the root beings. The next stage was going to various planets and starting the initial cultures. I'm going to put it just like that, "various planets," because names of planets here are pointless.

They're in other galaxies?

Yes, but they're in this universe, naturally.

But not galaxies we would even understand.

It's pointless to say it, because if you look at all the books that have been channeled by all the different beings, half the time you'll get the same planet or the same galaxy called fifteen different names from fifteen different people. I don't want to add to the confusion, so I'm going to speak generally about it. That's when beings, soul fragments, were beginning to experiment with bodies or body groups how to express individually: "I look like this" or "I look like that," as different beings. Then as a result of looking this way or that way and having or not having certain abilities, cultures would develop from that.

A physical anthropologist, for instance, could say that certain aspects of the human-being culture in your bodies are directly correlated to the way you look and to the capacities you have. For example, you have vocal cords, you can sing. Some other beings might not have vocal cords; they might not be able to make sounds, you understand. That kind of thing was being established—the way a being looks and the culture and what they can or cannot do—and the culture that grows out of that. The establishment of various civilizations and their cultures followed. These cultures had basically been set up without having contact with other cultures, so the next stage had to be contact with cultures unlike themselves—space travel, having the multibeing contact, seeing other beings.

Immediately after that a lot of people [chuckles] changed their occupations, saying, "Oh, I like what you're doing much better." At this point there hadn't been any termination of life; there wasn't birth, there wasn't death. That hadn't even started yet. Everybody was immortal. They would be what they are, then they discovered what other beings were and they wanted to try that. So they would stop being what they were and be the other thing. That was the next stage. (We're trying to condense it here.)

After that was the exploration of dimensional possibilities. All of this had been going on then right around the eighth or ninth dimension. Nobody had yet gone to the more physical dimensions and said, "But how about doing it here?" So the next stage was essentially a repeat of those first processes that I mentioned as beings descended into various dimensions all the way to the second. Most beings decided that the second dimension did not offer enough variety of experience in expression to be able to sustain life for a long time. It was too much of what I would call . . . not humdrum, but very predictable, a lot of sameness. At second dimension, beings, especially beings who have had vast amounts of variety, are able to be one thing for long periods of time. That is my perception of the second dimension. It is not less than the third dimension; it just has a different expression.

The Introduction of Birth and Death to Create Urgency and Purpose

So after going through those different stages that I mentioned initially and then descending into the dimensions (we've probably already passed eighteen civilizations), those same stages took place. It wasn't until the third dimension, followed quickly by the fifth dimension and significantly later in the fourth dimension that a limited term for life was experienced, brought about by birth and death. It was not that long ago in terms of the length of this universe.

Birth and death as you know it began, I would say, about two-thirds of the way in. Before that time birth and death didn't exist as you know it. The reason birth and death became so readily accepted by so many different dimensions was that even at the higher dimensions it introduced a sense of urgency. Now, if one is living for 1200 years, one could say, "Well, it doesn't seem like much urgency there," but that's only in comparison. It introduced a greater sense of purpose and of applying oneself to that purpose. You might say it was an idea that caught on.

Whose idea was it?

I think it was my companion's fragments that started it, and it caught on and spread very quickly. It is even experienced by beings who choose the experience at the eighth or ninth dimension. It doesn't *have* to be experienced, but it can be for beings who want it. It was recognized early on as a growth-stimulating experience, and since perhaps the ultimate intention of this universe is growth, it entrenched itself very fast. I'd have to say that from my perception, in terms of the evolution of the Explorer Race, the birth/death cycle is the last and most important stage. I don't consider separation or violence so important. Before then, growth would happen in a more lackadaisical fashion. For instance, you might be exposed to something that you were relatively interested in, but since you had, from your perspective, an indefinite amount of time, you could very easily say, "I'll do that later." Then you might or might not. But if you have a relatively predictable fixed amount of time for a life, and you're exposed to something you like, you might go and do that more quickly. That has been, I think, the last and most important change.

The Application of Ignorance

But what about the ignorance and the forgetting?

I don't consider even that so important. This is my perspective. But when did ignorance come in? I think it is a relatively recent experience. I think that the first true, applied experiment of ignorance was on Orion. That's when beings tried to understand the sacredness of the birth/death cycle as it would be seen then and really is. That's when beings considered whether there is any value in not knowing. Up to that point in time they were knowing more and more and more, but after a time of assimilating information, no matter how much more you assimilate, you don't feel like you're gaining any ground. It was really, I must admit, a revolutionary idea that some beings had.

"If instead of creating magnitudes or levels of expansion of gaining knowledge or wisdom, how about if we just do the opposite? What if we introduce a tension that blocks or slows the acquisition of knowledge or wisdom?" That's when that started—in the Orion culture, as far as I know. I must admit now that I have heard Zoosh's rationale on this, and it's very good, but I feel that ignorance was ultimately the cause of discomfort. I know that Creator has acquiesced to discomfort, and I understand that discomfort has its accelerating factor. I realize that I sound like I'm contradicting my first point of view, but I allow myself the privilege of changing my perspective.

If I had it to do all over again, I would have voiced an objection to including ignorance in such a way. If it had been up to me, I would have allowed or encouraged people and cultures to access at the deep meditative level greater knowledge and wisdom than they possess. Zoosh has told me, and I can hear you thinking it, that channeling or telepathy or inspiration accomplish that. That's true, but not all societies have accepted them as viable means of taking action. So I must admit to being closer to your Creator's camp right now, in terms of the idea that the veil of ignorance has created just a little bit too much mischief. Now, I didn't start out with that point of view; it is something that I shifted to. So I will be very happy when you get to the fourth dimension, because enough of the veil will be pulled away and individuals will be able to relax—deep relaxation, not even what you call meditation—and be easily inspired. I feel that is necessary.

Okay, so Orion was the first. What happened after that?

It wasn't the first. I have already passed through all of that. The first was what I told you initially, and then I compounded it going down through the dimensions. It was more than eighteen, but that is my perspective in terms of description. So Orion wasn't even the first, from my perspective.

But it was a more dense physical. It relates more to what we're doing.

That's right. It relates, and that's why I think Zoosh has told you only certain things. You know, Zoosh likes to tell you things about yourself, being the end-time historian. Speaking for him now, if I may, he's disinclined to wax on eloquently [chuckles], if I may use his term, about things that really aren't connected with you at this time.

I'm just trying to open it up a little bit more.

That's all right.

What can you tell us about the time from Orion to Maldek to here? Can you amplify that story a little?

I think you already did that. You'd have to be specific.

My Fragments

Let's leave that alone for a moment. As you split into fragments, did different fragments come from different parts of your personality?

No.

Or is it a holographic thing where every fragment is part of the total part of you?

Yes, and it's exponential. If I initially split into ten, and then from ten into a hundred and so on, or ten into a thousand (it's not to any powers, but it expands like that), at some point I'm always expanding, but everything is expanding in the same rhythm, meaning from one to ten, from ten to a hundred, from a hundred to a thousand. At some point, once I got from 10,000 to 100,000, the particles or the portions (ensoulments, if you would) started to understand the process. Having had experience in some levels of life, they were then given (by me and by Creator, of course) permission to fragment on their own, but not until they got to be 100,000. So one might fragment to ten and the others not and so on.

What changed as a result? Because that was all of you, did that filter down to all the parts of you?

I am all the parts of me *now*. I have always been all the parts of me, so that's always available, although at higher dimension.

I was wondering how the parts would be influenced.

The parts are not influenced. The parts have influenced the total, which is me. So the experience of my parts, if we can say that, because of their experience and because of having authority to duplicate themselves and go on in directions they wish to go, has influenced me. That is nice, because it is ultimately the intention. That which stems from something . . . the source is not always the one who provides. What goes on is more like this: You were birthed out by your Creator, you were colored and affected by your Creator, and you are intended to pass something back to your Creator. From my now perspective I see that this is the ultimate intent. It is not that we gradually reveal bits of the puzzle to *you*. It is more that by your experience you reveal bits to *us*.

That's another thing here that probably isn't in most creations. You split and fragmented, the three of you, to become us, but at the same time we are cloaked in the material provided by the Creator and are influenced by the friends of the Creator as to certain qualities.

Yes.

So we are more than what you were and bring all that back to you.

Yes.

But not to the Creator? But He also learned from us.

Yes, back to the Creator also—it goes back up the line. In my understanding, this cosmic-soup effect eventually goes back up the line all the way, meaning that no matter how magnificent beings are, sometimes they grow as far as they can grow on their own, and then other beings down the line, because of what they have learned, cause the beings up the line to grow more. I think every parent can understand that. Ofttimes your children do things that cause you to learn.

There's so much to talk about. Tell your fragments what you would like them to know, then maybe we can talk again sometime.

Well, this has been a most enlightening experience for me. I've learned a lot about companionship and letting go. I had to let go of my companion. I've learned that sometimes the sum is greater than the total of the parts, because you have assimilated knowledge and wisdom from which I have expanded and can see things differently. So never think of yourselves as less-than or smaller-than, because ultimately what is small in one moment can be very large in the next.

We'll talk to you again?

If you like.

The First Root Returns

March 3, 1997

an I go to the living library where the first root came from, then the temple where the other two came from, or do I stop with these root beings?

Zoosh: Keep going as long as you want to get material for this book. It's not a problem.

I have to confess that I taped over the first ten minutes of the first root of the Explorer Race. Maybe we could get him back again.

Well, let's do that now. Let him talk about where he came from.

All right. I am one of the roots of the Explorer Race. My point of origin is far, far from here, but I believe most of the Explorer Race roots do come from a considerable distance. My first recollection of any sense of self came about in what would look like a galaxy if you approached it from a distance, having that spiral shape. But as you approached it you would see that the lights, the colors within it, are not stars as much as concentrated light that has an almost crystalline appearance.

The Light Library of All Knowledge

This substance has the capacity to read light waves, vibrational waves and feeling waves. They have been in existence for so long that I cannot illustrate it with a number, even a type of number such as has been used for these books. I can only say that this place is primarily the library of all knowledge, as far as I know. It has been available for advanced beings to consult with for a long time.

The visits by advanced beings are perhaps not frequent, but they are thorough, meaning the exchange of knowledge is considerable. Most of the time the beings who come to consult the knowledge portions are creators or consultants to creators. Now and then a child who in a previous incarnation has gone near this place will dream of this place. When that occurs, the images given the child are benevolent and beautiful, and will often represent the seeds of ideas the child might have the capacity to bring about in some benevolent way or form wherever it exists.

The Pleiadian Child Who Dreamed Certain Symbols

For example, I remember on one occasion a dreaming child who used to live on the Pleiades and who in a previous incarnation had passed near this place in a light vehicle. At the time, the being felt the immense sense of wisdom emanating from this light library. Sometimes these exposures impact a soul so deeply that they dream of it in another life, the dream state being one in which the individual soul, even within a life, is functioning in an unlimited capacity. This dreaming child was given certain images, not what you would call visions, but symbols, and when she woke up these symbols remained in her consciousness. I will reproduce one of the symbols [draws]. This simple, innocuous, not unpleasant symbol (especially to a youngster and to many others) was given to her.

Being of an age where children like to decorate things and be artistic, that same day she put the symbols on a large graphic she was constructing. The teacher was fascinated (the teacher in this case being someone who guides but does not lead the child). On the Pleiades childhood is considered to be the sacred state of life in which children absorb their personalities and acquire traits for later in life, and also where they tend to reveal things. The dreams of children are paid close attention on the Pleiades.

When queried, the child revealed to the teacher that she had dreamed these symbols. The teacher, being knowledgeable in symbolic languages, had never seen any of these symbols before, so after the child had gone about her afternoon activities, the teacher called in one of the scholars of symbolics on the Pleiades. That individual had not seen them either. One might think that people would then come and copy the symbols, but that is not the case on the Pleiades.

There is a significant amount of respect paid to children, so the child was asked to reproduce the symbols on the side of a large, floating sculpture, which was lowered for her to reproduce them. This she did on all six sides of this particular figure. She was told she could reproduce them in any order and form. Although other people had produced graphics on this particular floating sculpture, she was also given the right to do so.

The scholars had noticed that the symbols caused them to feel good and rather excited, but they weren't sure why. So the sculpture was placed where it would be seen by young and old alike. As it happened, many people started dreaming and having visions, and an entire new form of higher-plane spirituality developed out of this. The observers, the scholars and those who monitor somewhat the spiritual life on the Pleiades noticed that when people studied or simply stared at these symbols, they were more quickly able to achieve deeper meditative states and visions relating to challenges or problems. (On Earth they would be only small things to be worked out, but on the Pleiades they might be considered problems.) These symbols proved to be a visioning aid.

Placing Root Origins on the Map

In relation to what the seed being who talked last said about where he was from, is where you're from beyond that or in the other direction or on top of it?

It's hard to give a point of reference, but if you were going out into space from this point in space, they are farther out.

Did you see the outside of the realms we've heard about here as you came this way? In other words, was it from beyond all these realms, or did you come through them?

I was beyond all these realms, yes.

And when you came here, you came . . .

. . . near them, yes. It wasn't necessary to pass through them, as a matter of fact.

So you and the other two can see them from the outside?

Yes.

And you're the one who had all the stories, right?

Yes.

I didn't know before that the other two were companions and you were alone. How did that feel during this whole experiment?

You have to understand that I was called, and I didn't really know that anybody else was coming. It wasn't a factor, so I don't think that I ever felt in any way separate from the others. They just happened to be companions, but now we are all contributing. I feel fine about it. [Chuckles.]

I'm just trying to expand what we learned from the other one. But you, I understand, were the first one out there. It's as if you started first and your extensions or fragments got through first. Is that a fair thing to say?

"Out there" meaning where?

You fragmented yourself first, and your fragments completed the process as members of the Explorer Race?

Oh, you mean, was I the first one out *here*?

Yes.

Yes, yes, and it was an interesting experience. But then you already know this.

So you didn't have any hesitancy, you just went for it.

Yes. Just because one is in many pieces does not mean that one is separated.

So you still had a sense of self even though there were billions of you.

Yes. You might say that you have a sense of thought even though there are many cells in your brain.

I know, but the cells aren't floating around out there functioning by themselves.

But from my perception there is no difference. I can look at the cells in your brain, and each one has its own distinct personality.

Really?

They choose to be in your brain. They like what they are doing, and if they ever don't like what they are doing, they simply pass out of existence in terms of that substance. Their energy or light goes elsewhere and they become something else. A physician might say that the cell died, but the cell doesn't think of it that way.

Your Creator's Two False Runs

Zoosh started to say something about this being the third time our Creator had attempted this. You three made the Explorer Race happen. Did He try this before without separate seed beings?

I think that your Creator made a couple of what Zoosh might have referred to as false runs—not being "wrong," but your Creator twice attempted to produce the Explorer Race entirely from Itself. The problem is that no matter how complex created beings are, creators can ultimately reproduce only themselves. They can't actually reproduce a being who has qualities beyond which the creator possesses or has access to. The Explorer Race needed to have qualities your Creator did not possess.

The first pass of the experiment that your Creator made was simply an attempt to put out particles of Itself, but this didn't work because the beings could not function in a circumstance of ignorance, however brief. They couldn't do it because creators are normally connected to many beings at once, and even if they're fragments of creators, they are still creators. If you suddenly separate and isolate them, they will immediately do what all creators do when they are isolated—shut down.

If a creator is isolated in a space in which it creates, it is not a problem; it will continue to create. But if it is isolated even within the parent creator's space and does not have the connections to its normal sources of wisdom, it will just stop until it is reconnected. That was the first pass. Your Creator did not know that, I might add, and just waited. It then attempted to give more and more energy to these beings, but kept the veil of ignorance there. After a while It realized that they were also waiting. So that was a failure.

Then your Creator reabsorbed the beings and thought about it for a while. [Chuckles.] Later It asked the consultants what they recommended. One of the consultants said, "How about stimulating the beings by giving them a strong bias to the future? This will surely cause them to want to bring some kind of future about."

Which consultant?

I think it was the dimensional master, yes [Synchronizer of Physical Reality and Dimensions, chapter 19 of *Explorer Race: Creator and Friends*]. Your Creator thought it was worth a try and tried it again. But it didn't work because those beings simply traveled far into the future, beyond which point this universe was no longer in this space, and proceeded to produce their own universe there. Creator was unsure what to do at that point and had to refer to the Council of Creators. You see, once a creator or even fragments of creators start to produce a universe, it is not all right to stop them.

The Council of Creators had to do something extraordinary, which is done occasionally. They had to re-create on their own the portions of energy that your Creator had spun off, manufacturing a temporary (in creator terms, temporary is a long time) space at a much higher dimension than is normally used for such creations, in order to envelop this creation and allow it to continue. It is there to this day, right around the sixty-sixth dimension—a dimension not normally accessed by beings in this space for *any* reason.

I might add that it is an interesting creation, not unlike the creation here, naturally, but with the exception that there is no Explorer Race there. Because these beings were given a bias to the future, they are constantly creating various alternative futures that every being they have created there can experience. A being might have a choice of a past they have made and a choice of a present they are in. But they have the conscious capacity at any moment to choose any of a hundred or even two hundred potential futures, having the complete understanding of where every one of those futures will go.

So will that be brought back into the Creator and absorbed now when we take over for him?

No.

That'll keep going?

It'll keep going as far as I know.

And what does that do to the Creator?

Nothing. The portion of the Creator that was spun off to create this was re-created in the Creator, and these beings, these creators that function as a group, have basically become their own creator, although with a bias. I expect that within a few hundred thousand years someone will come along and ask them if they wish to continue. They will be spelled if they wish it.

And they would then rejoin the Creator?

No.

They're totally separate?

Yes.

We Were Consultants First, Then Became the Explorer Race

But this doesn't make sense, because supposedly you three seed beings were perched in the Creator before He came to this space. So when did He do all that?

We came, yes, but He did not utilize us immediately. I believe your Creator initially considered that our energy alone would be enough to fuel this, so we were essentially consultants. You have to remember that your Creator was rounding up consultants during the time we joined and that your Creator did not send out a call for us. That's been covered—your Creator didn't send out a call.

Your Creator naturally assumed that someone else had sent out the call and that we would be consultants able to offer advice about the Explorer Race. Even we did not know at the time that it was intended that *we* become the Explorer Race. It was only after these two tries and another long wait that your Creator asked us if we would be willing to become the Explorer Race, since our experience was different from your Creator's and we did not have a particular job. The other consultants had a job. Your Creator initially thought that it was our job to advise Him on the creation of the Explorer Race, that's all. In one way, your Creator was assimilating beings to advise Him. So then your Creator thought that perhaps *we* were supposed to do this. "Are you open to doing this?" asked your Creator. We said yes.

They don't send a manual, do they? [Laughs.]

No. Interestingly enough, I might add that at the higher levels there is no manual either. The advantage you have as members of the Explorer Race is that at the level you are now functioning, you are used to not having a manual, whereas there is a manual in other more benign civilizations such as the Pleiades, Orion, Sirius—all of these places you are familiar with. The philosophy they are born into is planetary, sometimes even galactic, and the philosophy is essentially the manual.

Having No Manual

As the Explorer Race you do not have that. That is why *not* having a planetary culture is considered part of your education—so every parent must fend for him/herself. This is absolute training in being a creator, because every creator must fend for itself, yes. Creators can seek advice from the Council, they can go hither and yon and explore places, but ultimately, when it comes to their personal creations, there is no manual whatsoever. They have no idea what is coming, and they know absolutely that they must deal with the consequences, whatever comes. To a lesser degree that is exactly what *you* are doing here on this planet.

That is incredible! So you now understand that this is why you were called.

Yes, but it wasn't at all clear in the beginning—not to anyone, I might add. Well, I can't say about Zoosh, since Zoosh has been known to keep secrets. [Chuckles.] Certainly in the case of the others, as far as I know no one had any inside information. We were all just trying to understand what to do next. It just so happened that in this case, the third time was indeed the charm, as you like to say.

Fragmenting: Easy for Me, Harder for the Other Two

The other seed being talked about the temple fragmenting, so it had a model for this fragmenting. Had you seen that happen before, and how did you feel as you became several?

I didn't have a model, no. The other beings, as you say, did have a model, so for them it was a natural thing to do; they had done it before. Not having had a model, I essentially studied for a long time your Creator's creation of other beings on other planets, and I used that as a model for fragmenting myself.

Well, you seem to have done it in a way that got you through the lessons and out quickly.

Yes, but perhaps that was because I was open to it. I was particularly keen on the experiment. It's hard to say because I can't speak for the other beings, but I think that even though they had a model for fragmentation, the other beings still had a bias to being part of the whole. They hadn't wanted to be fragmented; it was a last resort. They felt like "here we go again," and they were not keen on that. So they waited, not unlike the way the temple waited. They waited till the last possible moment before they would participate, but I did not have that bias. Because I came from a place that was essentially made up of fragments, the idea of fragments was something natural to me.

Say more about that. You felt that you were a particular part of that?

Well, the place I'm from was a spiral shape, but there were bits in the spiral shape (not stars), individual condensed light droplets that would sometimes illustrate colors, action going on inside these objects that looked at one moment like crystals and another like liquid light.

So I was used to the idea of at least pseudo-individuality. And the idea of becoming many was also familiar, because in that structure I consider my home (at least from my now perspective), even though there were many, there was a body consciousness, a union of all portions. Each portion had its own job, you might say, even its own personality characteristics, but each portion was also a part of the whole.

You said my brain cells chose to be there.

Yes, exactly, and as such then I was perhaps more amenable to the idea of fragmentation.

Does this library of all knowledge work like a hologram, where you have all knowledge inside you, or did you have a piece you were interested in or specialized in?

Stories/Epics and Story-Gathering

Well, think of it this way: If you tell a story, each word within the story represents not only a meaning, but very often a nuance within the story itself, possibly even stimulating a mood or stimulated by a mood from the storyteller. If you look at the story as being a chemical formula derived from some previous or even future circumstance, one can see that stories are connected to all other nuances of knowledge. You can see cords going out from the stories to every place where stories that have any quality of any story within this place would fit in.

That's why I say it has all knowledge. If you have something that connects to something else, that something else will connect to many other things, and before you know it you have an exponential series of connections, and regardless of distance, time or what-have-you, if the connection is made, it is immortal. In that sense the stories themselves are immortal.

Would you say that these stories are lives lived by other beings?

Not exactly. I'd say they were more like epics. One might read an epic such as *The Odyssey* by Homer and enjoy the story. Yet one has the distinct feeling that more is being said than the story itself. Thus it has a clearly symbolic interpretation. That's why I referred to the stories as being epics more than simple stories.

Yet they came from experiences of beings someplace, sometime.

Yes, and if a place had not had its stories absorbed, the web from this place would not reach out to steal the story. The web would reach out and be receptive and ask to have the story told to it in some way. It might be interesting to know that there are storytellers who are like gypsies or even salesmen, if you would, who go all over every universe everywhere gathering stories for this being—emissaries, you might say. And it is not a one-way transaction. The emissaries from this being tell stories as well, and their payment is in the stories of individuals, groups of individuals, clans, tribes, peoples, planets, galaxies, universes. Their product is stories and their payment is stories.

But they would be more on the level of Star Wars *or* The Empire Strikes Back *than a soap opera. I mean, they would be vast, more like that.*

I think perhaps that is too small a container to describe them. Think of this: If you were able now to sit down and with absolute recollection tell your story from the beginning, it would be epochal in its nature. Not only because of all of your incarnations, but even if you were able to tell your story from the beginning of this life, you wouldn't simply say, "I don't remember that," because you would remember everything. You would be able to describe how every attitude, every expression on your face came about, how every thought was attracted to your consciousness. You would be able to explain everything about who you are.

That would be an epochal description of your life because it would explain in absolute detail who and what you are today as far as this life goes. And when the listener heard it, he would have a complete knowledge not only of who you are, but a pretty fair idea of how you would represent yourself five years from today even though you would have acquired more along the way.

Thus sometimes the story-gatherers and storytellers, especially in cases where beings are reincarnated, will tend to go to the same being (but in a reincarnated self) and ask for their story. Even if a being should reincarnate in another galaxy, a story-gatherer would go to him after a time and say, "And how would you describe your story of this life now?" then compare it to how they described their life in the previous incarnation. The gatherer would understand that if one individual with the capacity for total recollection (say an individual 50 or 60 years old) were to describe his story in detail, the story receiver would have a vast understanding of that civilization on that planet in that moment.

And these emissaries have been going out since the beginning of creation?

As far as I know, yes. Once they receive the stories, they send them up the line in cords to my point of origin, and the stories continue to travel. I might add that this is a nice job for certain individuals, a job that one is not assigned to in perpetuity. Storytellers and story-gatherers will sometimes do this for a time and then decide to do something else, because there are a great many individuals who seem to like to do this.

Have you been a story gatherer?

I have not, but I have known beings who have done it for a while, then other beings have come along to do it.

Then what do they go back to do?

I don't think it's a matter of going back; they go on to do whatever else is . . . understand that if one is a story-gatherer, one gets to go to far-flung places all over, and you might see something particularly appealing that you might wish to do. And when that particular mission is done, you can turn in your card, as it were, and incarnate there.

As a portion of that original spiral place, are you in touch with all these other beings? Is there some kind of a mental or a feeling connection to them?

There is a feeling connection, yes. It allows me to access certain knowledge they have, but I must admit that I do not have the capacity to reproduce at a moment's notice all knowledge that my source has.

Not all, but you can get whatever you need whenever you need it?

Yes, but I don't often need it.

Because?

Because I'm here. Here new things are being produced. In other places things are essentially being done as they've always been done, however wonderful they might be. The new thing is happening here, so I'm more inclined to be *producing* a story than acquiring one.

How were you chosen for this new thing, this exciting thing?

My Contribution: Stories

I think it's because of my connection to this being of stories. If you look at your culture and the culture of the Explorer Race, you can easily say that ultimately the past, present and future of the Explorer Race and all that it has been, is doing and will do can most easily be expressed in stories. If you look at all of your cultures that exist today and many that have gone before you as well as those that will come, almost all knowledge worth preserving for future generations is preserved in stories.

Look what has happened in the past in civilizations when attempts have been made to preserve valuable knowledge and wisdom. Invariably a succeeding civilization comes along and judges the wisdom of that culture less worthy than their own, and they will often destroy it, capture it or secrete it away. But stories are entertainment, and stories are easily passed on from generation to generation, and they are not often abridged.

That is why some of your scholars have looked at the modern works of Shakespeare, for example, and said, "Here you have basic story lines." As a scholar might say, "If you look to dramas produced today, they can easily be traced to the basic stories within this modern work of Shakespeare." Of course, Shakespeare also reproduced stories. Looking at whatever invisible hand invited me or a representative of my point of origin to participate here, it must have felt that stories in their own right would make a necessary contribution.

But it goes back even further. You said Shakespeare used old stories, but the Bible is full of stories of things that happened when we were on other planets and other galaxies, and they've been brought here.

Yes, the Bible has allusions to that. Certainly, documents—including ones that were cut out of the Bible, the Talmud and others because it was felt to be repetitive or for other reasons—are influential in your current time. Chinese writings of thousands of years ago are essentially about stories, even though they might be laws or suggestions on how to live—the Tao, for example. How to live, how it is best to live, are most often included in stories because it is infinitely easier to remember a story and its imparted moral message than to remember a book of rules.

You brought these stories here and shared them with the other two seeds. Everyone is living out these stories, yet we're taking them beyond what they were? Is that a fair . . .

No, I wouldn't say that. I would rather say that I brought with me the value, the essence, the institution of stories. And I did not tell stories unless I was asked. You have to remember that when you're dealing with consultants such as those you have heard from, many are creators. They might ask for your advice, but they won't ask you to explain why you are advising something. Even though I tend to speak in stories, they do not ask me to explain my position.

All right, let me get at this another way, then. When you fragmented, every fragment had access to all these stories?

No, but every fragment had a bias to the value of stories.

Well, could you say they lived more dramatic lives? What was the benefit of the stories to your fragments, then?

I think you still do not quite understand. That is because you have been raised in a society where stories in general are taken for granted. What I am saying here is that you might go to other universes where stories might not exist at all. One tends to take for granted, when one is raised in a certain context, that what is omnipresent is also universal beyond this universe. But in my experience that is never the case. For example, if you were a culture of bacteria living on sugar water, as part of that culture, that mini universe, you would assume that the sweetness of sugar was universal. Never having been exposed to salt, salt would come as quite a shock.

[Laughs.] That's a good way to explain it. We dream in stories. We learn by stories, we . . .

You *are* stories, but it is not a universal function of all universes, not at all.

But you did bring that to this creation, because many of the beings now on this planet are not your fragments, yet you gave this to all of the Explorer Race.

Yes, because of my involvement in your Creator (at the beginning of various creations, in any event), in the creation that took place here in this universe, many, many beings in this universe now tell stories. Certainly I did not invent stories, and stories are in many other universes, but I can easily think of several universes where stories simply do not exist. So it is not an absolute.

Would you say that we're laggards or that we're just down here for the ultimate in experience—because your fragments are already off watching us someplace, right?

No, there are about 1% of my fragments still here—no, let me restate that. If we pull back and look at this planet, 1% of the Explorer Race here on this planet are my fragments, to be specific. But the rest, as far as I know, have to do with the other two beings.

My Fragments More Imaginative,
99% Waiting for the Leap

All right. So how would we know your fragments from those of the other two roots? What is the differentiation, what clues?

This might be the common thread: At some point when my fragments were younger, perhaps even today, they would have been either accused or complimented (depending on their culture) or simply taken for granted for being dreamers. They might tend to be more imaginative, to fantasize more, to have greater depth of imagination. That's the only real difference.

Would they in many cases be the great writers or playwrights or . . .

Not necessarily. They might even be what your society calls escapists or other societies call visionaries. Some societies, if they have a problem, might ask for a vision. If the society is sufficiently sacred, the child who can most easily bring about visions will be trained to become the visionary or the seer for that tribe. That being will be asked what they see, and they won't see just one thing, but many possibilities. The seer's job within a tribal culture might be to mention the different things they see; then the leaders of the tribe or the wisdom keepers will, based on the different visions the seer sees, make a decision or choose a path to solve the problem.

The other seed being said that he and his companion were more practical, more physical.

Yes.

Since 1% of your fragments are still on Earth, what would you say the other 99% they have completed? What are they doing now?

Well, not to put too fine a point on it (as Zoosh likes to say), they are waiting.

But they can look at us, they can watch us?

Oh, certainly.

They see what we're doing?

Oh yes, if they choose.

And if they don't choose, what are they doing?

Whatever they wish. [Chuckles.] But they are waiting in this universe. Some of them are flying about looking at different things, but they are on call. [Chuckles.] And they are discouraged from incarnating.

Because?

Because they might be needed at any moment. Should the rest of you make the leap, they will all need to come, because you all need to come together quickly to make the shift to the fourth dimension, you understand.

What is your opinion on how close we are? Have we moved up from—where were we, 3.47?

I think you've made a fractional increase, but not enough to be considered 3.48.

Nobody knows, but is your guess a year, two years, five years, a hundred years? How long do you think those people have to wait?

I have to tell you that I personally (myself, my personality) have no personal experience with time, although my fragments have. But since I am speaking for my total self, to me a hundred billion years might be the same thing as a thousand seconds. So I would be hard-pressed to put a length of experiential time on it. Those are questions I leave to the end-time historian.

Merging the Three Roots and Clicking into Fourth Dimension

[Laughs.] There are a billion questions, but let's jump ahead to the leap, to the merge. How do you see that? Ultimately the three of you are going to be back together as total being?

Yes. If you were able to slow down the merge, it would seem like a sudden zooming together to a single point of brilliant light. It would be like astronomers observing the dawning of a new sun, where suddenly there's a new star in the sky. Perhaps an astronomer happens to look at the right time, which occasionally happens. It is thrilling for the astronomer and no less thrilling for the radiant beings.

This happens more than once, you understand. It happens as you make the click into fourth dimension, because everybody really has to be totally united to do that. If you were able to slow things down, you could see it. Then immediately individuals are individuals again. I know you are asking, what about when the Explorer Race ultimately becomes the Creator, yes? When that happens I would expect that we will all merge into one being—but that is strictly my best guess. What is happening here is new, and when new things happen one is reluctant to say absolutely with any authority what will happen or even place a potential on what will happen, because one might be subverting a larger thing. So I am disinclined to speculate.

But you had thought about it?

Yes.

So it's either three or one, probably?

Maybe. Or more. I really do not know, do I? Futures can only be limited from the present, not expanded—that's a law, by the way. You can write that one down. As far as I know, that is an absolute law. That is why very often beings who speak through all channels or even many inspirations will give you only broad definitions of futures. They know that even in those broad definitions they are potentially limiting your perspective, so they are reluctant.

Well, someone earlier said that because of who and what the Explorer Race is, they'll probably not want to hang around and maintain this place. They'll birth someone else and then go off and do something else.

This is a distinct possibility [chuckles].

But it's just one of the options?

Yes.

How Creator Made the Request for Us to Participate

I'd still like to get your feelings. The Creator said, "Do you roots want to . . ."—how did He say it?

Converting it to linear language, Creator said, "I wonder whether you" (referring to the three of us) "are intended to take a more direct role in the creation of the Explorer Race, because the other consultants are all working full time, whereas you are still within me. I already have an individual performing as a full-time consultant within me, and that is Zoosh. I wonder," the Creator might have stated in a linear function, "whether you are really intended to participate in this way. Other consultants are participating now, and as consultants you seem, much as I treasure your advice" (Creator is ultimately diplomatic, you see), "to be redundant." That is really how it happened.

How did you feel then? What was your reaction?

Well, when one is essentially promoted from being an advisor to being a participant, one is inclined to immediately seize the opportunity before it slips by. I for one said, "Yes, wonderful!" I was all for it; I was looking forward to it. The other consultants exhibited enthusiasm as well.

Our Merging, Compressing, Expanding, Fragmenting, Then Incarnating

What did you and the other two roots do then? What was the process, in a story?

Your Creator helped to radiate us out in the general space where we would be needed, and we allowed that. Then we merged briefly and concentrated our efforts toward moving in as far as we could. Then by compressing ourselves, we were able to more easily expand outward, and when we expanded we were more easily able to fragment. We discovered that if we tried to will ourselves to fragment, it didn't work. We needed something that would function somewhat as a catapult.

Once we were able to form initial fragments, then fragmenting from that point was easy. I think perhaps our total beings needed to know that even though we'd be fragmented, our personalities would in no way be separated from ourselves. We needed a little encouragement.

That's what we wound up doing. It was like a leaf falling into a stream. It was perhaps provided by your Creator. A stream of energy was there and we started moving in it. For a long time there were thousands, then millions of bits of light moving in the stream. Then we arrived at a galaxy. Some of us became beings on that galaxy and others went to other galaxies, all the while moving in this stream. That is how we came to be incarnated as beings of one sort or another.

But then you leaped into experiences, right?

Well, we incarnated as beings, and once we initially had an incarnation . . . you know, if you're a fragment of a being and go someplace—a planet, for instance—if you are there long enough, the chances of your becoming a being on that planet are greatly expanded. That's what we did. We went to different planets in different galaxies, wherever we were pulled, like the way a leaf is pulled to the shore when its voyage in the stream has been completed.

Once we incarnated again, it was another version of the experience. Even though we were incarnated and were having a life of some sort, that life functioned somewhat autonomously and we functioned at a higher level or a conglomerate level of that incarnation. As a root being, we have billions or trillions or more incarnations, but we still have a conglomerate personality connected to all of those incarnations, not necessarily flowing to the incarnations themselves, but flowing from the incarnations to us. We maintain our sense of personality and have access to what our incarnations are doing, but only sometimes do our incarnations have access to what we are.

This happens only if they are at a particular spiritual level where their advice might be needed. Then they would need to be able to tap into someone like ourselves in order to give advice for which they have had no personal experience in that incarnation. This is like what guides do. Here on Earth you all have spirit guides. When you are a spirit guide you can tap into all of your incarnations as you have lived them, and you can also tap into the advice of your teachers. At the spirit-guide level one usually functions with one primary teacher, but one can still access the wisdom gleaned from your incarnations, though in the case of spirit guides on Earth, one is usually in touch only with lives that have some relationship to Earth life.

Spirit Guides; Keeping You in the Experimental Group Lineage

That brings up something interesting. Are all of the spirit guides to humanity the part of the Explorer Race that is not physical, or are they from the Creator?

As far as I know, all spirit guides to the Explorer Race are members of the Explorer Race. We might trace that back to its apex if we look at it as a pyramid. In the beginning our personalities, our root personalities, were . . .

But when that became unnecessary, then as the pyramid expanded, those who followed would be the spirit guides, one life removed up the ladder, as it were. In this way the Explorer Race has been protected but at the same time isolated so that your experiences would remain within the context of the great experiment. Many of you have had incarnations beyond this, but if you have, your spirit guides do not have access to that wisdom even if *they* have had incarnations beyond this. Therefore they do not give you advice based on some culture that has been entirely separated from the Explorer Race. Their advice has to do only with *your* Explorer Race lineage.

It is not unlike the way scientists might keep a control group and an experimental group, you understand. In this way you always remain in the lineage of the experimental group and are kept isolated from your vaster experience so that you can become immersed in the experience of the Explorer Race; so that as you grow and expand you can become the best that the Explorer Race has to offer; and perhaps most important, so that you do not become polluted or colored in any way by other experiences, no matter how benevolent or wondrous they might be. If that were to happen, it would be interference.

My State When I Split from Creator

When you were at the point at which you left the Creator, what size were you? Were you a pinprick, the size of a planet or a galaxy?

It doesn't relate, really. Your Creator is this entire universe, yet if you were to go where your Creator hangs out, at any given moment the essence of your Creator might be in any one part of the universe. I know you are asking, "When you first came out, how big were you?" Recognizing the paradox involved here, this is a paradoxical answer. I was as large as all universes that I had ever been exposed to and more—and I was about the size of a soccer ball.

One must answer a question like that paradoxically, allowing for one's greater being. Many of you have incarnations that go way back. If you relate to me, you go way back, you see. Some of you might have gone way back before that; you might have been involved with us, yet have other things to do. Anytime you have ever been anything or a portion of anything, *that thing*, no matter how vast a space it might cover, *becomes a portion of your total self*. That is why, when one comes in touch with one's total being, even if it is a brief experience, one immediately has a sensation, an emotion, a feeling of vastness.

However big you were, as you split you were like infinitesimal sparks, because you

*were clothed in the material of the Creator, right? The Explorer Race uses the
material aspects of the Creator . . .*

Yes.

And it's the spark of Its soul?

To be more specific, Its energy body.

What do you call it in words we understand—the lightbody, the etheric body?

Lightbody is too limited because your energy body (you as an individual) might be vast beyond universes. Although your lightbody
would be something that could reach out beyond universes, in its normal state of being it tends to be encapsulated, perhaps a little beyond
yourself, but not much. So "lightbody" is too limited a term. Energy
body would have to do with all the Creator is, has ever been and (in the
case of a creator) knows about.

Once you achieve creator status, even if you haven't ever personally
been a part of a thing, just the knowledge of it is sufficient to have *been*
it, as it were. Thus "energy" means everything that makes you up—in
its space, dimension, thought, feeling, geography. We used the energy
body of the Explorer Race, but we used the personalities of ourselves.
In that way your Creator was able to produce a race of beings with
qualities beyond which It actually possessed. That was the intent.
Thus your Creator was able to do the greatest amount with the least
number and was able to utilize Itself. That is why your Creator says
your souls are portions of Itself and in a larger sense, as a member of the
Explorer Race, the spark of life—your soul—is definitely all from the
Creator. Yet since *our* personalities were involved, there is an element
of your personality that is a portion of us, your root beings.

*You mentioned that there might be other beings in the Explorer Race who did not
come from the three of you. Did they bring something to resolve, or did they say,
"That looks like fun"?*

I would be hard-pressed to answer that question. I think I would
have to suggest that you ask Zoosh or your Creator.

*Are there beings who came from someplace else and who just decided to play the
game?*

Not that I know of. You would have to ask somebody else.

I thought you said that some came from someplace else.

No. What I am saying is that you might have an incarnation that is
not involved in the Explorer Race at all. You might choose to have an
incarnation somewhere in this universe or even in another universe,
should you wish to have a life beyond this experience. But that life is
not allowed to contribute, even on the inspirational level, *when you are
a member* of the Explorer Race. Otherwise it would color the experiment. And certainly many of you have lived before this. That's what I
am saying.

Non-Explorer Race Lives

All Explorer Race beings come from you three, but some might have lived before. Can you explain that?

Yes, it is possible. In general, those of you who seek to know the absolute and unshakeable truth without any colorations, when you arrive at any absolute truth, you have achieved only a limit. Let that limit be temporary, and always know there is more to be learned. Absolutes tend to be limiting. That is a law of creation as far as I know. Yet as a member of the Explorer Race, you will tend to seek out absolute truths because you have a bias to do so, because you have been shielded from your experiences of other Explorer Race lives even on the inspirational level.

If you are in an incarnation where you are not in the Explorer Race, you will have absolutely no interest in seeking absolutes whatsoever. You will be perfectly open to the idea that truth is absolutely liberally interpreted, regardless of how absolute any particular thing seems to be. You are more of an artist or a philosopher in other lives, but here, as a member of the Explorer Race, you are purposely biased by your Creator to seek out absolutes. Why? Looking at all religions, all cultures, all philosophies, ultimately the Creator is identified as absolute truth, absolute wisdom, and you are biased to seek out that from which you have come. That is intentional so that your desire to know the truth will ultimately take you out into the stars to explore, to bring your wisdom elsewhere, to bring your survivability and your philosophy elsewhere.

When you become a creator, you will have a bias to follow in your Creator's footsteps, as it were. You will still feel that sense of absolute, and when you leave you will want to follow the exact direction your Creator went. In this way you will have all your questions answered. These things are designed into you so that no one is left with an unanswered question.

Where there's hope, eh?

Yes, you will ultimately know all, and even when you do you will know that there is more to know. It is a restless nature of life that is built in, so that even if one is stuck, one knows that there is more to know. Even in a benevolent life on some other planet perhaps, even if one is stuck in one's philosophy, one knows that there is more to know. One simply has to find that which can teach one.

That's a brilliant synopsis. Yes, that's the way it is.

Yes, and it is intentional. That's what ultimately gives the impetus to life. That is why individuals hang onto life so tenaciously. It is why they will be born even to lives that do not appear to be so wonderful on the surface. Life itself is not only its own answer, but is truly its own reward.

Do you think that the being from whom you have come could speak as a totality?

I don't need to very often, but it is certainly worth a try. I expect he would have many interesting stories to tell.

I'm hoping we can talk to you again. You're definitely not talked out in this hour and a half here.

[Chuckles.] Yes, some other time, yes.

But now, if you would just sort of give a parting message to your own fragments and all the other fragments.

A Story

All right. Once upon a time there was a very curious child. The child sought in all places and all faces and asked the question: What is the meaning of life? Ultimately the child grew up and was a pilot of a ship that traveled all over the galaxy. Every time the child/adult arrived at another planet, it would seek out the wisest being on that planet, asking that being, What is the meaning of life? and acquire the answers. When the child/adult had become quite old and aged, it had not yet found the total meaning of life that *felt* as if it were the meaning.

One day, having retired from having been an astronaut for many years, the child/adult was sitting on a park bench in a beautiful park on the Pleiades, as it was one of the places this being found most attractive and had retired to. While the being was sitting there, a child came up to this old person (from the child's perspective), who was considered by others by that time to be quite wise. The child, having been instructed by its parent, said to this individual, "Excuse me, but what is the meaning of life?" This person had explained as best it could to the child what the meaning of life was, drawn from all its experiences of speaking to all of the wisdom keepers and oracles from this being's many voyages.

This being finally understood that the true meaning of life was to be able to pass on wisdom of value to those who follow in its wake. Good night.

Good night, thank you very much.

All right. Zoosh speaking. Oh, these beings do get more eloquent when they are communicating longer, is it not so?

He—or she—is wonderful.

I've always been fond of that particular being, you know. Beings who know stories are very relaxed.

I can see how he rushed out there—you know, dived in exuberantly and got through first.

Yes.

I'm glad I taped him over so I got to talk to him again.

Well, perhaps we've done enough for one night, then.

Root Three, Companion of the Second Root

March 6, 1997

ll right, greetings.
Greetings.

I would speak now. My point of origin is the same as the other being, my companion, so I will skip over that part. Perhaps it would be good for you to ask a question, because my experience was so similar. I cannot say that the voyage was so different.

The Realms

He said that you were able to look down at the realms as you came by them, but that you came from an isolated spot far beyond them, the largest number we ever heard times five. The realms are between where you came from and where we are. Is that true?

It is a way to look at it.
Tell us how you look at it.

From my perspective, the realms are everywhere. One is passing from one realm to another but does not necessarily perceive it, depending upon the purpose of your voyage.
So the Temple is in a realm. Realms are everywhere.

Yes. If you were going from one point to another and passed through fifty realms, you might not notice that you were passing through them. On the other hand, if you were simply voyaging for the sake of voyaging, you would be very sensitive to your surroundings and would notice the passage through realms. My companion and I did not notice particularly, because we were going from, as you say, point A to point B.

And being literally pulled, not knowing where you were going.

Yes, we were being attracted, so we really had to let go of any manner or means by which we might guide or direct our journey.

The Fragmented Temple

Once the Temple fragmented, did all of it come on your journey or just part of it?

It all came, until that point of intersection where my companion and I were left. Then the rest of the Temple fragments, from my perspective of the moment, went that way [points to the left and chuckles]. All of it continued on in the same pattern. Since we were going in another direction, I cannot say where it went, but my impression is that it did not go very far. My feeling is that it is waiting for something, and my best guess is that it's something you are going to do. Since the Temple comprises all knowledge from everywhere as far as I know, it would possibly follow that certain beings might be able to gain something from this knowledge, even utilize it for the betterment of all beings. I do not know if it is ultimately intended to join you. If it is, it is most likely to do so after you leave this universe. But my distinct feeling is that it is waiting nearby, but beyond the boundaries of this universe.

It would experience the tenfold expansion then, like everything else would, right?

As far as I know.

But you have no telepathic or feeling communication with it?

We seem to be out of touch with it in that way, probably because of what we are doing here. Perhaps if we had that connection, as a root of the Explorer Race we would not be able to withhold it from you.

Aha! You have ignorance then, too?

No, not exactly. It's just that we don't think of it as ignorance. You must have the gift of ignorance; but we know who we are and can speak of where we came from and so on, whereas you cannot. So I cannot say that we are experiencing ignorance. I can only say that we do not have the full access we once had to this source of wisdom.

The Identity of the Temple, Its Connection to You

How did this source get its wisdom?

My understanding is that it was set there originally in the form of a very small image. The image itself was rather like what it came to look like, as this large temple, though it was not as complex. It was a simple-looking structure, quite small. It was assigned the task of acquiring all knowledge and wisdom that could be used to benefit all beings. That was really a simple thing, not a complex assignment. The being who put the Temple there, from what I gather, is actually from a future far distant from where you are now. That being came well back into the past in experiential time to set that in motion.

I believe, from what I have understood, that that being is somebody you now know. It might even be your total self, reengaged as the Creator you will be when you take over or inherit the job of running this universe. Perhaps at that time you will need to have access to vast amounts of wisdom not readily attainable from your experiences in this universe and before. Therefore I believe you might have gone forward into the future and back into the past to set this up to function as a reservoir for wisdom so you can reduce any possible mistakes you might make.

Think about this now for a moment: As the Explorer Race on Earth, you became accustomed to attaining wisdom and stimulating the creation and re-creation of your reality by using mistakes as an avenue to produce consequences that must be resolved and dealt with. But of course, once you become a creator, even though you will have had much experience beyond this planet, you cannot take the chance of making mistakes. You cannot be impetuous, as you would likely be now. And you cannot make a mistake that would lead to consequences that might keep you here for many thousands if not millions of years when there is much to be done beyond here. So I believe you set in motion—or someone did for you—the potential to have consultants whose wisdom runs deep enough that mistakes can be avoided.

When you talk about the total being from the future, that is you, your companion and the first seed being?

Yes, and all of you with all of *your* experience. One cannot rule out the experience you have had here, because (especially on Earth where you've got to essentially reinvent yourselves) the advantage of making mistakes is that you have to resolve them, and one tends to resolve them in *every* way possible, not just in any way possible. For those who, to your consternation, have had the experience of repeating some mistake over and over again, this occurs not only because you seem to be missing some point, but almost always because the way you previously resolved the mistake did not allow you to re-create yourself. Usually the last time you had this mistake in your life (and don't have it again) is because you have resolved it in some new way and have thus added to your wisdom, re-created your reality and generally grown and expanded yourself.

The Temple's Assignment

This small version of the temple was set out there in the middle of nowhere and assigned to amass all knowledge. How did it do that?

It was really very simple. It simply became highly receptive to certain types of knowledge and wisdom. It essentially had filters in place. Knowledge that was in any way self-destructive (as Zoosh says, that which hurts you or somebody else) was entirely screened out. Only knowledge and wisdom that was beneficial to you and others would be acquired. It was that simple.

It is essential to keep it that simple—cut and dried, as you say—because we're talking about vast amounts of knowledge and wisdom. If it were more complex than that, it would be easy to mistakenly acquire some knowledge which on the surface did not appear harmful but which would prove to be so after a time. But then the damage would have been done to one's entire being. So that simplistic editorial policy was set up.

How did the temple attain the wisdom, just absorb it from everywhere?

It is not difficult. You can be anywhere and acquire knowledge and wisdom. *You* would call it inspiration, but when you are beyond this planet and there is no veil of ignorance, it becomes the stream of available knowledge and wisdom. It becomes your normal way of thinking.

That's how it happened. It is very easy, although it is not easy for you to conceive of it now because of the veil of ignorance. The only time you experience your normal way of thinking now is through inspiration, but that is your actual method of thinking. This is the way it is for all beings who are reasonably enlightened everywhere. The acquisition is easy.

I'm still not really clear. Is there like a jet stream that goes through you, or are the air and space around you filled with it?

Think about it. You have been inspired before, yes? Is there a stream that comes to you?

It's just like suddenly knowing.

All right. There is a tendency, naturally, in the linear world to assume that all things must have points of connection. Even thoughts must come from somewhere and be traced back to somewhere. That is a manner of application available in the linear world, and one experiences the linear world in creator school so that one can more easily delineate consequences from other information. But in actuality—and I want to give you the clearest picture of how things are actually—there is no highway. It is just there.

Did you come there from someplace?

No.

Were you part of that temple and expanded with it?

Exactly that, as the other being said. I could repeat that word for word. That is because we were so close in the beginning that we were almost twins.

Why do you think there were two of you but only one from the land of stories?

It is easy to know that. If we were all three alike, how could we create or even apply to the creation of beings that would be in any way different from each other? There needed to be a base from which others can be built. You add a spice to make the food interesting. The food is nourishing without the spice, but perhaps not interesting. The other being is there to create interest.

The other being is the spice, then.

That's the way I see it, though it might not see itself that way. [Chuckles.]

Why You Need to Acquire Knowledge and Wisdom

You said we needed all that wisdom for what we had to do after we left this universe. What is your understanding of what that is?

As far as I can see it, you will follow along in the path of this Creator for a short time, but then there will come a point at which this Creator goes off elsewhere. You will probably follow this Creator until It goes off to do Its own creation, at which point you will then either continue onward in the same direction in which you were heading, or more likely you will begin a voyage of your own to acquire further wisdom, at which time the Temple will re-create itself, join you and be available to you—vast amounts of wisdom, even for creations, dimensions and levels of creation to which you will never go.

You see, you as a race of beings are ultimately designed to affect other beings even when you are at creator status. You will need to travel so they can touch you or be touched by you, and you will be driven to do this on your own because you will want to know. The ultimate expression of the Explorer Race is that *it wants to know.* If you take that to its logical conclusion, it means that the Explorer Race wants to know everything. This means that you will probably travel, possibly even for the rest of your existence. Maybe you will stop to make a creation, but I don't think so. I do not think that that is your intent.

In time I think that even though you have creator status, you will become more of what I would call a cloud of energy that travels to acquire wisdom. You will probably do this for a very long time because there are many places that need to be touched by you, and you will acquire wisdom and knowledge as your reward. Knowledge, you understand, is that which does not necessarily have an application, but when mixed with other knowledge might have one. So you will seek to acquire knowledge to see if some wisdom can work in application. That is the ultimate reward for knowledge—to become wisdom. I think this might cause you to become what you might now see as a wanderer, but as I see it, one who journeys, a traveler.

The Catalyst for Growth

This is an incredible aha! What you're saying is that the Explorer Race goes out in this creation to jazz it up a little bit, but as the three of you, with all of us as a total self, we do the same thing to other creations, other realms. Right?

Everything.

The spark, to bring it that lust for life?

Yes, because even if one is expanded by ten times, one simply becomes ten times the total capacity of oneself, but does not necessarily change or grow. One needs a catalyst to cause one to grow, and since you will be fulfilled by that experience, it is likely that you will want to have that experience over and over again, all the while acquiring more knowledge and more wisdom.

You're saying "you," but you're talking about yourself when you're saying that.

Yes, I am saying "you" for the sake of the reader and so on. If I say "me," the reader does not necessarily identify with it.

So that temple was set there and told to acquire all knowledge. You two, as part of that Temple, have the built-in drive to know. Was that the original instruction to the being from which you came?

Yes.

Why did it have to totally break into fragments if it simply needed to birth the two of you?

Because it would have been very difficult to travel in that form. When the Temple is complete and in that form, it is meant to be a place where beings can come to consult. If the Temple were traveling in that form, many more beings would have seen it and it would have been stopped so many times to be consulted by other beings that it would never have gotten here in time. [Chuckles.] It's simple.

The Future of Explorer Race and Temple

Is the Explorer Race going to rejoin it or travel with it, or will it take in what we've all learned and stay someplace and impart knowledge?

I already said that you would take this in and it will travel with you. Eventually, in not a very long time, you will have enough wisdom, including the temples and others that you will acquire, to be able to function as the Temple. But most likely you will choose to continue to travel. What you will probably do (and this has been done on Earth in the past, I believe) is go to various places such as planets and leave things there. You will go to planets energetically and impart the wisdom of the temple. You will include in an obelisk any other wisdom that feels appropriate for that place and the beings who might be there. You will leave the obelisk at a time in that planet's history far enough in the past of the prevailing society that it will become an object of attraction.

You will first encode symbols and designs upon it; you will make it possible for knowledge to be acquired from this obelisk through certain motions, gestures, colors and sounds. And when this society evolves to a point where it is sufficiently spiritually evolved in practicing that evolution, the obelisk will be readily available to all beings as a consultant. This you will do in many places, partially because your own experience here on Earth, Mars, Orion and other places has been very much like this.

It has worked well for you to have enigmatic objects from the past, which, as society grows and evolves and becomes more spiritually aware, also become more. First they are simply oddities, then they are often idols, then they are part of religions and then they gradually become studied and part of an educational system. As the society becomes more spiritual, it would unlock the secrets of these objects to provide wisdom for that society. This is something you are enamored of and will perpetuate in that manner.

So Arthur Clarke's 2001 *is based on realities?*

It is prophetic in that sense; however, I believe you will use the form of the obelisk, as it is more inclined to draw attention to itself.

What would be analogous to that here on this planet? The Great Pyramid and what else?

Yes, certainly the Great Pyramid and perhaps ancient wonders of the past, few of which are here anymore. I should think the Great Pyramid would be one of the more profound. Also, certain mountains have become considered that way, and certainly the archeological finds in Egypt and Central and South America and so on.

I can see how the first root being, with its desire to learn all these stories, would bring that same quality of needing and wanting to know through this mixture.

Since we were birthed out of the Temple, whose job was to acquire all knowledge and wisdom, that is the root of what tends to give you *your* insatiable curiosity. Children are born curious and remain so, whether you actually do anything about it or not.

This is a really big deal, then.

Yes.

Look at the effort and the time involved. But there are billions of individual personalities in this Temple? You don't think any of them went to other places? They're all just sitting there?

Yes. I can only tell you what I feel. I feel they are waiting.

There must be some additional reason for it. You said that to travel, it had . . .

Perhaps you could ask the Temple.

I plan to. Let's get to your experience now. Your companion and the other being explained how the Creator tried to do this two times on its own, and the roots didn't even know why they were here. Can you amplify that?

I am sorry; you see, being the companion, my story would be the same.

So you are that close? You are like identical twins?

Yes, that is a good way to put it. I think that might have been the origination of that experience for you as well.

So everything it said about hanging back and waiting, not jumping into the experience was true of you also?

How I and My Companion Differed

Well, that is where we differed. I felt it was necessary to go ahead, and my companion learned from *my* going ahead. You see, my companion couldn't learn from the other being because it could feel that the being was not itself. But my companion could learn from *my* experience and did so. So I went ahead, yes.

Talk about that a little. If you were the same, how could you if he couldn't?

We're not the same. Twins are not the same people.

What was your thinking? How did it differ from his? You felt that it was safe or that it was important?

I was celebrating the experience. I didn't see any reason to stop and wait. I can't really say why. It wasn't a why so much as a "Well, here it is. Let's do it."

Is that the only thing that you and he differed on?

I can't really say that. Generally we have the same or similar experience. I cannot say that that is the only thing we've differed on, but it seems to be the main thing.

Earth Individuals' Connections to the Different Roots

Are there about the same number of beings on the planet now that trace back to you as trace to your companion? Or are they more from your companion, since he started later?

No, I think there is more from me. What did my companion say—about 1%, no?

The one with the songs was 1%. The rest of them were you and he.

I think about 40% are mine.

Forty percent of what are or were here in the past?

What's here, yes.

Then how many are from your companions?

Do the math, yes? [Chuckles.]

You said most of them were yours. That doesn't compute.

It does to me, because I tend to think of my companion and myself as almost one person. Between the two of us, it is mostly us.

Right. But there's no significant difference between the two of you in the percentage of beings here? That is what I had asked.

I have about 40%.

That leaves 59% unaccounted for.

No, it does not.

The companion has 59% and the other one's got 1%. My thought was that since you had started earlier, there would be fewer of your beings here.

Yes, exactly.

Your companion said that you two were more practical, more physical, more in application. Would you say the same thing?

Yes, I think that that is a reasonable thing to say. We are more, perhaps, down-to-earth. (I do like your homilies.)

Well, they're yours. [Laughs.]

I don't think of them that way. You see, I think of myself as the point you stem from, but I don't think of your experience as my experience directly. I inherit your experience like an immortal parent, but I don't claim it as my own. If I were to do that, I would be saying that you are entirely myself, but I'm saying that you have the capacity to be independent of myself, or the veil of ignorance would destroy you. If you did not have the capacity to be independent, you see, when the veil of ignorance comes down, when you don't remember who you are, then you would not survive.

But you would not have that ability.

So I like to give you credit.

The Difference between Me and My Partner: Companionable and Individualistic

But you and the companion are close enough that even though you started first, there's no significant difference between the experiences of those who came from the companion and those who came from you? There's nothing you can trace, there are no qualities or kinds of experience that are more one than the other?

It is just possible that my beings might have the slightest predisposition, be just a little more likely to appreciate doing things in numbers or in teams rather than individually.

How would you explain that?

Perhaps because my sense of companionship with my companion is such that I think of the work I do with it as something we do together.

And that was a prime quality of those who sprang from you?

Yes.

So his beings are more individualistic.

A little bit more, yes.

You were there, then you traveled this vast, vast distance, and you were just sort of hanging around for this long time with no real job to do. How did you feel when it finally became obvious that you were to create this new race?

Oh, it was very exciting and joyful. It was a sudden realization, you know, as if to say, "Oh, *that's* why we're here!" Up to that point in time I don't think any of the three of us really understood why we were here. I'm not even sure your Creator understood it until that moment.

According to what everybody else said, you didn't.

I think it was more a sudden realization on everybody's part. Of course, we (I think I can speak for the three of us) were very excited, ready to go at a moment's notice because most of the time we had just been observing, occasionally advising.

Some of the advisors to the Creator didn't realize that you were different from the Creator even at the end.

Oh, that's very true. There were some who really did not notice—or else it was not their job to pay attention to it. That's understandable.

They all had things they had to watch very closely. Their job was demanding.

Yes, their job is so demanding that they really cannot be distracted even for a split second, you could say. I wish to say something here: I do not wish you to think me uncommunicative, but because in personality I am somewhat of an echo of my companion, if you ask me the same questions you have asked my companion, I will very often be inclined to refer to what has been said before.

Why would you be an echo of him any more than he's an echo of you?

Because that is how I am. I was attracted to him. He became aware of himself (or herself, as you wish) and I felt myself pulled to *his* being, not the other way. That is why I think the term "companion" evolved, because I feel connected to this being perhaps even more than it feels connected to me. I do not wish to say I am devoted, but I would say that there is a stronger sense of connection from me to this being than from this being to me. But my companion is loyal; we are still companions.

Pairings and Sex Divisions

Interesting. Were there other pairings like that within the fragments of the temple as it traveled?

I did not notice any, though there could have been. That is a good question for the temple. I have often thought that the root of the reason why coupling is so easily done here is not just because it preserves the species. It can't be, because if you look at civilizations on other planets where people do not couple but still preserve the species, there is a time when they come together for mating rituals, then move apart. They do not live together all the time, number

I think coupling is designed—myself with my companion—because this true coupling that you have here on Earth as the Explorer Race is truly intended. Perhaps it will make it easier for you to come together to reacquire all of your parts and be one because of your tendency and the ability for mutual attraction. Even the other root came together with us before we joined your Creator. So the attraction of one portion of the Explorer Race root to another is very strong, and Explorer Race beings will tend to be attracted to each other. I think this might be more than a coincidence.

[Laughs.] I don't think we've got any coincidences here. If we trace back far enough, there's a reason for it all.

In my awareness this is so.

Would the story-collecting being be equated to the third sex [see chapter 13, The Explorer Race] that Zoosh talked about?

It is certainly possible, but understand that on other planets *more* than three sexes are sometimes there. But I think you could utilize it.

Zoosh said once that had a representative of the quadrangle sex [see chapter 18 in Explorer Race: Origins and the Next 50 Years] *become a consultant, this whole thing would have gone by ten times faster. Are you acquainted with whatever that is?*

No, I am not.

You are more thoughtful and you have some very interesting things to say.

Thank you. [Chuckles.] Regardless of how few they are!

No, it's plenty. You've got much more knowledge and wisdom to look at. It's fascinating that the attraction between individuals in humanity is traced back to you and your companion.

I believe that this is possible. Even before people marry or are of an age to be attracted to the opposite sex, they have friends, and when they're older they have older friends. There's always a *very strong* desire to have at least one good friend amongst your other friends. This is what I would say is something akin to a drive. I believe it has to do with your eventual need to reconnect, because when you become the Explorer Race and go out all over the universe, you will spread out far and wide. Your Creator will probably inform you all; at some point you will become aware—and it will be only your ability to recognize other members of the Explorer Race energetically that will allow you to join with them, because after you spread out all over the universe, you might very well look entirely different from each other. You won't be able to say, "Oh, another Earth person" because you might not be Earth persons at all. So you must have that innate need, that drive to be with each other.

So we will go out and then might come to a planet and incarnate there.

Yes.

And look like them instead.

Absolutely. There is every reason to assume that will happen, because some races of beings you contact will be able to get all they need from a short experience, but others will need to have many, many years of exposure. When that occurs you will have to either incarnate as one of them or take up residence there for a long time.

For the hard-core ones who don't come around.

Oh, I don't want to call them that. I'd rather say the beings who need to understand.

The Ribbon of Inspiration from Your Future Being

How nice, how gentle. Can you see who originally waved that ribbon of inspiration by the Creator that caused Him to want to do this? Do you know where that came from?

Just a minute. I think I do. [Pause.] It seems hard to accept, but it seems to be your future being, when you are involved in that voyaging.

306 ✦ EXPLORER RACE and BEYOND

But I think you will have to ask others this. It is not the same being who put the Temple there, so this is a confusion. If it is your future being, it must be from a different future, a different point in your future. It might be somebody else, but I can see the being actually moving the ribbon. It is like an energy field. It is not exactly pushing it; it is pulling it past the Creator at a fairly quick pace. If you can give me a little longer . . .

You've got it.

[Pause.] It seems to be somehow a part of you.

Which would be part of you.

Yes—or more, since I am also more. We are all more since we have become a part of your Creator. And in the larger sense we are the temple, and in the sense beyond that we are all of the space that is around the temple. Ultimately we are everything.

How does the being who put the Temple down seem different from the one who pulled the banner by the Creator?

The person who put the Temple there appears to be more youthful than the person who moved the thread by. That is my best description.

The being who put the Temple there could have been one of the first steps, then further into the future it realized that it had to attract a creator? In other words, the one who put the Temple there would be closer to now, and the other one would be farther in the future—is that what you're saying?

Perhaps. Maybe. I think it would be good to pursue this with others.

We'll see if we can talk to those beings. I don't know how far out they would be yet, but they seem to be pretty far out.

It is possible that the being who pulled the thread by your Creator is you in the far-flung future, because what I see is a cloud of light. I am thinking that it is you as you voyage, as I mentioned before. It seems paradoxical, but it really isn't.

Because?

Because ofttimes one will observe one's present and say how one could be more if circumstances were broader. Sometimes, if you are very careful and have creator status and many levels of mastery, you can go into the past very carefully and change it. What I am suggesting is that you, in some wandering form in the future, bringing change and wisdom to many, might have decided to broaden your task and deepen your being. Conceivably you might have gone back in time to contact this Creator to re-create your past. That could be the explanation.

Creators ultimately tend to do that, in any event. When one makes a certain creation, there is a tendency to go back in the creation's history to change things in the present to make them broader. Occasionally one does this to make them less broad, but more often it is to make them broader, to do more, be more, have greater capacity or flexibility. Thus this kind of travel—traversing space and time for the expansion of ideas and ideals—is a regular, common thing, yes. Think how it makes such sense.

Let's say you are there in the future, traveling within a given period of space and time. At some point you realize you have gone to all the places you could to bring about all the change you can, and you can now simply go back and observe the results of your change. You can lean back and watch it for the rest of your existence. Or you could have available to you more places to go, more things to do, more of yourself, different ways to see things, different ways to apply what you do. But in order to do that you have to change the circumstances of what you have just completed, in terms of your journey.

The only way to do that would be to go back in the past to change your personal past and ask other beings who wish to be involved in the changing of your personal past to perhaps even expand what they too are going to do, especially if you can point to it and say that something good will come of it. And you do so by sending out threads to attract those who would be attracted to the thread of your intention. I feel that you might have done this to re-create yourself and your mission.

What I've Learned and How I Communicate

That's a beautiful explanation. What can you say to the parts of you here on this planet now? As you look at it now, what have you learned? How are you vastly more now than when you started?

I have learned the value of variety. I have learned to appreciate humor. This is, I think, a direct result of what you all have done, because in order to be as isolated as you are behind the veil of ignorance, a sense of humor is essential.

Survival?

Yes, and I have learned to appreciate its value more. I have learned to work in concert and cooperation better, and I have ultimately learned the value of a good story.

[Laughs.] I like that! So here's your chance to talk, through these words. You communicate to all the beings that we are through inspiration and love, right?

Usually through the deepest level of your dreams, ofttimes through your teachers and occasionally directly, should there be cause.

Only to your own beings? Or to anyone who needs it?

Only to my own beings, yes.

So when humans are praying, they're really praying to you or one of the other two?

Oh, I don't like to say that, not really. When one prays, one is praying within the context of one's religion and has a construct or a concept for God. I don't like to say they are praying to me or to others—no, let us not say that. It is rude, you know.

I'll acknowledge that. But on some level, when they ask for the deepest part of themselves, they're asking for you or whoever they sprang from.

If they ask it that way. Even that might not be so, but it might be.

And you are literally, as we're told God is, aware of every one of those you're connected to, that you created?

Yes. I am not generally aware of everything you have done, but I can be aware of you in the moment. After your life, then I can be aware of what you have done, because to be aware of what you have done I have to use a lot of your energy, and I don't think you have it to spare.

But if there is a desperate cry for help, it can reach you, right?

I can perhaps hear you. It begs the question, does it not?

Whether or not you're going to do anything?

It's not whether or not I'm *going* to do anything. My job is *not* to do anything. My job is to be the root for you, but it is not to change your experience, especially if you are attempting to acquire wisdom or re-create your reality.

What a Root Does

What is involved in being a root, then? Do you, even at this stage, give energy to the beings?

No, I do not need to give energy to you. The leaves and the branches of you have gone out far enough that you do not need to tap directly from the root.

You give inspiration or you are just there or . . .

I am the foundation upon which you have been built, but I do not feed you. If the foundation were removed, you could get along on your own.

Really? It works like that?

Not for every building, but in the case of *this* building it does.

For all three of you?

I can speak for myself only.

How did you do that?

I didn't do it. *You* did it by experience, by re-creating your reality sufficiently and by successfully, for many of you, completing creator school. In the case of the others, being open to attend creator school.

The Next Few Years

How do you see the next few years on this planet?

Oh, I think there will be a great many temptations. There will also be the tendency to let technology get out of hand, but fortunately I see now that there are those amongst you who see that technology cannot be the ultimate. It can only *serve* the ultimate. In the beginning ages of your technology (it is still very young) it is very easy to be seduced into the conclusion that technology is so much better than what *you* can do. But it isn't. It can only serve. To those of you who explore the ethics of whether technology is proper or not, I give you my total and hearty support and tell you that ultimately—if not in this generation, in some succeeding generation—your views will prevail.

Is there any direct reflection between civilizations we have heard about and the three root races?

I can't really answer that question because . . .

Wait, the civilization on Orion now and Sirius and Andromeda—they are not part of the Explorer Race?

Your Connection with Other Planetary Beings

No, not at this time, no. Once upon a time the Explorer Race went through some of those places, but they have been excused from that now. They can simply be as they would, be benevolent and . . .

They are direct reflections and creations of the Creator?

Yes, but then one can say that about many beings. I would say that their direct involvement in the experience of the Explorer Race is well into their past. They have on the one hand the advantage of saying, "This is in our past and we don't have to do it again," and on the other hand the disadvantage of no longer being in a growth cycle. Although their civilizations, of course, are benign, artistic, cultural, educational, interpersonal and many other good things, they are not what I would call growing.

Help me understand this. We as the Explorer Race had lives on Orion at a time of great, extreme energy during the time of the Black League and an empire. Were we the spice in that civilization, where most of them were not the Explorer Race but we were? Or was what was called the Orion civilization then made up of ourselves in past lives?

Most of that civilization was you at that time, the Explorer Race. If you look at the Explorer Race through a great many of your creations, you have had to experience some form of competition or separation in order to be able to question your deepest committed values. Competition or separation does require the confrontation of one's own values, because you are always attempting to do more or be more than you believe you can be. Thus you necessarily confront what you believe yourself to be or even what you might be. You were those beings at that time, and those beings did have confusion and conflict and so on. If you look around this universe to places that had some level of competition, separation or conflict in the past, generally . . .

That was us?

Not always, but ofttimes it was you. Some more extreme versions might have been attempted, but did not evolve into the Explorer Race.

The Pleiadians have some of that, but they cut it off and became benign.

Yes, the Explorer Race had some experience in the Pleiades, yes. But the Pleiadians decided that they did not wish to pay the price of that wisdom, and one cannot deny that there is a price.

There have always been civilizations on all of these places—Orion and the Pleiades and Sirius and others—but there were times when the bodies that were there were inhabited by souls who came from the three root races.

Yes.

And they moved on. It's like the play was in Philadelphia, then the actors moved to Baltimore and then someplace else.

Yes, that is exactly right. That allows you to understand why these races and planets are given permission to observe you or come close to you, because they are related in some way. You have gone on to do more and be more and have ultimately achieved what they could not in their societies and cultures at that time. There was a strong feeling, you know, when the Explorer Race departed and other beings took over.

Other civilizations were formed, more benevolent, benign civilizations. There was a strong feeling for a long time in the philosophical community that some great opportunity had been missed by excising this experience, because their conscious realization at the time was that they had simply suppressed something—not realizing, of course, that a whole mass of souls had gone on to incarnate elsewhere. There is no reason they *would* realize this.

If you look at the ancient philosophies on Orion and Pleiades and even other places where you've been, you will find a common ground in these places: Shortly after that time, for several generations they regretted and wondered what would have happened if—that kind of thing. Eventually, after establishing such benevolent societies as exist today on these places, it was easy to say, "Well, it's a good thing we didn't do that." But *at the time* there was a definite feeling that they had missed out on something, perhaps even failed in some purpose.

Their past unresolved problem allows them to come to observe you. Now it is at a distance, but in the recent past it was closer. This past connection also allows them to receive visits from you when you go out as the Explorer Race and give them a slight taste, essentially inoculating them to bring them into the growth curve, doing it in a way that they can accept, not in the powerful, dramatic way you have had to deal with it. Because of their ancient philosophies they will have some basis to say, "Look, this was predicted." All of those philosophies had that common prediction: "Some day we will have to do this again." So it will be very much of a messianic experience for them, not as if you are the messiah coming but as if a great vision were being fulfilled by your coming.

You are wonderful! You have much to say. Now you can't just say you are a carbon copy. [Laughs.]

Very kind of you.

It's the truth. Would you just talk to your beings this same way rather than the way you usually do?

So often I have encouraged many of you at the deepest levels of sleep to know that although your lives are so very fleeting on Earth at this time, your immortality is absolute. Many will be there to greet you at the end of your natural cycle, and you will know all. You have the opportunity to come to the hall of wisdom when you pass through the veils, where all will be revealed to you, as much as you wish to know about everything—your past, the lives you have lived in the past, how you came together to be with your family in this life, all your friends, all of the questions you have asked, "why, why, why" about so many times. You will then know it all. It will make complete sense to you. You will shed all regret and will be happy and exultant at the level of your accomplishments. Know that this is guaranteed. Good night.

Thank you very much.

All right, Zoosh here. Well, the joke's on you, eh? You have created yourself! You have come full circle. "Who is the Creator?" says you. Look in the mirror, says I! Full circle! Good night.

The Temple of Knowledge & the Giver of Inspiration

March 11, 1997

am the Temple of Knowledge. I speak to you at this time in my granulated substance, though even in this form I most definitely feel as if I am still in the shape of a temple. It is an interesting concept, because for a long time (to use this example), if a cell of skin should die and fall off of one of your bodies, even though it is returning to its native Earth, it still identifies itself as a skin cell for quite a while. You'd be surprised. Even after it has changed its form several times, it still feels somewhat more like a cell of skin for quite some time (of course, it would fall off in groups of many cells). For example, a cell might have been away from your physical bodies for up to three years, yet it still tends to feel more like a cell of skin from the human body than whatever it has become.

Extrapolating three years of your time into my experience, even though my experience is much longer, I still feel like the solid Temple. When I see myself in what you would call my mind's eye, I see myself as the Temple, but when I look at myself I see the seeds of the Temple. I do not see myself as the ground-down or crumbled residue, but as seeds. This is how I was able to dismantle myself. By inspiration I was led to believe that in time it would behoove me to drop various seeds in various places where they are needed, and like the seed or kernel of corn that reproduces itself in the corn plant (thence more ears of corn), each seed has the capacity to reproduce the Temple on its own.

Temple Seeds Can Reproduce the Temple

This is how the Explorer Race will reproduce its connections to all wisdom as well as become wise in your own right. When you reintegrate you will have at least two—one more than is needed—seeds of the temple. These seeds can reproduce in the etheric the wisdom and knowledge accumulated by the Temple. When the Temple is reproduced in such a way, it will be able to acquire all wisdom and knowledge since the Explorer Race experiment began. My perception is that these seeds are vital to your advancement to creator status.

Are you parked out there waiting for this experiment to be over?

Yes, parked, as you say. You see, in order to get to the universes, star systems, planets and people, I must wait, because places where this type of temple I represent is needed are not located in any of the dimensions in the reality in which I currently reside or even travel through. So I must wait until the ten-times expansion. When that occurs I will be greatly expanded. I will have considerably more range in dimension

Now I can easily travel to the 33rd dimension, briefly to about the 65th dimension (can't stay there) and have not really gone much past the 78th dimension (that was more a visioning process than an actual presence). But I believe that when the ten-times expansion comes, I will be able to easily access dimensions 200 through 210, where it is intended that I distribute the seeds to the residence of beings so that they can reproduce the temple and turn it into something like a crop (beings in that dimension have this capacity).

As the Temple grows and matures, it will reproduce itself in seed pods after gathering wisdom and knowledge of their societies. Then those societies will be given the mission (you see, they are looking for a mission) to take those seed pods that can produce temples (more than one) to other dimensions, delivering the gift of wisdom in that form to other dimensions, other cultures. The seed pods grow only when they are exposed to a culture of beings. They absorb the culture, understanding who the people are, their environment, how their souls came to be there and what they are expressing and learning and so on. When the pod has all of that, it will know how to express itself in a specific form of temple in order to best assist that society and be useful.

Dimensions Not Yet Accessible to Me

Help us understand dimensions. These are dimensions that are not yet created, but that the Explorer Race will create?

No. These are dimensions that exist but are not easily accessible.

Are they peopled now?

I am not certain, but I have been led to believe that they are, and that there is no ready access for beings such as myself. I believe that creators can visit these dimensions at least briefly, sometimes even stay at length if they are senior creators (having produced numerous universes). For beings such as myself, who represent really more of a library of consciousness, my ability to access such places with the staying power required to fulfill the purpose I have mentioned—there is no direct route by which I could stay there. I could be brought there by certain creator beings, but they are busy doing things elsewhere, and I need to be able to get there on my own.

My understanding is that the ten-times expansion will allow me to have ready access to dimensions well up to 350. Right now those dimensions, as I say, are very protected; they are so pristine that the tiniest thought or feeling would immediately be manifest in some way. Beings who frequent such places must be very disciplined in their feelings and thoughts (including their unconscious thoughts, should they have an unconscious), even the nuances of their feelings or gestures, because creations will naturally follow anything that is unspoken or incomplete, and emotions are ofttimes incomplete within your form of communication.

That is why generally only very high beings are allowed to go there. Beings created there will stay there but will not generally come to the denser dimensions because they do not have the capacity to protect themselves. For example, if one of these beings were brought here and any one of you were to desire something, completely unspoken, possibly not even conscious, that being would immediately *become that thing.* It would not be able to prevent it. This could, of course, cause a great deal of mischief.

Help me understand. Is that the creation we are in now? Do the dimensions go up to the 300s? Or is this some other creation?

Other.

Another Realm

Is it in this realm or other realms?

It is beyond this Circle of Creation, so I'd have to say, in terms of realms, that it is not really in this realm, because this realm has certain basic laws, the most basic of which is that *existence is its own purpose.* That's the foundational law of this realm. In other realms existence itself might not be the purpose. For instance, using as an example the realms in which the 310th dimension exists, the basic law there is that *flexibility interdicts all creations,* meaning that flexibility moves between and sometimes even interrupts all creations.

Does that realm have a name, just so we have something to call it?

Yes. You could, for the sake of simplicity, call it the preconscious realm. This tells you that beings in that realm might not actually experience individuality, though they might appear to be individuals. They would tend to act in unison, "think" in unison and experience in unison. Even though they might appear to be individuals, they are part of a unit.

How did you know? Do you have a teacher, or was it just a vision? How did you know to bring those two seed beings here?

My Early Existence

It started, you know, with a feeling of being unproductive. Here I was as the Temple, with so few visitors ever. The feelings of having visitors and the consultation of these creator beings was wonderful, but it was very rare—once every ten thousand millennia or something like that, very rare. I felt grossly underused and did not know what to do about it. Finally I expressed the need to have more fulfilling work. The moment I expressed it I was given this vision of changing myself into seeds in order to function in a cyclical re-creation, like the seeds from a dandelion.

So with great faith you dismantled yourself.

Yes. You know, it seemed like a good idea at the time. [Chuckles.] I had no reason to doubt its authenticity or veracity in terms of being a good idea, so I immediately went ahead and did it. I still have absolute faith that it was the right thing to do.

You didn't have any peers, you had no one like you. You didn't connect with any- one who did what you did anywhere?

No, but I know that these beings exist. Otherwise I would be sent around these realms where you are and go to universes here. Because I am not doing that, these places obviously have something like me now. I am needed elsewhere, where they *don't* have anything like me. That was a simple, logical conclusion.

That realm doesn't have anything like you.

Exactly.

The Two Seeds That Became the Roots of Explorer Race

How did the two seeds that ended up to be the root beings of the Explorer Race choose themselves, or how were they chosen?

Believe it or not (this will shock you), it was random.

Really?

Yes. It was strictly random.

Because they had an attraction?

Well, you have to remember that initially it wasn't going to be two. It was going to be one, but because the two had an attraction, they went as a set, if I can use that term. But it was chosen completely at random. The decision was made as the Temple began turning into the seeds, not later when we got to the point where they would depart. So they were chosen in the beginning. They didn't know, of course, that they were going to be dropped off, as it were, but I think they knew that they had more to do than be with the rest of the seeds. If they didn't, they know now.

So they are a holographic part of you in the sense that they are you, yet have their own individuality. There's a little difference between them; that's very interesting.

Yes, there's a little difference between them, and yet they were chosen completely at random. I realize that is not common where you are. You do not make many random choices, and perhaps that is just as well. Yet where I was, all the seeds were considered equal in value, and it was my job to simply designate one. By the time I designated it, it was two. So it was like, "Oh well, that's all right."

The Other Seeds

Do the other seeds know that they have a purpose? Have you explained this or shared your knowledge?

They *are* me, so they know. Remember, I still consider myself to be one being, and with that attitude, then they can know it. If I considered myself to be a collective of seeds, then I would have to have a larger personality that explained to all the pieces, but I do not. I do not need to have a separate personality that explains.

How will that work when the seeds are dispersed? Will you then be all of them, be aware of all of them and what they're doing?

I will know that when the time comes. I do not know.

You have tremendous faith. You don't know who sent you the vision?

I don't, but I have a feeling that I'm going to find out soon because you are pursuing it and, of course, we are all listening.

Well, why don't you just turn around and ask?

It isn't my job. That's *your* job.

My job! [Laughs.] Maybe curiosity is down the line from you, too? [Laughs.] Do you remember that one?

I haven't had curiosity before, so it isn't up the line, but it does beg the question. If I have all that knowledge, why did I originally accumulate it? Was it placed in me for safekeeping? Those might be good questions to ask of that which inspired me.

My First Awareness and My Accumulation
of New Knowledge/Wisdom

What was your first awareness?

My first awareness was as the formed Temple. I cannot say, "Well, I used to be this." My first awareness of being some *one* was when the temple was already constructed. I am not certain, but it is a possibility, though perhaps not a probability, that I was placed in the Temple *after* it was constructed. That might be a small point, but it is interesting to me.

So perhaps it is something you are ensouling or inhabiting.

It would suggest that I might be here temporarily.

If I remember, as the Temple you were simply there, and the streams of knowledge came through you and you absorbed them?

The knowledge was present when I became aware of being the Temple, and as more knowledge and wisdom was produced or discovered in other places, I would know it. I can give you an actual measured time (which is rare in the circumstances of this material): I would know when new knowledge or new wisdom (the application of knowledge) was discovered, rediscovered or practiced anywhere within one one-thousandth of a microsecond after it happened. So there was a measurable time; it wasn't simultaneous. It would seem simultaneous in terms of that description, but it wasn't.

A Temple As a Place of Culture and That Expands One's IQ . . .

Apparently I am tapped in that way. I have that experience even now in my granulated form, so I have to believe that each and every one of these seeds, which can grow into temples, can reproduce this body of wisdom in the form of a temple. You might ask why a temple. Is it a religion? No, it isn't. Is it a place of worship? No, no, not that. It is, perhaps, a place of culture—yes, closer to that. Think of the Temple as being like a place where one goes to see objects of beauty—a museum or even an arboretum where you can see rare and exotic flowers and absorb their fragrances.

The Temple is a beautiful being, a beautiful place, a beautiful presence that one is naturally attracted to. By simply being within the auric field of the Temple, you would feel the energy of it on a personal, physical level (where you are now) about a quarter of a mile away. In most higher dimensions the energy is felt anywhere from 225 to 100,000 miles away, and as you get closer to the Temple, you would absorb the knowledge to give you that concept in a practical application. If you were to do that in this world and this dimension, by the time you got within perhaps ten feet of the front door (not a door, but an opening), your intelligence quotient would have tripled. Then you would no longer be able to function in your society, because even though you would be brilliant and have great wisdom, you wouldn't be able to have much of a social life.

. . . and Accelerates a Soul's Evolution

That is why beings who come to experience the Temple are creators or else (as I believe will happen in the future, having given this some thought) will wear some kind of shielding device that will prevent the Temple from turning you into maximum geniuses and accelerate your personal soul's evolution. If a person came in totally unprotected, walked around the Temple for even an hour and a half like you would in a museum, when you were through your intelligence quotient would have been raised by almost a hundred times and your soul would have experienced *literally*, not just in energy or process, your next twenty or thirty lives! You would lose that moment-to-moment experience of a life, though your soul would evolve.

You might ask why such a thing would exist. I will tell you: For civilizations that have for some reason lost their bodies—meaning planets or occasionally even whole galaxies that have been disrupted by some disaster—then beings who cannot easily adapt to simply moving on and incarnating elsewhere and who have an agenda that needs to be carried out in that place would be allowed to come to the temple.

And experience the lifetimes they didn't get to have.

Exactly. Experience the lifetimes they were unable to complete, and have that in their soul reservoir of experience. This is the purpose, but there's more: It is ultimately intended that people walk around the Temple. By "people" I mean more than human beings or even humanoids, but I use the term "people" because it is a friendly term.

More personal.

How People Experience the Temple

Yes, but let's say people. They will walk around the Temple and absorb something. Ultimately people will wear a certain garb, some perhaps wearing special medallions for the sake of beauty and religious observance or philosophical expression placed over the chakras, front and back. This will decrease the impact of the full level of acceleration that one experiences there. One will wear a ceremonial garb over that, thus appearing to be wearing simply a beautiful, somewhat sheer garment. Thus one does not feel awkward walking pleasantly through the Temple. Let me tell you a little bit about the temple itself, all right?

Would you describe it at the beginning?

Yes, I want to tell you a little bit about it. If you walk through it, if you have no thoughts at all or any feelings other than calmness . . . let's say you have the feeling of calm. You will walk through the Temple. There are comfortable places to sit where a calm person might sometimes wish to sit and reflect. Around you the walls of the Temple look like granite but have a curious consistency that when touched, would feel softer, as if it had the ability to be personally expressive. The stones would feel like some one rather than some thing.

If you were feeling calm, there would be images or feelings that would appear in the stone or even float free in space, supporting and sustaining that calm. In your society it might be the image of a beautiful stream with ducks flying over it or swimming in it, something calming like that. Or if you had a problem and had 98% of the solution but not all, you would walk through the Temple and soon the solution would appear in many different ways. There would be a picture of the solution. If you stopped walking, the picture would become more elaborate. It would sequence itself either forward or back, depending on whether you wanted to see how it would work out or where it fits into the past (how it was solved or how it became a problem). You could explore the roots of the problem even before it was identified as a problem.

Let's say you were walking through the Temple feeling a little sad. Would the Temple support the sadness? No; by having that total link with you, it would attempt to cheer you up because it has an agenda: to either bring out the best in all individuals or help all individuals to find the best within themselves, not only the best thought, but the best feeling, the best experience, the best pleasure—all of that.

The best solution?

Certainly. So if you need it, even if you're wearing shields, the temple will give you an extra forty points of I.Q. (an arbitrary figure) as long as that does not take you out of the range of a socially acceptable person in your society. On the other hand (this happened once in the future) [chuckles], one time a person came (seeing from a farther future) who was overly brilliant; his I.Q. would have been 225 in your society. Although he had a great deal to offer and was considered almost an oracle—people would go with problems and he would always have good resolutions—he was very lonely. No one was his intellectual equal, one with whom he could express his type of humor and have it appreciated, who would understand its nuances and subtleties. He missed that very much.

We waited until he was able to program a wisdom keeper (a crystal) with all of his knowledge, which he was able to do in a fairly short time simply by holding the crystal to his various chakras, front and back, for about ten minutes. Then we lowered his I.Q. by about sixty points. Although he felt different, his personality was much more amiable and he was able to make jokes that were less complex and more easily understood by members of his society. He was able to get married and have children and friends—all the things you cherish.

Did he later access the wisdom crystal to solve problems?

Oh, no. He left the crystal. It was taken somewhere and left as a resource for all beings, who would then come and utilize the crystal, not unlike an oracle.

Your Seeds' Wisdom-Gathering Currently on Hold

That's incredible! Let's jump to the time you're spending out there parked. Are the two seed beings constantly receiving all the wisdom from everywhere while they're here, or is that put on hold until they're through here?

Exactly. It's put on hold. The seed beings will receive wisdom if it is pertinent to what they are doing with you, as long as that wisdom does not in its own right solve problems that you, the Explorer Race, are intended to solve. You cannot have your roots know how to solve something that will necessarily limit your creation of the solution, so to some extent what they are able to absorb is censored.

At what point will they get it back? When they're ready to do a creation of their own, or after this one is over?

If they desire it—that is always a factor—they will, shortly after the ten-times expansion, be able to reacquire that wisdom. I think that after the ten-times expansion they will not feel the need to do so. They might very well have capacities that connect them in other ways to wisdom. It is like a library of knowledge. In your own town or village you have libraries where there is available knowledge, but you do not always use it nor do you always need it. It is there for you, however, should you desire or require it.

You must have something beyond our comprehension that allows you to absorb wisdom from realms that are so unrelated, so opposite and so complex. They're all different, right?

How I Gather Wisdom

What if I told you I don't know how *not* to do it? Then would you say I am so wise? When I say that, it tells you something very important: that my ability to absorb this is not something I worked or strived to attain, but is rather part of my natural function. As you naturally breathe, so I acquire wisdom.

Do you compartmentalize it?

No.

It comes from so many different sources. Are there billions of realms? How do you classify creation?

I don't. It all just goes into a big hopper, as you might say. It's all right for it to go in in a total jumble, because the only time it ever comes out is when other beings have needs for it, and their needs pull it out in a sequence they can absorb. I am not responsible for being anything other than a vessel. If it does not relate to me personally or if it is something so esoteric from my perspective that I cannot relate to it, I pay no attention to it.

But can't you be amused and interested about the stuff that comes in?

Oh, certainly, certainly. Many times at least 30 to 35% of the wisdom and knowledge is interesting enough for me to pay attention to and follow up wisdom on those subjects. Yes, I am not a disinterested bystander, but like you or others, I am not interested in all things at all times.

I don't know what to call it because it keeps expanding, but possibly you can see more of creation than anybody we've talked to so far.

"See" is in quotes.

Well, feel, know . . .

Feel-know is perhaps closer to it. Feel-know, because seeing is not happening physiologically. I can feel-know something, *then* I can "see" it, as you might imagine something. But I do not see it as it's happening.

Only when you focus on it.

Only when I focus on it, that's right. If something is happening somewhere and a split minisecond later I become aware of it, even if I'm interested and pay attention to it, I'm still not seeing it in the exact moment of its happening.

Well, it's pretty close.

It might be close, but it is not the exact moment. Do you know why? There's a reason. Because of all the knowledge and wisdom I have, if I were present in any form energetically . . .

. . . you could change it.

Yes, I could very easily—completely unintentionally—by the radiation of my energy and knowledge, change what the person or persons are doing to develop *their* wisdom. So I'm not *allowed* to be present.

So you're more like a recording device that feels, sees, knows, hears, understands.

Yes. I am a conscious record player.

The Way I See What Is

We have the idea of realms. The one we're in, the paradoxical, this one, that one. How can you describe What Is? Are there any words you can say that would help us understand?

I don't think it would help you, but I've always considered What Is to be anything that can be felt, done, seen, experienced or imagined. The concept of limits is much less likely to be real than to be needed by certain individuals.

Needed as an educational tool?

Yes, or needed as a means by which to keep you on the direction you are moving so as to not distract you. What Is is beyond your current mental capacity to understand, but not beyond your *true* mental capacity, your natural way of thinking.

Every universe has a creator and there are billions of creators within just this little Circle of Creation, then there's God knows how many circles in this realm. Do you think there's some ultimate creator?

Oh, yes, I think there is. There must be an invisible creator, an invisible energy, because otherwise how would I have been inspired? I didn't think to turn myself into seeds. That wasn't *my* thought. I had the need and someone answered the need. If that wasn't from the being you referred to, it certainly was someone who was very helpful. Yes, I have faith that there is some ultimate creator, but this is my belief. My belief of the ultimate creator is visual here. I will show it for the sake of . . . perhaps I will do it from the top down. [Draws.] Off the paper, but

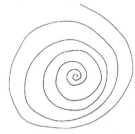

it continues, yes? [Indicates which side is up, then draws a spiral seen from the side.] It goes on much farther, but . . .

It looks like a spiral.

[Connects the two ends by a dotted line.] What does that suggest?

That there's an equal and opposite on the other side?

No, that the ultimate creator is that which has been created, re-creating ad infinitum to recycle and cycle more and more. So if a creation begins here [at bottom] and cycles up through all of these (and it's much longer than that), at some point it cycles back down here and continues to cycle on, on and on, up, down, on and on and around. Of course, if we look at that another way, then it doesn't seem to have an up and down. The main thing is the recycle point. My belief is that the ultimate creator has more to do with where we came from . . .

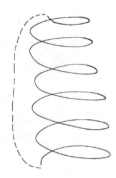

. . . than what we're doing now.

The Ultimate Creator Seems to Be Us

Yes, and so I'm saying that in my experience, the ultimate creator does seem to be us somehow. By "us" I mean not only all beings, but all levels of all beings. This is by way of saying, again using the analogy of your own bodies, that if a cell within your body is connected to all other cells within your body, then the total amount of cells expresses a single body. We know that all of the millions of cells within your body are individual and unique, yet they are one being. In my experience, such microcosms that the analogy represents are absolutely equal to the macrocosm of all being.

I am saying that if that apparent recycling coil represents all beings (for the sake of this discussion), if you could stand back far enough, then at some point you would be able to see that it is some *one*, and that some function of someone is providing that inspiration. After all, if future memory is a total fact as well as past memory, one might discover something to be true in the future of one's existence, and if it could be delivered into the past, one might relive one's life. So you could say that inspiration might be an aha! from the future delivered to your past—which in that moment is your present—which causes you to alter your life from that point on, allowing you to become more in the future, even as the future allows you to become more in the past. It just depends where you put your focus.

So you can move at will.

I feel that we are all this. That is my model for creator at this time.

That's the best one we've heard so far. Would you do an experiment with me?

Certainly.

Sort of move over and ask who put you in the Temple, who created the Temple. Then come back and ask if the being who gave you the vision would talk to us for a moment. Then listen.

All right. I will try. [Pause.]

Giver of Inspiration: I am that which reconnects ideals to the origin of their being, in this way providing inspiration that simply aligns you to the origin of the original purpose of whatever is your current interest. Even if it is a facet of that interest, all I really do is help you keep on line with what you are doing and help you keep from moving too far off the line. It is my job to provide inspiration to all beings. I do not always create this inspiration, but it is my authority to disseminate it.

I Give Inspiration to All, Including Your Creator

You're the one who gave the inspiration to the Temple?

Yes, and to everyone else. It is my authority. I think perhaps you say it is my "job" to provide inspiration. I do not always have it to provide. About 15% of the time I must ask for the inspiration, because I do not always have it.

Who gives it to you?

[Chuckles.] Further up the line. There is always more.

[Laughs.] You give inspiration to everyone, so you're not intimately connected to the Temple being? We were trying to find out his source, his origin.

No, I give inspiration to the Temple just as I give it to a child with a mathematics problem.

Did you give it to the Creator?

Yes.

Did you give it to Him, or did you get it from someone else?

I gave Him the thread because I felt that in order for an expansion to take place that would allow the original purpose of all beings to be fulfilled—and the original purpose is always to re-create yourself in a greater or more magnificent fashion—it would be necessary for you to become your own creators. Then when that ten-times expansion takes place, many more beings will achieve creator status, not only Explorer

Race. Explorer Race acts as a catalyst for expansion, and because this universe created by your Creator (who loves variety) has so much variety, then it is mathematical simplicity.

The amount of variety increases the exponential rate of expansion. If there is no variety, then expansion is slow even if one exerts great energy. But the more variety there is, even stress in that variety (some species not fully understanding others), the greater the exponential increase in the expansion energetically, requiring less energy to stimulate the expansion in the first place. So the energy the Explorer Race experiences through its own expansion need not be a burden for it or for your Creator. It is for you a very minor expression of expansion, but because of *where* the expansion is taking place, it is greatly expanded.

Who wanted this expansion? Whose idea was it?

You Requested This Expansion in an Alternate Future

You mean who requested this expansion?

Yes.

This expansion was requested by your future selves, who, in an alternate future (but real to them), are experiencing the ending of the Explorer Race scenario, and they didn't get far enough for their own satisfaction. So instead of the creation they experienced in their reality, they asked what they could do to have a creator who would be more excited—as it turned out, one who loved variety. The creator they had in that experience, that evolution, was one who was interested in single experiences, not variety, so the ultimate expression of the Explorer Race in that reality did not go very far.

You mean these three seed beings are going to affect everything everywhere?

No, no. Back, back. Before the Explorer Race was started, a call was put out. I am linking, not in theory but absolutely, as one connects a lever to another lever with a piece of steel, not even a chain. I am linking the future solidly with the past, stating that *the future must change the past, and what is changed in the past will change the future.* The tension between the past and future creates the present, but the present does not exist in any form of kinetic society without a past and future even in theory. But you have a real one, and that tension creates the present, and in the present one can make choices.

You have a more expansive understanding than the temple. Can you help the temple and myself and the readers understand how the temple got there? Did it suddenly wake up there?

The Individual Who Became the Temple

That being who now knows itself as the Temple was once a very ambitious individual, allowing for his society, one who was easily able to assimilate knowledge and wisdom in his job at the library of wisdom in that future of the Pleiades. That being, albeit very young and what you would call a prodigy, ran out of wisdom. Because that being truly lived on experiencing new wisdom—food, air, companionship, the joy of the consumption or absorption of wisdom—and it had run out, he was dying. As a dying wish he said, "I wish I were someplace where I would never run out of new things to know."

Who created his next body, his next incarnation?

He simply left his body. He did not die. The body has been preserved all these many years in case he comes back. The Pleiadians are truly an advanced and loving race that they would maintain that body for so long.

A Temple's Function

Are there many of these temples everywhere, or is this the only one?

A temple's function, in terms of that which gathers and provides wisdom and knowledge if needed, is expressed in many different places and forms, but *this* temple form was such that it would be more readily accessible by a broader range of beings. The Temple is not simply an oracle but an experiential phenomenon, should beings walk through it, fly through it, swim through it or be through it.

What an awesome thing! He said that as all those seeds of the Temple go out, the wisdom will be spread everywhere.

Yes, yet there are other wisdom keepers. The wisdom will go to a place that needs to be inspired and given a mission for being—these higher dimensions, where beings have accomplished all they can accomplish and are essentially bored. They need to have a sacred mission so that they might serve in a capacity in which they are truly needed and appreciated and can experience something that has been lost in their societies for a great deal of time. That is *fulfillment through service.*

So this one being who so dearly loved wisdom is going to affect the whole creation.

Yes.

Well, we kind of stumbled on you. Would you like to talk more and come back another night?

Yes, come back another night.

What do we call you—the One Who Gives Inspiration?

Yes.

We'll ask for you next time.

As you wish. [Pause.]

All right, here is the Temple again. Can you not appreciate now the value of your role? The questioner must actually need to know, and when the questioner needs to know, the answer ofttimes will provide an answer to many who also need to know but for one reason or another are unable to ask it.

How do you feel about what he said?

Very good. Something new to know, eh?

Oh, it's wonderful! It just gives me goosebumps. What would you like to tell these readers, who are really expressions of you? The Explorer Race is ultimately an expression of you also.

Yes, all right. Know that your service as the Explorer Race is profound indeed, for the ability to expand and create and provide so much more is often done for others you might never meet. An inventor creates something and it is accepted and cherished worldwide, but she does not meet most of the people. Her invention has served nevertheless. Know that in your role and capacity as the Explorer Race you will serve many more beings than you will ever meet, yet in the final experience of all life you are them and they are you. You will *feel* their joy, and this will multiply your personal joy in your ultimate accomplishments.

The One Who Gives Inspiration basically confirmed your model of creation.

It is always satisfying to know that one can extrapolate. Thank you.

Thank you, thank you so much.

Good night.

The Voice Historian, Who Provided the First Root

March 13, 1997

I am the speaker of the stories, the Voice Historian. I can be referred to that way—the Voice Historian—for it is my job to speak of that which provides and preserves sacred systems. In this way stories with a meaning or moral message have been perpetuated on your world.

The Being Who Desired Expansion

Some great time ago I worked with a being who was traveling by. This being told me of a great plan it had for providing the wisdom needed to move the history and the cultural levels well past their current expansion possibilities. As you know, since you live in a physical world, there is a limit on how far things can expand physically. In those days this limit was in place mentally and, in a great many cases, spiritually as well. This is because that which created all universes, all places, everything, had departed for a realm that exists beyond all dimensions discussed so far in this historical set of books and all that has not been discussed as well.

When that being had established a viable working creation that could reproduce itself and expand and become more on its own, it set into motion the mechanisms by which universes, circles of life—all that has been discussed in Explorer Race books and more—have been able to create and perpetuate levels of creation only slightly imagined from this point. That being, deciding that it would attempt that level of potential in another realm, departed to that realm.

Sometime later this being happened by and said it was traveling about to various universes to enlist the aid and cooperation of various beings in an attempt to form a consensus whereby there would be sufficient cooperation to prompt the change within beings who were more than happy, who even had wishes, hopes and dreams to establish the potential for expanding all life as you know it. This refers not only to the ten-times expansion associated with the Explorer Race, but to a certain amount of graduated exponential expansion that will occur at irregular times beyond the ten-times expansion resulting from the Explorer Race's actions and deeds with your Creator. This expansion is necessary for occupying and accessing higher dimensions that are largely without life as you know it, even without life as you *don't* know it [chuckles].

This being came by. I thought it had happened by, but much later I realized that of course it came by on purpose because I was the storyteller, one who acquired and dispatched stories to souls or individual entities. Now, I do not want to suggest that I am somehow solely responsible for all stories told everywhere, no, no. Many of them are imaginative creations, and that is very good. But I am responsible for certain stories that perpetuate or expand benevolent spiritual and/or sacred societies designed to transform or maintain spiritual integrity in societies that have lost their way or societies that wish to leave something behind (if they are disseminating) or simply wish to share their stories with others who might want them. Thus it has largely been my task to seek the transformative circumstance and society that might require such assistance.

Expansion Based on Tension, a Worthwhile Risk
Based on Vast Potential Rewards

This being said that it desired to create an expansion based on tension. I was surprised to hear that because so much work had gone on in benevolent civilizations to eliminate stress, tension and discomfort. Yet here was a being coming along, saying that tension had some innate value that was heretofore unrecognized in sacred societies in all of these creations that we know to be All That Is (though I can attest to the fact that there are more).

Here I was confronted with a conundrum, something entirely new, wherein someone I had reason to respect was stating that there was value in tension. I am not talking about physical tension used for benevolent purposes, but tension that potentially leads to some action that might or might not be destructive to someone. Here was a being saying that even though there is a risk of some destruction, the risk is worthwhile because of the vast rewards the reaction to this tension will bring; and that the purpose of the tension is to stretch people (I'm saying people, but it's souls) into a direction that is not native to their natural purpose.

If one being is stretched this way, he might stretch this way for a long time and not snap back right away. A great many beings will be stretched this way, including to some extent beings on other planets and nearby star systems because of their proximity (thus they are involved whether they like it or not). For example, the Pleiadians in the future will go through 2% negativity, which they really don't want to do, but they *have* to do it to stimulate their growth cycle and also because of their proximity to what is happening here and their relationship to you as genetic cousins.

When the being first began speaking to me of this, I had a high degree of what I can only call resistance, because it was clear to me that some suffering would be inevitable. This being was saying that the only way it could see to expand the universe and other universes—and apparently all universes, from what this discussion has implied—is for the tension and the response to be more than physical. The response had to be based on the spiritual line. From this being's perspective, the entire Explorer Race experiment is not only to prepare an entire group of souls to quickly achieve creator status and allow your Creator to go on plus all that has been discussed, but it is to do much more: to build up a tension in the souls and the light of these beings.

It is not natural for beings such as yourselves or beings anywhere to experience the degree of discomfort that you perpetuate on yourselves and on each other. It's totally unnatural. There are a great many stories in your religions and philosophies underlying how unnatural it is. Even in your present metaphysical stories being told of the death experiences of people who come back to life, they all go to the other side where they feel how benevolent it is there and are disappointed to come back to physical life, yet strengthened to know they will rejoin their natural state of being at the end of their natural cycle. They tell others, which is very reassuring for people to hear. You have people constantly telling each other in one way or another that to be of discomfort or to be destructive to yourself or others is wholly unnatural, yet you are doing it.

Explorer Race Experiment: Souls Volunteering for Tension Anchored in Your Spiritual Identity

You could ask yourselves why. "This is not who we are—it makes no sense!" Those of you who have read Explorer Race books could say, "Well, it's because we have a veil of ignorance" and so on. But I'm going back before that and asking, "But why? Why all of this?" I'm saying that in order to create the tension reaction, as in the slingshot, you must pull and stretch it back. You know this. That's what's happening for you. In the whole Explorer Race experiment, the invisible hand, if you would—the spirit—is pulling you back and putting you into a place. You are cooperating because you have volunteered for this unnatural situation, where it is not one person but billions who are being put in this unnatural position. In terms of the entire Explorer Race, it is trillions of individual souls in this state of tension.

This tension is anchored in your spiritual identity. Yes, it has effects in your emotional, physical and mental, but it's anchored in the spiritual because the spiritual is that which remains relatively the same. Oh yes, your spirit can advance and grow, but the nucleus of being you are all related to, that nucleus of love and benevolence and magnificence—your soul—is not changed. That is on purpose, so that there will always be a tension to want to flip back.

This being said to me a long time ago that we would have no trouble getting volunteers to do this, and that even though it would affect many, many lives and there would be a lot of suffering, everybody would volunteer on the soul level. No one would be involved who didn't volunteer, and that would be that.

Now, that being might have been a little idealistic, because I have seen some beings involved who *didn't* volunteer; those beings are on other planets and have been affected because of their proximity. For a time, extraterrestrials have come to Earth to try to get you to transform, but it is difficult, this communication between you and them. Without mass communications of their benevolent message, the message has largely gone unheeded because it has been unheard. But very soon now, not soon in eons but in years—as your friend says, experiential years—this tension will snap back. I will describe the phenomenon, because it will be that.

After Your Snap-Back, Euphoria, Sleepiness Forgetting of War, etc.

When the snap-back occurs, everyone on Earth, which is where the Explorer Race is concentrated right now, will feel out of your bodies for about a week. You'll be very disoriented. You will feel on the one hand euphoric, and on the other hand you will have a curious feeling of being tired all the time. You will have the extraordinary sensation of feeling euphoric and uplifted (the euphoria, of course, is from snapping back to your normal state of being), yet your physical body, having been so affected by all the discomfort, will feel like it needs to rest. These are some landmarks so you will know when this is happening.

Everybody, whether they are in your level of consciousness or in some other level, will be very much out of their bodies and disoriented —everyone, all of you. And everybody will want to go to sleep. People will go to bed at night and sleep sixteen, eighteen hours (their first experience of this). That will be usual, and then they will get up and try to stay awake, but two hours later will go back to sleep for another six or eight hours. It will be like that, gradually tapering off so that at the end of the week you will still be sleeping from eight to twelve hours a night. For some people eight hours a night is a lot, but they will still feel a little groggy.

After three weeks have gone by you will feel fine. Things you have taken for granted—wars between neighbors, wars between beings who were originally part of the same clan, such as in the Middle East—will be no more. People will literally put down their guns and forget how to load them. If you could look at this circumstance from now (if I might make a cartoon out of it for a moment, though it's not funny in your present), you would see people looking blankly at bullets and guns after only two or three months, trying to understand what to do with the gun. Some people will understand that the bullet has something to do with the gun and they'll try to shove it down the barrel. [Chuckles.]

You see, people will forget, and after a while they'll gather up all the guns, as the Bible story goes, and literally turn them into something that people enjoy more. In the old days they said spears and so on would be beaten into plowshares, but nowadays that might not be practical. They will probably melt them into something that can be used to build a bridge or something useful. This won't happen for any moral reason or because of a sudden conversion to some morality. It will happen *because you will be your natural self.*

Now, I know you want to know when it's going to happen. If I told you when it's going to happen, that would take away the tension. But I have been made a convert by this person. [Chuckles.] I have been made a convert that this tension is useful. When that being came to talk to me to say that tension is useful and that all of the discomforts that would come as a result of being separated from your natural selves had value, I couldn't even imagine considering that then. Even now I feel some sort of internal fascination with the idea, yet a significant repulsion to the suffering that has gone on.

The Burning Snap-Back Fuse Will Travel to Rest of Explorer Race

Of course, when you move beyond the veil into your natural state of being after your death at the end of any life, you shed all of that and become your natural state of being. But this process of snapping back will, of course, take place while you're still alive. The snap-back process will occur *first* on Earth because Earth is the place where kinetic energy can be most easily expressed by the Explorer Race. So think of yourselves as the fuse. When all beings on Earth snap back, all the

Explorer Race beings everywhere in this universe will also snap back. But *you* must snap back first because you have the kinetic energy.

When that snap-back occurs it will be very much like a fuse, and the emanation will travel up the line to where the Explorer Race is waiting for you. They will snap back and then the whole universe will be affected; it will begin to snap back and so on. For the rest of this universe where the rest of the Explorer Race is waiting, the extremes that are going on on Earth and the memory of those extremes is like a weight. The rest of this universe is benevolent, and for these areas it's like having a cancer. It's weighing them down; it's disproportionately uncomfortable because they are in such benevolent societies. For anyone in such a benevolent society, the slightest discomfort is appallingly uncomfortable compared to what for you would be hardly noticeable.

Final Click into Fourth Dimension, Then
Your True Purpose Revealed

When this snap-back occurs, one would assume that there might be a time of vibration, but there won't be. You literally snap back, expelling the tension. Others will snap back, transforming the discomfort, and that energy will continue outward. You easily click into the fourth dimension, and that's what's going to allow that last click to take place from about 3.75 to 4.0. Just like that [snaps fingers], not a long time. The only benchmark I can give you about when this will take place is that you will have been at 3.75 for a few experiential years and then it will happen.

You probably want to know who the being is who came with this idea. (I will see if I can get permission to talk about it, because timing is important.) This being is running through its many disguises to show me which it will present. [Pause.] This being does not wish to reveal his/her identity to you at this time, but will say that it has the utmost capacity and ability to love you for all you have done as Explorer Race. It appreciates your great contribution to this expansion and says that after the expansion the true purpose of the Explorer Race will be revealed to you in every detail so that you can understand more easily the value of this experience, not only for yourselves but also for others. At that time, if not a little sooner, that being will state who it is, but does not wish to do so now.

Are you saying there's a true purpose beyond what we know now, an additional purpose for the Explorer Race?

Yes. That is my opening statement.

My Constant Testing Would Keep the Experiment on Track

You sent something to be one of the root beings of the Explorer Race?

I think it's because—and this will surprise you—I so resisted the initial proposal of this project (from that being who wishes not to have its name revealed at this time) that the being, whose invisible hand is behind this whole project, felt that if one of the core emissaries came from me, not only would the primary cultural aspects of my being contribute to the Explorer Race, but my resistance and my questioning would test the experiment constantly to make certain that it remained on track.

Getting off track would be much easier without a constant testing to make sure that the purpose of the Explorer Race and the magnitude of its impact were kept small while you were going through your suffering. The impact would be allowed to be very large after you had passed beyond the bulk of that suffering. The best could come out of the circumstance and you would have the least impact on others while you were going through your struggle to cocreate with Creator. I believe that this being had so much faith in its design and idea that it desired to use that which would truly challenge the idea and be a constant voice of conscience within the experiment.

Then how did it work out?

After the being left me to solicit more support for this radical, revolutionary idea, I pondered for some time, "Do I even want to be a part of this?" I truly considered leaving this All That Is and allowing some other part of myself to carry on in my place, but I didn't. I even went so far as to create myself into a binary system. I can still leave, but I don't plan to. As a binary system I could separate like an egg in a human would separate to become identical twins. I set up the idea that I would leave a twin here who would be prepared to go along with the experiment. But the vaster part of me did not desire to do that. I got up to that point and decided to wait and see. I'm glad I waited. [Chuckles.]

A consensus was reached by this being who had come to visit and a great many creators that the experiment would be allowed to go on unless it became intolerable. If the suffering were to spread beyond the Explorer Race (wherever you might be), affecting other galaxies in some permanent way—where even if you moved on to some other galaxy to evolve your total being, if any of those galaxies remained in any way negative or had and perpetuated discomfort—the experiment would be immediately terminated, and all beings involved with the experiment would be uncreated, including that being who came to me initially.

Yes, we recently learned of this.

With that in mind, if the uncreation had taken place (for the sake of visualization), your universe would not exist. In terms of the Circle of Creation—all the orbs and everything within your entire Circle of Creation—about two-thirds of it would be missing. It would not have been a death; the beings involved in any way in the experiment would have been uncreated, *remaining* uncreated in any form for the term of experiential years equaling the half-life of any Circle of Creation, which is a vast amount of time—in which to ponder (it wasn't punishment) how you might have done it differently. So it was a tremendous risk by all beings involved.

And that applied to you also?

No. In the beginning I was not involved. I was planning to cast a no vote. When the being left me, I admit I was intrigued by the idea, but I was not so intrigued that I would have cast a vote for it. This being was able to assemble 200 high-status creators (ones who had been involved in at least two or more vast universes, some significant experience)—a few more, actually—so I felt that if *those* beings could see the value in this, then I would simply abstain. I never voted. I know of several other beings who also abstained. We were basically in a wait-and-see mode. We felt that the risk for permanent, perpetuated suffering was too high. In hindsight, because of what is being created now, I can see that you are going to succeed and that the risk of your not succeeding is so low as to be minuscule. But I do not regret my decision.

A Portion of Me Joined the Experiment

So that moment came and that portion of me moved off (even though I was binary, I allowed another portion to move off). I don't think I knew at the time that that portion, which was basically the conscience of the experiment, was going to be that which tested it, but I am happy with that role. I am glad that portion of me became the conscience of the Explorer Race, an advocate to the being whose idea this was and to your Creator as well as others that extreme vigilance be taken with the experiment so that other societies would not suffer permanent damage. I am proud of that portion of myself; I feel it has done well. When it split off to become many different personalities, some of which are still on your Earth, I believe, many of these beings became known for their moral . . .

. . . certitude?

Perhaps certitude, moral convictions. They're not all that way, but they're not all true believers either. [Chuckles.] They are, many of them, beings who have strong feelings and passions about what is right.

It seems to me that a much larger portion of your total beingness, personality and wisdom came to be one of our three roots than the roots from the Temple. The other two from the Temple of Knowledge fragmented into billions of grains of sand, only one of which became the two other roots or seeds.

I understand that it would appear that way, but I would have to say no. The portion of me that came to be one of the root beings was no greater a portion than the two grains provided by the Temple. It is like this: If the seed of a child grows within the mother, the mother contributes nutrients to that child's growth, yet when the child leaves the mother, is the mother diminished other than in her physical appearance? I do not think so. I would rather say that I, as a mother, birthed that portion.

Rather than sending a third of you?

Yes, I birthed that portion and I was not diminished.

I want to go in two directions, forward and backward. Let's go back first. What is your perception of where you came from? When did you first become aware? Did you create this position, or did you find yourself in it?

My Parent and My First Memories

It is an irony, that. The being who came to me with the idea of this intentioned experiment was my originator. It placed me there to do the job I did and have been doing. I am sorry to be coy with the readers, but I will simply say that the being who came to me, even though a parent to me, like a father or mother, I could not in good conscience support and I did not. This being was the individual from whom I originally sprang.

What are your memories of events?

My memories were of becoming aware initially of myself as a part of something larger, in which I was seemingly most involved with memory functions—remembering. The context of the memory was in some narrative form that pointed to the essential qualities that were intended to be remembered, whether the story was absolutely factual or illusory (created to remember things of value, but fictional). I became conscious of myself as part of this other being, as an awareness, a being of legends or a mass of mythology (to be alliterative). I was there for some time while this being traveled about, and this was well before the being had the idea. (I do not remember that idea when I was within that being, and I would have known about it.)

I became gradually more focused in what I was doing, and looking back, I feel that this being allowed me to clone myself (if I can use that buzzword of the moment) so I could be elsewhere if needed. I believe this being wanted to park me somewhere where this knowledge, wisdom, mythology, legend—the stuff of dreams, if you would—would be permanently and safely stored, like downloading data onto a storage disk, somewhere where I would be out of harm's way. So that's what happened. I was parked at such a great distance that to find me, you would have to be a creator or have creator status. Otherwise you could pass right through me and not even know it and without harming me either intentionally or accidentally (which would be more likely). I will go this far and say that I am an outer reflection of an inner reflection. I cannot say more than that or you could easily find me.

What was your experience while you were parked?

How I Deal with Incoming Material

You mean my initial experience?

No, your overall experience. You had a memory of all the stories. Did they continue to flow into . . .

Yes. They continued to come in. Even now as I'm speaking to you, the stories are still coming in, because mythology, legend, knowledge, wisdom and so on are constantly being created, re-created and perpetuated everywhere. If it is myth and legend that supports the perpetuation of something disturbing or discomforting, I classify it and drop it into a certain file [chuckles] that might be technological. If it is what I consider normal (spiritual, benevolent), I will let it flow into me entirely. If I were to give a percentage of my storage in terms of discomforting myths, the number is as follows [writes the number]: 0.00001%. That small portion of me stores all the discomforting or potentially discomforting negative-creating or anomaly-creating myths. I use the term "anomaly" to mean a disquieting story or myth that does not really have a beginning or an end and that would be represented as a statement of fact that is not really factual, otherwise known as cynicism. Stories such as these, which I consider anomalous because they rip a hole in the fabric of what is your essential goodness—a hole that leads to the perpetuation of such anomalous, abstract ideals as cynicism—I have dropped into my category of stories that perpetuate discomfort.

Yet you are able to handle that small percentage?

Yes, if I isolate it. I have it isolated in a portion of me that does not allow access by any beings except high-status creators, who can tolerate it. But it *does* allow me to have such wisdom that when it is desired I can, through inspiration, provide to societies or to individuals who will get their information out to societies, stories that would tend to countermand myths exemplified here as cynicism. No matter how cynical you might find your society becoming, you will always have a benevolent reaction within yourself when you see something endearing, no matter how cynical you are. You will have the capacity to have a benevolent reaction.

You called them myths and stories. The seed root being said they were true life stories of beings.

Yes. But to me, a myth is that which contains the truth and fictions of that truth that make the story more understandable to any group of people such as you have now. A typical example in the Western world is your Bible stories of Jesus and so on. Those stories are told in many different ways, perhaps most rarely the way this being truly was, but most of the time in a way that a given society can hear it. They appreciate the value of this being even though the story itself might not be true. That's why I will take the truth and legends, group them together and call it myth.

They come into you as someone's experience, then you amp them up a little bit?

No, I do not alter it. It is unnecessary. The passion of the experience is sufficiently powerful, whereas the stories that grow out of it . . . the legend of Jesus, if I might say, I do not amp up either. It is all equal, because to me stories are just as useful as facts, sometimes more so. How rare that a student remembers facts from his or her grade school, for example.

But they remember the stories.

But they do remember the stories, yes.

Our consciousness creates stories; we can read something with pieces left out, and we'll fill them in without even realizing it. We're story-creating beings, right?

Yes, you are *intended* to do that. You are intended to be able to tell what is essentially the same story in many, many different ways, so that when you go out to explore the stars and meet beings from other planets, you will be able to tell stories, quickly adapting them to those societies even though you have only just met the people. Thus one of the essential people on all ships that go out to do this will be the storyteller, also known as the wisdom keeper. In that way you will easily be able to create a bond between yourselves and your new friends. And you will find as you travel to other planets that stories are much more important than facts, because it is understand there that since these people have no resistance, they don't have to grow. It is understood there that the wisdom of the story is best felt in the impact it has in an individual's life, forming that individual's values, morals and even mores.

That is why you have so many stories that are root stories or even great and powerful stories that live for thousands of years and from which you can easily see many, many variations. The multicolored coat [of Joseph], the Bible story, and his betrayal by his brothers—can you not see this Bible story in many of your modern stories that have little to do with the original characters? Yet the root story is still present.

Archetypes

This leads to something more interesting. We have what are called archetypes, which to me are like role models or something to aspire to, beings who hold qualities we hope to emulate. Because part of you told stories, did those stories get into our culture from all over creation? Are some of our archetypes from everywhere?

Most archetypes are based either in the angelic world or at the higher philosophical levels of other planets you passed through on your journey as the Explorer Race. They are most apparent in the mythological cultures of tribes or clans of people that have managed to keep the bulk of their wisdom together: native Americans or native Africans or aborigines and so on, who are recognized as still having a primary culture with primary values and, most important, myths. But these are myths, mythological stories, that perpetuate the values of those groups of people.

Yes, archetypes come largely from off Earth, but I suppose I can single out one or two that might be associated with Earth, stories having to do with temptation. They are associated with Earth because on Earth polarity is such a real daily experience; on a momentary basis it is right there. You can do something benevolent or something self-destructive and everything in between and all around. Thus temptation archetypes are associated with this place. Understand that I am including as archetypes not only ones you might look up to, but also those that are perhaps less benevolent and represent actions or behaviors of individuals or groups of individuals.

Potentials or seeds.

Yes, potentials. Exactly.

But did some of our myths come from other realms, from other creations far away? Did the part of you that brought the stories here share them, then did people live some of the stories? How did that get down into the creation?

Stories and Myths Were Universally Seeded by the Explorer Race

Primarily he brought with him the archetypes or the nucleus of legend, myth and fact. Being such a foundational element of the Explorer Race, he was able to seed the storyteller or wisdom keeper amongst all beings in this universe. Even though the Explorer Race has tended to concentrate itself in certain places, beings who have been a member of the Explorer Race at some time have almost always reincarnated someplace else in the far reaches of the universe not directly associated with the Explorer Race. Thus they seeded those areas of the universe with storytelling myth and legend that might not otherwise have existed in that way. Some individuals in some very benevolent and balanced societies do not have stories, myth, legend, song, dance, none of that. They have only the perpetuation of their benevolent society. But the value of story, myth, legend, dance and song has been perpetuated by former Explorer Race beings who might choose to have another Explorer Race life in their future, understand? This whole system has been seeded throughout this universe in this way.

You've got little carbon copies of you everywhere.

I know what you're saying. They might have been carbon copies once upon a time, but I have evolved and they have evolved. It is important to mention it this way because your child, for instance, might be very much like you, presenting and representing your attitudes, opinions, feelings and so on, but as it develops its own personality and has its own experience, it becomes itself.

What I meant was that you have had an incredible influence on this entire universe.

I hope so. I say that in all modesty because, being the tester in the Explorer Race, I feel that my main contribution has been to help keep the experiment on track.

That is interesting. You're the tester, yet that seed being part of you jumped right in and went for the fragmenting and creating of beings immediately, whereas the other two held back a lot.

That is not surprising, is it? In order to saturate the areas where beings would be manifesting themselves, you cannot trust the slow route. You must take the expeditious route.

Which we're doing here.

Yes, and I think that was wise.

So the experiment's going to be a success. What is that going to mean to you personally? How do you plan to use the expansion?

I have no idea. I cannot imagine what it would be for me. You have to understand that unlike yourselves, I do not have an unconscious. I do not have a subconscious. I have only that which I am aware of. Even though I am a repository for stories and for that from which future stories might be made, I am largely in the present. To perpetuate a potential for the future is much more difficult for me, so I do not know.

What is your social life like? How do you interact with beings? Do they come to see you because you're in touch with everything?

I'm on the Creator/Storyteller Net

I can make a joke?—I am on the net. I am on the creator and storyteller net. Anywhere there is a storyteller or a wisdom keeper, I will dream with these people. Whether they are visioning or simply in their dream state, very often they will see me and I will see them. I am also, as I say, on the net with creators and beings who might want suggestions about foundational elements for the myths, legends and factual stories of a given place. Whenever they need to access any level of my wisdom or knowledge, they just punch up my handle on the computer net, yes?—on the creator net, how's that?

But it is interactive. You absorb all of this, but at the same time there is interaction between you and the creators when they ask your advice.

Yes. Usually they tell me of their creation if I am not aware of it, or bring me up to date on their creation if I have not been informed recently. Then they ask me to recommend, as any consultant does (though they might already have plenty of ideas), foundational elements for wisdom and myth and so on for their societies existing in that time. I will make recommendations, but they do not always take them. As any consultant must know, you cannot be attached to your advice necessarily being carried out to the letter. They ofttimes do that, sometimes just using parts of my advice, which is fine. That is the nature of creation. Ultimately, as you know, creation must be creative.

Where I Exist

I want to know where you are. Part of you talked about how far it had to come from where you are. You are beyond the realms that we know of, but are you inside some realms?

I am at the outer boundaries of All That Is in this experience of creation, that being which created all of this. I am at the outer "boundaries" (not barriers) of that. It is quite open, but I am so far away that in order to get to the first Circle of Creation, a realm where there are life forms that you might recognize as being part of your world or a discernible life form) . . . well, I live beyond the point of colors, so I must produce my own.

About All That Is, My Grandparent

What relationship do you and the being who birthed you have to the All That Is who moved up?

My impression is that the being who birthed me is the offspring of that being, so I can trace my lineage to that being, which is I why I have some small knowledge of it. That is the easiest way to describe it.

What do you know about this being? He created everything here and then decided he wanted more, right?

No, it was not exactly that he decided he wanted more. He/she created everything (we don't become too sexist, eh? [chuckles]) up to its capacity to create that which you could easily absorb or understand. It created everything it could think of, everything it could imagine based on what it could think of, everything it could feel. It created everything that was a part of it in any way, and that took some time. And when it got to the point where further creation would have been duplication, it stopped. Then it said, "I would like to have the wisdom to come back here." Because there was so much space created, it was going to take almost an infinite amount of time to occupy that space with various creations. But the being wanted to go on for further training, possibly become involved in creations at some other realm. In order to come back here and create on some other level it wasn't aware of, it asked to be taken to some other place beyond this mass creation for the application of such training, creating something there, then come back either to perpetuate its creation here or possibly teach others to do it.

We've been using the idea of realms as horizontal; the being mentioned realms. How do you know how he . . .

In any event, realms are neither horizontal nor vertical; they are simply zones of experience.

. . . with a little different rules or laws of physics or experience.

Yes, exactly. Therefore I am saying that this All That Is of which we are a portion is in a larger sense a realm of being created with many zones of existence. But in the larger sense it is a Realm, too (a capital R realm). We must believe that there is something else, because when that being desired to do so, it did in fact leave this place and it is some-place else now. I can feel it; it's there somewhere, but I do not know where . . . I cannot even imagine. I have not the depth to imagine where it is, but I know just from my feelings that it is alive somewhere.

Do you think that what our Creator has learned it is tethered to has a relationship to where All That Is went?

It is possible. That is not an unreasonable theory, because since this being created this All That Is and then moved on to some other place, as far as I know (in terms of my discussions with other creators), all other creators are interested about that other place. None of them has ex-pressed a great desire to go there, since it is virtually unknown, but the reason this creator being who created this All That Is wanted to go on was to come back here and serve in some greater capacity. None of the other creators has that need, so this pioneering effort has not produced another follower. I do not know if your Creator actually desires to fol-low there. We must understand that the core of your Creator's person-ality is associated with variety, and variety can always be traced back, forward or sideways in some way to curiosity. One cannot assemble and accumulate variety without having some desire to do so, which I would loosely put in the category of curiosity.

Do you think that in its desire to serve this level of All That Is, that the All That Is inspired the being who came and talked to you about this expansion?

This I do not know. It is a reasonable extrapolation, but I do not know this.

Your connection to the seed being here means that you're intimately connected to the Explorer Race and our experiences?

Yes, and it is ironic, because my original attitude, although it has been changed by your performance, was less than a Dutch uncle and perhaps more of a stern teacher.

What would you like to be known as? The Wisdom Keeper?

What did I say in the beginning? Voice Historian. I like that term.

Here's where you get to say whatever you want to those reading this book.

I wish to talk especially to those of you who have been called dream-ers. If you are ever referred to as a dreamer, regardless of how the word is stated, whether as a compliment or (more often the case) as a derisive statement or a putdown, decide that "Dreamer" is capitalized. All great societies, sacred societies and societies that are visionary in their results and capacities were established by people who were honored as dream-ers. Know that to be a dreamer is not truly a putdown; sometimes you might have to [chuckles] apply yourself to some other activity, but never believe that being a dreamer is any less than being a visionary. Good night.

Thank you very, very much. We will be talking to you again!

Yes. All right. Zoosh speaking.

This being said that a portion of him came here to help as a conscience and that some parts split off and became personalities who were like testers. Some of these beings might have been historical; are there any we might recognize as teachers or strict moralists or whatever?

I will give you one or two, far enough back so that they are more mythological than a sense of a person you might visit. King David, the biblical story, goes way back to the Old Testament. King Solomon is one. Let's see . . . all right, Mary of the Magdalene. I might give you more some other time in the future, so hold that question. There are more recent individuals, but I do not wish to state their names because they have relatives alive today.

One-third of the Explorer Race was attributable to this being, so . . .

Oh yes, but we need to pick out figures that are recollected or remembered or who are known to you. We can't just say, "Oh yes, Gus, you know, he lived several years ago." That would be meaningless to you. The question was framed, in any event, as historical figures, all right?

Creator of All That Is

March 18, 1997

I am the energizer of the current expression of all you can experience in your diorama of life. I have moved beyond this diorama in order to discover what else there is and apparently to prepare the way for others who will follow. When I moved past all of this, I felt at first that I was in a very small place. At first I wasn't sure whether there *was* a place, then as I became more omnipresent there, the place started to get bigger, either to accommodate me or perhaps simply in reaction to being activated. This is a possibility. I decided it was essential to not start creating there, but to wait. To create is what is where *you* are. I thought perhaps I would wait, so I waited and I have been waiting.

A Recent Creation—a Passage to Beyond

I have only recently begun to create something: Instead of creating planets, atmospheres and so on, I have created a passage. This passage will allow your Creator and others to follow through this area, and it will give them the option to pause in this area if they choose. They have considered now that this area might be a way station, an area meant for rest and relaxation but not necessarily to create anything. I have briefly created something unpopulated to see if it is amenable to creation, and it is. But I uncreated it and returned it to its original elements because I think it is not for me to create this. I will wait for your Creator to pass through this channel by which I have perpetuated here, and if your Creator stops here, I will either go on or make my decision then whether to go on. For now, I am waiting to support your Creator on Its passage through this realm and beyond.

What gave you the idea that there was someplace beyond?

It wasn't an idea so much as an assumption. When you look at what has been delivered so far, you can see clearly that there is something beyond. I had no evidence, not a shred, that there was anything beyond, but I created a small fold in the outer boundaries of what I had created and eased into that fold, entirely sealing the space behind me so that wherever I went would not penetrate this mass creation. In that way I ensured safe passage both for myself and all of you so that there would be no rent or tear. Once I got into that small space, I simply emitted a desire to know if there was more. Not unlike yourselves, I simply said, "If there is more, open up the side of this envelope that faces away from this creation so this creation will be undisturbed and allow me to emigrate toward the more."

It happened the moment I completed that emission, and when I squeezed into this space it was like a closure behind me. I was here for a long time, at first squeezing around to explore it, because it was very thin. I began to think that it might be a space between things. My natural reaction was to continue, but for no particular reason I can express, I decided to wait. After some time I felt I was waiting for your Creator, so the space gradually accommodated me by getting larger. So I have been waiting.

Will the tenfold expansion reach you, and if it does, will it propel you then?

I am not sure it will reach me. It is possible it will impact only all that exists where you are. I do not at this time have reason to believe it will reach me. Part of the reason I put in the passageway from where you are through this space and beyond was so that the propulsive effect of the expansion will have a way to express itself and your Creator will be able to move easily without having to propel Itself. When you do not actually know where you are going, like your Creator, propelling yourself is a disadvantage, because no matter how advanced you are, you will have a certain bias as to where or how you get there. If on the other hand you are being attracted, you will be attracted to what is right for you and how you are right for what attracts you. I felt it was best to create a passageway that your Creator might travel, with an access to this space if your Creator wished to step out of the transitional point for any reason. But it is not required.

Cords and Peers

Why this Creator? Because He's the only one besides you who has expressed a wish to go? He's corded. Is He corded to you?

He's corded above, which is why I say it's easier for Him to be pulled along toward something but not so good to push.

Are you corded to something above you?

No. And why this Creator? Partly because He has an opening or desire to go. But also because this Creator has made the necessary sacrifices and fulfilled Its obligations in the creation, manifestation and, ultimately, completion of the Explorer Race. So this Creator has earned the right.

Everyone we've talked to up till now has a peer and they came from someplace. It appears you have no peer. Do you remember where you came from?

No, I cannot say I have no peer. I would have to say that in the All That Is where you are there might not be a direct peer, but since I am in a way station, there is every reason to believe there is a peer. I am waiting, really, for your Creator. But I cannot say.

My First Awareness, Identity

You ask, "Where are you from?" I think I became aware of myself while I was involved in the creation of All That Is where you are, and my impression was that I once was many beings who joined to become one being. So I cannot say where I am from as much as who I am. And part of the who that I am is associated with your Creator. I have assimilated all of the other creators who joined to make myself, which means that they finished what they wished to do. But I am waiting for your Creator, which is a portion of me, and It will either stop in this way station where I am or, if It does not stop, I will follow It because It is a part of me. Thus I have to say *who* I am from, not *where*. There is no tracing back. It is more of a combined state of personality.

Do you include everything we have talked about in this book series—all the realms, all the places beyond the realms, everything?

Yes. I am initially made up of about 100 creator personalities, 99 of which are now encapsulated in me because they finished what they needed to do. The hundredth is your Creator. I do not wish to go on incomplete, so I wait and rest until your Creator has finished.

Your Creator's (and 99 Others') Connection to Me

Can you help trace the line from you to our Creator? What is the lineage? Is there any way to understand why this Creator and not some other?

The lineage is not a blood lineage such as you would know or even a spirit lineage that would make some semblance of sense. It is a lineage more associated with feelings, desires, interests and to some extent thoughts. All of the creators of which I am made up have the basic desires, feelings and even thoughts toward variety and expansion of life; moving beyond the unknown; and faith or trust in the unfoldment of life. Those qualities connect us and, like friends who find each other due to traveling spiritually or even physically from one end of the universe to the other or beyond, you gravitate to each other because of your similarities. What connects the hundred creators of which I am made are our similarities, but it is not a lineage as you understand it.

I can see it's the qualities in this Creator. Even though we know about the Creator's creator and the creator of that creator, there's no connection to those. It's the qualities that this Creator exhibits.

Exactly.

His courage, and what He's created.

Yes, using a diagram of a molecule or an atom with pictures of a molecule, each circle is a creator. For the sake of building a model, the connections would be our similarities and the similarities in the creative procedure, basically what we like and what we are inclined to do to create it.

What is your fantasy or imagination? What do you think lies ahead?

What do I dream of? It is my opinion that what lies ahead will be something completely different from what exists in the space you now occupy. Perhaps the difference will be how things are created or uncreated. Perhaps the difference will be how thoughts or feelings come together. Perhaps when I go there I will feel like a novice; perhaps I will feel comfortable and adapted. The most important thing is that it will be *new* to me. That's important.

So do you think our Creator has a tether He can follow, yet none of the other 99 do who are integrated within you?

They don't need to have a tether in me because they are connected. Your Creator needs to have a tether so that It can find Its way.

Is that tether to you?

Yes. That tether you're talking about is to the rest of the Creator's self. But from there, the rest of the Creator's self is tethered to me. It would be like this, for the sake of simplicity [draws]. This is C [Creator] to more of C [the rest of Creator] (obviously, the distances are longer) to I—or, if I may, to eye. It is not an accident that the eye is considered the God symbol. One always assumes, naturally, that it has to do with what the god sees, but what is less understood is that it is *not* the eye looking at you. It's the *other* side of the eye.

How Creation Works

Let us consider for a moment creation and how it works. Creation is beamed energetically through the self, in your case having to do largely with your needs, your soul's aspirations or your day-to-day structures of life. Yet on the creator level it has to do with inspiration, because creators are, in a nutshell, as you say (I

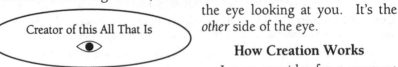

Creator of this All That Is

more
of
Creator's self

Creator

like that), inspiration and application—that's it. Take a look at the back of the dollar bill, understanding that the Creator's eye is not looking at you. What is on this side of the Creator's eye is actually *behind* the Creator's eye. It contributes to the inspiration of the Creator, what the Creator will create in any given point.

The energy of whoever looks at that picture—who they are, the whole world and beyond, the stars and so on and all that is within the Creator (you are in the Creator, yes?)—is projected out through the eye, which is the focus of the Creator in any given moment somewhere. It would be useful to understand that the mystical picture on the back of the dollar bill is not about what *is*. It is about the future—what could be, what might be, what will be (not what should be—no bias). This might be worth putting out, because the promise of looking at the picture this way is that nobody is stuck. You can change; things can be different for the one or the many.

The Next Place

You talked about the place you're waiting to go to as a "there." Is that analogous to the way we think of higher dimensions?

Yes, I think that is a reasonable analogy, because one tends to project toward higher dimensions some similarity of what you now have. For example, you might think of your physical self, and at a higher dimension think it is your white or lightbody or your gold body or even your blue or green body—however you might think of the higher dimensions. There is a tendency to project dimensionally some similarity or sense of relation. But this is different. This is not a dimension, although there is a similarity in that ability to say how one connects to the other.

It's like a jump between octaves, it's totally . . .

Yes, since I require that it be new for me—new and wonderful, yes? Whatever it is, it will give me that. Regardless of what I know now, I can be certain that it will be new and wonderful. Remember that when I was in the fold of what I had created, I did not know whether there was anything beyond; yet the beyond, which was barely there in terms of my being able to be there, opened up and I was able to access it. Although it was small, it gradually expanded so that I could be comfortable.

One has to assume from that experience that where you go and what you do and what you discover there has significantly less to do with what is there than *what you need*. It is a constant reassurance of the loving presence of some benign, benevolent being who will give you what you need. So obviously there is something beyond! Somebody is providing this for me. I must assume there is more. Especially at the creator level, if I may say this, it is *essential* for a creator's existence to know that there is something beyond, because creators often experience a variation of what they themselves are doing as they visit one creation or another. It might be beautiful, it might be wonderful, but it is not really new. So just like you (we are reflections of each other, yes?), a creator requires the ability to go somewhere and find something new and wonderful, and it has to be new to that creator. I have every reason to believe that infinite newness is available.

And you are creating the passageway so that ultimately we can experience that?

Yes, of course. What is the point of being the Explorer Race if everything is everything? You must find *something* new, yes? Ultimately you have to have the passage to the entirely new. If it is new to me, I gather that it might be new to you, but who can say?

So we've reached the end, then. There's no one else at this time until you make contact? You will come back and tell us, then we can talk to somebody else, right?

Definitely. But from this passage I would have to say, "This far and no farther."

Creating All That Is

Talk a little bit about All That Is. Does it work the same out there as it does in a smaller . . . did you create the realms? How did you start? How did this process start?

Not unlike the way it works for you. I created essentially the means of creation, giving out large amounts of autonomy to individual creative processes that could duplicate and create variations of those processes without being influenced by anything discomforting, so that there could be no disease creation. It was necessary to do that. If I might describe what I did as management, I didn't individually create a world here, a world there. I would set up prototypes—create a galaxy, for example, and planets, star systems, masses of potential creation, gases and so on. Then, granting that others might also wish to create that prototype, as long as it followed certain general benevolent guidelines they could go ahead and create.

Then (as an example) encapsulated beings who have an apparent self (such as yourself) might draw increasing realms beyond, and the consistency of expanded versions of beings would be carried out like the solar system and the galaxy. Beings would have their inner light, then their energy body expands beyond them, their feeling body beyond that, their needs beyond that, and their ability to create their needs beyond *that*. Drawing a silhouetted figure, one can draw realms and light realms beyond that. For instance, the average human being's creative energy runs from about 50 (it's rarely closer than that) to 75 feet (more likely) away from your physical self to (usually) the outer boundaries of the galaxy you are in.

This allows you within your lifetime (this encapsulation) to interact with the entire galaxy on the creative level in order to create what you need. This is often the interaction between yourself and someone or something else to support what you are attempting to do in your life. Of course, there are some individuals whose creation energy goes out beyond the galaxy, but I mention the boundaries of the galaxy because it is typical for the average human being, who has a short life (a hundred years or so), to go no farther than that. This doesn't mean that your energy links do not go beyond that, but your creative energies usually find their outer boundary at the galaxy you occupy. Of course, all that is in the galaxy bears some similarity in some way to who you are and what you are doing in that life. That is a type of creation.

I created prototypes like that, including basic laws. I don't wish to make "laws" sound intransigent, you know—stuck—but these would be basic physical or emotional laws so that things do not manifest chaotically. Chaos before creation is acceptable, but not manifested chaos, because that can rip apart the psyche of any individual and render his physical life useless. To be a physical human being and a functional creator at the same time would cancel the benefit of being a physical human being, so certain laws are necessary to get the most out of one's momentary experience.

Prototypes for Realms

Did you set up the prototype for each realm? The little we've learned is that this linear realm is straight and easy to understand, but some are so far beyond our ability to comprehend . . .

No. I set up the prototype for the first realm and made it available for others either to reproduce with their own particular bias or to duplicate the functional aspects of that prototype realm. Some creators wanted to simply duplicate it to see how it felt (of course, if you duplicate it, you're responsible for it). Other creators wished to put a little spin on the structures and mechanisms of the realm, so they would create the realm with little differences. But anytime you create a realm, just as anytime you create anything, really, you are responsible for the outcome. They would have to go there.

That is why some realms, even if they are really unusual, are not always filled with vast amounts of life as you would understand it but are often like big hollow rooms, because the creator responsible for that realm has to get used to its own definitions of how that realm functions. Very often the creator will simply spend time in the balloon (if I may call it that) of this realm, getting used to it, then gradually make creations and give those creations some authority to reproduce themselves—not unlike what I've done here—so that the creator can slowly get used to the consequences of the creation process in that realm. I recommend that; I think that's the best way.

The Paradoxical Realm and the Crystal Nearby

Which was the first one you made?

The first realm was the paradoxical realm. That was necessary, because in the paradoxical realm it is possible to have infinite reflections. One has the potential, especially as a creator, to go to such a place and see how many different combinations would work out that would not ordinarily come together. If, say, two polar opposites were in some momentary concordance, you would be able to see, within the paradoxical realm, if these apparent opposites could function in the same realm and how. So the paradoxical realm was necessarily first.

Was ours one of the later ones?

Yes.

How the Crystal Functions

Would you describe the crystal [see chapter 10, page 185ff] and why it's there?

The crystal functions primarily to store all that has been produced in the paradoxical realm at any moment, no matter how slight or how long. Then if something isn't in the realm when a particular creator or any being might visit (but it usually requires a certain level of creator status even to function in the paradoxical realm and keep one's sanity), the crystal is a storage mechanism through which a creator might study for long periods of time (if I may use that word) a particular combination, like the example I gave you.

As you know, in the paradoxical realm things are always moving and changing, but one can go and study it within the crystal. That is the crystal's purpose. I don't wish to call it data storage because that is too simplistic; it is a multilevel creation storage.

If you study something inside the crystal, you will actually experience it, so it is not something that one is separated from. To study it is to *be* it. But you do not have to create anything, because it will be infinitely moving through various levels of the creative process as you study it. Thus you can have that creative process going on within you as a creator, but it does not affect or even infect the crystal itself. You can study the process within yourself to see if you feel compatible with it, and if you as a creator can feel compatible with it, then it is likely that you will be able to produce beings who will also feel compatible with it.

Ultimately it is intended to be a gateway by which a creator will know that it has achieved some level of creation abilities. To simply function within such a crystal with such massive amounts of stimuli going on at all moments, you have to be very focused. Also, in the longer range it maintains compatibility within all the realms, because within it is that of the paradoxical realm and also that on the functional level of all the realms. Thus a creator could stop off there, study all life in all the realms, assimilate all of it in less time than it takes to do this [snaps fingers], then exit the crystal and study it elsewhere. A creator can get massive input, then take a great deal of time afterward to compare and consider what it might wish to create. So it functions as a massive experiential system.

Someone mentioned that the crystal has the authority to send beings to different places where they are needed.

Yes, beings (not necessarily creators) on the path toward becoming creators can go there, but they must enter from one of the poles (if we can call them that). The crystal is not polarized, but beings must enter from the top or the bottom so that they are not assaulted with a massive amount of what this crystal does, allowing them to tap into things more gently. Thus the crystal has the capacity to guide you.

If you do not know yourself sufficiently to go to the best realm for you or the best creation within that realm and so on, it can get you there very quickly or it can allow you to remain there until you complete some process you need to work with, then transfer you to where you wish to go. Equally, that level of the crystal can attract to you that which you might need so you can go where you wish to go on your own. Generally a being would not go there for such a purpose unless he had achieved spiritual mastery, material mastery and teaching mastery. Now, he might be working on dimensional mastery or quantum mastery, but he must have achieved those three levels of mastery to be able to be sufficiently comfortable within that crystal not to be affected by what might otherwise feel like maximum chaos.

Now, let's look from our level at the awesome, incomprehensible complexity of what you have created—laws, realms, everything—life force. How do you think we can learn how to do that?

Explorer Race's Gift: To Re-create Your Reality

Well, it is an interesting thing—and this compares very nicely to people living on other planets beyond the purview of the Explorer Race experiment. When you are born on other planets, you don't question the how. It is there and you can do it. It is as if you walk up to a bicycle for the first time, look at it, look at your body, then get on the bicycle and ride it. No one shows you how; you don't see any examples because no one has told you that you need to learn. You don't get up on the bicycle and fall down; you maintain your balance.

What I am saying is that it is unnecessary to know you can do something if you have never been told you can't. In order to fulfill your destiny as a human being in the realm where you are now, in any given life you must have completed at least one experience (most of you will do more than one) of re-creating your reality so that it will affect all your lives and incarnations beyond even this universe. That is the gift of coming here, of course. But it is a rare gift.

In most places in this universe one does not have such a gift. One has a benevolent reality, but one does not grow, one does not have the opportunity to re-create, and a given life will not necessarily affect one's other lives, at least not to the extent of a life where you are. That is why Earth experience as it is now is so much the finishing school of exposure to consequences.

It is common, if not universal, to want to work on quantum mastery, which is the mastery of consequences, because one has been exposed to so many levels of consequences here that one not only wants to know how to deal with it but to have the patience *required* to deal with it. Now, you all know (except for those of you who have been working intensely spiritually for many years) that patience is one of the most difficult and challenging crises you will face, yet you learn patience here even if your life is very short.

To simplify, I did not know I could *not* do it, so I did. That tells you that I have not gone through the process of ignorance. Of course, in a larger sense you are a portion of me, so I could say, in the larger sense, that I have experienced ignorance because I can feel it within *you*. Yet what I feel within you is not my own personal experience. I cannot say that I remember how it feels to be ignorant, whereas you can say, "I know how it feels to be ignorant," meaning, "I know how it feels to not know something." Obviously, when you are not incarnated here on Earth in this school, you cannot say that because you know everything according to your cultural bias where you are.

When Elsewhere, You Won't Remember Here

As I say, it is an interesting thing. The gift of ignorance, as Zoosh refers to it, works both ways. You are ignorant of your life beyond this Earth plane when you come here so you can re-create your life. But equally, when you are beyond the Earth plane and not in this school, you are ignorant of what you have done *here!* That is essential because you are benevolent, you are open, you are vulnerable, you are pure, you are sweet. You cannot be allowed to remember your Earth experiences, or you would be wounded, and we can't have wounded beings running around amongst totally open beings.

So you will have assimilated knowledge and wisdom through re-creation, but you won't be able to pinpoint something and say, "The reason I've changed and the reason I feel differently about that now is because of this experience on Earth." You will simply have grown. So the gift of ignorance, or the buffer zone, works both ways.

That's a new concept. So all members of the Explorer Race who have already finished and who are waiting for us have no memory of their Earth lives?

No. They can't have it. They have expanded, they have become more, they have integrated wisdom, but if you were to pin them down and say, "Well, how do you know that?" they would say, "It just came to me one day" or something like that. Or "As I discussed it with other beings, they seem to feel the same way, so we have reason to believe it is so." But they would not be able to say, "Well, one day I fell off the bicycle and skinned my knee, and that's when I discovered that I need help in learning how to do new things." They can't tell you that.

Shifting from Third to Fourth Dimension

But we're the only ones going through this experience of moving from third to fourth density in the physical body. Won't we remember?

Well, when Earth shifts dimension, all the rest of this universe is shifting dimension at the same time. It's easier for them, because if you're in the fifth, sixth or seventh dimension and click into the eighth dimension, it's no big deal. But if you move from third-dimensional Earth to fourth-dimensional Earth, it's a *very* big deal. It feels like a massive thing to you, but for other beings in this universe it doesn't. For them it is a variation on a theme and they get to do more, be more, experience more. It is a benevolent switch, like, "Oh, we've been eating mint and now we can have chocolate." It's the addition of something, but it is mild.

I always thought it was a question of focus, that you could focus on an Earth life once you were beyond it, and remember some of the people and situations.

Creator Status

Once you get to creator status you are allowed to remember that, because by the time you get to that status the pain of learning will no longer be present as pain. You will understand that pain has a function, albeit an unpleasant one, which is to point out a change that must be made in some way or other. You can remember once you get to creator status. When I say "creator status," it doesn't necessarily mean that you are a creator, but that you are capable of being a creator, though you might not wish to be one in that moment.

Creator status would require spiritual mastery, material mastery, teaching mastery and probably dimensional mastery. You would need to be well on your way through dimensional mastery and have already started and made a significant impact into quantum mastery in order to have a creator status. Your planet Earth, for example, has a creator status. She is a spiritual master, material master, teaching master and now she has achieved dimensional mastery. She is well on her way through the experience of quantum mastery; this is how she is able to put up with the circumstances that prevail. After all, the Garden of

Eden is not a place, it is a planet, and this is the planet here.

Eden Planets

There are other planets named Eden. The real name for this planet, in terms of those who perceived it (this relates back to the ship that Jehovah arrived on [see chapters 4 and 5 in *The Explorer Race]*) is New Eden. That was their name for it, and that's how they managed to suggest the story that has come to be known as the Garden of Eden. Planets generally referred to as Eden are of that garden type, where life is nurtured and encouraged and does not block out other life. You can have a tall tree that might normally give shade, but plants that require sun aren't beneath it. All life is nurtured and encouraged and lives compatibly with all other life. That's what you call, roughly, Eden status, or an Eden-class planet.

Where did that group experience that? What planet were they referring to?

Well, there is an Eden planet not far from their own system [Sirius] of planets where they came from. It was always studied from afar because they came from a place where there was a lot of polarity. They couldn't approach it because they had that polarity. If it hadn't been for the long journey to get here, they would have retained that polarity. When they escaped from that place and started coming here, they left a lot of that energy behind them, and Jehovah and others amongst the group were able to teach everybody methods not unlike meditations, living meditations where they were able to shed a lot of that.

They could now, of course, go to Edens. There is an Eden in the Pleiades and several others scattered about. In the Sirius star system, for example, there are many Eden planets. So the idea of calling this New Eden was appropriate, especially since it was their intention (at least Jehovah's initial intention as a social engineer) to create an Eden planet where one had not existed before. I'm skipping over some things, of course, but I wanted to give you a little background.

We didn't know that you could talk to us so directly. You could fill several books by yourself.

Well, the advantage of having potentials here through this particular being is that it opens up and broadens the spectrum. Many of the beings who have spoken are perfectly capable and open to the idea of giving more.

The Initial Inspiration—from a Need

Yes, but you are the one to talk to. Did you come up with the idea of the Explorer Race experiment and inspire the one [the Voice Historian] who went around and inspired everybody else?

I'd have to say that that wasn't my thought. It's hard to get this kind of precision, because inspirations often hit beings at the same time. I have to say that when I considered this, someone else had considered it before, so I was probably getting a reflection of their creation. In my management course, if I were to give one, I would start creative beings on things, giving them basic latitudes in which they can work so that as beginners they don't make any horrendous mistakes. The more they learn, the more I broaden their latitude.

I believe this idea came from some other beings. It started out as a need, and once you have a need, as I had, the creationism process itself, with all beings of free will, will attract beings within the infinite spectrum of life. The building blocks of life would be attracted as well as whatever would enjoy fulfilling that need and be fulfilled by fulfilling that need in some being. This allows for perfect harmony and balance.

Where do you think the idea came from, then—the one that inspired all those beings, who went around and talked about it?

I think that it came initially as a need. Then I think that the idea began to put itself together in pieces, because when the need was expressed, it was expressed like growing pains. "How do we move beyond, how do we expand?" So it was essentially a need. Once that need came to consciousness, it was simply a matter of creating the means to expand, and those who had that means filled in the details. This is like creating or delegating. You have the nucleus of the idea, then you delegate others to contribute their intuitive visions.

Don't you think that your need to go beyond everything that you had created here could have somehow stimulated this need?

Certainly, because I needed more and got the more I needed in the way station, though not exactly. It's very possible that that might have been what triggered the need.

How Creator's Friends Were Drawn

Maybe you can fill in some of the blanks. We don't know how yet, but Zoosh and the other eight friends of the Creator were drawn by the need of the Creator for their skills. From your point of view . . .

Well, they were drawn to the Creator, not by the Creator's need to have their skills, but by the Creator's future awareness of the challenge of creating the expanding mechanism—the Explorer Race.

They were drawn by the challenge?

They were drawn by the need, though within the context of time it was a future need. They were drawn by the need, which is why the consultants would often meet . . .

They were pulled.

Some of them were pulled at great speed. They were initially pulled in concordance with the need, leading to the Creator's need for their input within any moment. So they drawn by the need, not by your Creator's need for *them*. When a being comes along that seems to be attracted to you and you are attracted to it, you invite it, as any creator would, to come along because you assume that you will probably need it. Creators believe in synchronicity, not coincidence. That's why the Creator was open to that.

How do you feel about the ones He asked to come? Zoosh said [in Creators and Friends, chapter 24] that had there been more of the third sex, it would have taken a much shorter time and less suffering, and that had the quadrangle sex come as a consultant, it would have taken 10% of the time. How do you perceive that?

But in my experience faster is not necessarily better, so I would say that the need to progress slowly, to experience the maximum variety available in order to learn thoroughly, is much more important than to get there quickly. Generally speaking, mastery is not achieved by quickness. It is achieved by thoroughness. I would say that it was essential to keep the experience moving at a rate slow enough that thoroughness would be possible.

I Left before Your Creator Was Birthed

There's no time, but in the sense of duration, had the Explorer Race already manifested and started to fragment before you started looking for the route to this other place somewhere? At what point did you leave in relation to the Explorer Race?

I left slightly before your Creator emerged from Its creator.

Yet you knew what was going to happen?

I had some small idea of what might occur. You have to remember that when you create something, it can be vast or it can be more condensed, but ultimately you will do everything with it that you can consider doing. Once you have gone as far as you can with the creation using your own capacities within it, you must then consider (at least this is my logic): Is the management in place? Can they oversee themselves? Are they safe? Once you have satisfied those questions in the affirmative, then you can proceed with the certainty that someone else will be available to do more with what you have created. Once you've done all you can do, you must pass it on. So I left right about the time when I realized I needed to pass it on. At that point I was certain that the creation process was safe.

But in this case they had to give outrageous guarantees to uncreate themselves and everybody else should it fail. This was unlike anything that had ever happened in your creation before.

Yes, but this happened *after* I left.

Oh, that's why it was allowed to happen.

Yes, because I did not have the capacity to create something that would risk causing great harm for ultimate gain. I had already left when that was going on. I could hear all of that from where I was; I could be aware of it. I can be aware of what you're doing now, but to actually have stimulated that, to have said, "Okay, let's try that," that is not mine. One must understand that the process of creation, creativity in anything you do, might be entirely different. You might be a potter producing pots rather similarly throughout your career. You might train an apprentice how to create pots, and they will create them rather like yours, but eventually they will include their own designs, which you might or might not like. The creative process is at the core of existence in this All That Is. It is intended that all beings come from the creative process and eventually evolve into creator status on their own, by their own experience and by the accumulation of that experience and the consequences that come from it.

This is highly interesting, because the Council of Creators was intimately involved in this. They had many meetings, they went back and forth. Always before, my sense is, they could look to you for a final word or some correction.

Yes. But they couldn't, you see . . .

Being without Your Teacher

But now they have the most unusual thing that's ever faced them, and you're not there to guide them.

Yes, but don't you know—and I think all mystical people know this: The point where you feel you need your teacher the most is often the point when your teacher is no longer available. The time when you feel you need your teacher the most is when you become dependent. The whole purpose of creation and being a creator is to be able to do it on your own with the confidence that you can deal with all consequences. You might ask others for advice, but it is your responsibility to work with the consequences.

There's a point here that's very interesting: you left right at that time when we were faced with the most unusual thing that had ever happened.

I left a little before that, not right in that moment, and that allowed them to do something new, even with the qualifications they approved. It allowed them immediately to do something new. You could say it was because they couldn't consult with me, but on the other hand you could also say it's because they knew they had to be creative on their own and felt they must give it a chance. They gave it a chance, but I can tell you, many's the time they wanted to terminate it!

Yes, I know. Zoosh has told us about the incredible guarantees that had to be made by everyone involved.

The guarantees were very deep and long-lasting.

Would you talk to us again? These sessions go by so quickly that sometimes we don't get to absorb everything.

Oh, certainly.

If we have questions, could we come back and talk to you later?

Certainly.

Well, I've about run out, so if you want to say something to humans . . .

Resolve Your Consequences within a Lifetime

Let me simply say this. Your personality is guaranteed to be immortal. Anything you do in your life, since you are in creator school, is guaranteed to have consequences. But you are no longer in the thread of karma, which means that the future of this planet as it has existed will not exist indefinitely in that way into the future. In other words, you cannot have karma as you have known it, so you cannot be guaranteed that you will be able to work things out in the future as you have in the past. Thus you have the opportunity to resolve consequences *within a given life.*

Many of you are having very powerful dreams and your sleep state is entirely topsy-turvy because you are doing so much at other levels of your being to resolve the consequences of what you have done or been involved in even on the periphery in this life right now. This is because you cannot be guaranteed that such conditions and polarity and challenges and rewards that are available now will be just as available in some future life. Your sleep cycles, the food you eat, the friends you are attracted to, the family you do or don't get along with, are all in complete flux right now to allow you to create, to re-create—and in some cases even to uncreate—something that needs to be resolved before the end of your life.

You are actually beginning to experience to some degree, although you do not have creator status yet, the responsibility and consequences of being a creator. The reason you are allowed to do this is not only because you are involved in the Explorer Race, but because you are doing this resolution in combination with other members of the Explorer Race on your planet. This is why when you wake up from a dream you will often feel briefly that you are with old and dear friends, but their faces do not relate to people you know here and now. These are beings you have known elsewhere at other times and often in other guises you would not even recognize as human. Know that you are getting your initial apprenticeship in creationism these days, even though you might not be aware of it.

Thank you very much.

Good night.

Keep that passageway open, because we're coming, okay?

I'll be lookin' for ya.

◆ BOOK MARKET ORDER FORM ◆

BOOKS PUBLISHED BY LIGHT TECHNOLOGY PUBLISHING

Title		No. Copies	Total
ACUPRESSURE FOR THE SOUL	$11.95	___	$___
ARCTURUS PROBE	$14.95	___	$___
BEHOLD A PALE HORSE	$25.00	___	$___
CACTUS EDDIE	$11.95	___	$___
CHANNELING: EVOLUTIONARY . . .	$9.95	___	$___
COLOR MEDICINE	$11.95	___	$___
FOREVER YOUNG	$9.95	___	$___
GUARDIANS OF THE FLAME	$14.95	___	$___
GREAT KACHINA	$11.95	___	$___
I'M OK, I'M JUST MUTATING	$6.00	___	$___
KEYS TO THE KINGDOM	$14.95	___	$___
LEGEND OF THE EAGLE CLAN	$12.95	___	$___
LIVING RAINBOWS	$14.95	___	$___
MAHATMA I & II	$19.95	___	$___
MILLENNIUM TABLETS	$14.95	___	$___
NEW AGE PRIMER	$11.95	___	$___
PATH OF THE MYSTIC	$11.95	___	$___
POISONS THAT HEAL	$14.95	___	$___
PRISONERS OF EARTH	$11.95	___	$___
SEDONA VORTEX GUIDE BOOK	$14.95	___	$___
SHADOW OF SAN FRANCISCO PEAKS	$9.95	___	$___
THE SOUL REMEMBERS	$14.95	___	$___
STORY OF THE PEOPLE	$11.95	___	$___
THIS WORLD AND THE NEXT ONE	$9.95	___	$___
ROBERT SHAPIRO/ARTHUR FANNING			
SHINING THE LIGHT	$12.95	___	$___
SHINING THE LIGHT — BOOK II	$14.95	___	$___
SHINING THE LIGHT — BOOK III	$14.95	___	$___
SHINING THE LIGHT — BOOK IV	$14.95	___	$___
SHINING THE LIGHT — BOOK V	$14.95	___	$___

Title		No. Copies	Total
ROBERT SHAPIRO			
THE EXPLORER RACE	$25.00	___	$___
ETS AND THE EXPLORER RACE	$14.95	___	$___
EXPLORER RACE: ORIGINS . . .	$14.95	___	$___
EXPLORER RACE: PARTICLE . . .	$14.95	___	$___
EXPLORER RACE: CREATOR . . .	$19.95	___	$___
EXPLORER RACE AND BEYOND	$14.95	___	$___
ARTHUR FANNING			
SOUL, EVOLUTION, FATHER	$12.95	___	$___
SIMON	$9.95	___	$___
WESLEY H. BATEMAN			
DRAGONS & CHARIOTS	$9.95	___	$___
KNOWLEDGE FROM THE STARS	$11.95	___	$___
LYNN BUESS			
CHILDREN OF LIGHT, CHILDREN . . .	$8.95	___	$___
NUMEROLOGY: NUANCES . . .	$13.75	___	$___
NUMEROLOGY FOR THE NEW AGE	$11.00	___	$___
RUTH RYDEN			
THE GOLDEN PATH	$11.95	___	$___
LIVING THE GOLDEN PATH	$11.95	___	$___
DOROTHY ROEDER			
CRYSTAL CO-CREATORS	$14.95	___	$___
NEXT DIMENSION IS LOVE	$11.95	___	$___
REACH FOR US	$14.95	___	$___
HALLIE DEERING			
LIGHT FROM THE ANGELS	$15.00	___	$___
DO-IT-YOURSELF POWER TOOLS	$25.00	___	$___
JOSHUA DAVID STONE, PH.D.			
COMPLETE ASCENSION MANUAL	$14.95	___	$___
SOUL PSYCHOLOGY	$14.95	___	$___

Title		No. Copies	Total
BEYOND ASCENSION	$14.95	___	$___
HIDDEN MYSTERIES	$14.95	___	$___
ASCENDED MASTERS	$14.95	___	$___
COSMIC ASCENSION	$14.95	___	$___
VYWAMUS/JANET MCCLURE			
AHA! THE REALIZATION BOOK	$11.95	___	$___
LIGHT TECHNIQUES	$11.95	___	$___
SANAT KUMARA	$11.95	___	$___
SCOPES OF DIMENSIONS	$11.95	___	$___
THE SOURCE ADVENTURE	$11.95	___	$___
PRELUDE TO ASCENSION	$29.95	___	$___
StarChild Press ★ ★ ★ ★			
LEIA STINNETT			
A CIRCLE OF ANGELS	$18.95	___	$___
THE TWELVE UNIVERSAL LAWS	$18.95	___	$___
ALL MY ANGEL FRIENDS	$10.95	___	$___
ANIMAL TALES	$7.95	___	$___
WHERE IS GOD?	$6.95	___	$___
JUST LIGHTEN UP!	$9.95	___	$___
HAPPY FEET	$6.95	___	$___
WHEN THE EARTH WAS NEW	$6.95	___	$___
THE ANGEL TOLD ME . . .	$6.95	___	$___
COLOR ME ONE	$6.95	___	$___
ONE RED ROSE	$6.95	___	$___
EXPLORING THE CHAKRAS	$6.95	___	$___
CRYSTALS R FOR KIDS	$6.95	___	$___
WHO'S AFRAID OF THE DARK	$6.95	___	$___
BRIDGE BETWEEN TWO WORLDS	$6.95	___	$___

BOOKS PRINTED OR MARKETED BY LIGHT TECHNOLOGY PUBLISHING

Title		No. Copies	Total
ACCESS YOUR BRAIN'S JOY CENTER	$14.95	___	$___
AWAKEN TO THE HEALER WITHIN	$16.50	___	$___
EARTH IN ASCENSION	$14.95	___	$___
GALAXY SEVEN	$15.95	___	$___
INNANA RETURNS	$14.00	___	$___
IT'S TIME TO REMEMBER	$19.95	___	$___
I WANT TO KNOW	$7.00	___	$___
LIFE IS THE FATHER WITHIN	$19.75	___	$___
LIFE ON THE CUTTING EDGE	$14.95	___	$___
LOOK WITHIN	$9.95	___	$___

Title		No. Copies	Total
VOICES OF SPIRIT	$13.00	___	$___
WE ARE ONE	$14.95	___	$___
LEE CARROLL			
KRYON–BOOK I, THE END TIMES	$12.00	___	$___
KRYON–BOOK II, DON'T THINK LIKE.	$12.00	___	$___
KRYON–BOOK III, ALCHEMY OF . . .	$14.00	___	$___
KRYON–THE PARABLES OF KRYON	$17.00	___	$___
KRYON–THE JOURNEY HOME	$15.00	___	$___
RICHARD DANNELLEY			
SEDONA POWER SPOT/GUIDE	$11.00	___	$___

Title		No. Copies	Total
MSI			
ASCENSION!	$11.95	___	$___
FIRST THUNDER	$12.95	___	$___
SECOND THUNDER	$17.95	___	$___
ENLIGHTENMENT	$15.95	___	$___
PRESTON B. NICHOLS WITH PETER MOON			
MONTAUK PROJECT	$15.95	___	$___
MONTAUK REVISITED	$19.95	___	$___

Books

Title	Price	Amount
Mayan Calendar Birthday Book	$12.95	$_____
Medical Astrology	$29.95	$_____
Our Cosmic Ancestors	$9.95	$_____
Out-Of-Body Exploration	$8.95	$_____
Principles To Remember and Apply	$11.95	$_____
Song of Sirius	$8.00	$_____
Soul Recovery and Extraction	$9.95	$_____
Spirit of The Ninja	$7.95	$_____
Temple of The Living Earth	$16.00	$_____
The Only Planet of Choice	$16.95	$_____
The Pleiadian Agenda	$15.00	$_____
The Transformative Vision	$14.95	$_____

Title	Price	Amount
Sedona: Beyond The Vortex	$12.00	$_____
Tom Dongo: Mysteries of Sedona		
Mysteries of Sedona — Book I	$6.95	$_____
Alien Tide — Book II	$7.95	$_____
Quest — Book III	$9.95	$_____
Unseen Beings, Unseen Worlds	$9.95	$_____
Merging Dimensions	$14.95	$_____
Sedona in a Nutshell	$4.95	$_____
Barbara Marciniak		
Bringers of the Dawn	$12.95	$_____
Earth	$12.95	$_____

Title	Price	Amount
Pyramids of Montauk	$19.95	$_____
Encounter in the Pleiades . . .	$19.95	$_____
The Black Sun	$19.95	$_____
Lyssa Royal and Keith Priest		
Preparing For Contact	$12.95	$_____
Prism of Lyra	$11.95	$_____
Visitors From Within	$12.95	$_____
Amorah Quan Yin		
Pleiadian Perspectives on . . .	$15.00	$_____

ASCENSION MEDITATION TAPES

Joshua David Stone, Ph.D.

Title	Code	Price	Amount
Ascension Activation Meditation	S101	$12.00	$_____
Tree of Life Ascension Meditation	S102	$12.00	$_____
Mt. Shasta Ascension Activation Meditation	S103	$12.00	$_____
Kabbalistic Ascension Activation	S104	$12.00	$_____
Complete Ascension Manual Meditation	S105	$12.00	$_____
Set of all 5 tapes		$49.95	$_____

Vywamus/Barbara Burns

Title	Code	Price	Amount
The Quantum Mechanical You (6 tapes)	B101-6	$40.00	$_____

Taka

Title	Code	Price	Amount
Magical Sedona through the Didgeridoo	T101	$12.00	$_____

Brian Grattan

Title	Code	Price	Amount
Seattle Seminar Resurrection 1994 (12 tapes)	M102	$79.95	$_____

YHWH/Arthur Fanning

Title	Code	Price	Amount
On Becoming	F101	$10.00	$_____
Healing Meditations/Knowing Self	F102	$10.00	$_____
Manifestation & Alignment w/ Poles	F103	$10.00	$_____
The Art of Shutting Up	F104	$10.00	$_____
Continuity of Consciousness	F105	$25.00	$_____
Merging the Golden Light Replicas of You	F107	$10.00	$_____

Kryon/Lee Carroll

Title	Code	Price	Amount
Seven Responsibilities of the New Age	K101	$10.00	$_____
Co-Creation in the New Age	K102	$10.00	$_____
Ascension and the New Age	K103	$10.00	$_____
Nine Ways to Raise the Planet's Vibration	K104	$10.00	$_____
Gifts and Tools of the New Age	K105	$10.00	$_____

Jan Tober

Title	Code	Price	Amount
Crystal Singer	J101	$12.00	$_____

SUBTOTAL: $_____

BOOKSTORE DISCOUNTS HONORED — SHIPPING 15% OF RETAIL

SALES TAX: $_____ (8.5% – AZ residents only)

SHIPPING/HANDLING: $_____ ($4 Min.; 15% of orders over $30)

CANADA S/H: $_____ (20% of order)

TOTAL AMOUNT ENCLOSED: $_____

NAME/COMPANY _____

ADDRESS _____

CITY/STATE/ZIP _____

PHONE _____ FAX _____

E-MAIL _____

☐ CHECK ☐ MONEY ORDER

CREDIT CARD: ☐ MC ☐ VISA

_____

Exp. date: _____

Signature: _____

(U.S. FUNDS ONLY) PAYABLE TO:

LIGHT TECHNOLOGY PUBLISHING

P.O. BOX 1526 • SEDONA • AZ 86339
(520) 282-6523 Fax: (520) 282-4130
1-800-450-0985
Fax 1-800-393-7017

All prices in US$. Higher in Canada and Europe. Books are available at all national distributors as well as the following international distributors:
CANADA: DEMPSEY (604) 683-5541 FAX (604) 683-5521 • ENGLAND/EUROPE: WINDRUSH PRESS LTD. 0608 652012/652025 FAX 0608 652125
AUSTRALIA: GEMCRAFT BOOKS (03) 888-0111 FAX (03) 888-0044 • NEW ZEALAND: PEACEFUL LIVING PUB. (07) 571-8105 FAX (07) 571-8513